More praise for *Something in the Soil*

"No one writes more shrewdly or with more elegance about our shared past than Patricia Limerick does—and no one has a better time doing it. *Something in the Soil* is vintage Limerick, which means that easterners as well as westerners are guaranteed a good time, too."
—Geoffrey C. Ward

"Patricia Nelson Limerick has been a dominant voice among New Western Historians for close to two decades. In *Something in the Soil*, she delivers rigorous, thought-out opinions, often iconoclastic, always on the side of inclusiveness, in vivid, memorable prose. This book is a must for those who want to understand recent thinking about the past of the American West, and its future."
—William Kittredge

"Patricia Nelson Limerick is blazing the trail toward a new understanding of the history of the American West. Her sparkling essays in *Something in the Soil* show with sharp insight how forgotten dramas of our frontier past shape actions, ideas, and dilemmas of the western present."
—Arthur Schlesinger, Jr.

"An excellent précis of Limerick's work since *The Legacy of Conquest* and of the major thrusts in new Western history as a whole over the past decade."
—*Chicago Tribune*

"Patricia Limerick is simply one of the best writers alive—and the astonishing thing is that she thinks as clearly and logically as she writes."
—Garry Wills

By the same author

THE LEGACY OF CONQUEST

19 April 2002

Dear Trish,

As the back cover says, the West has a history as a magnet for dreams of a better life. That's a big reason why I came here, I wanted

SOMETHING
IN THE SOIL

*Legacies and Reckonings
in the New West*

*to chase my dreams. They sure paid off, because I found you.
With all my love, Brad*

PATRICIA NELSON LIMERICK

W·W·NORTON & COMPANY
New York · London

To the memory
of my brother-in-law,

Louis William Ingram,

whose impatience for justice
is a renewable resource

Copyright © 2000 by Patricia Nelson Limerick

First published as a Norton paperback 2001

The author gratefully acknowledges the University of Washington Press for permission
to reprint poetry from *Island: Poetry and History of Chinese Immigrants on Angel
Island, 1910–1940*, eds. Him Mark Lai, Genny Lim, and Judy Yung; and Rutgers
University Press for permission to reprint poetry from Mitsuye Yamada's *Camp
Notes and Other Poems*. Copyright © 1992 by Mitsuye Yamada. Reprinted by
permission of Rutgers University Press.

The text and display of this book is composed in Sabon
Composition by Allentown Digital Services
Division of R. R. Donnelley & Sons Company
Manufacturing by Haddon Craftsmen, Inc.
Book design by Jacques Chazaud

Library of Congress Cataloging-in-Publication Data

Limerick, Patricia Nelson, 1951–
Something in the soil : legacies and reckonings in the New West /
by Patricia Nelson Limerick
p. cm.
Includes bibliographical references and index.
ISBN 0-393-03788-6
1. West (U.S.)—History.   2. West (U.S.)—Historiography.   I. Title.
F591 .L57 2000
978—dc21   99-047246

ISBN 0-393-32102-9 pbk.

W. W. Norton & Company, Inc., 500 Fifth Avenue, New York, N.Y. 10110
www.wwnorton.com

W. W. Norton & Company Ltd., 10 Coptic Street, London WC1A 1PU

1 2 3 4 5 6 7 8 9 0

Contents

Acknowledgments

For help, inspiration, encouragement, and instruction in these writing projects, I am in debt to a crowd of people. The University of Colorado's Center of the American West is a promised land of intellectual community, and I thank Tracy Ainsworth, Dave Armstrong, Susan Avery, Ryan Bernard, Steve and Sharon Binder, Gene and Judy Bolles, Jane and Carl Bock, Ken Brengle, Rutt Bridges, Dick Brown, Nancy Carlston, Cathy Cameron, Jim and Susan Cargill, Annie Gilbert Coleman, Bud Coleman, Sharon Collinger, Jim Corbridge, Linda Cordell, Tobey Cho, Dan Cress, Peter Decker, Richard Delgado, Phil Deloria, Peter Dietze, Ruben Donato, Ed and Jennie Dorn, Michael Dorsey, Leslie Durgin, Hubert Farbes, Jr., Chuck Forsman, John Fredericks, Eleanor Gehres, Marcia Goldstein, Nicki Gonzales, Jule Gomez de Garcia, Hannah Gosnell, Jim and Lucy Guercio, Bill Gwaltney, Julia Hobson, David Hoffman, Barbara and Bill Hornby, Carmine and Margaret Iadorola, Roni Ires, Brad Johnson, Kathleen Kelley, Roger Kennedy, Bill King, Patrick Kneeland, Rick Knight, Lee Krauth, Lisa Ledet, Steve Lekson, Brandon Lerch, Leviticus Za'mien, Bill Lewis, Pat Long, Ed Marston, Peter Michelson, Kathryn Mutz,

Lisa Penaloza, Michelene Pesantubbee, Patricia Raybon, Tom Riis, Brenda Romero, Walter Rosenberry, Lynn Ross-Bryant, Charles and Karen Scoggin, Reg Saner, Pat Shea, Bob and Nancy Sievers, Jean Stefancic, Pete and Julie Steinhauer, Sven Steinmo, Steve Sturgeon, Jamie Sudler, Lucien Taylor, Neale Ward, William Wei, Jim Williams, Wren and Tim Wirth, Sid Wilson, Sharyn Yeoman, and especially my teammates and coauthors, Bill Riebsame and Charles Wilkinson. I am grateful to President John Buechner, Chancellor Richard Byyny, Vice Chancellor Phil DiStefano, Dean Carol Lynch, and Dean Peter Spear for their support for the Center. The MacArthur Foundation Fellows Program, though not explicitly in the business of institution building, gave me the "positioning" I needed to get the Center on its feet and running. And I am grateful to the Ford Foundation and the Hewlett Foundation for their interest in the Center.

In the history-oriented hallways of Hellems Hall, I benefit regularly from the company and the example of Lee Chambers-Schiller, Vine Deloria, Jr., Steven Epstein, Bob Ferry, Julie Greene, Camille Guerin-Gonzales, James Jankowski, Diane Johnson, Susan Johnson, Susan Jones, Padraic Kenney, Susan Kent, Ralph Mann, Kellie Matthews-Simmons, Marjorie McIntosh, Scott Miller, Chidi Nwaubani, Bob Pois, Tim Weston, Marcia Yonemoto, and Tom Zeiler. Pat Murphy, as she did with *The Legacy of Conquest,* stepped in to save the day—and the manuscript—in its final stages, while Bill Wyman and Luana Vigil kept me from sinking beneath the tide of new technology. Meanwhile, Alphonse Keasley and the Minority Arts and Sciences Program Scholars offer consistent reminders of why an affection for universities is a sane and reasonable sentiment.

In the field of Western American history, I have some of the world's finest teammates. This is a very limited list of those to whom I am in debt for all sorts of ideas and inspirations: Alison Bernstein, Bill Cronon, Bill Deverell, Neil Foley, David Gutierrez, Ramon Gutierrez, Beth Hass, Robert Hine, Yvette Huginnie, Al Hurtado, Howard Lamar, Valerie Matsumoto, Maria Montoya, Katherine Morrissey, Peggy Pascoe, Martin Ridge, Vicki Ruiz, George Sanchez, Virginia Scharff, Jan Shipps, Quintard Taylor, Elliott West, Richard White, Donald Worster, David Wrobel, and John Wunder.

For advice on the essays that appear here, I am in debt to Dana Asbury, Leonard Arrington, Ken Burns, Lavina Fielding Anderson, Jesse Embry, Mary Jane Gormley, James Grossman, Steven Ives, Roger

Launius, Michael McCone, Monica McCormick, Rich Nicholls, Gail Nomura, Richard Orsi, Kenneth Owens, Ed and Martha Quillen, Mark Pittenger, David Ransel, Allyn Roberts, David Thelen, Geoffrey Ward, and William Wei. For help in research, I thank Shreka Anderson, John Coleman, Tracy Brady, Kim Gruenwald, Elinor McGinn, Hannah Nordhaus, Ken Orona, Jeremy Shelton, Stephen Sturgeon, Mike Uihlein, and Clark Whitehorn. For her close attention to the manuscript, I am grateful to Carol Loomis. For help in proofreading, I thank Brad Cartwright, Wendy Cunningham, John Grider, and Elizabeth Shook.

In the category of "friends without whom life would be unimaginable," Gloria and Jack Main and Sallye and Michael McKee always rank at the top, as does Ed Barber, without whom, as a matter of stark and incontrovertible fact, neither *The Legacy of Conquest* nor *Something in the Soil* would have happened.

Grant and Patricia Nelson, Carole Nelson Ingram, Francine Nelson Brookins, and Sunnie, Jim, Jay, and Michael Bell continue to set a high standard for good humor, compassion, and human interest. I am honored to be their kin.

Jeff Limerick is a fine architect, a good-natured recipient of ideas up for testing, and a world-class pal. I am, as he has been known to remind me, lucky.

My biggest debts are to the good hosts who invited me to speak and the audiences who listened to me and talked back over the last ten years. You gave my life unexpected meaning. (And thanks to Airport Specialists who literally got me places and to Keith Lewis, the UPS man, who got me books.)

Introduction
Something in the Soil

> Before it can ever be a repose for the senses, landscape is the work of the mind. Its scenery is built up as much from strata of memory as from layers of rock. . . . And though it may sometimes seem that our impatient attitude for produce has ground the earth to thin and shifting dust, we need only poke below the subsoil of its surface to discover an obstinately rich loam of memory.
> SIMON SCHAMA, *Landscape and Memory*

The land of the American West isn't what it used to be. Weeds and other exotics have been remarkably aggressive in competing with native species; plowing has encouraged erosion; grazing livestock have transformed groundcover; mines have ripped the ground and leached minerals into streams and rivers; irrigation has deposited minerals and salts in farmland; buildings have stacked themselves up on parts of the surface; roads and highways have linked distant tracts of land into a global social and economic network.

Harder to see but just as telling, an accumulation of stories and memories has also transformed the land. At some places—Yellowstone National Park, Sutter's Fort, Sand Creek, Little Big Horn, the Grand Canyon, Salt Lake City, the Oregon Lava Beds, Glen Canyon Dam—narratives have piled themselves up into moraines, deltas, and heaps of memory. Even though some Western landscapes practice a trickster's habit of presenting themselves to newcomers as if they were fresh, untouched, vacant spaces, nonetheless, stories have become quite literally something in the Western soil. As well as rock, soil, plants, animals, water, and air, the American West is composed of layers and layers of accumulated human activity and thought. Traveling around the West for the last decade, exploring the region's past, present, and future with a wide range of audiences, I have kept oriented by reckoning with these strata of memory.

These travels have proceeded from and returned to the History Department and Center of the American West, in Hellems Hall, at the University of Colorado in Boulder. Thirty-five years ago, when I first visited a campus with one of my older sisters, I fell in love with universities. From then on, I became codependent with colleges; placed on a campus, I am instantly both enabled and enabling. I like classrooms and I like students, but the situation is worse than that. I am absolutely wild for professors and their works. To hear a thought-provoking conference paper or to read a lively new academic book permits, in my judgment, an ahead-of-schedule visit to heaven.

As in all relationships overcharged with affection, an open and declared love for universities also involves agony. In the late twentieth century, public conversation on the role of universities has taken a disheartening turn. Critics condemn professors for a variety of sins: a preference for research over teaching, a refusal to submit to demands for accountability and evaluation, a writing style that shuts out nonacademic readers, a refusal to connect with the issues of real life, a stubborn determination to hold on to the privileges of tenure, and a commitment to enforce that mysterious state of expression called "political correctness." Stung by these charges, professors do not always shine in their response. A prickly refusal to change and a snooty defense of academic turf have the sorrowful effect of seeming to verify the charges. To many members of the public and, worse, to many members of budget-controlling state legislatures, "academic" becomes a synonym for "arcane," "pointless," and "self-indulgent."

And yet I know many professors who cheerfully work with public school teachers, who plan museum exhibits and documentary films, who talk at service clubs and retirement homes, who answer questions from journalists, who make their research accessible to policymakers, activists, and officials in government agencies. While it may be premature to declare this a movement, a significant number of academics do defy the stereotype of the ivory-tower captive, sequestered in a world of abstract, irrelevant research.* The practice of the applied humanities—using history to step away, at least momentarily, from the bitterness of current controversies and to place those controversies in a more reflective context—offers enormous growth opportunities.

As academic bashing has flowered into a national sport, I have regularly and repeatedly had a glorious time in travels outside the walls of the university, and I begin to think that my experience may be not an anomaly but one indicator of a significant change in professorial practice. It is a rare public audience that holds my "professordom" against me, and even the occasional cautious or suspicious group can be disarmed with gestures of respect and a demonstrated willingness to attend closely to their thoughts. Moreover, in these outings, I have drawn heavily and explicitly on what I have learned from journal articles, monographs, and conference papers; contrary to stereotype, the research done by academics has a great deal of bearing on current dilemmas. And, in appraising the congeniality of these encounters, it is important to remember that I have been speaking on a subject matter often judged to be one of the most violent ideological battlegrounds. I have been talking about the history of the American West, a topic carrying a heavy investment of national vanity and sensitivity.

These pleasant travels and instructive encounters began after publication of *The Legacy of Conquest* in 1987 and escalated a couple of years later. After the "Trails" conference in Santa Fe in 1989, media attention to Western American history skyrocketed, and opportunities to pursue public conversation followed the same trajectory. The purpose of the Santa Fe conference was not, actually, to proclaim a new historical movement; on the contrary, it was to launch a modest but peppy exhibit called "Trails through Time." A meditation on routes of travel in the Rocky Mountain West, "Trails" was itself a traveling exhibit, visiting many communities in Arizona, New Mexico, Col-

*In the field of American history, some of the notable participants in this "movement" include William Cronon, Eric Foner, Andrew Gulliford, James O. Horton, Barbara J. Howe, Michael Kammen, Edward Lilienthal, James Loewen, Patricia Mooney-Melvin, Gary Nash, Anna Kasten Nelson, Kenneth Owens, Roy Rosenzweig, Arthur Schlesinger, Jr., David Thelen, Janelle Warren-Findley, Richard White, and Donald Worster.

orado, Utah, and Wyoming. To fit in the funding requests, the title of the launching conference had to use the word "trails." And yet all of us who had worked on the conference were already suffering from overexposure to the history of trails, and the prospect of sitting through two days of trails talk was discouraging. So we decided to make the conference into a general appraisal of the field's changes, and thus the Santa Fe conference carried the title "Trails: Toward a New Western History."

In no time at all, that accidental phrase declared its independence from its authors and developed a life of its own. After stories in the *Washington Post,* the *New York Times,* the *Christian Science Monitor,* the *Los Angeles Times, USA Today, U.S. News and World Report,* and many other news publications, I found I was hitched to an untamed and badly groomed intellectual entity called the New Western History. At this point, I began to feel a sense of camaraderie with Dr. Frankenstein, who surely watched with comparable alarm as his creature lurched out of the laboratory to frighten the townspeople. The only workable strategy seemed to be to accompany the creature out into the world and try to act as its translator, if not, alas, as its master.

What was the New Western History? Definitions proliferated. Every now and then, the content of these definitions matched my own understanding of the changes in the field.[1] Other times, definitions of this movement and of my own role in it entirely mystified me. An unusual partnership of journalists and a few disgruntled Western historians created a portrait of a very grim movement that cast white men as wicked and demonic and envisioned the history of the American West as an unrelieved tragedy. Reading one or two newspaper articles supplied a number of people with all they needed to know about the matter. A friend, working in a bookstore in a resort town in Colorado, saw an elderly gentleman browsing in the store's Western history section. My friend approached him and said, "If you are interested in this field, I'd recommend Patricia Limerick's *The Legacy of Conquest.*" At this, the old gentleman drew himself up and replied, "*I* am on the other side of *that* question."

"That question" evidently hinged on the level of cheeriness one wanted in one's story of the region's past. To a surprising number of journalists, as well as a few historians, paying attention to the injuries and damages wrought by the United States's westward expansion seemed inherently grim, disheartening, and unpatriotic. "Historians

Accent Dark Side of Frontier," the headlines said; "Historians Paint Gloomy Picture of the Old West." In a foreword to a picture book, *The Old West* (1990), one alarmed historian offered a typical summary of the New Western History. With our attention focused on the "dark strains" and "splatters of mud" in Western history, the New Western Historians offer "a picture of unrelieved bleakness," "a somber West, devoid of light, marked by hardship, suffering and failure," peopled "by victims of institutionalized brutality and avarice." We judge Western history to be "a profoundly disturbing and negative aspect of the nation's past," a "most destructive heritage of which Americans should be ashamed."[2]

Passages like this helped me realize that the New Western History had become a kind of Rorschach test for people ruled by strong, unexamined emotions about the West. Just as those who administer the ink blots in psychological tests would achieve little by trying to "correct" the weirdness projected on the images, why bother trying to correct the agitated misreadings of the New Western History? In hindsight, I recognized that it would have been a great deal more instructive to explore these revelations of projected fear and anxiety by breathing deeply and saying, "How interesting that you find what we write so negative. Let's talk about why you feel that way."*

In truth, the rumored gloom of the New Western History has often worked to my advantage. The situation matches a story told by Joseph Wood Krutch, the important writer about Southwestern deserts. In 1929, Krutch published a book called *The Modern Temper,* declaring that science and rationality had stripped faith and meaning from the lives of sophisticated Americans. A year later, he was scheduled to speak in Detroit to a women's club. Arriving at the train station, Krutch waited for the woman who was to meet him. "She approached me," Krutch reported, "only after every other descending passenger had left the platform."

---

*The charge of negativity usually came in a package with alarm over the undertaking called "revisionist history," a term that could benefit from rethinking. Every normal human being is forever recalculating, reorienting, reorganizing information and reaching for new understanding. Thus, if you know a historian who is not a revisionist, indeed, if you know any human being in any line of work who is not rethinking, reappraising, and revising her or his previous assumptions, then charity requires you to summon the paramedics and get that nonrevisionist examined fast, on the chance that there might still be time to get this party's heart restarted.

"Are *you* Mr. Krutch?"

"I am."

Her face fell.

"But you do not look as . . . as . . . *depressed* as I expected."[3]

I have many versions of this story, in which people come up after I've spoken to tell me that I am nowhere near as depressed, glum, bitter, or angry as they had expected, or hoped. An advance reputation as the Wicked Witch of Western History can leave audiences easily disarmed, when the author surprises everyone by showing up with a personality that bears a much closer resemblance to Judy Garland's Dorothy than to Margaret Hamilton's witch.

The desire to transcend some of these misapprehensions led me to develop a four-word summary, exemplary in brevity and directness, of the changes in this field of history. Responding to the questions of a skilled interviewer from *People* magazine (a periodical with an underrecognized potential for bringing professorial understandings to a wider audience), I was able to pack the New Western History into four words beginning with "c": continuity, convergence, conquest, and complexity.[4]

CONTINUITY

Twenty years ago, right at the heart of the dominant version of Western history, stood a big discontinuity between the nineteenth-century West and the twentieth-century West. As Frederick Jackson Turner had declared, the frontier closed in 1890. Frontier stories came to a halt; in the end of the Indian wars and the creation of national forests and parks, frontier issues reached resolution; the West lost its distinctiveness. These assumptions remained orthodoxy in college history textbooks into the 1990s.* Nearly all of the textbooks stopped indexing any usages of the word "West" after 1890 because, to their authors, the frontier was the West, the West was the frontier, and both had departed as significant subjects of study before the twentieth century started. Most unhappily, this closing of the frontier and the West, in a stroke, declared the work of Western historians irrelevant to any

---

*See "The Case of the Premature Departure," the third essay in this volume.

understanding of the West today. To study the frontier was to study an era that had definitively and solidly *ended,* with no narrative or causal ties connecting the past to the present.

Nearer the soil, Western life told quite a different story. There was more homesteading after 1890 than before. A number of extractive industries—timber, oil, coal, and uranium—went through their principal booms and busts after 1890. If one went solely by the numbers, the nineteenth-century westward movement was the tiny, quiet prelude to the much more sizable movement of people into the West in the twentieth century. Even more important, any number of conflicts and dilemmas, stirred up in the nineteenth century, remained to haunt Westerners in the twentieth century. Conflicts over water use, public lands, boom/bust economies, local authority versus federal authority, relations between Mexico and the United States (as well as between Mexican Americans and Anglos), Indian land and water claims, as well as freedom of religious practice—most of the issues that had agitated the nineteenth-century West continued to stir things up a century later. The assertion of continuity in Western history, along with the discounting of the belief in "the end of the frontier," could reunite the pieces of a fragmented story and help Westerners steer their way through dilemmas which seemed to come from nowhere but which actually came with long pedigrees.

CONVERGENCE

In earlier versions of Western history, the doings of white people, especially white men, controlled center stage. With attention fixed on the westward movement of white Americans, the older Western history could only recognize Indian people as obstacles or barriers to the big process of frontier expansion, while Chinese and Mexican workers could find relevance only as they contributed to the building of railroads and the developing of agriculture. White Americans were the leading men (and, much more rarely, women) of Western history.

In practice, the American West looked dramatically different. The West was, in truth, a place of extraordinary convergence, one of the great meeting zones of the planet. In the Trans-Mississippi West, people from all over the planet met, jockeyed for position with each other, and tried to figure each other out. The westward movement of white Americans was unquestionably important, but so was the westward movement of African Americans, the northward movement from Mexico, the eastward movement from Asia, and the prior presence of Indian people.

CONQUEST

The word "frontier" was the essential term for Western historians in earlier generations. In 1893, Frederick Jackson Turner wisely passed up the opportunity to pin down the term, but its meaning was, in fact, quite clear. If historians were willing to merge their point of view with that of English-speaking white people, heading into the interior from the Atlantic Coast. From that angle of vision, the frontier *was* the edge of civilization, the area where white domination had not yet been consummated. Saturated with nationalistic pride, the emotional and ideological associations of the frontier had the curious effect of exempting United States history from world history. In popular understanding, places like South Africa, the Belgian Congo, Algeria, New Zealand, and Australia had unmistakably undergone invasions and conquests, and the United States, meanwhile, had a frontier, an ever-expanding zone of freedom, opportunity, and democracy.

As Western historians grew more uncomfortable with the problems built into the term "frontier," a number of enterprising souls set forth to salvage it, trying to redeem it for continued use by reducing its ethnocentricity and increasing its inclusivity. My own preference was to give up on these time-consuming exercises in redefinition and, instead, to place Western American history back into global history with an explicit and honest use of the word "conquest." In the last five hundred years, the biggest story on the planet has been the movement of Europeans from Europe into every other continent. Like many other parts of the planet, the American West had been transformed by this story, as the seizure of resources and the imposition of colonial dominance, along with often more benign processes of collaboration, intermarriage, and syncretism, have reshaped the lives of native people. Calling this process "conquest" cleared away the fog.*

COMPLEXITY

The desire for a telling of Western history in which good guys are easily distinguished from bad guys is deep and persistent. Mythmakers have shaped thinking all over the planet; residents of other nations, as well as many Americans, want the Old West to be the place in the past where we go to escape complexity. Black hats should mark the heads of villains, and white hats the heads of heroes, and yet the moral reality of Westerners makes gray hats the appropriate headgear. Human behavior in the American West, both past and present, has shown the same level of moral complexity as human behavior in any other part of the planet. To make a comparable statement about the South would surely elicit a heartfelt "Ho hum."

Describing the West as morally complex, I have had many opportunities to observe, will elicit a chorus of dismay and protest against such a negative point of view. Thus, a major project of the New Western History had to be the assertion that benefits often came packaged with injuries, good intentions could lead to regrettable outcomes, and the negative aspects of life wove themselves into a permanent knot with the positive aspects. The deeply frustrating lesson of history in the American West and elsewhere is this: human beings can be a mess—contentious, conflict loving, petty, vindictive, and cruel—*and* human beings can manifest grace, dignity, compassion, and understanding in ways that leave us breathless.

Underlying all four "c"s was the assertion that the history of the American West was important, and it is a source of the greatest satis-

---

*Curiously, the rejection of the word "frontier" set off a wonderfully unnecessary scholarly debate over the comparative validity of analytic preferences for place or process. The New Western History, the advocates of process contended, unjustly prohibited the study of the frontier process and required that all our attention must now go to the study of region, or place. In fact, the goal of substituting the word "conquest" for the word "frontier" was to have a better grounded discussion of the process that shaped the West. The squabble over place versus process was, as my colleague Richard White has observed, one of the few scholarly debates to die purely of its own fatigue, a very encouraging precedent.

faction that this assertion now seems unnecessary. Twenty years ago, obituaries for the field of Western history were frequent. Specialists seemed demoralized; attendance at the Western History Association seemed to be shrinking; respect for this scholarly turf seemed to contract ever faster. From the mid-1980s, I recall vividly a conversation with a professor who was leaving the University of Colorado for the University of North Carolina and who saw this move as a great stride in upward mobility. At a farewell reception, the departing faculty member remarked, "Since I'll be moving to North Carolina, I'll have to do a lot of reading in Southern literature and history." "When you moved to Colorado," I asked him, "did you have to do a lot of reading in Western literature and history?" The professor and everyone else taking part in the conversation (except me!) took this as a joke, and a pretty funny joke at that. To their minds, Western history's status as a playpen for antiquarianism and nostalgia was a common understanding. Our goal was to make that understanding much less common.

By nearly any measure I can think of, the movement met its goals. Attendance at the Western History Association is hearty and substantial; mainstream organizations like the Organization of American Historians, the American Historical Association, and the American Studies Association energetically recruit Western historians for offices and positions; significant numbers of talented graduate students have been drawn to the field. To many of these younger scholars, the squabbles of the late 1980s and early 1990s look strange, distant, and puzzling. Was it not obvious that race and ethnicity occupied a central place in Western history? And equally obvious that the "end of the frontier" had not resolved conflicts begun in the nineteenth century and persisting into the twentieth? Of course, case studies from California or New Mexico carried equal weight and validity as case studies from Massachusetts or Virginia. Why put so much effort into proclaiming the obvious?

"When shifting paradigms," a student once wrote, "it is important to remember to put in the clutch." The clutch, in this case, proved hard to find; the shifting of the gears in Western history will not be remembered for its grace and fluidity. But it was certainly rapid. The transformation of young rebels into established authorities is always a deeply weird one, and performed at a high speed, it leaves the head spinning. On behalf of my credentials as a young rebel, it is a matter of some pride to me that I finished writing *The Legacy of Conquest* before I had tenure. Of the various souls who felt obliged to warn me of the risks—resentment, retribution, ostracism, denial of tenure— that I was courting in challenging orthodoxy, no one thought to warn me that *becoming* orthodoxy posed an even greater threat. Why did things move so fast? Because so many people had, independently, decided that the old model of Western history was stretched to the point of snapping. The situation was a textbook case of Kuhnian paradigm shifting. Particularly because of work in ethnic history, women's history, environmental history, and legal history, the pressures had built up to where the plates were going to shift. The publication of *The Legacy of Conquest* and the presentation of the "Trails" conference benefited from impeccably fortunate timing.

If Western American history was revitalized, then the question still lingered: where or what was the American West? Was the West primarily an idea floating from place to place according to time and imagination? Was the West a disparate collection of pieces and parts, localities and areas with little in common? Could anything much in the way of regional distinctiveness survive the tidal wave of homogenized mass culture? Was the West really a definable region?

Asked these questions on several hundred occasions, I prepared my reasons for treating the West as a region, defining it with flexible borders at the Pacific and at the hundredth meridian, where rainfall drops below the twenty inches a year needed to sustain irrigated agriculture. This West is not, heaven knows, a unit of homogeneity and internal consistency. But much of this territory shares common characteristics, characteristics that do not appear in every part of the West but that overlap in enough Western places to give the whole some conceptual unity.

1. The West is prone to aridity and semiaridity, and this is a fact full of consequences, because most of what Anglo-Americans considered and consider normal in a landscape requires much more water than the West would provide. The scarcity of water would inspire a distinctive regional campaign to change nature: to build—with heavy support from the federal government—a vast network of dams, reservoirs, and canals to "normalize" this anomalous landscape.

2. The West contains many Indian reservations and many visible, unvanished Indian people. This is not meant to take anything away

from the significance of the Mohawk people or the Eastern Cherokee or the Pequots. This is a matter not of denying the significance of Eastern Indian people or of asserting the West's uniqueness, but simply of saying that the center of gravity in American Indian affairs is in the West, with the bulk of the land that is still under tribal sovereignty and with the majority of the descendants of the conquered people.

3. The West shares a border with Mexico, and has been and is the entry point for Mexican immigrants. In Mexican immigration, people do not have to cross an ocean, and the relationship between immigrant and home country is thus substantially different from other forms of U.S. immigration. Moreover, the conditions of the Mexican–U.S. border are distinctive and remarkable, as a place where a prosperous, developed nation shares a land connection with a developing, Third World nation. Equally as important, much of the West was once under the sovereignty of Spain and then Mexico and was acquired by the United States in a clear war of conquest against another nation. Originally participants in an invasion and conquest of Indian territory, Spanish-speaking people thus came to share, with Indian people, the status of a minority by conquest, with their rights theoretically guaranteed by international treaty.

4. The West reminds us that the United States is a bicoastal nation, making attention to the Pacific Ocean as necessary as attention to the Atlantic Ocean. It was, and is, the entry point for Asian immigration; it was the center and staging ground of anti-Asian agitation. It is the focal point for the shift in the balance of U.S. trade, from Europe to Asia.

5. The West contains the bulk of the land still under federal control. The Eastern states privatized the public domain, and privatized it *fast*. The Western states followed another track entirely—in part because the aridity, or sometimes the elevation, of much Western land made it unsuitable for conventional Anglo-American economic development and in part because the federal government made a massive swing toward permanent ownership of the public domain, beginning with the creation of the forest reserves in 1891.

6. As point 5 suggests, the West is a particularly illuminating case study in state power, in showing how the United States as a nation conducted conquest. In the permanent control of public lands, in the subsidizing of private businesses like the railroads, in the construction of federal dams, in the reckoning with the treaty rights of Indian people (as well as rights awarded Mexican Americans under the Treaty of Guadalupe Hidalgo), the operations of the federal government are crucial and central. In many ways the Department of the Interior began as, and continued to be, a special state agency for the governance of the West. Any discussion of the powers of the federal government that does *not* include this distinctive regional relationship will be incomplete to the point of serious distortion.

7. The West has a particularly dramatic, though certainly not unique, long-term involvement with the boom/bust economies of extractive industries (mining, logging, ranching, oil drilling, and commercial farming), cycles of prosperity that the federal government has sometimes moderated but never tamed.

8. The region has an equally long involvement with the commercial, intentional mythologizing of the West as a place of romantic escape and adventure. This mythologizing has, indeed, created a nearly intractable dilemma in regional and national self-knowledge. It has, as well, given the region a particularly heavy dependence on the uncertain industry of tourism and on the effort to meet the expectations generated by this myth.

9. The West has a long history as the nation's dumping ground—either for troubling populations of Indians and Mormons or for toxic and radioactive substances. It was, for instance, surely no surprise to anyone when Western sites won the finalist's position for permanent national nuclear waste dump.

10. As a result of a number of these factors, the West is particularly prone to demonstrate the unsettled aspects of conquest, to show in the late twentieth century more than its share of the evidence that the conquest of North America came to no clear point of completion. From the presence of the majority of the conquered people and the un-

resolved status of their rights to the ways in which aridity refuses to mask the impact of conquest, leaving everything from abandoned mines to the effects of erosion exposed and unmistakable, the West displays the ongoing legacy of conquest in everyday life.

Incorporated into speeches and essays, these factors worked when field-tested with Western audiences. For years, I had wished that contemporary Westerners would include historians in their discussions of contemporary issues. In the absence of historians, a fuzzy nostalgia usually substituted for the historical events that shaped the present. When, for instance, public officials called for immigration restriction, they often used the phrase, "We have lost control of the Mexican border." "But when," I would wonder, "did you or anyone else ever *have* control of that border?" Imagining and then yearning to recapture a lost era of control did not seem a very sound basis for contemporary policy.

For quite a long time, I had no idea how to get directly into these conversations. The ultimate armchair quarterback, I began my project to inject historical perspective into contemporary issues by muttering at television sets and newspapers. But then, quite abruptly, invitations started to appear—invitations to speak to living human beings about real-life dilemmas in the West. Here, in chances to address groups like the Western Governors Association, the Western Association of Fish and Wildlife Agencies, the Bureau of Land Management, the Society of American Foresters, the International High-Level Radioactive Waste Management Conference, the Colorado County Commissioners, and the National Conference of State Legislatures, was a dream come true. The realization of a dream, I was soon able to report, delivers equal portions of happiness and major-league anxiety.

Many of these audiences had a touching faith that historians, having come to understand the past, were thus equipped to explain the present and to predict the future. In truth, any "operator's license" that I received in graduate school was restricted to the use of the past-tense verb. When I tried to shift to the present tense or, weirder still, the future tense, I was quite literally operating without a license. I am, moreover, no particular believer in the proposition that "those who do not study history will be condemned to repeat it." Every historical situation seems so distinctive that the idea of repeating cycles of events can only work at a very abstract level. Presenting the lessons of history is a lot more complicated than discovering and describing a great Ferris wheel of historical cycles.

I had many occasions to think of a memorable correspondence my college roommate had shared with me. After graduation, she wanted to get a job in theater production, and so she wrote around the country, asking for advice and prospects for jobs. She got one letter back from a director in Pittsburgh, a man with odd and cryptic handwriting. But the last line of his letter seemed very clearly to say, "I am a fraud; I cannot help you." What a refreshingly honest man, we all thought; you wouldn't expect such honesty from someone in his position. And then we looked at the letter more carefully and realized that the last line actually said, "I am *afraid* I cannot help you." Afraid or a fraud, if these groups had invited me to give them historical perspective, how could I say to them, either indirectly or directly, that they had made a big mistake? So I gave it—and I use the term advisedly—the old college try. The field-testing of the New Western History, along with a number of the essays in this book, was the result.

Ten years ago, opportunities to declare the relevance of history to current dilemmas seemed fantasies. Now they are almost a daily experience. When I was writing *The Legacy of Conquest,* I mistakenly thought I was on my own; only after its publication did I realize that I had actually been part of a team and a movement, with colleagues and collaborators that I hardly took time to notice. In my hopes for the reinvigoration of the academic world through engagement with public audiences, I no longer labor under any illusion of individualism. I know there are lots of professors who are involved in similar enterprises. Members of the public are hungry for perspective, and a journey in time seems one of the most practical ways for them to get it. University-based public intellectuals have opportunity spread out before them, and Part V of this book sums up what ten years of experience have taught me about techniques and strategies for seizing that opportunity. The field-testing of the New Western History maps out one easy and practical route to redeem higher education, to increase appreciation for university-based work among voters and taxpayers, to reacquaint academics with the value of their work, and to have a good time in wonderfully mixed company.*

---

*For techniques and strategies for this kind of work, see part V-A of this volume, "A How-to Guide for the Academic Going Public."

Nearly thirty years ago, as a student at the University of California, Santa Cruz, I took my first venture into the world of public discourse. For years, Santa Cruz had been a quiet resort and retirement community. Then, in 1965, to the horror of many of the elderly residents, a new University of California campus opened, and young people with long hair and alarming habits soon arrived. In my case, responding to the mandate of the times and becoming active in the community came to mean trying to mediate between these hostile camps of young and old. My passion for visiting old folks eventually got me written up by Associated Press, portrayed as a kind of good teenager, sitting attentively in nursing homes, while bad college students neglected personal grooming and raised questions about Richard Nixon's conduct of the Vietnam War. This good-teenager business, appearing on front pages of newspapers across the nation in 1970, was not easy to take. Surely the most bothersome part of the whole operation was an unpleasant letter I got from an old person in Boston, who thought that I was condescending to the elderly.

Having assaulted my character in every other way, this unpleasant soul turned to picking on my birthplace and hometown, Banning, California, which had been briefly referred to in the article. My correspondent knew nothing about Banning, but she wrote a damning line, a sentence that seems to deepen in the memory with the passage of two decades. Banning, she said, "sounds like something in the soil."

Something in the soil?

What my critic meant by "something in the soil," I never figured out. But the phrase has stuck in my mind. Anyone who thought that Banning was something in the soil would most likely think that I was something pretty close to the soil myself. This suggested that my hometown—and other peripheral, or marginal, Western communities like it—and I had a common cause. As a Western American historian, I have tried to provide a more-grounded and down-to-earth version of the history of the American West. Of course, the West has had a very full life as an abstraction, an ideal, and a dream. And yet the West is also actual, material, and substantial—"something in the soil," a set of actual places now holding layer upon layer of memory.

PART I

—◆—

FORGETTING

AND

REMEMBERING

Western American history presents an extraordinary study in the operations of human memory. The memory of the Western past runs the spectrum from obsessive fascination with details of the Old West—trails, outlaws, Pony Express, ghost towns—to full and complete denial of the harsh realities of invasion and conquest.

Asked to write an essay about photographs taken at the sites of major events in Indian-white relations (battles, massacres, treaty negotiations, routes of flight), I had to look closely at the ground-level workings of conquest: episodes of brutality and violence that make amnesia seem an attractive option. In writing *The Legacy of Conquest,* I had purposefully left the battles and wars out, ostensibly because they seemed inconsequential in light of the fact that tribes who did not fight the U.S. Army underwent the same loss of power and territory as those who took part in direct combat. To write "Haunted America," I had to give up evasion and look at the patterns revealed in the bloodshed by which white Americans gained possession of the continent.

The shift in tone in the next essay, "The Adventures of the Frontier in the Twentieth Century," may well disorient readers; it certainly disorients me. For a catalogue accompanying an exhibit at the Newberry Library, "The Frontier in American Culture," I tracked the ways in which late-twentieth-century

Americans think about the frontier. In their use of the word, Americans reveal the ways in which they remember the history of westward expansion. The lightness of this pattern of memory should make for quite a contrast to the heavy weight of the wars remembered in "Haunted America."

History textbooks may or may not shape our memories. I am in some doubt on this matter, having struggled to get under-graduates to read the often bland and homogenized prose. In any case, textbooks do offer a telling glimpse of historiographic orthodoxy. Editing a series appraising textbooks in *The Journal of American History*, Roy Rosenzweig asked me to look at their treatment of the West. The degree of standardization in text-books was its own surprise; in our classes, we are forever as-suring our students that historical interpretation is a fresh and spirited adventure of the mind, a message quite wonderfully mocked by the textbooks we have assigned. As "The Case of the Premature Departure" argues, official historical memory of Western history is nearly as distorted as popular memory; in every textbook available in 1992, the West appeared as a pass-ing, ephemeral historical interlude, departing on schedule in 1890 with the end of the frontier.

I-A

Haunted America

If there be one principle more deeply rooted than any other in the mind of every American, it is that we should have nothing to do with conquest.

THOMAS JEFFERSON,
letter to William Short, 1791

. . . you will soon find it theologically and factually true that man by nature is a damn mess.

NORMAN MACLEAN,
A River Runs Through It

THE SHARP POINT OF CONQUEST

If you place yourself at a distance, there is no clearer fact in American history than the fact of conquest. In North America, just as much as in South America, Africa, Asia, and Australia, Europeans invaded a land fully occupied by natives. Sometimes by negotiation and sometimes by warfare, the natives lost ground and the invaders gained it. From the caves in the lava beds of Northern California, where the Modocs held off the United States Army for months, to the site along the Mystic River in Connecticut, where Puritans burned Pequots trapped in a stockade, the landscape bears witness to the violent subordination of Indian people. These haunted locations are not distant, exotic sites set apart from the turf of our normal lives. Neither time nor space, it would seem, can insulate us from these disturbing histories.

And yet distance makes these facts deceptively clear. Immerse yourself in the story of the dispossession of any one group, and clarity dissolves. There is nothing linear or direct in these stories. Only in rare circumstances were the affairs that we call "white-Indian wars" only matters of whites against Indians. More often, Indians took part on both sides, tribe against tribe or faction against faction, and whites sometimes played surprisingly peripheral roles in the working out of relationships between and among Indian groups.

Moreover, if Indians were often divided against each other, the same shortage of solidarity applied to the other side. In the tense and unpredictable circumstances before, during, and after a war, whites often squabbled bitterly with each other, presenting something one would not begin to call a united front. In virtually every case, the story of how the war got started and how it proceeded is a long, detailed, and tangled business. These are narratives designed to break the self-esteem of storytellers. You can be the world's greatest enthusiast for narrative history, and you can still lose your nerve at the prospect of putting yourself and your readers at the mercy of one of these tales from hell.

They are tales from hell because they are stories so loaded with tiresome detail and pointless plot twists that narrative art bends and breaks under their weight. They are tales from hell, as well, because they are stories that drive their tellers and readers to a confrontation with the darkest and grimmest dimensions of human nature. Torture, maiming, rape, mutilation, murder—all of the worst injuries that human beings inflict on each other serve as the capstones to these stories. Whites did these things to Indians, and Indians did these things to whites. Invaded or invader, conquered or conqueror, nearly every group had occasion to use terror as a memorable method of communication.

The person who contemplates these tales ends up feeling a kind of nondiscriminatory moral shock, unnerved by nearly everybody's behavior. Of course, one can never lose sight of who started the whole business. Indians never invaded Europe; Indian tribes did not cross the Atlantic to seize the homes, fields, and sacred places of Europeans. It is perfectly clear who started this fight. And it is also perfectly clear who, when the dust had settled, had maneuvered whom into surrendering land, food, and the weapons of aggression and self-defense. But in between those two points of clarity lies a great stretch of historical turf in which people of all ethnicities and backgrounds embraced brutality and committed atrocities. In this disorienting turf, neither victims nor villains came with consistent labeling.

In the muddled events that lie between the beginning of invasion and the invaders' consolidated domination, historical lessons are hard to come by. Morals to the story that lift the spirit and inspire hope simply do not appear. On some occasions, historians are quick to make cheerful remarks about how the understanding of history will help us to understand ourselves and to cope with the dilemmas we have inherited from the past. It is hard to pipe up with one of those earnest declarations of faith in the value of historical knowledge when you are thinking of the water at the junction of the Mississippi River and the Bad Axe River. That water, on August 2, 1832, was reddened with the blood of the wounded Sauk and Fox people trying to escape the bullets of American troops. In Indian agent Joseph Street's description, "The Inds. were pushed literally into the Mississippi, the current of which was at one time perceptibly tinged with the blood of the Indians who were shot on its margin & in the stream. . . . It is impossible to say how many Inds. have been killed, as most of them were shot in the water or drowned in attempting to cross the Mississippi."[1] Those Indians who survived the crossing at Bad Axe did not leave brutality behind them when they escaped from the white soldiers. The survivors were attacked a few days later—by a party of Sioux.

What good can knowledge of this miserable story do? Is the principal lesson simply that the winning of Illinois was as tangled, brutal, and bloody a process as the winning of Massachusetts or the winning of Oregon? What exactly does knowledge of this event add to American self-understanding and well-being?

When I went to college, I had a fine professor in my freshman course in Western civilization. Jasper Rose was from England and given to the use of terms of address like "ducky." One day in class, we talked about the Calvinist belief in the evil that had lodged in the human soul after the fall of Adam. The way that Mr. Rose discussed the topic of human depravity puzzled me to my core.

"When you were talking about the way people used to believe in the evil in humans," I said to him after class, "you sounded as if *you* believed there is such a thing. But how could a modern person believe in human depravity?"

"Just wait, ducky," Mr. Rose sighed. "Just wait."

Jasper Rose was doing his best to get me braced for the Battle of Bad Axe. But there is no way to be truly braced for the dreadful reality of these events. The Mystic Fort Fire, the Ohio River Wars, Black Hawk's War, the Mountain Meadows Massacre, the Bear River Massacre, the Sand Creek Massacre, the Modoc War, and the Nez Perce War—all these events have me flummoxed. Yes, these stories are part of our national heritage; yes, they shaped us as a people; yes, we have to know our past to understand our present. But, by remembering these stories, what do we gain besides a revival and restoration of the misery?

A Twelve-Point Guide to War

In graduate school, we were trained to be finders of themes. Where others might see a bunch of unconnected facts, we were obligated to locate the underlying patterns. Like any exercise, this was hard at first but easier with practice. And, unlike many exercises, this one was addictive. In a world so overloaded with complexity and contradiction, the activity of getting a grip on themes and patterns is genuinely comforting and soothing. This ability of generalizations to bring calm is particularly appealing when one confronts ugly forms of human behavior. In that spirit, I now put forward twelve patterns of white-Indian wars. These are not universal laws; readers will, no doubt, think of many exceptions as they read. But the most that one can ask of one's historical patterns is that they are true more often than are not, and these easily meet that qualification.

To give these general patterns a clear tie to reality, I have prefaced each point with a story from the Modoc War of 1872–1873.[2] I have chosen this war because it clearly and directly embodies most of these patterns; because it makes a geographical break from the usual Great Plains–centered tellings of the Indian wars, reminding us that these wars occurred all over the nation; and because it is a representatively agonizing war story.

Modoc Story, Part 1

The Modoc War began on November 29, 1872. Interaction between whites and Modocs began long before that. In the 1820s, traders from the Hudson's Bay Company came into Modoc territory, at the border of what are now the states of California and Oregon. Like many tribes, the Modocs enthusiastically adopted European-introduced horses. In the late 1840s, white settlers in Oregon laid out wagon roads through Modoc territory, providing both a route to and from California and a more southern line of access from the Oregon Trail. These roads provided opportunities for raiding and killing, as the Modocs and other Indians of the area responded to the presence of white travelers with livestock and well-packed wagons. Both civilian vigilante groups and federal troops reacted to these attacks, sometimes "punishing" Indians who had taken part in the raiding and sometimes simply attacking any Indians they could find. Gold discoveries brought miners into the area, and ranchers and farmers also settled in.

Newly founded towns were magnets for Indians as well as whites; Modocs were frequent visitors to the town of Yreka. Some Modoc women served as prostitutes, and both Modoc women and men proved susceptible to the appeal of alcohol. Modocs worked, as well, as cowboys on some of the local ranches. By the time of the war in 1872, the denim and calico clothes worn by many Modocs were only one of the marks of change in their habits. In battles during the war, the men shouted insults at white troops, expertly wielding their familiarity with the English language to rile up the enemy.

PATTERN 1
Before a war happened, there was already a great deal of water under the bridge.

Before whites and Indians would feel inclined to fight each other in a sustained way, they had to get to know each other. Before prolonged violence came disease, exotic plants and animals, traders and trade dependence, intermarriage, missionaries, representatives of the federal government, and, often enough, white emigrants, farmers, miners, or ranchers. Before they took up arms against each other, Indians and whites had to go through a substantial "getting to know you" phase. But, unlike the pattern in the musical *The King and I,* "getting to know you" in these situations often meant "getting to dislike and distrust you," "getting to realize that, even though I thought I could use your presence for my benefit, it is not working out that way."

The "getting to know you" phase was often so long and consequential that the border between whites and Indians became blurred. Intermarriage was the most obvious example of this blurring. Where

traders had been present for a while, children of mixed heritage became important figures in society, sometimes caught uncomfortably
between groups, sometimes finding their status in between to be the
source of considerable advantage. After a generation or two, the terms
"Indian" and "white" had become more matters of political loyalty
and cultural practice than lines of biological descent. Through intermarriage, natives and invaders had become, in the broadest sense,
relatives; under those circumstances, Indian-white wars looked more
like a quarrel between neighbors than a collision of strangers.

Interaction with whites, moreover, reshaped tribal economies and
politics. Decades, sometimes centuries, of diplomacy, exchange, and
negotiation preceded warfare, and Indian economies and forms of
leadership showed the impact. Every time an Indian fired a gun in a
battle, the use of a manufactured firearm offered another reminder of
how intertwined the lives of the participants had already become.

Modoc Story, Part 2

In 1864, representatives of the federal government tried to negotiate an understanding with the Modocs and the other Indians of the
area. But confusion was built into the process. In February of 1864,
Elijah Steele, a judge and Indian agent for northern California, took
part in discussions with the Modoc and two other tribes. By the terms
of the Steele treaty, the Indians would cease to fight each other; they
would not interfere with white settlers; and although they would re-
tain the right to travel, they would agree to be regulated by the officers at Fort Klamath. The Steele treaty did not address the question
of whether the Modocs would have a reservation near the Lost River,
their home area; it did not, by the same token, suggest that this was
impossible.

While the Steele treaty was at least moderately compatible with
the Modocs' preference, it never received approval by the Indian Bureau or ratification by the United States Senate. Instead, in October of
1864, another negotiator—J. W. Pettit Huntington, superintendent
of Indian affairs for Oregon—presided over a second set of discussions. The result was a second treaty, setting forth very different terms,
terms much less acceptable to the Modocs, since this treaty would
send them away from Lost River.

The second treaty created one reservation for both the Klamath and the Modocs. This land that made up the reservation was entirely Klamath land; the Modocs would have to leave their homes and move into the homeland of another, sometimes hostile tribe. The Modocs divided over this prospect: some of them followed the leader Old Schonchin to the reservation and agreed to live there, despite frequent friction with the Klamath people. But another group left the reservation and returned to Lost River, repudiating the second treaty of 1864, while keeping their allegiance to the unratified Steele treaty. Kientpoos, or Captain Jack, emerged as the leader of this group.

White settlers in the Lost River country were not happy to see these original inhabitants return. Badgered by settlers' complaints of property damage and threats from the Modocs, federal officials succeeded in getting the Indians to return to the reservation—briefly. In the winter of 1869, A. B. Meacham, now the superintendent of Indian affairs for Oregon, persuaded Captain Jack and his fellows to go to the reservation. Then, in late April 1870, to the dismay of the settlers, Captain Jack's Modocs left the reservation and returned to Lost River. To Captain Jack and his party, the Steele treaty was the agreement with which they were still complying, and nothing in that treaty required them to live far from home in the company of the irritating Klamath. The treaty, the reservation, and all the various efforts to control the situation, launched by the officials of the United States Army and the Indian Bureau, had finally produced a perfect muddle.

PATTERN 2
Before a war occurred, some men representing the federal government declared that they were going to settle everything and instead left everyone confused. That confusion was often the trigger for the war.

The Constitution declared the centrality of federal responsibility in Indian affairs, giving Congress the power "to regulate commerce with foreign nations, among the several states, and with the Indian tribes." Thus there was a constitutionally based reason for federal officials to swing into action in anticipation of conflict and to try to arrange a peace that would serve two not very compatible goals: the expansion of white commerce and settlement, and the protection and assimilation of the Indians.

And so a phalanx of territorial politicians, Indian agents, military officers, and humanitarians and reformers called for and attended hundreds of meetings with Indian people. At those meetings, the white officials declared their good intentions and their hopes for harmony between whites and Indians. While some of them were cheerful liars, veiling land grabs under the rhetoric of paternalistic helpfulness, many others believed the things they said.

Frequently the outcome of these councils and negotiations hinged on the honesty and efficiency of one person: the interpreter, who had to translate not only two very different languages but also two very different systems of property and law. Opportunities for confusion were unlimited. Merely identifying who, on either the tribal or federal side, had the authority to ratify and to enforce an agreement could be the most difficult part of these negotiations. White officials fell into the habit of selecting and identifying certain leaders as "chiefs," and then declaring that a whole tribe had agreed to cede territory and retreat to a reservation, when, in fact, only a few, not-always-respected individuals from the tribe had signed an agreement.

From these federal efforts to anticipate conflict and reach a resolution came agreements that carried very different meanings for different individuals and groups. With their multiple meanings, the agreements were very difficult to enforce. On the federal side, a breakdown of enforcement was built into a policy stretched to the point of snapping; an official goal of benevolence to Indians pulled in one direction, and an insistent white demand for lands and resources pulled in another.

Federal officials had visions of sharing the benefits of civilization and Christianity with grateful Indians; Indians had visions of maintaining their sovereignty and traditional economies; white settlers had visions of owning and using land without Indian interference. The federal negotiators and commissioners were placed exactly at the point where those visions clashed. It was not, therefore, unusual to find federal commissioners playing the part of the recipients of everyone's wrath, since both Indians and whites cast these negotiators as the bumblers whose negotiations had delivered everyone into confusion and conflict.

The effectiveness of federal intervention was undermined, as well, by the weakness of the government's power through the first century of the nation's existence. American citizens had a principled distrust of an established, well-funded army. Monarchies and tyrannies relied on standing armies. But democracies and republics called up citizen militias to deal with emergencies and then disbanded those militias when the emergencies were resolved. Here, then, was a curious reluctance to face up to the fact that the nation was engaged not in occasional military emergencies but in a prolonged and concerted war for the continent, a war that would not be won without a serious army, seriously funded. The ideology of expansion may have offered an image of inferior Indians who would simply melt away as white settlements expanded, but few tribes chose to melt and many chose to fight. The cost of war weighed on the federal treasury, principled opposition to a standing army or not. At the end of a war, the supporters of thrift would reappear, cutting back the army's funding and size and leaving the federal government in a chronic position of weakness when it came to enforcing its laws and standing by its promises.

Expenses aside, it was an awkward matter to use the United States Army against United States citizens. Even though the Army did sometimes try to remove white squatters and intruders from Indian territory, this was hardly the way to make the Army more popular. Unable to deliver on many of its promises and guarantees, the federal effort to get the jump on conflict and to negotiate peaceful agreements frequently added up to the achievement of giving all the partisans someone to blame when those agreements fell apart.

Modoc Story, Part 3

In November 1872, the pieces and parts of the federal government geared up for action. Replacing A. B. Meacham and too recently arrived in his job to know much about the Modocs, Thomas B. Odeneal, the new superintendent of Indian affairs for Oregon, asked Colonel John T. Green to send troops from Fort Klamath, to arrest Captain Jack and return him and his people to the Klamath Reservation. Selected by Green, Major James Jackson and thirty-eight soldiers took a long, miserable ride through rain and sleet. Several armed civilians joined in the enterprise.

Early on the morning of November 29, 1872, the Lost River Modocs were camped at two sites. The Army prepared to enter the larger of the two camps, the one with Captain Jack in it, while the civilians took on the smaller camp. Jackson and his men proposed to disarm the Modocs; the Modocs held on to their guns and rifles. In this tense situation, shooting suddenly started. Finding that they were in way over their heads, the civilians retreated—fast—from the smaller camp. The regular troops held on to the larger camp, but the Modocs fled and the troops did not pursue them. After burning the village, with Captain Jack now far beyond the reach of the Army, Major Jackson led a retreat of his own to a neighboring ranch.

While most of the Modocs headed off to take refuge in the nearby lava beds, a small group of men rode off to vent their anger on the nearby settlers. In his retreat, Major Jackson had not tried to warn settlers in the area, much less to offer them protection. A group including Hooker Jim, Boston Charley, Long Tim, and others—*but not Captain Jack*—stopped at several neighboring ranches, killing men and male children but sparing women. At their first stop, Hooker Jim and his allies killed a settler named William Boddy, along with Boddy's son-in-law, Nicholas Schira. Abruptly and terribly widowed, Mrs. Boddy and Mrs. Schira hid during the night and fled to refuge the next morning, while the Modoc party went on to attack other whites, killing fourteen altogether.

The bungled attempt to arrest Captain Jack triggered the war. The vengeance imposed by a few Modocs on the unwarned and unprepared white settlers made the momentum for war irreversible.

PATTERN 3

The first acts of violence usually were more accidents of impulse and passion than the considered and chosen opening acts of an intended war.

At the end of a war, it was common for leaders—both white and Indian—to offer some version of this sentiment: "We did not want this war; it happened in spite of us." When they said this, they were not lying. On the contrary, they were recording the fact that at the start of the war, the preferences of the leaders did not carry nearly as much weight as the impatience and anger of a few individuals. On the Indian side, the first acts of violence were often committed by impulsive young men, driven by their ambition as warriors and defiant of the restraints imposed by their elders. Hunger was also a common provocation for violence. In the gritty details of daily life, invasion and conquest meant, at the bedrock, a loss of traditional sources for food for Indians, and there are few better triggers for desperate acts than the prospect of starvation. On the white side, the triggering acts of violence often came from a similar impatience in white settlers who felt that the United States Army was far too slow in coming to their aid and who therefore took it upon themselves to "punish" Indians for various "crimes," especially for theft. These acts of retaliation were often committed in defiance of white officials, who had a better grasp on the proposition that white American notions of "crime" and "punishment" made an uneven fit to the complex reality of incompatible groups with conflicting ambitions trying to live as neighbors.

Individualistic in their origins, these opening episodes of violence placed leaders in positions where their range of choice was much diminished. Repeatedly, the heated acts of a few individuals carried more weight than the restraint and caution that leaders had tried to maintain. Here came the turning point in the escalation of violence: white settlers and officials chose to take the acts of a few impatient Indian people to represent the will of the whole group. With that assumption embraced, everyone—women, children, and men who had not picked a fight—had to be punished for the actions of a few. Once that choice was made, the unrolling of the war might have seemed inevitable. But it is crucial to remember that there were *two* paths leading from this fork in the road, and neither was inevitable. Humans, in circumstances like these, have the capacity to distinguish individual actions from group actions and to calibrate their responses with that distinction in mind. Here is the clearest contribution of hindsight: if that capacity to make distinctions had been more often in play, the mortality and misery rate in these wars would have been much diminished.

Modoc Story, Part 4

When Hooker Jim's party, reacting to the soldiers' attack on their camp, killed some of their white neighbors, rumors spread in all directions. In towns and in ranch houses, settlers panicked, anticipating brutal surprises from all directions. From the security of hindsight, it is clear that whites who settled in Modoc territory had been taking a great risk, insisting on their right to live in contested terrain. But the killings committed by Hooker Jim's party cast the whites as undeserving victims, delivered by their innocence and trust to the knives and bullets of treacherous Indians. For most settlers in the area, the

Lost River killings settled the question. *All* the nonreservation Modocs had to be punished, and what hindsight would call a war of conquest proved, at the time, to be a conflict in which the whites felt that *they* were the ones who had been mistreated and who were fully justified in defending themselves before the next outrage could occur.

PATTERN 4

If Indians tried to terrorize settlers into leaving contested territory, whites instantly saw themselves as the innocent victims and Indians as the guilty aggressors, and thus the question of justification seemed settled.

Throughout history, humans have found various ways to communicate the message, "Get out; we don't want you here." Snubbing, shunning, segregation, economic boycotts, eviction notices, elimination of a food supply, threats, property destruction, torture, and murder—all of these gestures have been used to say to their recipients, "We'd just as soon you got out of here." When whites moved into territory that Indians claimed, and especially, when white settlement interfered with Indian food growing and food gathering, Indians turned to these various devices of communication to say, effectively and memorably, "Get out."

At various places and times, delivering this message to white intruders, Indian people used the full vocabulary of terror: fire, kidnapping, rape, murder, and mutilation. Because of the brutality practiced in these episodes, moral judgment of the Indian wars will never be pure or clear. Rather than trying to be saints of nonviolence and passive resistance, Indians could be cruel and arbitrary in their attacks on white families whose ambitions had led them to the wrong place at the wrong time.

Contemplating these attacks, historians become "equal opportunity cynics," seeing neither nobility nor brutality as the exclusive property of any group. While Indian attacks on white families have mixed and blurred the moral vision of historians, they sharpened and clarified the moral judgments of white settlers and officials. Once the Indians tried to terrorize settlers into leaving, in the minds of Anglo-Americans, the roles of aggressor and victim instantly reversed. Whites ceased to register as invaders and provokers of conflict and occupied, instead, the status of innocent victims. With this shift, the question of justification was settled: Indians had started the trouble and had asked for punishment, and whites could do whatever they had to do, in order to defend themselves.

Modoc Story, Part 5

After the violence at Lost River, the Modocs crossed Tule Lake and took refuge in an extraordinary place, the lava beds of northern California. When he heard the news of the bungled arrest and the flight of the Modocs, Colonel Frank Wheaton, Green's and Jackson's commanding officer, felt considerable confidence in his understanding of what to do next. He would assemble a force composed of units of both regulars and California and Oregon volunteers, and he would march into the lava beds toward the Modoc stronghold in the center, encircle the renegades, and defeat them. "I do not believe we need anticipate a continued resistance from this little band of Modocs," Wheaton told General E. R. S. Canby.[3] Canby, in turn, reported cheerfully: "I do not think the operations will be protracted."[4] In Washington, General William Tecumseh Sherman synthesized the various messages of confidence he had received from the West Coast and told the Secretary of War that Canby "is in actual command of all the troops and resources of the country and will doubtless bring this matter to a satisfactory end."[5]

In January 1873, Colonel Wheaton tried to put this confident plan into action. But a clumsy troop movement the night before had alerted the Modocs and sacrificed the advantage of surprise. On January 17, a dense fog covered the ground. The troops started forward and presented themselves as targets for Modoc bullets, often expertly delivered. The soldiers could see the injuries and deaths produced by these bullets, but with the thick fog and the rocky, ridge-broken landscape, they could seldom see the Indians who were firing on them. Demoralized, the troops ground to a halt; officers could not or would not follow the original plan to encircle the stronghold. By nightfall, the United States forces were in a disorderly retreat, leaving behind, for the Modocs' use, many of their firearms and much of their ammunition and abandoning many of the wounded. The January 17 attack proved to be a complete disaster for the whites, as the advantage shifted to the Modocs, who did not lose one warrior. Fewer than sixty Modoc men had defeated three hundred soldiers.

PATTERN 5
The wars often began with an Indian victory, frequently because whites were overconfident and thought that fighting a primitive, unsophisticated enemy would be easy and quick.

By all the tenets of white American pride, it should have been easy to beat a set of disorderly, undisciplined primitives. That excess of confidence, however, often led to an initial defeat, as white troops plunged into battle confidently, certain that they had a clear advantage over a simple foe. A belief in one's own intrinsic superiority, these early battles demonstrated, could be a dangerous, even lethal delusion. The defeats put American forces through a rough period of reassessment, leading to the necessary recognition that Indian war was serious business, requiring substantial commitments of leadership, discipline, equipment, and, especially, funding. The defeats reinforced, moreover, the vision of the whites as the embattled, besieged victims, further obscuring the bedrock reality of white invasion, encroachment, and aggression. Perhaps most important, these losses made whites furious, determined on vengeance and unwilling to consider alternatives to the escalation of the war.

Modoc Story, Part 6

During the war, a significant number of Modocs stayed on the Klamath Reservation; some were sympathetic, some simply neutral, and some opposed to Captain Jack and his group. While the Army decided not to try to use Modocs against Modocs, some Klamath Indians took part in the January 17 attack on the lava beds. When the battle turned against the Army, officers placed some of the blame on the Klamaths for fighting halfheartedly. The Army then recruited a number of Indian auxiliaries from the Warm Springs Reservation. These Indians found cooperation with whites to be, on occasion, a life-threatening challenge. On one occasion, late in the war, the Warm Springs Indians tried to come to the aid of a group of soldiers who had been ambushed by Modocs. Panicked and unthinking, the soldiers fired on their rescuers. Despite every effort on the part of the Warm Springs Indians to identify themselves as friends, they could not get their allies to stop shooting at them.

By the end of the war, any notions of tribal solidarity had been shattered. Captain Jack had never been an enthusiastic advocate of war. The impulsive acts of Hooker Jim's party, in killing the Lost River settlers, had forced Captain Jack into a war he did not want. In the spring of 1873, as federal officials tried for a negotiated resolution to the war, the Modoc militants pressured Jack into taking part in a treacherous attack on the peace commissioners. On April 11, 1873, the Modocs killed Reverend Eleazar Thomas and General E. R. S. Canby (the only general killed in the Indian wars) and seriously wounded Albert Meacham. In May of 1873, Hooker Jim, Steamboat Frank, Shacknasty Jim, and Bogus Charley, members of the war party, left Captain Jack and surrendered to the Americans. Over the next weeks, the Modoc men who had pushed Captain Jack into war and assassination now served as his betrayers, helping the Army track him down for a final capture.

In July of 1873, Captain Jack and five others were tried and convicted for the murder of the commissioners. Hooker Jim and others of the original war advocates were not tried for either the murder of the Lost River settlers or the killings of the commissioners. On the contrary, the Army rewarded them for their betrayal of Captain Jack by exempting them from punishment, in order to set an example that would encourage other Indians to change sides. Captain Jack was obviously very much troubled by this chain of betrayal. "I didn't know anything of any settlers being killed until Hooker Jim came with his band and told me," he said at his trial. None of his own people "had killed any of the whites, and I had never told Hooker Jim and his party to murder any settlers; and I did not want them to stay with me." Hooker Jim was "the one that always wanted to fight, and commenced killing and murdering." But now, Captain Jack said, "I have to bear the blame for him and the rest of them."[6]

PATTERN 6
The idea of an Indian war as a conflict of whites against Indians seldom had much to do with reality because Indians were usually on both sides of the conflict.

Intertribal conflict began long before the arrival of Europeans or Euro-Americans. In some areas, the introduction of horses and guns increased the stakes and intensity of intertribal raiding and war. All over North America, the expansion of white settlement escalated the conflict among tribes, as they struggled for control of a reduced supply of territory and resources. Under those circumstances, it made perfect sense for members of one tribe to see whites as helpful allies in campaigns against the common enemy of another tribe. It made sense, as well, to exercise a warrior's skills and take advantage of the opportunity presented by the Army's need for scouts and auxiliaries who knew the terrain and the ways of the enemy.

Divisions in war came, as well, from the presence of factions within tribes. The boundaries of identity and loyalty to a particular tribe were flexible; the band or the clan or the family was more likely to be the primary unit of social cohesion. Conquest placed, moreover, a terrible strain on leadership. To some leaders, going along with whites and their treaties and reservations seemed like the wisest response to an unhappy situation; to leaders of a different persuasion, resistance—armed if necessary—seemed the best way to serve their people's interests. In some cases, missionaries had split the tribe between those who had converted to Christianity and those who held to the traditional beliefs and practices. And, true to human nature, conflicts of personality and of individual ambition played their role in dividing tribes.

Facing up to the divisions inside and among Indian groups requires one to pay attention to one's own unexamined sentimentality. Many late-twentieth-century Americans, of all ethnicities, remain susceptible to a romantic wish that the victims of white American aggression had stood together, measuring up to a standard for saintly, noble, heroic solidarity that any human population, living in perfectly happy and tranquil times, would have had a hard time meeting. Put humans under the terrible pressure of conquest, and the record discloses the great muddle that is human nature.

Modoc Story, Part 7

In the course of the Modoc War, the whites did not do much better than the Indians at maintaining solidarity. Blaming each other took nearly as much of their time and energy as did fighting Modocs.

Before the war began, some federal officials put considerable effort into arguing that the whole situation had been produced by the actions of "bad" whites, who had given the Modocs bad advice and encouraged them in their resistance. When the plan to arrest Jack exploded into war, some whites blamed Superintendent Odeneal for acting in ill-considered haste (and for keeping himself at a safe distance from the scene of danger). Some blamed Major Jackson for letting the arrest action get out of control, for refusing to pursue the Modocs, and for failing to warn the neighboring settlers of their danger.

After the January 17 defeat of the Army, blamers and faultfinders launched into a second round of activity. After that debacle, Wheaton was replaced by Colonel Alvan C. Gillem. Not a particularly charismatic fellow, troubled by ill health, Gillem gained a reputation for reluctance to take on the Modocs and evoked considerable hostility from his officers. For the rest of the war, divisions ran in all directions: officers of the Army against representatives of the Indian Office; regulars against volunteers; the governor of Oregon against the appointed officials of the federal government; Oregonians against Californians (judged by the Oregonians to be too sympathetic to the Modocs); officers against local merchants and farmers who sold the Army provisions and supplies for a handsome profit; Eastern humanitarians standing up for the Modocs' rights against both the Army and the settlers.

The effort to form the Modoc Peace Commission was itself a fine demonstration of the disunity of whites. When A. B. Meacham was asked to serve with Thomas Odeneal, his successor as superintendent of Indian affairs in Oregon, Meacham, who felt Odeneal was responsible for the whole mess, held up the process until a commissioner more agreeable to Meacham could replace Odeneal. Long before they tried to negotiate with the Modocs, the peace commission had a hard enough time simply finding personnel who could peaceably talk with each other.

The Modoc War's most-distressing examples of the breakdown of white solidarity came in a few episodes in which uninjured soldiers refused to help the wounded during retreats. During the retreat from the January 17 defeat, the soldiers scrambled up a bluff to safety: "No one," Keith Murray notes, "helped anyone else, and the walking wounded were left to climb the hill as best they could." After another Army defeat, the soldiers lost their way in the night and those who could still walk "tried to avoid helping to carry the stretchers" of the wounded.[7] White Americans did not march in unity and harmony to the conquest of the continent. White Americans did not retreat in any better order.

PATTERN 7
Whites were often quite disunited themselves, so disunited that white Americans sometimes looked as if they might kill each other before the Indians got a chance at them.

The impact of Indian war on white society resembled the impact of a rock on a window, a window that does not shatter entirely but still shows cracks that spread in all directions. The fractures ran right through the center of the federal government; the Office of Indian Affairs and the War Department were jealous of each other's turf and often opposed in their policies. The president often received conflicting advice from the various officials working in Indian affairs; these were not the circumstances to give rise to a coherent and consistent federal policy. In some cases, the lack of coordination and communication between Indian agents and Army officers was, directly and concretely, the cause of war.

The Army on its own was a fissured society. Personal rivalry and conflicting ambitions divided the officers. Personality conflicts were often heightened by the conditions of isolation and remoteness; it is not too much to say that some of these men truly hated each other. Young officers were often impatient with the restraints imposed by older officers; especially after the Civil War, as opportunities for promotion narrowed, a sense of frustrated ambition spread through the officer corps. Some of the most-heated conflicts centered on supplies, as officers out on the front lines struggled with inadequate food, firearms, clothing, and transportation. Enlisted men, in the meantime, felt varying degrees of enthusiasm and loyalty for their officers and for the whole cause and campaign in which they were employed. Sometimes the soldiers experienced true crises of confidence, convinced that they were trusting their lives to leaders without wisdom or sense. The most unmistakable expression of discontent and demoralization came in a high rate of desertion.

The greatest division in the fighting force was the gap between regulars and volunteers. Local citizens who joined militia units or who simply rode along as informal volunteers often saw the Army as plodding, cautious, and too easy on the Indians. Raids, retaliations, and acts of terror had built up strong currents of racial hostility; local volunteers often wanted to hit the Indians hard, fast, and indiscriminately. On the other hand, volunteers stood a good chance of being undrilled and undisciplined, susceptible to panic and flight at the most crucial moments. When volunteers complained about regulars, and regulars complained about volunteers in this tense and angry relationship between two elements of the white American population, there seemed to be little room left over for any attention to the Indian enemy.

Another important element of white disunity appeared in the dissenters, whites who for various reasons disapproved of the course of action taken by the Army. Sometimes these were settlers who had gotten to know Indians under tranquil and collaborative circumstances. Men and women like these sympathized with the misfortunes of their Indian neighbors, tried to help them secure permanent land claims, and complained of the Army's inflexibility and harshness. Another group of dissenters wore Army uniforms. It was not uncommon, after a massacre or vicious battle, to find a few soldiers or officers who were repelled by what they had seen or taken part in. In some cases, officers felt that their own honor had been violated; they had taken a group of Indians to be peaceful, had promised them safety, and then been unable to protect them from attack. These officers were surprisingly outspoken in expressing their dissent.

The loudest objections came from men and women far from the battlefield—humanitarians who registered their dismay and disapproval when they looked at the actions of the Army and hostile Western settlers. After the Civil War, these humanitarians coalesced as a significant lobby with real power. Army officers thus spent part of their time anticipating criticisms and denunciations from the humanitarians. These agents of Manifest Destiny could feel themselves to be besieged on all sides: constantly challenged and often outfoxed by the Indians, denounced by the Eastern humanitarians for their cruelty, and damned by Western settlers for their unwillingness to punish the Indians with proper harshness.

From time to time, the United States government has been denounced for its "genocidal" policies against Indians. But once you have examined the intensity and range of division within the white population, and even within the forces officially detailed to Indian affairs, then there is one clear defense against the accusations of genocide: even though some individuals did call for the extermination of the Indians, white Americans were simply too divided and disorganized to implement such a policy, even if a majority had supported it.

Modoc Story, Part 8

The Modoc people knew the landscape of the lava beds, and the whites did not. The lava beds provided the Indians with pockets of water and ice, with places to hide cattle, and with caves that could withstand bombardment. The landscape was shaped by parallel ridges of rocks which worked perfectly to the Modocs' advantage. The rock ridges were natural fortifications; the passages between the ridges served as corridors and pathways that permitted the Modocs to keep shifting their sparse number of warriors to new and unexpected locations. On January 17, 1873, as the regulars and the volunteers sat miserably in the mist and absorbed bullets that seemed to have been fired by the fog itself, the Indians' advantage in knowing the turf was the most compelling reality that the soldiers had to contemplate.

On April 26, 1873, a party of soldiers under Captain Evan Thomas went to the lava beds on a reconnaissance. In the early afternoon, the party sat down for an unguarded lunch. The Modoc ambush that came down upon them caught them completely by surprise. Many of the soldiers died on the spot; many more *would* have died if the Indians had not stopped the attack, when the Modoc leader Scarfaced Charley called out, "All you fellows that ain't dead had better go home. We don't want to kill you all in one day." Twenty-three of the Americans were killed, and nineteen wounded. Thomas's force, in historian Keith Murray's words, "had lost almost as many men in two hours as the entire army had lost thus far in the war." Just as they had during the January 17 battle, the Modocs "suffered no losses."[8]

The moment of the Modocs' cease-fire was by no means the end of the surviving soldiers' distress. Still to be reckoned with was the landscape. The relief party coming to their aid got lost. The doctor, traveling behind the relief party, also got lost. Walking the next night in a storm, carrying the wounded, the relief party tried to follow "guides" who "had no idea where they were going," putting the wounded through an awful, aimless ordeal of jostling and bumping against rocks. Knowing where you were, how to get out of there, and how to get to where you would rather be added up to a large element of success and survival in this campaign, and this was an element very much balanced toward the Modocs. "We seem," one of the Army's high-ranking officers telegraphed after the Thomas incident, "to be acting somewhat in the dark."[9]

PATTERN 8
The fact that the Indians knew the landscape, terrain, food supply, and water sources put the whites at a considerable disadvantage.

A century after the Indian wars, "the lessons of Vietnam" became a commonly used phrase. The lessons of Vietnam hinged on the maddening realities of fighting a guerrilla war. The more confident Americans were of their technological superiority and greater wealth, the more vulnerable they were to an enemy who relied on other strengths entirely. In the jungles of Southeast Asia, Americans finally had to recognize the crippling disadvantages of being the intruders and strangers, trying to impose their will in a terrain the natives knew far better.

And yet it is no easy matter to distinguish the lessons of the Indian wars from the lessons of Vietnam. In the territory that would become the United States, the natives knew the terrain, the travel routes, the easily defensible locations, the climate, the location of water, and the sources of food. Their knowledge formed a great contrast with the ignorance, on all these topics, of most Army officers and soldiers. The Indian population could, moreover, shift back and forth between hostile and friendly, enemy and ally, in a way that left whites puzzled, jumpy, and frustrated. In the space of a few hours, a warrior raiding a settlement or fighting hard against the Army could become a family man, relaxed and at peace in his village.

Whatever whites may have thought about the superiority of their technology or their civilization, those assumptions of superiority did not do them much good on the battlefield. If anything, their excess of confidence played into the hands of the enemy. When full of confidence, whites were set up to fall for decoys and predisposed to cooperate with ambushes. Imagining the course of the war, far from the actual battlefield, officers could convince themselves of the effectiveness of their own grand plans and strategies, and then watch those visions dissolve under the pressure of difficult and disorienting terrain, impossible supply lines, and an enemy who simply knew more than they did about the place of contest.

The lessons of the Indian-white wars and the lessons of the Vietnam war were strikingly similar because they were both the lessons of guerrilla war, the kind of war in which the local, insider knowledge held by the natives gave them a great advantage. The invaders, by contrast, were decidedly out of their place. They had to work with the constant burden of overstretched and overstrained chains of communication and supply. At the most awkward moments, the invaders simply lost their bearings. Contemplating the Indian-white wars, one cannot avoid the conclusion that much of what we have taken to thinking of as the lessons of Vietnam was available for learning a century or more ago.

Modoc Story, Part 9

When the Modoc men fled Lost River for the lava beds, there was never a question of dividing families. Women and children went with the men; women and children occupied the stronghold along with the warriors; women and children, despite the close presence of soldiers, escaped from the stronghold with the warriors in April of 1873. There were no exemptions on the basis of gender or age from the migrations and hardships of this war.

For the first rounds of the war, the Army's inability to close with the Modocs limited any opportunity for injuring or killing noncombatants. On April 16, 1873, when the Modocs left the stronghold and the Army occupied it, hostility toward noncombatants boiled to the surface. Three old Modoc men were found alive in the stronghold, and one woman. Two of the men and the woman "were shot by soldiers," Modoc War historian Richard Dillon reports. "The third man was stoned to death by the Warm Springs" Indians. White soldiers "kicked the severed head of a Modoc like a soccer ball." Trooper Maurice Fitzgerald reported that he saw an aged "woman begging piteously for her life. 'Me no hurt no one, me no fight,' she whined." According to Fitzgerald's report, an officer then said, " 'Is there anyone here who will put that old hag out of the way?' A Pennsylvania

Dutchman stepped forward and said, 'I'll fix her, lieutenant.' He put the muzzle of his carbine to her head and blew it to pieces." Here, again, one has a hard time distinguishing the lessons of the Indian wars from the lessons of Vietnam.[10]

After Hooker Jim's party had killed the Lost River settlers at the start of the war, civilians in southern Oregon were wild for revenge. At the end of the war, one party of Modocs surrendered to a white man, John Fairchild, who had tried to be a peacemaker. John Fairchild's brother James started off with the captives in a wagon to take them to the Army. Two white men stopped the wagon, forced Fairchild away, and "fired into the wagon at almost point-blank range," killing four men and wounding one woman.[11] In circumstances like these, individual guilt or innocence could not be the determinant of one's fate; being Modoc and falling into the hands of vindictive whites were the two key components of a death sentence.

People writing with disapproval about violence toward noncombatants in wartime can, intentionally or not, come close to trivializing or dismissing the terrible effects of violence on actual combatants. It is, therefore, important to take a moment to remember what it might mean to be injured in legitimate, certified combat. This is a description of the ordeal of Jerry Crooks, a member of the California Volunteers, during the retreat from the January 17 defeat:

> He had taken a rifle ball in one leg, which broke the bone so badly he could not be carried in a blanket. So he rode a pony with his leg dangling loosely. When it struck boulders or even stubborn sagebrush, the pain was terrible. Finally, his comrades tied a rope around the leg so that it could be lifted when his mount came to an obstacle. Still, [a companion] wrote, "It was sickening to see the expression on his face, and the pain he must have endured was excruciating."[12]

PATTERN 9

While some warriors and soldiers tried to keep a clear line between combatants and noncombatants, those efforts often broke down, in part because of confusion and in part because of pure hatred.

The conditions of guerrilla war carried their own grim logic. The invaders foundered in making distinctions—hostile from friendly, guilty from innocent, combatant from noncombatant. Demoralized and disoriented troops were men in the mood for scapegoating and not much interested in distinguishing between warriors and nonwarriors, men and women, adults and children. Moreover, Indian warriors were most often living in the midst of their families, because protecting the women and children was one of the principal obligations of the warriors and because the wars were taking place in their homelands, in the areas where these families lived. If the Army tried to make a surprise attack on the warriors, striking at dawn, women and children would be among the ones surprised. To the Army, fighting Indians who were often nomadic, the greatest challenge lay in locating them. Give them advance warning, try to separate the combatants from the noncombatants, and you could lose all the advantages of surprise; you could, for that matter, lose your entire opportunity to attack. Given the greater knowledge the natives had of the terrain, it might well be a long time before that opportunity arose again.

These reasons, in part, explain the violence inflicted on noncombatants. Beyond reason, however, lies passion—an intensity of hatred and an embrace of brutality that could make a man see a child or an infant as an appropriate target for murder. For many historians, writing of these wars, it has been tempting to avoid these troubling issues, by taking the position that we cannot permit ourselves any moral or emotional responses to these events, because we cannot judge the events of the past by the standards of today. According to this line of thought, the people who enthusiastically killed Indian women, children, and noncombatant men were simply men of their times, who operated under the standard attitudes and values of those times—attitudes and values that we, as creatures of another century, have no right to judge. But this argument is, finally, both inaccurate and dangerous.

It is inaccurate, because white American men of the nineteenth century had a wide range of attitudes and values, and we do them a considerable disservice when we write about them as if they had all submitted to the same, Manifest Destiny, attitudinal cookie cutter. Before adopting the "men of their times" model of moral homogeneity, one has an obligation to consider this haunting episode from the Bear River Massacre in 1863. Following the commands of his grandmother, the twelve-year-old Shoshone boy Yeager Timbimboo spent most of the day lying on the snow-covered ground, pretending to be dead. But at a crucial moment, he disobeyed his grandmother, and opened his eyes.

> A soldier came upon him and saw that he was alive and looking around. The military man stood over Yeager, his gun pointing at the young boy's head ready to fire. The soldier stared at the boy and the boy at the soldier. The second time the soldier raised his rifle the little boy knew his time to die was near. The soldier then lowered his gun and a moment later raised it again. For some reason he could not complete his task. He took his rifle down and walked away.[13]

"What went through this soldier's mind will never be known," said the Shoshone woman who told this story, but what went through this man's mind must be respected. It would be dangerous and chilling to say that we dare not use our own standards to respond to this man's moment of restraint and to find it heartening and impressive. If an ideal of historical detachment and objectivity requires us to hold to a scrupulous neutrality on the question of whether soldiers should shoot young children, then this is a professional ideal that corrodes the humanity of the historian.

The judgment of violence toward noncombatants is not, in any case, a matter of nineteenth-century standards in opposition to twentieth-century standards. It is just as much a matter of differences and conflicts among nineteenth-century white Americans themselves. In a number of the most violent episodes in this history, individual white officers and soldiers spoke out vigorously in opposition to what the majority had done. In Colorado in 1864, white officers opposed John Chivington's plan to attack at Sand Creek the day *before* the event; in the days and weeks after the massacre, some men in the Army and some civilians continued to speak out against Chivington and his supporters. In 1871, a Tucson citizen named William Oury led a massacre of Apache families at Camp Grant, Arizona. Royal Whitman, the officer at Camp Grant who had promised the families a sanctuary, instantly and persistently protested the attack. Twentieth-century Americans owe Royal Whitman the recognition that he was not a creation of twentieth-century moral hindsight. Royal Whitman, denouncer of the Camp Grant Massacre, was just as much a nineteenth-century man as William Oury, leader of the attack.

Modoc Story, Part 10

Captain Jack was a war leader who had not wanted war. He was, moreover, a leader with very limited power to impose his preferences on his people. On the contrary, he was often outmaneuvered by the war enthusiasts, pressured either to join them or admit to cowardice. Thus, even when the war had turned into a losing proposition, Captain Jack found it virtually impossible to persuade his people to reach a consensus for surrender. But Captain Jack confronted a relatively unusual situation in Indian war: a disposition, on the part of the federal government and its immediate representatives, to receive peace initiatives with some eagerness.

The result of these conditions was a pattern no doubt maddening to everyone involved: frequent indications, delivered through a variety of emissaries, that Captain Jack would like to surrender; optimism, on the part of some officials, that this might prove to be a route away from further carnage; and then a retreat on Jack's part, with the declaration that he could not surrender if it would mean that his people would have to leave Oregon or that some would be tried and executed for the killings of settlers or commissioners. Two propositions were clear and impossible to reconcile: Jack wanted out of the war, and yet he could find no way out.

PATTERN 10

It was no easy matter to surrender; getting out of a war was a lot harder than getting one started.

When Indians decided they had had enough of a war, whites were often reluctant to receive that message. These are agonizing events to contemplate; in the Black Hawk War in 1832, the Sauk leader Black Hawk tried three times to tell the American troops that he wanted this struggle to end, and each time, he was rebuffed and his people were attacked again. Reaching the decision to surrender was by no means an easy one for an Indian leader, but getting the whites to agree to recognize that decision could often prove even tougher.

Why this reluctance to take white flags seriously? Differences of language and custom made it difficult to communicate clearly any message at all, whether of belligerence or of peace. Suspicions of treachery preoccupied both sides; a white flag could be, and sometimes was, a trick, a way of getting the opponent to drop his guard be-fore a duplicitous attack. Perhaps more important, after investing many lives and much money in a war, whites wanted to get the most out of that investment. They wanted the enemy pushed to the margin, forced to make an unconditional surrender and to accept whatever terms the winners wished to impose. The clearest way to make certain that a group would never fight again was to reduce them, materially and psychologically, past the prospect of recovery. And, perhaps most important, a spirit of revenge and retaliation so powered white actions that the implied response to surrender was this: "You want to make peace *now,* but it is too late; you should have thought of this before you started fighting."

Modoc Story, Part 11

In July 1873, after some debates over the legality of a trial, a mil-itary hearing took place, with Captain Jack and five other Modoc men accused of murdering the peace commissioners in violation of a truce. The transcript of the hearing makes for painful reading. The presiding officer seemed willing to give the Modocs a chance to pre-sent their story, and an interpreter attended to translate for the ac-cused. But the interpreter was also a witness for the prosecution, the Modocs had no attorney to represent them, and the whole procedure was clearly a foreign and discouraging process for them.

Early in the hearing, the transcript records this exchange: "The prisoners were then severally asked by the judge-advocate if they de-sired to introduce counsel; to which they severally replied in the neg-ative; and that they had been unable to procure any." After each witness's testimony appears this notation: "The judge-advocate then asked the prisoners severally if they desired to cross-examine the wit-ness, to which they replied in the negative." The feelings of men awaiting a life-or-death judgment from a process that was out of their control come through most strongly in Captain Jack's interruption in his address to the court. Speaking through an interpreter, Jack sud-denly made this remark: "I hardly know how to talk here. I don't know how white people talk in such a place as this but I will do the best I can."[14]

Kept in a guardhouse at Fort Klamath after their conviction, Jack and his five comrades were taken out for hanging on October 3, 1873.

When he was asked, the day before, if he had a last request, Captain Jack said, "I should like to live until I die a natural death."[15] Two of the younger Modocs had had their sentences commuted from death to life terms in Alcatraz, but the Army had adopted the curious custom of refusing to reveal this clemency until the moment scheduled for execution. All the Modocs were required to watch as Captain Jack, Boston Charley, Schonchin Jim, and Black Jim were hanged. That night, someone removed Captain Jack's body from its grave.

The rest of the nonreservation Modocs—thirty-nine men, fifty-four women, and sixty children—were put on a train, with their destination concealed from them. They were temporarily placed at Fort McPherson, Nebraska; then moved to Baxter Springs, Kansas; and then finally permitted to resettle in Seneca Springs, at the Quapaw Agency in Indian Territory (present-day Oklahoma). In 1909, thirty-six years after their defeat, the Modocs who so chose were permitted to return to the Klamath Reservation or, for those born in captivity, to go there for the first time.

If one goes by "the number of Indians involved," Keith Murray has observed, "this was the most expensive Indian war the United States ever fought."[16] In these matters, "expensive" carries a host of meanings.

PATTERN 11

Exultation and a sense of achieved glory were hard emotions for the victors to feel at the end of a war; the Indians, at the time of the surrender, looked more like a pitiable and battered people than a fierce and terrifying enemy, valiantly defeated.

When the survivors of war decided to give up, they were likely to be hungry, tattered, demoralized, and, often enough, injured and wounded. Seeing them in this condition, some officials, officers, soldiers, and civilians responded to the end of the war with fits of regret and wishful hindsight, wondering, "Was all this really necessary?" The same outcome could have been reached, many participants would end up thinking, with much less in the way of expenses and suffering, using negotiations rather than bullets.

The moment of surrender creates an unsettling dilemma, as well, for historians. Brought together in Helen Hunt Jackson's *Century of Dishonor* (1881) and welded into place by Dee Brown's *Bury My*

Heart at Wounded Knee (1971), the standard, sympathetic version of Indian-white history casts Indians as victims, passive people who stood frozen in place as a great wave of white expansion crashed down on them and left them broken and shattered. This story, of course, was of a piece with a broader approach to the history of people of color, an approach which accented the actions of whites toward the others, and virtually ignored anything that these others did for themselves and on their own terms.

In the last twenty years, the rejection of this model of passivity and victimization has become an article of faith among most American historians. Indians—and African Americans and Mexican Americans and Asian Americans—were not passive victims, we all recognize now; they were active participants in making and shaping their own history. We did Indian people a disservice when we adopted what one might call the "hanky at the eye" school of Indian history, thinking of Indians as melancholy victims, boohooing over the injuries of the past, lamenting the Indian plight, and seeing the whole story as very, very sad.

And yet, at the end of an Indian-white war, reduced by the hardships of life in chronic battle, sometimes betrayed by other Indians, often forcibly removed from the place they considered home, bullied into giving up ownership of that home, the Indians often *did* look like victims, and the whole story does indeed seem very, very sad. It would be silly to ride the pendulum swing back to the version of history in which the Indians were victims, and nothing but victims. As many of these twelve points of war suggest, these stories would not make an ounce of sense if one did not see Indians themselves as active forces in the shaping of history. But one ends up shaken in one's orthodoxy. Consider the condition of Indian people at the end of the wars, and the term "victim" keeps coming back to mind. Reciting a declaration of faith—"we just don't think of Indians as victims anymore"—will not drive the word out.

Modoc Story, Part 12

On November 29, 1872, Mrs. Boddy and Mrs. Schira were suddenly and bitterly widowed when Hooker Jim's group killed their husbands. In June 1873, while the Modocs were held as prisoners of war at Fort Klamath, Colonel Jefferson Davis, the commanding officer at the fort, responded to an alarm. Mrs. Boddy and Mrs. Schira had entered the prisoners' compound. "Mrs. Schira had a double-edged knife in her hand which she was trying to use on Hooker Jim. Mrs. Boddy had a gun which she did not know how to cock."[17] Colonel Davis restrained them and took away their weapons.

The depth of bitterness—Modoc to white and white to Modoc—seemed beyond any healing. And yet the American public's fascination with the West and with Indians offered an odd alternative to vengeance. Indians associated with wars of resistance were instant celebrities. Both the Nez Perce Chief Joseph and the Hunkpapa Sitting Bull had barely surrendered before they were being hosted and lionized, interviewed and celebrated, by white Americans. If Captain Jack had *not* taken part in the murder of commissioners during a truce, one suspects that instead of being hung in October 1873, he might well have been on a tour of the East Coast, watched by crowds in New York and hosted at a presidential reception in Washington, D.C.

Trying to capitalize on the commercial opportunity presented by the wars, the former superintendent of Indian affairs for Oregon and former peace commissioner Albert Meacham made the most of his injuries. When the Modocs killed Commissioner Eleazar Thomas and General E. R. S. Canby, Commissioner Meacham had been left for dead. Recovered from his many wounds, Meacham went on a prolonged lecture tour, displaying the wounds he had received from the Modocs and sometimes displaying the Modocs themselves. Shacknasty Jim, Steamboat Frank, and Scarfaced Charley joined Meacham on his tours. The war turned colorful, quaint, and marketable in an amazingly short time.

PATTERN 12
These Indian wars were often so bitter and so brutal that it is hard to imagine either how they ever turned romantic, picturesque, or fun in the works of American mythmakers or how the survivors and their descendants were ever able to live in peace with each other.

In the hands of novelists and filmmakers, the Indian-white wars became spectacles with great entertainment value. Here is one of the greatest mysteries of the commercial manipulation of the story of westward expansion: historical episodes in which human nature appeared at its worst provided novelists and moviemakers with the material for escapist fantasies. Escapist? In their true character, these stories raise profound questions about the reality of evil in human life, questions made even more compelling when they arise in a nation which has struggled to paint its history in shades of innocence. Rather than permitting the reader to escape the sorrows and troubles of the real world, these events force the reader's attention to the grimmest facts about American origins. They are moral and spiritual muddles, in which the lines between good guy and bad guy, victim and villain, twist and meander and intertwine. And yet by the powerful alchemy of selective storytelling, in American popular culture, narratives of great complexity became simple stories of adventure and heroism and triumph, with, perhaps, just a tinge of melancholy.

Just as mysterious is the process by which peace was restored and a kind of coexistence arranged. When you have been thinking about the injuries and outrages committed in the course of these wars, a century does not seem like enough time to restore the peace.

A story that Westerners tell to make fun of Easterners brings this issue to a focus. A car full of tourists from New Jersey pulls up at a gas station in a remote Western setting. "We notice there's an Indian reservation up ahead," the tourists say to the gas station attendant. "It's getting close to sunset; are we going to be safe if we try to cross the reservation after dark?"

"Well," says the gas station attendant, whose sister owns the motel next door, "I'd be very careful about that. But your timing is good; the weekly Army convoy leaves tomorrow at seven in the morning. If you wanted to get a room at the motel tonight, then you could be sure you'll be safe tomorrow."

This story usually presents a fine opportunity to laugh at the fools of the Eastern United States. But when you have been reading the stories of Indian-white warfare, considering the full measure of bitterness and brutality in those events and recognizing how short a period of time a century is, the notion of waiting for the 7 A.M. convoy does not seem like such a foolish idea.

And yet, at some point, the participants in these wars and their descendants broke the cycle of revenge and retaliation and ceased to think of each other's destruction as a desirable goal. In the United States of the late twentieth century, the descendants of the Modocs and the descendants of the white settlers of northern California and southern Oregon are not killing each other. We take that turn of events for granted, but for someone immersed in the history of the Indian-white wars, this outcome appears remarkable, surprising, and even illogical. Continued theft and manipulation of Indian resources, restrictions on Indian religious freedom, arbitrary and damaging federal intervention in reservation affairs, poverty, unemployment, alcoholism, discrimination, prejudice, and bitter memories—there is nothing cheering in those various manifestations of the legacy of conquest. But it is still a considerable relief when the flow of blood slows down, and the guns, by and large, fall silent.

AFTER THE WARS:
THE CHARACTER OF AMERICAN SUNLIGHT

> In America, the Indian is relegated to the obligatory first chapter—the "Once Great Nation" chapter—after which the Indian is cleared away as easily as brush, using a very sharp rhetorical tool called an "alas."
> RICHARD RODRIGUEZ, *Days of Obligation*

Immerse yourself in the history of Indian-white wars, and you gain one advantage that others around you will not have. Along with your neighbors and associates, you may well be disheartened by the alarming violence of the late twentieth century—the urban gangs, the drug warfare, and the drive-by shootings that leave many feeling precarious and vulnerable. But while others imagine a happier age in the past, when times were less brutal and better values prevailed, the person who has been thinking about the Indian-white wars will waste no time in yearning for a prettier time in the past when humans treated each other better.

If you have been reading descriptions of the careful, detailed, exquisite, and very personal torture and mutilation that characterized Indian-white encounters on a number of occasions in the eighteenth and nineteenth centuries, then drive-by shootings acquire a different shading. They are terrible things, but they are not any more terrible than the killings of the Indian-white wars. By some measures, if you compare a nineteenth-century death by torture and mutilation to a twentieth-century death by a comparatively quick and impersonal shooting, the terribleness of violence may seem to be shrinking over time.

Readers may well find themselves rendered unhappy and unsettled by this line of reflection, and especially that curious word "measures." What, in heaven's name, are the proper measures for judging and comparing levels of horror and terror? Numbers are, for many people in the late twentieth century, the standard way of measuring everything: economic well-being, social values, educational achievement, the effectiveness of leaders, success or failure, progress or decline. But should number set the level of our response to brutality? Should there be some sort of direct correlation in which the numbers of dead and injured provide a precise setting for our horror and outrage?

Nearly everyone who writes about battles and massacres wrestles, at least briefly, with the problem of numbers. This episode of numerical reflection usually begins with the problem of disputed numbers: battles and massacres are occasions of passion, and passion works against precision in numerical records. Thus, calculating how many were killed, how many were injured, and how many in both of those categories were women and children is no easy matter.

There is a moment when this quantitative exercise strikes the more reflective writers as odd and troubling. Historian Juanita Brooks, writing about Utah's Mountain Meadows Massacre, offers what may well be the only clearheaded conclusion: "The total number [killed at Mountain Meadows] remains uncertain. We can be sure only that, however many there were, it was too many."[18]

While it certainly made a difference to the individuals involved, should it really make a difference to our judgment of an event if the total number of casualties at a given massacre added up to 214 or to 198? By the measure of numbers, the comparison between violence in the nineteenth century and violence in the twentieth century clearly works to the disadvantage of our times. In the wars of the twentieth century and the Holocaust in Nazi Germany, the numerical indices of brutality soared off the charts. If you went by the numbers, the violence of the Indian-white wars would hardly register when you put the totals of their casualties up against the millions in the twentieth century.

Whatever else we learn from numbers, we learn that twentieth-century human beings do not have much in the way of moral high ground. With its record of wars and holocausts and threatened atomic annihilation, the twentieth century provides no viewers' grandstand on which we can sit in self-righteous judgment of the cruelties of the nineteenth century. Thus, when the writers of a recent American history textbook tell us that "By twentieth century standards, [Andrew] Jackson's Indian policy was both callous and brutal," one cannot help wondering, "And which twentieth century standards are those?"[19]

There is, in any case, not much in the way of opportunity or originality left for late arrivals in the business of moral condemnation. By the 1970s, the federal government, the United States Army, the volunteer regiments, and the resource-grabbing settlers had taken just about every blow that printed words can inflict. The Modoc War, wrote historian Keith Murray in 1959, was "a perfect case study in American maladministration of its Indian affairs." This was "a government that did not know where it was going or what it was doing." The "most serious aspect" of the war, Murray concluded, was that "the federal government clearly learned nothing."[20] In a later history of the war, published in 1973, Richard Dillon was even more outspoken in his criticisms. The "land-lust of white settlers" gave the Modoc War its context, while the "immediate causes were the usual combination of civilian duplicity and pressure on government, a worthless treaty, Indian Bureau bungling (more stupidity than perfidy) and Army folly and overconfidence."[21]

Reading older, no-punches-pulled condemnations of the white-Indian wars, one feels a bit like the nineteenth-century prospectors who arrived late for a gold rush. Very much like a miner arriving at a placer site months after the first discoveries, one finds that earlier arrivals have already taken all the good lines. As much as the latter-day critic might like to land an original blow, the duplicitous federal government and the greedy white settlers have already been beaten around the post, and there is not much left for late arrivals to do, besides regret their timing.

The book reviews that responded to the publication of *Bury My Heart at Wounded Knee* in 1971 provide remarkable evidence of how completely condemnation of the wars had become a litany, a formula, a chant. The periodical *Book World* characterized *Bury My Heart* in these terms:

> Custer may have died for our sins, but Indians still have much to reproach the White Man for. A chronicle of lies, torture, and slaughter on the plains that exhausts anger, pity, and regret. Never again.[22]

Recommending Dee Brown's book as one of the "best books for young adults" for the year, the *Booklist* summed up its content:

> Battle by battle, massacre by massacre, broken treaty by broken treaty, this is a documented, gripping chronicle of the Indian struggle from 1860 to 1890 against the white man's systematic plunder.[23]

To a writer for *Newsweek,* the "appalling" story that Brown told, "with plenty of massacres and genocide overlooked by our traditional history texts," was "essential history for Americans, who must learn that this sort of thing was quite acceptable to the government in Washington."[24] Writing, as well, in *Newsweek,* Geoffrey Wolfe called *Bury My Heart at Wounded Knee* a "damning case against our national roots in greed, perfidy, ignorance and malice."[25] For Peter Farb, in the *New York Review of Books,* Brown's "account of one horror after another endured by the reds at the hands of whites" showed the Indian wars "to be the dirty murders they were."[26] The book reads like "a crime file," *Life* magazine said, telling the story of the "30-year slaughter of Indians; the broken treaties that stole Indian hunting grounds; the inhumane treatment on reservations; . . . the systematic blood lettings, including the massacres of Sand Creek and Wounded Knee—Mylais of a century ago."[27]

These writers, it is clear, had Vietnam on their mind. But the United States got out of Vietnam and the recitation of wickedness hardly paused. Even when you turn to the kind of historical writing in which blandness and inoffensiveness have been the most prized of virtues, the condemnation of white behavior in the Indian-white wars proves to be severe and unforgiving. Examine these quotations from recent college-level American history textbooks:

> Grasping white men were guilty of many additional provocations. They flagrantly disregarded treaty promises, openly seized the land of the Indians, slaughtered their game, and occasionally debauched their women. . . . On several notorious occasions, innocent Indians were killed for outrages committed by their fellow tribesmen; sometimes they were shot just for "sport."[28]
>
> The Western tribes were also victimized by the incompetence and duplicity of those white officials charged with protecting them. . . . The history of relations between the United States and the Native Americans was, therefore, one of nearly endless broken promises. . . .

As usual, it was the whites who committed the most flagrant and vicious atrocities.[29]

The whites took away the tribes' sustenance, decimated their ranks, and shoved the remnants into remote and barren corners of their former domain. . . . No historical equation could have been more precise and implacable: The progress of the white settlers meant the death of the Indians. . . . The Indians had no chance against the overwhelming strength of the soldiers and the relentless white settlement of the land.[30]

The government showed little interest in honoring agreements with Indians. . . . [The attack at Sand Creek] was no worse than many incidents in earlier conflicts with Indians and not very different from what was later to occur in guerrilla wars involving American troops in the Philippines and more recently Vietnam.[31]

The whites cloaked their actions with high sounding expressions like "civilization against savagery" and "Manifest Destiny." But the facts were simple: The whites came and took the Indians' land. . . . American policy towards the Indians was a calamity.[32]

Just a brief tour through these simple declarations from both book reviewers and textbook writers produces strange and unexpected results. "Now just a minute here," one surprises oneself by thinking. "Let's not get carried away; it's really quite a bit more complicated than that."

The biggest puzzle in these summations is, of course, their astonishing assumption of simplicity. The stories of the wars are narratives so tangled and dense that they defy clear telling. In these summations, every ounce of that complexity disappears. The diversity of white people and their responses to war are gone. Instead, a coherent, linear, and, most improbable of all, systematic process of eliminating Indians takes the place of the actual jumble of motives and intentions, communications and miscommunications, actions and reactions.

The most distressing element of these set pieces of condemnation is the finality of their plots. Nearly every textbook crashes hard into the massacre at Wounded Knee in 1890; the bodies of the Lakota people left in the snow stand for the end of the Indians as significant and distinctive figures in American history. One textbook gives the section on the Indians in the late nineteenth century the title "The End of Tribal Life." From this book, students learn that, in the late nineteenth century, the Indians "lost their special distinctiveness as a culture."[33] "In the end, blacks were oppressed," summarily declares one

textbook published in 1989, while "Native Americans were extermi-
nated."[34] In offering this picture of a strange and dreadful finality, the
textbook writers no doubt think that they are showing great sympathy for Indians. They are also, of course, killing them off with a thor-
oughness that the United States Army did not, thank heavens, match.
This, surely, is what writer Richard Rodriguez had in mind when he
referred to the habit of getting rid of the Indians with "a very sharp
rhetorical tool called an 'alas.' "

Read some of these textbooks, and you want to shout, "Hold the
presses! These obituaries are premature!" But more surprising, even
the best-credentialed, sixties generation, consistent, white, liberal historian responds to the textbook litanies with an urge to defend the
Army. Take this summation from a Western American textbook published in 1984:

> The army was at the center of a vicious spiral of hatred, one level of
> fury escalating into a tier of bloodletting. The highest levels of com-
> mand of the army should have been held accountable for not pro-
> tecting Indians against white settlers. Though lesser officers and
> enlisted men often sympathized with the native, there is not one sig-
> nificant example of the army protecting the Indian under the law.[35]

"Not one significant example"? It was a common pattern, after a
war, for white civilians to want to kill Indians who had surrendered
and for the Army to refuse to give them that opportunity. The characterization of the wicked Army does not begin to acknowledge the
many occasions on which the soldiers ended up in the middle, trying
to resist the settlers' demands for unrestrained violence while still trying to control the Indians. The Army, of course, did terrible things, but
the greater truth about the Army was that it was inconsistent—equally
inconsistent in both honor and dishonor.

While the peaks of moral condemnation had already been
climbed, claimed, and occupied by the early 1970s, no one had made
much of a start on the project of fitting the wars into a broader understanding of American history. On the contrary, some of the writers most committed to lamentation over the injuries done to the
Indians were also the most effective at declaring the topic closed and
finished. With the massacre at Wounded Knee, authors have drawn
the curtain on the whole sad story of the conquest—drawn the curtain, driven the audience out of the theater, locked the doors, and put

up a "CLOSED; WILL NOT REOPEN" sign. With the year 1890 standing not only for the end of the Indian wars but virtually for the end of the Indians, the whole subject is isolated, stripped of relevance, and denied any consequence for the present.

With Indian-white wars quarantined from significance, American history looks a great deal more appealing. Consider the portrait of westward expansion offered in 1993 by an American historian, called a "national treasure" by his interviewer. Here is Daniel Boorstin's declaration of faith in an inspiring and uplifting version of American history, resting on a cheerful rendering of westward expansion. In the midst of the divided and violent world of the 1990s, Boorstin said,

> community—an emphasis on what brings us together—is what I think is called for in our time. It's what built the American West: People coming by wagon trains, where they made their own systems of law and cooperated in going up and down the mountains and across the prairies to build new towns.[36]

To ask, "What's missing from this picture?" is to belabor the obvious. The tougher question by far is to ask how such a picture of history could carry any credibility at all. Knowledge of the brutality of the Indian wars has been widely distributed for centuries. And yet Daniel Boorstin carries considerable weight and influence when he places the opportunities and achievements of white people at the center of American history and pushes the conquest of Indians to the margins of the picture.

On behalf of those who join Boorstin in straining for a prettier picture of the nation's past, one has to say this: it is hard to find a way to tell the national story that does justice both to those who benefited from conquest and to those who literally lost ground. Consider what might seem to be the most remote subject from the history of the Indian-white wars: the history of white pioneer women. Men, conventional thinking goes, fight the wars; on this topic, of all topics, it ought to be permissible to concentrate on men's history to the exclusion of women. And vice versa: one ought to be able to write the history of white pioneer women with, at most, a few brief references to the unpleasantness of the Indian-white wars.

Indeed, separation and segregation have been the pattern in the writing of both the histories of Indian wars and of white pioneer women. Here, one can see the fragmentation of the history of the conquest of North America at its peak. That split appears most clearly and concretely in the writings of Dee Brown. Best known for *Bury My Heart at Wounded Knee,* Brown was also the author of another widely read book on the American West: *The Gentle Tamers: Women of the Old Wild West,* a set of portraits of pioneer women. Neither the word "Indian" nor the word "war" appears in the index of *Gentle Tamers.* In the chapter on "The Army Girls," the focus is on the hardships and travels of Army wives. There is no attention to the larger process of conquest which brought them those experiences, and no attention to the impact that the "Army Girls' " husbands had on Indian people.[37]

In Brown's strangely unconnected publications, we have the clearest and starkest example of a common pattern. The history of westward expansion has ended up divided into two, utterly separate stories: the sad and disheartening story of what whites did to the Indians, and the colorful and romantic story of what whites did for themselves. The very same writer can, on different occasions, write both of these stories, with no sense of self-contradiction or inconsistency.

These stories, however, move back together the moment one gives up the campaign to keep them apart. The history of pioneer women and the history of Indian war, to use the examples that seem the most separate, are very much intertwined. Women may have carried some technical status as noncombatants, but that status gave them no exemption from injury. Both white and Indian families were the targets of direct attack, and the deaths of soldiers and warriors in battle left widowed women on both sides facing very tough times. Women could, as well, be powerful forces in demanding revenge and retaliation. The seizure and rape of Indian women or the forced captivity of white women were often primary motivations for going to war. For Indian men, the mistreatment of Indian women could be the last straw in the insults of conquest; for white men, the idea of a white woman vulnerable to an Indian man's sexual desire could produce wild and irrational anger.

These connections between women and war are, however, the easy ideas to grasp. The tougher part is recognizing the connection between the wars and the white women settlers who were not direct participants in combat but who were nonetheless beneficiaries of the opportunities, resources, and lands opened up by the conquest and displacement of Indians. To call white pioneer women "beneficiaries of conquest" is by no means to say that their lives were easy or privileged; on the contrary, their hardships were often grueling. Moreover, many of the pioneer women, whose diaries and memoirs are now available to us, were likable women, women on whom the labels "cruel conqueror," "thoughtless invader," or "villainous displacer of native people" would sit awkwardly. They seem, truly, to have lived in a world apart from the world of massacre, mutilation, torture, and murder.

But did they?

"Although they do not ignore the reality of racist attitudes among white women," historian Antonia Castaneda has said of recent historians writing about white pioneer women, "their accounts are remarkably free of intercultural conflict in a land bloodied by three centuries of war and conquest." These writers ignore "the economic and other privileges that women of the conquering group derive from the oppression of women and men of the group being conquered." Conquest was not the exclusive enterprise of white men: "Within their gender spheres and based upon the power and privilege of their race and class," Castaneda writes, "Euro-American men and women expanded the geo-political–economic area of the United States" and played their part in establishing the dominance of white Americans.[38]

Even if the vast majority of them never fired a gun on a battlefield, much less took part in mutilation at a massacre, white pioneer women were members of a civilian invading force and beneficiaries of the subordination of the natives. A recognition of the moral complexity of their position in history does these women no disservice; on the contrary, it gives a much deeper meaning to their lives by restoring them to their full, tragic context. Putting the history of white pioneer women back together with the history of Indian war is in truth a matter of uniting American history, not disuniting it.

Cease to quarantine the Indian-white wars, battles, and massacres, and you take an essential step toward the uniting of American history. Nineteenth-century white pioneer women and twentieth-century white career women, exploiters of natural resources and celebrators of natural beauty, rural cowboys and urban businessmen, bluebloods of Boston whose ancestors arrived in the 1620s and Mexican immigrants who arrived yesterday—a whole range of people who see each other as alien and who feel that they have no common ground, benefit from the tragic events of conquest. Conquest wove a web of consequences that does indeed unite the nation.

We live on haunted land, on land that is layers deep in human passion and memory. There is, today, no longer any point in sorting out these passions and memories into starkly separate forms of ownership. Whether the majority who died at any particular site were Indians or whites, these places literally ground Americans of all backgrounds in their common history. In truth, the tragedies of the wars are our national joint property, and how we handle that property is one test of our unity or disunity, maturity or immaturity, as a people wearing the label "American."

For a century or two, white American intellectuals labored under the notion that the United States was sadly disadvantaged when it came to the joint property of history. The novelist Henry James gave this conviction of American cultural inferiority its most memorable statement: "The past, which died so young and had time to produce so little, attracts but scanty attention." "The light of the sun seems fresh and innocent," James wrote, "as if it knew as yet but few of the secrets of the world and none of the weariness of shining."[39]

The sun that shines on North America has, it turns out, seen plenty. A claim of innocence denies the meaning of the lives of those who died violently in the conquest of this continent, and that denial diminishes our souls.

I-B

The Adventures of the Frontier in the Twentieth Century

The year 1988 signified the fortieth anniversary of humanity's escape from zippers and buttons. In May 1988, a journal of science and technology called *Discover* published an article commemorating this occasion. "Velcro," the headline read: "The Final Frontier."[1]

To the specialist in Western American history, this is a title to ponder. In what sense might Velcro constitute a frontier? In his 1893 essay, "The Significance of the Frontier in American History," Frederick Jackson Turner left his central term curiously befogged: The word "frontier," he said, "is an elastic one, and for our purposes does not need sharp definition."[2] But Turner did join the United States census director in offering one clear and concrete definition: the frontier was a place occupied by fewer than two people per square mile. Thus, if the headline writer were a strict follower of Turner's quantitative definition, then the Velcro frontier would be a place where fewer than two people per square mile used Velcro. The writer, on the other hand, might have been following one of the more poetic and less precise Turnerian definitions, finding in a society's choice of fasteners a symbolic line of division between wilderness and human culture, backwardness and progress, savagery and civilization. The habit-bound users of zippers would now represent the primitive and backward people of North America, with the hardy, adventurous users of Velcro living on the cutting edge of progress.

Historians of the American West might puzzle over the shifting definitions of the word "frontier," but few readers experience any confusion when they see this headline. To them, the frontier analogy says simply that makers, marketers, and users of Velcro stand on the edge of exciting possibilities. Velcro is a frontier because Velcro has thousands of still-to-be-imagined uses. No normal reader, if one defines "normal reader" as a person who is not a Western American historian, would even notice the peculiar implications of the analogy. For most Americans in the twentieth century, the term "frontier" is perfectly clear, reliable, and simple in its meanings.

"Frontier," the historian David Wrobel writes, "has become a metaphor for promise, progress, and ingenuity."[3] And yet, despite the accuracy of this summation, the relationship between the frontier and the American mind is not a simple one. Clear and predictable on most occasions, the idea of the frontier is still capable of sudden twists and shifts of meaning, meanings considerably more interesting than the more conventional and familiar definition of the frontier as a zone of open opportunity.

Conventional thinking is at its most powerful, however, in twentieth-century reconstructions of the nineteenth-century experience of westward expansion, reconstructions quite explicitly designed for sale. To see this commercialized vision of the Old Frontier in concrete, three-dimensional form, the best place to go is Disneyland in Anaheim, California. When they enter Frontierland, visitors might ask Disneyland employees for directions, but they do not have to ask for a definition of the frontier. The frontier, every tourist knows, was the edge of Anglo-American settlement, the place where white Americans struggled to master the continent.

This frontier, as everything in Frontierland confirms, was populated by a colorful and romantic cast of characters: mountain men, cowboys, prospectors, pioneer wives, saloon girls, sheriffs, and outlaws. Tepees, log cabins, and false-front stores were the preferred architecture of the frontier; coonskin caps, cowboy hats, bandannas, buckskin shirts and leggings, moccasins, boots, and an occasional sunbonnet or calico dress constituted frontier fashion; canoes, keelboats, steamboats, saddle horses, covered wagons, and stagecoaches gave Americans the means to conquer the rivers, mountains, deserts, plains, and other wide open spaces of the frontier; firearms, whether long rifles or six-shooters, were everywhere and in frequent use. These images are very well understood. Tourists do not need any assistance in defining Frontierland.

And yet, even in the tightly controlled world of Disneyland, the idea of the frontier has encountered complications. At the Golden Horseshoe, Frontierland's saloon, every show had a "spontaneous" gunfight, with Black Bart and Sheriff Lucky blazing away at each other. In 1958, as a reporter for the *Saturday Evening Post* watched, the gunfight underwent some slippage at the joint that connects fantasy to reality: "As the sheriff advanced toward the wounded bandit," the writer said, "a tow-headed five-year-old, wearing a cowboy suit and holding a cap pistol, came running from the crowd," asking earnestly, " 'Can I finish him off, sheriff, can I?' " The sheriff consented, and everyone fired. "Black Bart shuddered, then lay deathly still. The lad took one look, dropped his gun and fled, screaming, 'Mommy, mommy! I didn't mean to! I didn't mean to!' "

Scholars with a penchant for interpreting signs, symbols, and signifiers could go to town with this incident, pondering the way in which the appeal to mommy follows hard and fast on the attempted initiation into the manly sport of gunplay. But my own attention fixes on the line, "I didn't mean to!" If the child wanted to kill Black Bart and, with an impressive deference to authority, asked the sheriff for permission to kill him, why would he then claim, "I didn't mean to"? His worries of intention and outcome were, in any case, soon ended: "His tears stopped a moment later, however, when he turned and saw Black Bart and Sheriff Lucky walking into the Golden Horseshoe to get ready for their next performance."[4] Rather than feeling soothed, another sort of child might at that moment have conceived a long-range ambition to kill *both* Black Bart and Sheriff Lucky for their complicity in tricking him.

In the twentieth century, as this boy learned, the image of the frontier balances precariously between too much reality and too little. Properly screened and edited, the doings of the old frontier are quite a bit of fun. But when matters get a bit too real, when encounters with death or injury or conflict or loss become unexpectedly convincing and compelling, then fun can make an abrupt departure, while emotions considerably more troubling take its place.

The outlaw-killing lad was not the only child encountering the limits of Frontierland's fun, not the only one to stumble in the uncertain turf along the border between the imagined and the actual. As the *Saturday Evening Post* writer described it, one "seven-year-old boy was certain he could tell the real from the unreal."

> As they jogged along on the burro ride, the leathery mule-skinner warned, "Look out for them thar cactus plants. Them needles is mighty sharp."
> The skeptical boy leaned over and took a swipe at the cactus. On the way to the first-aid station, he decided all was not fantasy at Disneyland. The management has since moved the cactus out of reach.[5]

Moving the cactus—finding the place where its thorns could *look* sharp and scary but not *be* sharp and scary—can serve as a fine representation of the whole process of getting authenticity into the proper adjustment at Frontierland. When too many surprised innocents make visits to the first-aid stand, the frontier is clearly out of alignment, and a repositioning is in order.

And yet, in other parts of Frontierland's turf, wounds and injuries were a taken-for-granted dimension of frontier life. At Tom Sawyer's Island, as the *Saturday Evening Post* writer put it, kids "can fire air-operated, bulletless rifles at the plastic Indians. . . ."[6] "From the top of a log fort you can sight in with guns on a forest in which Indians lurk," a writer for the *Reader's Digest* described the same opportunity in 1960. "The guns don't fire bullets—they're hydraulically operated—but the recoil is so realistic that you'd never guess they aren't the genuine article."[7]

The Indians of this frontier were not, however, the sort to hold a grudge. Visitors could fire away at the Indians and then move on to a voyage in "Indian canoes paddled by real Indians."[8] "Realness" was not, in this case, an easy matter to arrange. "Wanting authentic Native Americans to paddle canoes full of guests around the rivers of the theme area, Disneyland recruited employees from southwestern tribes," historian John Findlay writes in his book, *Magic Lands*. "These Indians, of course, came from the desert rather than a riverine or lakes environment, so they had to be taught how to paddle canoes by white employees of the park who had learned the skill at summer camp."[9]

Over the decades, life at Frontierland has become, if anything, more confusing for those rare individuals who stop and think about what they are seeing. There is, for instance, the question of the frontier's geographical location. On one side of a path, a roller coaster ride rushes through a Southwestern mesa, carved into a mine. On the other side of the path, the great river, with its stately steamboat, rolls by. Where is the frontier? Evidently where New Mexico borders on the Mississippi River, where Western gold and silver miners load their ore directly onto steamboats heading to New Orleans.

In recent times, even the ritualized violence between whites and Indians has become a matter of some awkwardness. On the various rides along the Rivers of America, one passes a settler's cabin, wildly in flames. In my childhood, the guides announced that the cabin was on fire because Indians had attacked it. In current times, the cabin is just on fire, usually without commentary or blame. At the further reaches of cultural change lies the recent experience of an acquaintance: the guide told his group that the cabin was on fire because the settler had been ecologically and environmentally careless.[10]

Consider, as well, the curious politics of the shooting gallery encountered at the entrance to Frontierland. Visitors can take firearm in hand and shoot at a variety of targets, including a railroad train, winding its way through a sculpted landscape. But if you are shooting at a railroad train, then *who*—in this frontier role-play—*are you*? Which side are you on? If you are firing on the train, then you seem to be either a hostile Indian or a murderous and larcenous outlaw. Is the visitor receiving an invitation to play with point of view, to reconsider the whole question of the identity and interests of good guys and bad guys, champions of progress and opponents of progress? Or is this casting of the railroad as target simply the product of Disneyland's designers working under the mandate to create a scene chockful of the shapes and forms that will say "frontier," with the assumption that any visitor so stimulated visually will fall into step with the mythic patterns of frontier life, pick up a gun, and blast away at whatever is in sight?

If professional Western American historians find themselves conceptually without anchor when they visit Frontierland, there is a clear reason for this: with the possible exception of the suggestion that environmental carelessness produced the settler's cabin fire, the work of recent academic historians has had virtually no impact on either Disneyland's vision of the frontier or the thinking of Disneyland's visitors. That cheerful and complete indifference to the work of frontier historians may, in truth, be the secret of the place's success.

For several decades, some historians have earnestly campaigned to redefine the frontier as a contested zone of cross-cultural meetings.[11] These careful requests to stretch the term "frontier" to accommodate ethnic diversity have not carried far beyond walls of universities. Consider, for instance, the license plates of Alaska. Alaska is a state with an enormous amount of unpopulated land, but, by the same token, it is a state where the vast majority of the people live not outdoors in nature but in cities. In that very urbanized state, each automobile sports a license plate with the words, "Alaska: The Last Frontier." Not a single one of the drivers, I am willing to bet, understands this to mean, "Alaska: The Last Zone of Cultural Interpenetration and Contested Hegemony."

PRESIDENTIAL POLITICS
ON THE FRONTIER

Presidents and presidential candidates are a distinct minority in the American population. And yet their circumstances render them useful as case studies in popular attitudes. In the last half of the twentieth century, electoral politics makes a presidential candidate into the navigational equivalent of a bat, sending off signals, reading the signals as they bounce back, and attempting to set a course based on what these signals reveal. When presidential candidates and presidents put the frontier analogy to use, there is a broader lesson available on the persuasive powers given to that analogy by particular styles of presentation at particular times.

On July 15, 1960, in Los Angeles, California, John F. Kennedy faced "west on what was once the last frontier" and accepted the Democratic presidential nomination. In midspeech, he retold the familiar, Turnerian story of westward expansion:

From the lands that stretch three thousand miles behind me, the pioneers of old gave up their safety, their comfort, and sometimes their

> lives to build a new world here in the West. . . . They were determined
> to make that new world strong and free, to overcome its hazards and
> its hardships, to conquer the enemies that threatened from within
> and without.

These enemies were, presumably, a combination of natural forces,
natives, and cautious naysayers who dragged their feet against the
currents of Manifest Destiny. The success of John F. Kennedy's
rhetoric rested in part on oratorical skill but also on historical timing:
he gave this speech before the rise of environmentalism, the resurgence
of Indian activism, and the onset of widespread queasiness over American overseas imperialism shifted the terms of national opinion of
those "enemies that threatened from within and without."[12] Kennedy
was free to offer an image of the New Frontier, premised on the assumption that the campaigns of the Old Frontier had been successful
and morally justified.

Like Turner, most Americans in Kennedy's audience assumed that
the frontier had closed in the nineteenth century.[13] "Today," Kennedy
proclaimed, "some would say that those struggles are all over—that
all the horizons have been explored, that all the battles have been
won, that there is no longer an American frontier." That notion, however, could no longer stand: "For the problems are not all solved and
the battles are not all won—and we stand today on the edge of a
New Frontier—the frontier of the 1960s—a frontier of unknown opportunities and perils—a frontier of unfulfilled hopes and threats."
Here was an image of the frontier that seemed to be composed of
equal parts of Buffalo Bill Cody and Frederick Jackson Turner: half a
frontier of violence and inverted conquest, in which innocent Americans defended themselves against the attacks of savages, and half a
frontier of peaceful, pastoral Americans seeking a better world. "I
tell you," Kennedy declared, "the New Frontier is here, whether we
seek it or not."

> Beyond that frontier are the uncharted areas of science and space, un-
> solved problems of peace and war, unconquered pockets of igno-
> rance and prejudice, unanswered questions of poverty and surplus.
> It would be easier to shrink back from that frontier. . . . But I believe
> the times demand invention, innovation, imagination, decision. I am
> asking you to be new pioneers on that New Frontier.

And then, with the topic of foreign affairs, the analogy made a clear shift toward the violent frontier of Cody:

> For the harsh facts of the matter are that we stand on this frontier at a turning point in history. We must prove all over again whether this nation—or any nation so conceived—can long endure; whether our society . . . can compete with the single-minded advance of the Communist system.

On this "race for mastery of the sky and the rain, the ocean and the tides, the far side of space and the inside of men's minds" hinged the prospects of the New Frontier.[14] Drawn from both Cody and Turner, the 1890s vision of the frontier as the triumphant but demanding crusade of the American people made a nearly perfect match with the 1960s search for language to direct and motivate the American public in the midst of the Cold War.

Twenty years later, one might have expected a few things to have changed in the usefulness of the frontier analogy. Indian people were active in pressing their rights; the environmental prices of conquest were visible and publicized; the imposition of American will by force had stumbled in Vietnam. But none of this added up to any discouragement for President Ronald Reagan. The imagery of pioneers and frontiers echoed through his speeches and through his lifestyle, as he vacationed on the ranch in southern California, with horse and cowboy hat in conspicuous display. In a memorable conflation of Washington, D.C., and the West, the Secret Service named the riding trails after streets in Washington, D.C., and code-named the president "Rawhide." Thus, the phrase, "Rawhide entering Pennsylvania Avenue" meant that the president was "entering the main trail" at his ranch. "Rawhide" rode down "Pennsylvania Avenue" with some frequency. "There is nothing better for the inside of a man," Reagan was fond of saying, "than the outside of a horse."[15]

On the fourth of July, 1982, greeting the return of the space shuttle to Edwards Air Force Base, Reagan gave his fullest tribute to Turnerian frontier history. "The conquest of new frontiers for the betterment of our homes and families," he said, "is a crucial part of our national character." Like Kennedy, Reagan parted from Turner to affirm the openness of America's frontiers: "There are those who thought the closing of the Western frontier marked an end to America's greatest period of vitality. Yet we're crossing new frontiers every day." With the specter of a closed frontier disposed of, Reagan returned to the Turnerian terms of basic American character; the space shuttle's astronauts "reaffirm to all of us that as long as there are frontiers to be explored and conquered, Americans will lead the way."[16]

In his second inaugural address, Reagan pitched into a celebration of westward expansion:

> . . . the men of the Alamo call out encouragement to each other; a settler pushes west and sings his song, and the song echoes out forever and fills the unknowing air.
> It is the American sound: It is hopeful, bighearted, idealistic— daring, decent and fair. That's our heritage, that's our song. We sing it still. For all our problems, we are together as of old.[17]

Twenty-five years after Kennedy's New Frontier, could such rhetoric still work? The columnist William Safire felt that it certainly did. The song of the settler, Safire thought, was "a lovely metaphor, and enabled [the President] to use the half-dozen adjectives that describe his vision of America: 'hopeful, bighearted, idealistic—daring, decent and fair.' "[18] In his State of the Union speech two weeks later, Reagan stuck with the frontier, celebrating "a revolution carrying us to new heights of progress by pushing back frontiers of space and knowledge."[19]

And yet an embrace of the frontier metaphor was no guarantee of electoral success. In 1988, running for the Democratic presidential nomination, Massachusetts Governor Michael Dukakis adopted the slogan "The Next American Frontier" and repeated it assiduously in his stump speech.[20] He began with the requisite quotation from John F. Kennedy on the New Frontier. This race in 1988, Dukakis said, "must not be about succumbing to shrunken ambitions. It must be about building the future we want, and conquering the next American frontier." What was this frontier? Here rhetorical force faded, as Dukakis simply proceeded through a catalogue:

> [T]he next American frontier is a vibrant, growing economy that provides good jobs at good wages for every citizen in the land. . . .
> The Next American frontier is in the marketplace of our international competition. . . .

The next American frontier is the American mind. . . .
The next American frontier is the millions of Americans who have been left behind. . . .
The next American frontier is the health of our people. . . .
. . . the next American frontier [is] in the democratic leaders of Central and Latin America who want to work with us for peace and economic development.[21]

Something, it seems clear, was not working in this speech; the energy that Reagan could pull out of the frontier metaphor was simply not available to Dukakis. He could not go beyond a formulation of equivalence: "frontier" equals "social or political issue." For reasons one can only guess at, Dukakis would not carry through on the analogy. He would not say, "The next American frontier is in the marketplace of our international competition, and we shall fight the barriers that obstruct American trade just as our pioneer ancestors fought the wilderness and the Indians." The Democratic presidential candidate in 1960 could follow the frontier analogy all the way up to an attack on "enemies that threatened from within and without"; the Democratic presidential candidate in 1988 showed a perfectly understandable reluctance to go all the way. Dukakis could only repeat his mantra of diminished power, "the next American frontier," and hope for the best.

THE HEADLINE FRONTIER

The headlines in 1986 looked as if they had been coauthored by Frederick Jackson Turner and the director of the 1890 census:

Frontier's Fate Still Uncertain
Frontier Still Has a Chance for Survival
Frontier Verges on Collapse
Time Runs Out for Frontier
Frontier Shuts Down
Too Late for Frontier
Frontier Throws in the Towel
Frontier Files for Bankruptcy
Politics Killed Frontier
Frontier Legacy Lives[22]

The entity in question was Frontier Airlines, struggling for financial survival. For readers in Colorado in 1986, the fate of the airline was a subject of some anxiety; the ironic historical resonance of these headlines did not offer much in the way of consolation or diversion.

Seldom recognized for its ironic implications, the word "frontier" makes frequent appearances in headlines. To serve their function, headlines have to convey some trustworthy clue as to the contents of the story they introduce. But headlines are very short; they are virtually a freeze-dried form of communication. Thus, their writers tap out their message in a kind of code. In the necessary economy of the headline, the writers go in search of words that will convey big meanings. They have, under those circumstances, little interest in treacherous words, words that stand a chance of betraying their users.

Headline writers are, predictably, heavy users of the words "frontier" and "pioneer." They trust those words, and the words repay that trust. They are words that carry the master key to the reader's mind; with that key, they can slip into the mind and deposit their meanings before anyone quite knows they are there.

To assemble a set of artifacts of this mental behavior, I looked at roughly four thousand headlines, from 1988 through the first half of 1993, that made use of the words "frontier" and "pioneer." The first time through, I made a strategic error and simply looked to see how silly these references were. This was an easy exercise, because many of the usages are indeed goofy. But at the end of the exercise, I had to realize that simply chuckling over these phrases was not accomplishing much for the cause of understanding.

The next time, then, I tried to find the patterns in the usage of these words. What seemed to be going on in people's minds in the late twentieth century when they called someone a pioneer or referred to an activity or an enterprise as a frontier? In answering this question, even the sillier usages can be illuminating, showing just how far from historical reality this historical reference has strayed. This exercise works best if the reader picks a nineteenth-century pioneer and then imagines how that pioneer might respond to his or her twentieth-century descendants. Or one might think only of Frederick Jackson Turner and imagine his response to what the twentieth century has done to his favorite term and his favorite people.

Let us begin on the comparatively neutral frontier of food. "Eating to Heal: the New Frontiers," the *New York Times* put it in 1990.

Apparently fighting on the wrong side of this frontier was the "Cookie Pioneer," "creator of the fortune cookie folding machine and a line of risque fortune cookies." The Cookie Pioneer may have held only a superficial kinship to the Cinnamon Roll Pioneers, but all of them could have joined forces with the Fast Food Pioneer and the Pioneer of the Snack Food Industry, to defend their turf against the insinuations of the Natural Foods Pioneer, the Vegetarian Pioneer, and the Pioneer of the Edible Landscape. Occupying less-contested territory were the Pasta Pioneers, the Potato Pioneer, and the Microwave Popcorn Pioneer, and surely the most memorable of the food pioneers—the Pioneer of the South Philadelphia Hoagie.[23]

As striking as the food pioneers are the lifestyle pioneers: the Passionate Pioneer of Fitness Franchising, the woman who founded Jazzercise Inc.; the Surfing Pioneer, "he pioneered a whole way of surfing for thousands"; the Psychedelic Pioneer; the New Age Pioneer; the Sex-Change Pioneer; the Porn Pioneer; the Pioneer in the Crack Business; and the Peekaboo Pioneer, the founder of Frederick's of Hollywood. Frederick's pioneering work did not exhaust the possibilities of the underwear frontier: "Underwear Pioneers Targeting Men," one headline reads, and the story opens with this promising line: "The two designing women who revolutionized the bra industry in the 1970s with the invention of the first jogging bra have turned their talents to men's underwear." On the subject of fabrics and new materials, there is the memorable Polyester Pioneer, as well as a Pioneer of Plastic and the Stainless Steel Pioneer.[24]

Forced into the discomfort and disorientation of time travel, Frederick Jackson Turner or any of his contemporaries would have to experience astonishment at the applications of the word "pioneer" in the late twentieth century, at this implied kinship between overland travelers and marketers of underwear, stainless steel, and hoagies. Of all these contestants, the award for the most unsettling pioneer would have to go to Dr. Louis Irwin Grossman, Pioneer in Root Canal Dentistry. And if there were an award for the twentieth-century pioneer of the product that nineteenth-century pioneers would have had the most occasions to appreciate, then that prize would go to Bernard Castro, described as the Pioneer of the Sleeper-Sofa.[25]

Beneath and beyond the silliness of these references lie a clear set of patterns. The pioneers and frontiers cluster in particular areas and enterprises. Art, music, sports, fashion, commerce, law, and labor activism get their full share of the analogy. Technology holds the biggest cluster: technology of transportation (bicycles, automobiles, helicopters, airplanes, rockets, and spacecraft); technology of communications and information (radio, television, talk shows, CD players, laser discs, computers, software, and programming); technology of medicine (heart transplants, plastic surgery, headache treatment, weight reduction, and gene therapy); technology of weaponry (rocketry and atomic bombs). Indeed, it is impossible to read all these references to the frontiers of technology without recognizing that the American public has genuinely and completely accepted, ratified, and bought the notion that the American frontiering spirit, sometime in the last century, picked itself up and made a definitive relocation from territorial expansion to technological and commercial expansion.

In November 1944, nearing the end of World War Two, President Franklin Roosevelt asked Vannevar Bush, director of the Office of Scientific Research and Development, to report on the prospects for American science after the end of the war. "New frontiers of the mind," Roosevelt said, "are before us, and if they are pioneered with the same vision, boldness, and drive with which we have waged this war we can create a fuller and more fruitful employment and a fuller and more fruitful life."[26] Called *Science, The Endless Frontier,* Bush's response to Roosevelt's request set the agenda for federally funded science. "It is in keeping with basic United States policy," Bush wrote, "that the Government should foster the opening of new frontiers," and federal investment in science "is the modern way to do it."[27] Casting science as the nation's new frontier, a frontier maintained by hearty federal funding, Vannevar Bush captured and promoted the terms of popular understanding of the frontier's relocation after Turner.

Certainly the space program has provided the best example of this pattern. The promoters of space exploration and development may well qualify as the nation's most-committed and persistent users of the frontier analogy. *Pioneering the Space Frontier,* the 1986 Paine Commission Report on the future of the space program, shows the analogy at its most fervent. The story of the American nation, as imagined by the Paine commissioners, was a triumphant and glorious story of success, with the complex stories of Indian conquest and African American slavery simply ignored and eliminated. "The promise of virgin lands and the opportunity to live in freedom," the commissioners declared, "brought our ancestors to the shores of North America."

The frontiers have not closed, and Manifest Destiny has just taken a turn skyward: "Now space technology has freed humankind to move outward from Earth as a species destined to expand to other worlds." The best that the Paine commissioners could offer in the way of a recognition of the fact that frontiers might not always be vacant was this memorable line: "As we move outward into the Solar System, we must remain true to our values as Americans: To go forward peacefully and to respect the integrity of planetary bodies and alien life forms, with equality of opportunity for all."[28] If one thinks of the devastation of Indians by disease, alcohol, war, loss of territory, and coercive assimilation and then places that reality next to the Paine commissioners' pious intentions, one feels some obligation to take up the mission of warning the alien life forms, suggesting that they keep their many eyes on their wallets when they hear these intentions invoked, especially the line about "equality of opportunity for all."

However this frontier experience plays out for alien life forms, the equating of the frontier of westward expansion with the development of space proved to be an enterprise that ran itself. In the selling of space as "the final frontier," the aerospace industry, the National Aeronautics and Space Administration, presidents, the news media, and the entertainment business collaborated with perfect harmony, with no need for centralized direction or planning, with a seamless match in their methods and goals. The split infinitive was regrettable, but the writers of *Star Trek* came up with the phrase to capture the essential idea brought to mind at the mention of the words "frontier" or "pioneer": "to boldly go where no man has gone before."

MEANWHILE, *LA FRONTERA*

The attention of Anglo-Americans has been fixed on the definition of the frontier drawn from the imaginative reconstruction of the story of the United States and its westward expansion. But North America has, in fact, had two strong traditions in the use of the term. There is the much more familiar, English usage of the frontier as the place where white settlers entered a zone of "free" land and opportunity.

But there is the much less familiar but much more realistic usage of *la frontera,* the borderlands between Mexico and the United States. This is not simply a place where two groups meet; Indian people have been influential players in the complicated pattern of human relations in the area. In the nineteenth century, trade, violence, conquest, and cultural exchange punctuated and shaped life in the borderlands. In the twentieth century, with conflicts over the restriction of immigration, with disputes over water flow and environmental pollution, and with a surge of industrial development and population growth from American-owned businesses *(maquiladoras)* operating in northern Mexico, conditions along the border remain far from tranquil.[29]

In the idea of *la frontera,* there is no illusion of vacancy, of triumphal conclusions, or of simplicity. As the writer Gloria Anzaldua puts it, the United States–Mexican border is "where the Third World grates up against the first and bleeds."[30] It is a unique place on the planet's surface, a zone where an industrialized nation shares a long land border with a nation much-burdened by poverty. "Ambivalence and unrest," Anzaldua says, "reside there and death is no stranger."[31] Any temptation to romanticize *la frontera*—as a place of cultural syncretism, a place where the languages of Spanish and English have learned to cohabit and even merge—runs aground on the bare misery of poverty in the border towns.[32]

The idea of the frontier is extremely well established as cultural common property. If the idea of *la frontera* had anywhere near the standing of the idea of the frontier, we would be well launched toward self-understanding, directed toward a realistic view of this nation's position in the hemisphere and in the world. "The struggle of borders is our reality still," Anzaldua writes.[33] One can tinker a bit with that line to draw the crucial contrast: "The adventure of frontiers is our fantasy still; the struggle of borders is our reality still."

In truth, this idea of the frontier as border has made some inroads in popular thinking. If you are reading a headline for a news story set outside the United States, there is a chance that the word "frontier" will carry a completely different meaning from its usual one. References to the "Romania-Bulgaria frontier" or to the "Lebanese-Israeli frontier" are quite a different matter from references to the frontier where the pioneer stands on the edge of vacancy and opportunity. These are frontiers in the old, concrete, down-to-earth sense, much closer in meaning to *la frontera:* borders between countries, between peoples, between authorities, sometimes between armies. When the newspaper writers tell us that "Algeria and Morocco reopen their frontier" or the nation of Turkey decides it "will close its frontier with Bulgaria," these are references to borders that are full of possibilities for both cooperation and friction, places where "opening" and "closing" mean things quite different from what Frederick Jackson Turner and the director of the census meant in the 1890s.[34]

In these references to international borders and boundaries, the word "frontier" takes a firmer hold on reality. Reading my collection of headlines, the frequent appearances of this definition of "frontier" caught me by surprise. Perhaps, it began to seem, there is more hope for this word than it seemed at first; perhaps popular thinking has already dug a sizable channel for thinking about the frontier in a manner quite different from the *Star Trek* mode.

One other pattern of usage, however, struck me as equally surprising: the omnipresence in headlines dealing with African American achievements. Here, the usage was again closer to the *Star Trek* definition, with pioneers boldly going where no one like them had gone before. Pioneers in civil rights—"Desegregation's Pioneers"—were everywhere, from A. Philip Randolph to Rosa Parks, from Julian Bond to Charlayne Hunter-Gault. The range of African American pioneers covers a great deal of turf: a Pioneer Black Professional Golfer; a Pioneer of Black Pride; the National Football League's Pioneer Black Coach; a Pioneer Black [Theatrical] Producer; a Pioneer Black Announcer; Negro League Pioneers; a Pioneer Black Ivy League Teacher; a Black Radio Pioneer; a Black Foreign Services Pioneer; a Pioneer Black Los Angeles Judge; a Pioneer Black Journalist; a Pioneer in Black Film; and Sidney Poitier, the winner of the "coveted Pioneer Award," bestowed at the Black Oscars Nominees dinner in 1989. As all these headlines suggest, the idea of the pioneer as an appropriately complimentary way to refer to African American people who traveled with dignity, courage, and determination where no black person had gone before has become an established part of the American cultural vocabulary. When, in 1989, Secretary of Health and Human Services Louis Sullivan "told the graduating class of A. Philip Randolph Campus High School in Manhattan that they will become 'pioneers' if they meet the challenges of fighting inequality, racism, and poverty in the 21st century," Sullivan was employing the term in its standard usage.[35]

This usage was so well understood that it gave rise to one of the few cases where a person interviewed in a newspaper article actually engaged and questioned the meaning of the term and its application to him. "National League President Plays Down 'Pioneer' Talk," the headline read. The opening sentence explained, "National League President Bill White says he's getting tired of people referring to him as a black pioneer. . . . 'I'm not a pioneer,' White said. 'Jackie [Robinson] was the pioneer.' "[36] To Bill White, "pioneer" was the term reserved for the unusually courageous person who went first, and the one who faced the worst and the most intense opposition and resistance.

The African American applications of the pioneer analogy caught me completely by surprise. They took the ground out from under any remaining inclination I might have had simply to mock or make fun of the use of the analogy. The lesson of these references is this: the whole package of frontier and pioneer imagery has ended up as widely dispersed intellectual property. One could argue, as I probably at other times *would* have argued, that African Americans would be well advised to keep their distance from the metaphors and analogies of conquest and colonialism, that there are other and better ways to say that someone was a person of principle, innovation, and determination, without calling him a pioneer.

Even though they have been significant participants in the westward movement and in the life of the American West in the twentieth century, African Americans barely figured in the traditional tellings of frontier history; the history of pioneering Americans was for far too long a segregated, whites-only subject matter.[37] The image of the heroic pioneer was in many ways a vehicle of racial subordination, exalting the triumph of whites over Indians. Jackie Robinson, A. Philip Randolph, and Rosa Parks were people of great courage and spirit, and getting them entangled in the whole inherited myth of Manifest Destiny, nationalistic cheerleading, and justifications for conquest does not seem to be the best way to honor them.

But it is a bit too late to avoid that entangling. Greatly troubled by the problem of violence inflicted by blacks against blacks, Reverend Jesse Jackson pled with people to "Stop the violence!" The campaign to end the violence, he said, is "the new frontier of the civil rights movement."[38] Logic and history say that the frontier was, in fact, a place where violence served the causes of racial subordination, but a more powerful emotional understanding says that the frontier is where people of courage have gone to take a stand for the right and the good. For people of a wide range of ethnicities, when it comes to the idea of the frontier, logic and history yield to the much greater power of inherited image.

This is the curious conclusion that these headlines forced on me: a positive image of the frontier and the pioneer is now implanted in nearly everyone's mind. It would not surprise me to see headlines referring to an American Indian lawyer as "a pioneer in the assertion of Indian legal rights," "pushing forward the frontier of tribal sovereignty," even though it was the historical pioneers who assaulted those rights, even though it was the pioneers' historical frontier that charged head-on into tribal sovereignty. And yet Indian people have adopted any number of white-introduced items. They wear cowboy hats, drive pickup trucks and automobiles, shop in supermarkets, study constitutional law in law schools, and remain Indian. In all sorts of ways, Indian people put Anglo-American artifacts, mental and physical, to use for Indian purposes. There is no very convincing argument for saying that they must put a stop to their adopting and incorporating when it comes to the idea of the frontier and the image of the pioneer.

Many Americans in the late twentieth century have taken to lamenting "the disuniting of America" through the expansion of multicultural history.[39] We hear frequent expressions of nostalgia for an imagined era of unity, before an emphasis on race, class, and gender divided Americans into contesting units and interests. Reading several thousand headlines about pioneers and frontiers, however, gave me the conviction that matters are by no means as disunited as the lamenters think. When African Americans turn comfortably to the image of the pioneer, then the idea of the frontier and the pioneer have clearly become a kind of multicultural common property, a joint stock company of the imagination. As encounters with scholars from other countries usually demonstrate, this is not just multicultural; this is international. People from the Philippines, people from Senegal, people from Thailand, people with plenty of reasons to resent the frontier and cowboy diplomacy inflicted on their nations by our nation— many of them nonetheless grew up watching Western movies and yearning for life on the old frontier and the open range.[40]

As a mental artifact, the frontier has demonstrated an astonishing stickiness and persistence. It is virtually the flypaper of our mental world; it attaches itself to everything—healthful diets, space shuttles, civil rights campaigns, heart transplants, industrial product development, musical innovations. Packed full of nonsense and goofiness, jammed with nationalistic self-congratulations and toxic ethnocentrism, the image of the frontier is nonetheless universally recognized and laden with positive associations. Whether or not it suits my preference, the concept works as a kind of cultural glue—a mental and emotional fastener that, in some very curious and unexpected ways, works to hold us together.

The frontier of an expanding and confident nation; the frontier of cultural interpenetration; the frontier of contracting rural settlement; the frontier of science, technology, and space; the frontier of civil rights where black pioneers ventured and persevered; the frontiers between nations in Europe, Asia, and Africa; *la frontera* of the Rio Grande and the deserts of the Southwestern United States and northern Mexico—somewhere in the midst of this weird hodgepodge of frontier and pioneer imagery lie important lessons about the American identity, sense of history, and direction for the future.

Standing in the way of a full reckoning with those lessons is, however, this fact: in the late *twentieth* century, the scholarly understanding formed in the late *nineteenth* century still governs most of the public, rhetorical uses of the word "frontier." If the velocity of the movement of ideas from frontier historians to popular culture remains constant, somewhere in the next century, we might expect the popular usage of the word to begin to reckon with the complexity of the westward movement and its consequences. Somewhere in the mid-2000s, the term might undergo a crucial shift, toward the reality of *la frontera* and away from the fantasy of the frontier. That shift in meaning will be the measure of great change in this nation's understanding of its own origins.

I-C

The Case of
the Premature Departure:
The Trans-Mississippi West and
American History Textbooks*

In *America: Past and Present*, Robert Divine and his coauthors tell a story about the "Eastern provincialism" of presidential candidate Al Smith in 1928: "When reporters asked him about his appeal in the states west of the Mississippi, he replied, 'What states *are* west of the Mississippi?'"[1] Writers of the current crop of American history textbooks have a certain amount in common with the ill-fated Smith. A few of them run into moments of trouble in keeping these big, square, evidently interchangeable states straight. Wyoming, most commonly, is the state injured: Irwin Unger, in *The United States*, moves the Fetterman massacre from Wyoming to Nebraska, and R. Jackson Wilson and his collaborators, in *The Pursuit of Liberty*, remove the Union Pacific Railroad from its accustomed route through Wyoming and send it south across Colorado.[2] Such bloopers, however, are no novelty to Westerners, who find it an equal challenge to keep the tiny states of the East Coast in some semblance of named order.

---

*Readers should be alert to the fact that many of the endnotes in this essay are not only amusing but also worth reading.

The textbooks, more often than not, put Western states in their proper geographical place; indeed, the maps are sometimes more illuminating than the written narrative. The problem arises, instead, with the Trans-Mississippi West's place in national history. Laboring under their own version of Al Smith's "Eastern provincialism," nearly all of the authors are content to let their point of view, as well as most of their narrative, rest in the Eastern United States. When some of them use the phrase "the Far West" to describe Utah, Oregon, New Mexico, or California, no one has to ask, "Far from what?"

In other sections of these books, intellectual revolutions have taken place. In the writing of colonial, Southern, African American, and labor history, the texts keep up with new information and new interpretation. As Wilson and his colleagues announce in the opening of *The Pursuit of Liberty,* "Nowadays, of course, everything about learning history has changed."[3] But not quite everything: the story of the westward-moving frontier has, to a remarkable degree, resisted change. The presence of Indians and Hispanics may have become more noticeable, but the basic model of the American West as a westward-moving frontier, coming to a halt in the 1890s, still sets the terms of the narrative.

Tracking the frontier in its erratic movements, no textbook shows even a momentary recognition that the term itself has become problematic. In fact, some of the most-determined loyalists to the concept of the frontier are, by other measures, the most receptive to revision and reinterpretation; it is a particular surprise to see the word used frequently, and without definition or reflection, in Mary Beth Norton, et al., *A People and a Nation.* The risks inherent in the word—the reduction of a multisided convergence of various peoples into a model of the two sides of a frontier line—do not concern any of the writers. Every textbook uses the term "frontier" freely, and no textbook defines it clearly, evidently on the assumption that its meaning is so well known that it needs no clarification.[4] The West is the frontier and the frontier is the West, and that, for the textbooks, is all anyone—writer, reader, lecturer, or student—needs to know.

Coming after the chorus of calls for the inclusion of minorities, women, gays and lesbians, and the poor, a call for a more realistic treatment of the Trans-Mississippi West cannot be a welcome sound to the textbook writers' ears. While it is, in truth, disorienting to sit in Colorado and read about the disappearance of the American West in the 1890s, the point of a more comprehensive treatment is not to help Westerners increase their sense of self-worth. The point is that the Trans-Mississippi West is more than half of the country. This does not mean that it should, by some equivalence of size and significance, occupy half of each textbook. As a teacher of the American history survey course, I have full sympathy for the textbook writers' problems with the allocation of space. But I would ask them to reconsider their present strict economy in allocating significance to the Trans-Mississippi West and to explore the ways in which a more fully realized and recognized West might add to the educational power of their books.

With very few exceptions, the textbook treatment of the West follows a deeply worn set of ruts. The opening section on Indian people before the arrival of Europeans usually has a reference to the Pueblos and the Plains tribes. The summary of Spanish colonization includes Francisco Vasquez de Coronado's 1540 expedition to the borderlands, with, perhaps, a few words more on the colonization of New Mexico, or even California. These brief courtesies observed, the action moves to the Atlantic Coast, where it stays for at least two centuries.

With the creation of the American republic, the West gains importance, but it is no longer the homeland of the Pueblos and Plains Indians or the site of the Spanish settlements in New Mexico. The region between the Appalachians and the Mississippi River—Kentucky, Ohio, Indiana, Alabama, Mississippi, and their neighbors—now constitutes the West. But when a more-interesting candidate appears, as it does with the Louisiana Purchase, the West takes a sudden leap westward across the Mississippi, becoming the territory of Louisiana and of Meriwether Lewis and William Clark's travels. Then, with Lewis and Clark's successful return, the West springs back to its cis-Mississippi location.

In the chapter on Manifest Destiny and the struggle over slavery in the territories, the West returns to its trans-Mississippi meaning. The Texas Revolution, the Mexican-American War,[5] the discovery of gold in California all have one clear claim to significance: they ignited the fuse that set off the Civil War in the Eastern United States. The story of the colonization of this Far West is thus subordinated to the story of the struggle between the North and South over slavery. When last seen in the first volume of the textbook, the West has returned to the eastern side of the Mississippi River, where Vicksburg and Shiloh represent the Civil War "in the West."[6]

In the second volume, the West crosses back over the Mississippi. This is now the last West, the "folding frontier," and "the final phase of the westward movement."[7] The Trans-Mississippi variety of the West thus shares the sad fate of Jenny Cavilleri in *Love Story*, along with any number of young people in a well-established genre of melancholy movies and novels. Like those unlucky fictional characters, this West lives a hard, fast, and colorful life before its abrupt death. For a few years, though, the pace of life is wild indeed, as mining frontiers, cattle frontiers, and farming frontiers radiate in all directions. Independent prospectors race from boom to boom, ironically leaving their antithesis—corporate, industrial mining—in their wake. Cattlemen pour north from Texas, speculate wildly, overstock the Plains, and emerge from the dreadful winter of 1887 a chastened, shaken-down set of businessmen who will henceforth raise their cattle with rational methods. The Plains Indians, judged to be "the most important" Western Indians, are chased from pillar to post, from Sand Creek to their final destruction at Wounded Knee.[8] Farmers, meanwhile, rush to the Plains, prosper briefly, and then, besieged by drought, grasshoppers, demoralized farm wives, failing prices, and debt, collapse in the direction of the virtually omnipresent Mary E. Lease and her fellow Populists.[9] With or without a direct quotation from Frederick Jackson Turner announcing the end of the frontier, the West is over and done with, even if four or five hundred pages remain in the text.[10]

The index tells its own story of a West with a limited lifespan. When "West" appears in the textbook's index, it is not only mobile, sliding to and from the Trans-Appalachian West to the Trans-Mississippi West, it is also terminal. Indexed references to the "West" stop before the twentieth century begins. Regardless of the politics, methods, or age of the textbook's authors, the West registers as a transitory phase of national history and not as a permanent place. In a number of books, the index makes this subordination of place to process crystal clear: for "frontier," the index entry says, "see West."[11] In other books, the word "West" does not even appear in the index, and the phrase "westward expansion" takes its place.[12] The West has its only meaning as an ephemeral zone on the edge of Anglo-American imagining and settling.

Any Western resource booms and busts occurring after 1890 have simply missed the deadline. As late arrivals, the timber business in the Pacific Northwest and the Rockies and the uranium rush in the Four Corners area and the Black Hills are absent from the textbooks. The word "oil" is so tightly linked to the name John D. Rockefeller, and thus to Pennsylvania, Ohio, and the Midwest, that the Western oil industry has to settle for a sentence recording its most recent rise and fall in the 1970s and 1980s, or the vexing problem of oil spills.[13] The Western tourism industry, which has become, in many parts of the American West, the most important support of the economy, has no history. Similarly, the ongoing instability of Western mining and cattle raising cannot register in textbooks where those two industries turn corporate, calm, predictable, and dull before 1890.

Some books do make an effort to include examples from the entire country to illustrate national trends and events; on that count, Boyer, Clark, Kett, Purvis, Sitkoff, and Woloch's *Enduring Vision* is the textbook most consistently *national* in its scope. When, for instance, Boyer describes Americans celebrating the end of World War Two, he mentions festivities in San Francisco, Salt Lake, and San Diego, not just in Boston and New York.[14] But even with examples drawn from the region, the West departs as a unit of study after 1890, and important regional characteristics and patterns cannot even be named. None of the textbooks note the Trans-Mississippi West's status as the region with the greatest urban concentration of population. No textbook remarks on the West's good fortune as the region receiving the greatest *per capita* benefits from the New Deal, and no author notes the West's particularly strong association, arising out of World War Two, with military and nuclear enterprises. No author discusses the West as a region where, except for the coastal Pacific Northwest, scarce water remains a permanent challenge.[15] The West as the only part of the nation that shares a land border with an underdeveloped country, the West as the part of the nation with the most direct Pacific Basin ties, the West as the site of the vast majority of the public lands and of the largest Indian reservations—these are regional characteristics and qualities that the textbooks leave for students to notice on their own.

Curiously enough, in spite of their model of the vanished West, the textbooks provide enough information to permit enterprising students to begin to construct a more realistic model of regional history. This opportunity is clearest in the contradiction between the information conveyed by words and the information conveyed by maps. Many of the books have a map showing the topography or climate of the nation, and the higher altitudes, mountainous landscapes, aridity of the Western half of the continent make an unmistakable impression of distinctiveness.[16] The maps show a kind of terrain, and an evolving history, that cannot fit neatly in the concept of a westward-moving frontier or in the concept of a thoroughly homogenized, postfrontier nation. By the 1840s, with Mexican settlements in New Mexico, Texas, Arizona, and California, with the travels of fur traders throughout the region, with American settlements in Texas, Oregon, and Utah, the idea of a frontier "line" is no longer workable.[17] In the same way, the maps mock the idea of a completed conquest. The text says the frontier is closed and the West is gone; the maps show an enormous amount of unsettled space in the Trans-Mississippi West in 1890 and later.[18] Why declare the mastery and occupation of the Trans-Mississippi West to be complete in 1890, when so much of the terrain had not yielded (indeed, by virtue of its aridity and altitude, still has not yielded) to conventional American settlement? When the text says the West is settled and tamed and the map tells another story, the best plan may well be to trust the map.

The written text itself offers students other clues that the traditional approach to Western history is ripe for rethinking. No sooner is the obituary recorded for the West than certain puzzling signs of regional life go on record, offering hints of another, more inclusive, and more interesting way of writing Western history. There are, for instance, a number of events, arising out of Western conditions, that have made it into the canon of significant United States history. They make a substantial list: California newspaperman Henry George's distress over the perils of land monopoly; the Credit Mobilier scandal and the Union Pacific Railroad; the Chinese Exclusion Act of 1882; the early successes in the campaign for women's suffrage; Gifford Pinchot, Theodore Roosevelt, and the origins of federal conservation; Oregon and California Progressives; the Industrial Workers of the World; the judicial attack on the Northern Securities Company's concentration of railroading power; the border activities of Pancho Villa; Frank Norris and John Steinbeck; the movie business and Hollywood;

Albert Fall and Teapot Dome; the Dust Bowl; the repatriation of Mexicans in the 1930s; the Japanese American internment camps of World War Two; the zootsuit riots in wartime Los Angeles; the bracero program; the design, development, and testing of the atomic bomb; *Brown v. Board of Education of Topeka;* the Watts riots; Mario Savio and the Free Speech Movement; Cesar Chavez and the farmworkers' movement; the early careers of Lyndon Johnson, Barry Goldwater, Richard Nixon, George McGovern, and Ronald Reagan. These people and events make an appearance in virtually every textbook.[19] They are, however, usually presented without any regional context, as if the fact of their national significance released them from the handicap of their setting.

Each of these examples poses the question: Why not recognize both levels of significance, regional and national? More important, why not let the implications of these Western events build a more instructive model of Western history than the floating frontier approach? Consider a few examples. The Chinese Exclusion Act of 1882 arose out of a West Coast pattern of immigration and nativism and set a crucial precedent for the limiting of immigration on the basis of race and ethnicity. Conservation, whether in the creation of forest reserves and national parks or in the building of dams by the Reclamation Service, had particular implications for the Trans-Mississippi West. The Northern Securities concentration of power carries a message about a national trend toward monopoly, and also a message about the particular vulnerability, by virtue of remoteness, vast distances, and raw material economies, of Western locations to manipulation by transportation businesses. Albert Fall and the Teapot Dome scandal carry a lesson about the perils of federal land management of Western resources, not just a lesson about the perils of Warren Harding's presidency.

Most consequential for the rethinking of the place of Western history are two recent events, both of them almost always included in the textbooks: the rise of the Sunbelt and the shift from Europe to Latin America and Asia as the principal source of immigration, with Hispanics on their way to becoming the nation's largest minority. Noting these developments, even the textbooks that banned the word "West" from the index are forced to refer to a region by that name: how else can they record the crucial fact that, in the 1980s, the population of the South and the West came to outnumber the population of the

Northeast and the Midwest? In the same way, while Hispanic American and Asian American people live all over the nation, their longest history, their most visible presence, and their frequent point of arrival lie in the American West. "Like Hispanics, Asians were concentrated mainly in large cities and in the West," Brinkley and his coauthors observe, in a sentence that, true to the indexer's policy of terminating the topic in the 1890s, will not appear under the listing "West."[20]

While they all note the late-twentieth-century geographical rearrangement of the nation's population, the textbook authors have not begun to explore the implications of this new demography for the writing of national history. In the comparative sparseness of its pre-twentieth-century population, one suspects, lies a principal reason for the short shrift the region gets from the textbooks. This, also, helps to explain why the entry of social historians into the textbook-writing business did so little to change the basic treatment of the West. If an earlier generation of textbook writers followed the presidents and Congress, the more recent generation follows the crowds. The numbers of a certain population, in a rough way, suggested how much attention they should receive. For historians struck by the remarkable rate of population growth in the English colonies in the eighteenth century, Spanish settlement in the West in the same period could only make a weak claim for attention. In the same way, in the second half of the nineteenth century, the scale of European immigration would make Asian and Mexican immigration of the same period look, by comparison, small and dismissible.

In the mid-1960s, when California replaced New York as the most populous state, the door opened for a new way of thinking about national history. The maps that show the redistribution of population by the 1980s, maps that make a dramatic case for the proposition that westward migration has a history extending long beyond 1890, are each graphic invitations to rethink the "Eastern provincialism" of the textbooks.[21]

To suggest that the distribution of national population in the late twentieth century is an argument for expanding coverage of the nineteenth-century Trans-Mississippi West (or of the sixteenth-, seventeenth-, and eighteenth-century West) may at first seem too much a matter of hindsight and presentism. And yet hindsight rules the structure of American history textbooks.[22] The colonies of Massachusetts and South Carolina, New Jersey and Virginia are brought into the same story because the authors and their readers know that these disparate colonies were on their way to becoming a nation. The approach of the Civil War sets the terms and tones of what goes under the name of the antebellum period. A Western American application of hindsight is as legitimate as these other, well-established forms of structuring the narrative on the basis of knowing "how it all turned out." In those terms, one might well broaden the terrain of colonial history in response to the fact that New Mexico, Texas, California, and Arizona eventually joined up with Massachusetts and Virginia, and, moreover, became a populous and powerful part of the United States.

Just as important, the West offers textbooks prime opportunities for developing comparisons and thus for encouraging an interpretative cast of mind in the students. Comparing Spanish New Mexico to the English Atlantic colonies could cast a spotlight on both the common characteristics of colonies and the distinctive styles of particular empires.[23] Comparing English colonial governments to Western territorial governments or comparing Western territories to Southern state governments under Reconstruction could shed a valuable light on the norms of democracy and self-government, as they respond to the stress of abnormal situations. Comparing the Indian and Mexican experiences as minorities by conquest to the African American experience as a minority by forced migration and enslavement could give American race relations its full range and interest. Comparing Mexican American and Asian American labor history to African American and European American labor history could broaden the picture of industrial relations and of social class. Comparing overseas immigration to immigration over a land border, as well as trans-Atlantic immigration to trans-Pacific immigration, could give the traditional Ellis Island–centered model of immigration history a broader and more thought-provoking context.

Serious attention to the American West, in other words, permits an accessible, manageable kind of domestic comparative history, sparing the textbook writer the time and trouble of presenting the history of another nation for purposes of comparison, while offering many of the same advantages in defeating a narrowly nationalistic perspective.

"Through most of the nation's history," Brinkley, Current, Freidel, and Williams write, "Americans had been accustomed to thinking of

themselves as essentially a society of two races: whites and blacks."
The proposition may well have some application to the Eastern United
States (though, even there, its dismissal of Indians is puzzling), but it
makes no sense at all for the Western United States. And, now that
Asian Americans and Hispanic Americans are as visible in the rest of
the country as they have long been in the West, the situation is transformed. As Brinkley notes, it is "no longer possible to think of America" in terms of two races.[24]

In all the textbooks, one can hear the gears strain in this effort to
go beyond a black-white model of American race relations. Discussions of Mexican American and Indian history still trail behind the
longer, more substantial sections on African American history, with
Asian American history appearing much less regularly.[25] This is most
noticeable in discussions of activism in the mid-twentieth century; as
Henretta puts it, "The civil rights movement influenced other groups,
such as Hispanics and native Americans, to organize to press their
claims."[26] While no one would deny the powerful influence of the
African American civil rights movement, activism on the part of Western American minorities has a history that long antedates the 1950s
and 1960s, a history obscured by the suggestion that they remained
passive and quiet until Eastern African Americans gave them a better
idea.[27] The textbooks thus remain several stages away from a truly national view of the movement against racial discrimination, a project
of historical description and analysis made much more difficult by the
usual eastward tilt of historical significance.

Of equal value is the opportunity Western history offers for environmental history. At present, environmental history is one of the
weakest elements of the textbooks.[28] Most books allot a paragraph or
two to Theodore Roosevelt, Gifford Pinchot, and the origins of federal conservation; a few sentences on the Dust Bowl and the activities
of the Civilian Conservation Corps in the 1930s; and then a few
words at the end of the book on the growing popularity of the environmental movement and the rise of anxiety over oil spills, Three
Mile Island, and global warming. Quite in contrast to the perfunctory
treatment the textbooks give environmental history, students taking
American history courses give every sign of eagerness to hear more on
the subject, and this, unlike some others, is a client demand well
worth meeting.

Because of the West's dramatic and distinctive landscapes, its aridity, its long-term dependence on natural resource extraction, and the federal control of so much of its land, the history of the human relationship to the physical environment is one of Western history's strong suits. Maps of American settlement in the West show, down to the present, large areas with sparse populations, where the human relationship to nature is virtually spotlit. As the nation's common property, the national forests, the national parks, and the lands under the jurisdiction of the Bureau of Land Management have functioned as focal points for conflict and change in American behavior toward nature. But only a student miraculously capable of reading between the lines could learn much of anything about the history of the public lands from any of these textbooks.[29]

The invisibility of the Taylor Grazing Act of 1934 provides the best example of how the conventional narrative of Western history leaves out crucial stories in environmental history. Responding to the continued problems of overgrazing on the public lands, the Taylor Act created the Grazing Service, which evolved into the Bureau of Land Management. By establishing federal supervision of most of the remaining public domain, the Taylor Act stood for a fundamental change away from the unregulated use of resources on federal lands. The Taylor Act is, however, completely unseen in the textbooks, for obvious reasons of narrative structure. According to the "end of the West" model, the cattle business settled down in the late nineteenth century; livestock raisers took to the use of fenced-in pastures and winter feed crops. "Cattle raising," as Gruver puts it, "ceased to be a spirited, individualistic enterprise and became an efficiently managed business." Or, as Norton and her colleagues describe the 1890s, "big businesses" took over "the cattle industry" and applied "scientific methods of breeding and feeding. Most ranchers owned or leased the land they used."[30] With the cattle business apparently tamed and off the public lands by the 1890s, there is no imaginable reason for the Taylor Grazing Act in 1934 or for the continued, bitter, sometimes violent conflicts over grazing on Western public lands in our own time.

Like the struggles over the public lands, many of the most important stories of the American West fall outside both the chronological and conceptual limits of the story of the westward-moving frontier. Consider, for instance, the array of nuclear events and enterprises in the region. The Los Alamos laboratory oversaw the design of the bomb, the Hanford Reservation on the Columbia River provided key production facilities, the desert at Alamogordo offered the right conditions for the first test and, into the Cold War, the Four Corners area and the Black Hills supplied the uranium, the Plains and mountain states provided much of the missile-sitting terrain, the Nevada Test Site absorbed the repeated shocks of bomb development, Rocky Flats in Colorado and Pantex in Texas assembled bombs, and, finally, the West was reliably the winner in national contests for choosing the site for nuclear waste disposal. American atomic affairs have long carried a Western emphasis.[31]

The assumptions that now guide the textbook treatment of Western history exclude most of the region's most crucial stories. Why, then, would the authors stay loyal to a model with such narrow limits? The situation brings to mind the remark of an exuberant conductor in Los Angeles' Union Station twenty years ago. Announcing the departure of the train running from Los Angeles to Seattle, the conductor said, repeatedly, "This is the best train to Seattle." Asked to explain, he responded, "This is the best train to Seattle—because it's the only train to Seattle."

The story of the westward-moving frontier has remained the best version of Western history because, for most of the textbook writers, it was and is the only version.[32] In the last thirty years, revision and rethinking in Western American history have taken place, primarily, in the arena of the monograph. In Trans-Mississippi studies, specialized inquiries into gender, minorities, physical environments, labor, and twentieth-century events thoroughly undermined the traditional framework of frontier history. But it would have taken a particularly determined set of textbook revisers, scholars with time on their hands, to read through all those monographs and assemble a more realistic presentation of the American West. No wonder they took a more economical approach to the use of their time and held on to the old plot of the mobile and vanishing West.

Should the textbook writers throw out the old plot and adopt a consistently regional meaning for the word "West"? On the contrary, after reading fifteen fundamentally similar treatments of the West as frontier, an enthusiasm for orthodoxy decreases, while a yearning for novelty rises. My wish is that the textbook writers might reconsider a number of their standard assumptions about the West. If the results of that reconsideration vary considerably, all the better, as long as some fresh air comes to circulate in these currently stuffy passages.

If, for instance, the authors decide to stick with their mobile and transitory model of the West, they could distinguish clearly among their various Wests; consistent use of the adjectives Trans-Appalachian and Trans-Mississippi would add considerable clarity. The writers could explore the advantages of a truly comparative approach to colonial history, an approach that would not only use the Spanish colonies to illuminate the distinctiveness of the English colonies (and vice versa); this would counter the notion, to which students are already susceptible, that the history of the Spanish and Mexican settlements springs to life and gathers significance only when, at long last, Anglo-Americans arrive on the scene.[33] The authors could, as well, reconsider the nearly complete subordination of Western events before 1861 to the theme of sectional struggle over slavery. They could explore the implications of the fact that this is a bicoastal nation; with the increase in Asian immigration and Pacific trade, the importance of the United States's Pacific Coast gets clearer every day. They could entertain the possibility of a more-detailed presentation of the origins of the national forests, the national parks, and Bureau of Land Management lands, as well as a fuller and more thoughtful treatment of the contradictions and paradoxes of the movement broadly labeled "conservation." Most important, they could rethink their common practice of terminating the West and Western history in the 1890s.

"America," in Irwin Unger's phrase, may have "had many 'Wests,' "[34] But American history textbooks have had only one way to tell the story of those "Wests." That strategy has had the unhappy side effect of canceling out the existence of the West that is still with us. American history is surely big enough to include both the story of national expansion and the story of the increasingly important western half of the nation.

PART II

——◆——

BELEAGUERED

GREAT

WHITE MEN

With the exception of an occasional bore, powerful white men are people of great interest and certainly people of consequence. In recent times, making up for a longstanding imbalance in historical practice, the attention of many professional historians shifted toward the history of minorities, women, and workers and away from the holders of power and influence. The time seems propitious to return to the study of the famous, prosperous white men, with their stories now enriched and deepened by a recognition of the people whose subordination made possible the prosperity of the elite. In truth, the stories of the less powerful cannot make complete sense without an intense reckoning with the stories of those white men who exerted power over others. Of course, white men themselves are hardly birds of a feather. The disparity of wealth separating a mining magnate from a working miner, a railroad baron from a railroad worker, or a senator from a hardscrabble farmer remind us that different white men have lived starkly different lives.

These three essays explore lessons from the lives of three famous European or Euro-American men in Western American history. The citizens of Poncha Springs and Salida, Colorado, hold an annual Anza Day, to commemorate the fact that the site of Poncha Springs represented the farthest northern travels of Juan Bautista de Anza, the capable Spanish borderlands official who led the first civilian settlement in California and who served as governor of colonial New Mexico. Given in 1997, this talk was wonderfully interrupted by thunder, lightning, and a total downpour, leaving only the hardiest to make it through all thirteen historical lessons of Anza's life.

To commemorate the 150th anniversary of John Sutter's settling in the Sacramento Valley, Kenneth Owens of California State University, Sacramento, organized a speakers' series. In pious presentations of state history, Sutter operates as *the* Founding Father, the pioneer who made possible the Americanization of California. In "Prototype for Failure," I make the case that Sutter proves to have been a great deal more interesting—and more complicated—than his placement on a pedestal ever permitted him to be.

For many Western historians, Frederick Jackson Turner remains firmly settled on his own pedestal, the Father of the Field of Western History. Because Turner played such a central role in the early years of the American Historical Association and its journal, the *American Historical Review,* the editor asked for a fresh appraisal of Turner and his impact on the historical profession for the *AHR*'s centennial. Turner believed that historians should keep up with the times and rethink their understanding of the past in response to current events. As anyone who adopts this faith soon learns, this program is a lot easier to declare than to practice. Working on this essay led me to the unsettling recognition that Turner and I had more in common than either of us might have liked: hence, the title, "Turnerians All."

II-A

Historical Lessons on Anza Day

Juan Bautista de Anza is not a household name, but I wish he were. Why did celebrity status and name recognition come to some figures in Western American history and not to others? A biography of a figure like Meriwether Lewis can become a fixture on best-seller lists. As a book trying for comparable popularity, a biography of Juan Bautista de Anza would seem defeated before it started, with no way to appeal to nationalistic pride or even to basic name recognition.

My own sense of defeat in these matters settled in a few years ago. I was flying to Durango, Colorado, and I was looking at a *New York Times Book Review*. On the inside front page, there was a prominently featured advertisement for a book, called *Heart of the West*, by a woman named Penelope Williamson. The ad featured a lurid Western sunset as background and these words at the top: "Wild, Raw, and Beautiful." At the bottom, the ad gave a summary of the book: "Nothing had prepared this New England bride for the harsh realities of the frontier. Nothing could prepare her for a love beyond reason." And then, very portentously, at the bottom, stood the words: "Montana Was Not the Only Frontier." When I got to Durango and met with some students at Fort Lewis College, I showed them the ad for Penelope Williamson's book. Then I asked them to assess the proportion of influence here: on a scale of 100, how much influence over popular thinking would they assign to Penelope Williamson's image of the West, and how much influence would they assign to Patricia Nelson Limerick's image of the West?

The students gave ninety-eight points to Penelope Williamson and two points to me. Then, under a little pressure, they admitted that they only gave me the two points in order to be polite and kind.

After that trip to Durango, life has been a lot more restful. For years, I had struggled away, insisting in every possible forum that the real stories of the West were much more compelling than the stories cooked up to meet the desires of those who love the Western myth. I actually believed, for quite a long time, that Western fact could hold its own against Western myth. Thus, there was something very restful, something really quite soothing, about recognizing, facing up, and submitting to defeat. But every once in a while a fit of nostalgia for the old campaign flares up. What would happen if I decided to give the Western popularizers a run for their money and make a case, pitched to the ever more frenetic marketing concerns of mainstream publishers, for the life of Juan Bautista de Anza as thrilling, blockbuster material?

What sort of ad could we design for such a book? There is certainly nothing lacking in the available scenery. We could have a shot of the haunting landscape of New Mexican mesas, towering mountains in the Southern Rockies, or life-threatening stretches of deserts west of the Colorado River. But how do we word this ad? Honesty would probably require, in the place of "Wild, Raw, and Beautiful," something closer to "Well-Organized, Effective, and Disciplined." And, in contrast to "Nothing had prepared the New England bride for the realities of the frontier. Nothing had prepared her for a love beyond reason," we would have to say, "*Everything* had prepared the colonial officeholder for the realities of the frontier. Everything had prepared him for promotions beyond his original rank." And then there is the final line, counterpart to "Montana Was Not the Only Frontier": "The Settlement at San Francisco Was Not the Only Achievement."

Certainly the characteristics disqualifying Anza from celebrity status are considerable. First of all, he was working for the wrong empire, the empire that worked its way northward instead of westward,

the empire whose descendants did not take part in the writing of the
Declaration of Independence in 1776 or in the writing of the United
States's history until quite recently. And then there is the problem of
Anza's timing. Leading an overland party to found San Francisco was
one thing; having the poor luck to do this in 1776 was another. When
it comes to paying attention to events that occurred away from the
Eastern seaboard in the 1770s and 1780s, most American historians
will claim that they have a prior engagement. The American Revolution holds onto the limelight. With the revolt of the British Atlantic
colonies in full swing during Anza's peak period of activity, it is very
hard for him to escape from the narrative framework, "Meanwhile,
as these consequential and world-changing events unfolded on the
East Coast, off in the middle of nowhere some other things of dramatically less importance were going on." On the days when the cir-
cus is in town, it is very hard for even very interesting performers in
another show to drum up an audience.

One factor may outweigh the others in reducing Anza's name
recognition value, and that factor we might call an excess of good
sense. Too much good sense can be a tremendous handicap when it
comes to achieving fame. Examples like John C. Fremont or George
Armstrong Custer persuade me of this point. For Fremont and Custer,
good sense was never in surplus. They specialized in pushing their luck
and in bragging—or, sometimes, having others brag for them—about
how well their gambles paid off. Anza played the game in another way
entirely, using careful preparations, discipline, and steadiness to reduce risk. In his expeditions, Fremont led small parties of men along
trails that others had pretty much explored and laid out. In taking
colonists to California, Anza led a big horseback party including children and women—and pregnant women, at that. Despite the considerable difference in the scale of the burden of leadership resting on
them, it was Fremont who huffed and puffed about what a courageous and daring enterprise he had embarked on, while Anza just did
the job.

Anza was certainly not shy about reporting his achievements to
Spanish officials, but the tone of his reports is entirely different from
the tone of Fremont's reports, with almost nothing to match Fremont's self-dramatization. While this is a difference in temperament,
it is also a difference in audience. Fremont had to court the American
public and Congress, while Anza had to solicit support and approval

and funding from a much more limited and clearly defined chain of officials and authorities. Can we generalize that those who are short on good sense have a proportionately greater ability to woo Congress? It is certainly verifiable that individuals playing to Congress and the American public often generate the kinds of documents that also play well to posterity and to historians. So poor Anza, he never got the chance to write a properly self-dramatizing report to the United States Congress.

If we were looking at this contrast between Anza and Fremont and trying to distill from it advice to ambitious young people, then one item of advice would have to be this: "Brag. Be the first to pat your own back. When it comes to making your reputation, actual achievement is only a small part of the package, while saying, 'Hey, look at me!' is a much bigger part."

At this moment, one hopes—probably safely—that young people are not attending to this line of thought. In this instance, watching TV or listening to rap music or renting videos might well pose less of a threat of corruption to their values than paying attention to the lessons of history. If young people pay attention to the lessons of history, as they seem to be presented by the comparison between the life strategies of Juan Bautista de Anza and John C. Fremont, then we are all at terrible risk. In my line of work, if students were to take the Fremont lesson seriously, they would take to handing in brief, perfunctory papers that barely met the requirements set out in the assignment, but attached to each of these minimal papers would be long, vivid, dramatic statements about how hard it was to write this paper, how much daring and courage had to be brought to bear on this assignment, how demanding and strenuous the journey to the library was.

If history really does offer lessons, is there any reason to think that those lessons would be worth learning? Is there any reason to think that learning the lessons of history would make us a better, more ethical, more-civilized people?

In "The Story of the Bad Little Boy," Mark Twain mocks the usual Sunday school books that tell about the doings of little boys who do bad things and get immediate and appropriate penalties for their misdeeds. Jim, Twain's bad little boy, does everything awful and escapes every penalty. "Once he climbed up in Farmer Acorn's apple trees to steal apples, and the limb didn't break, and he didn't fall and break his arm, and get torn by the farmer's great dog, and then languish on a sickbed for weeks, and repent and become good. Oh, no; he stole as many apples as he wanted and came down all right; and he was all ready for the dog, too, and knocked him endways with a brick when he came to tear him. It was very strange—nothing like it had ever happened in those mild little books with marbled backs. . . ." Jim's whole life worked out that way: "he grew up and married, and raised a large family, and brained them all with an ax one night, and got wealthy by all manner of cheating and rascality; and now he is the infernalest wickedest scoundrel in his native village, and he is universally respected, and belongs to the legislature."[1] History matches Twain's tales with plenty of stories of virtue punished and vice rewarded, with goodwill and hard work producing frustration and a sense of wasted effort.

Thus, the mystery and anomaly of the life of Juan Bautista de Anza: his is a story in which there is, more often than not, a match between will and outcome, between deciding to do something and getting it done. In truth, it is quietly hypnotizing to see somebody decide and act, promise and deliver, intend and achieve, in such a regular and reliable way.

Anza wanted to join the Spanish military and rise in the ranks, and he did. Anza wanted to show his courage and skill as a warrior against the Apache people, and he did. Anza wanted to find an overland trail from Sonora to Coastal California, and he did. Anza wanted to transport a party of colonists safely to settle in California, and he did. Anza wanted to play a key part in the organizing and uniting of the northern borderlands, and he did. Anza wanted to be an effective governor of New Mexico, and he was. Anza wanted to give the Comanches a clear, resistance-breaking military defeat, and he did. Anza wanted to end decades of destructive and draining warfare between the Spanish and the Comanches, as well as between the Utes and the Comanches, and he did. Anza wanted to reduce the distrust of the Comanches, a distrust triggered by Spanish cheating and corruption at trade fairs, and he did. Many, many times, when Anza willed himself to do something, he did it.[2]

No wonder a few of the men who outranked him in the imperial bureaucracy did everything they could to ruin him.

It gets even more striking when we look to see how a number of his achievements proved difficult, or even impossible, for his successors to maintain. The revolt of the Yumas in 1781 shut down Anza's overland route to California. The network of alliances and diplomacy that Anza knit together in New Mexico began to fray pretty soon after his departure, breaking down entirely by the time that revolution in the Spanish colonies drew attention—and money—away from the borderlands. It didn't take long at all for that familiar split between will and achievement to reassert itself after Anza's departure.

It is important, in order to get ourselves to the maximum state of recognition of Anza's distinctive story, to remember what a horrible job this office of colony governor was. As governor, you stood in the center, trying to find some harmony in the conflicting agendas of soldiers, settlers, missionaries, traders, and leaders and followers in various conquered and converted tribes, as well as leaders and followers in various unconquered and unconverted tribes. As governor, you were placed, as well, at the intersection where colonial ambition and colonial disappointment collided with each other, and the person who got the blame for that collision, more often than not, was the governor. Through all this, people placed thousands of miles from you—people sitting secure in offices in Mexico City or Spain—were setting your goals, writing your orders, and evaluating your performance.

Field work, or direct personal observation, of the dilemmas of colonial governors might seem hard to come by. And yet, nearly ten years ago, some adventurous students persuaded me to try a classroom exercise that deepened my understanding of the dilemmas of the governor, even as it deepened my own reluctance ever to try such a classroom experiment again. The students convinced me that we should devote one class period to playing a game they had created, called "The Conquest Game." To simplify a very complicated scenario, the desks in the middle of the room were North America, and they were quite fully occupied by native people. Starting from the four corners of the room were four empires, Spanish, French, English, and Russian. Each empire had a certain percentage of settlers, traders, soldiers, and missionaries, presided over by a governor. Each governor began the game with strict instructions from his empire, telling him to keep control of his colony.

The game began in quiet chaos, chaos that grew louder. Missionaries attempted to convert natives, and, often enough, to seize their desks in the process. Settlers took desks from natives, and then demanded that soldiers come protect the settlers and drive the natives from the area. Perhaps most memorably, the traders went to work;

since the students had persuaded me that alcohol was a trade good of unquestionable historic significance, the traders wielded the little bottles of liquor more often wielded by flight attendants. To my surprise and sorrow, despite this being a 10 A.M. class, natives, traders, and settlers, and, for all I know, missionaries, began testing the trade goods. The governors, meanwhile, still had their orders to keep the colony under control. They tried—they designed policies, they issued orders, they set out prohibitions—and none of their colonists paid an ounce of attention. Mercifully, this was only a fifty-minute class. The Conquest Game came to a much-valued halt. The legacy of conquest, this time, proved to be a room that we barely had time to clean up before the next, much more satisfactorily subdued and conquered class arrived, no doubt puzzled to find trash cans rich with the material culture of trade good containers. I had begun with a pretty good appreciation of the difficulty of a colonial governor's job, but the Conquest Game deepened my appreciation considerably. Anza, I can say with even greater certainty now, had a very tough job.

As remarkably as Anza rose to the challenges of that job, as persistently as he applied determination to challenges, it is still not clear to me that the historical lessons of his life are lessons that we would necessarily like to see widely adopted in our society. To show what I mean, let me call to your attention an example of the drawing of historical lessons, a quite extraordinary book, published in 1993, by Emmett C. Murphy with Michael Snell, called *The Genius of Sitting Bull: 13 Heroic Strategies for Today's Business Leader.* This book takes stories from Sitting Bull's life and draws from them applications for today's business world. Here are the basic terms of the analogy:

> The historic Battle of the Little Bighorn took place on June 25, 1876. It represented the most ignominious defeat ever suffered by American armed forces. Today, more than 100 years later, America's economic and social forces have come dangerously close to a similar humiliation.[3]

Does this make sense? If it was Sitting Bull who inflicted that ignominious defeat in 1876, then, by analogy, would not the application of Sitting Bull's strategies serve the goal of defeating the United States once again? This apparent contradiction does not trouble the authors, nor should it. It is a fundamental aspect of the romanticizing of Western history, that you simply dissolve context and encounter Sitting Bull, not as a person engaged in serious warfare against the United States but as an abstract, courageous, inspirational figure from the colorful Western past.

So Sitting Bull's life story teaches us various business lessons. First, lessons of preparation: create commitment, build trust, increase power, live the experience of your people, be a healer, and communicate on many levels. Take the fuller working out of that last item: "An extensive network of scouts and continuing intertribal contact give the Sioux minute-by-minute intelligence on Bluecoat activity." Here is the direct statement of the lessons (a passage which also offers the occasion to wonder why academics and not inspirational business writers carry so much of the blame for awful writing): "Multilevel communication comprises the first of two pivotal strategies that transform the potential energy assembled through the mobilization process into laserlike projections of force."[4] Next, there are the Sitting Bull lessons of implementation: think strategically; respect your competition; redefine the rules of battle, know the terrain; my favorite of them all, rightsize your forces; welcome crisis; and measure the results.

Even a brief glance at *The Genius of Sitting Bull* can make the academic historian giddy with possibilities unexplored, with options never imagined. Thus, I present *The Genius of Juan Bautista de Anza: 13 Heroic Strategies for Today's People of Ambition*. These heroic strategies, however, carry a kind of surgeon's general warning. Some of these lessons may be dangerous; some may be morally unhealthy; some may be strategies that deliver effectiveness at a cost we choose not to pay. Others, however, are so rosy and heartwarming that they are ready for adoption by service clubs. Remember, I am simply drawing the lessons, not advocating them.

ANZA LESSON 1

Keep your private life private. No one needs to know about your inner struggles to live with the loss of your father at an early age or about your relationships with your wife, who must have some pretty strong feelings about, for instance, your habits of travel. Biographers tell us that Anza's father was killed by Apaches in 1739, when Anza himself was four years old, and biographers tell us that Anza married a woman named Ana Maria Serrano. That's about all that biographers know of those matters. Of course, it is possible to take these thin and straitened facts and speculate about them. Anza believed that his principal Comanche enemy, Cuerno Verde, was driven by rage and resentment over the fact that the Spanish had killed his father. Anyone who wanted to could say that Anza's lifetime hostility to the Apaches, killers of his own father, must have given him a certain emotional kinship to Cuerno Verde, the man whose death he engineered. But Anza's historical lesson for us is this: people can and probably will speculate about your private and emotional life, but you are under no obligation to supply them with material for those speculations. Contemporary American leaders might profit by following Anza's example. Dare to be dull.

ANZA LESSON 2

If you are going to whine, do so in private and not for the public record. If you set out from Santa Fe in August, heading north, and the weather is unseasonable and you encounter cold and rain and even snow, you can note this in your report, but that is it.[5] If this weather makes you feel miserable, keep that to yourself. Maybe a refusal to whine will reduce the drama of your adventures and lessen their appeal to future filmmakers, but the dignity you preserve, by not complaining, will remain impressive for centuries afterward.

ANZA LESSON 3

Accept the fact that you have to work with people you have every good reason to dislike. On the trip, with the settlers to California, Anza had in his company one of the great pills of Western America, Padre Pedro Font. Padre Font was enormously gifted at complaining. When the settlers and soldiers celebrated the success of their journey, Padre Font condemned them for their inappropriate and far too secular festivity. Just reading Padre Font, more than two centuries later, can make you want to kill him. But there is the striking fact: on a long, draining journey, Anza did *not* kill Padre Font, or even show much irritation with him. Thus, with this historical lesson in mind, we are empowered to go to work on Monday, look around our workplace, turn our attention to the coworker who most directly seems to be channeling the spirit of Padre Font, and say to ourselves, "Well, I guess I can put up with him."

ANZA LESSON 4

Find a way to shift rapidly between independence and deference to authority, even when this means showing loyalty and submission to people you have never laid eyes on. Anza could take charge in the situations in which he was on his own, and yet he could also, in other situations, perform all the proper gestures of deference, submission, and subordination, as required by the Spanish hierarchy. This was, remember, a man whose family had lived for at least three generations in the northern borderlands. And yet Anza seemed perfectly comfortable, talking about the King and recognizing and invoking the King's authority, even though the distance from Spain to Sonora was beyond imagination. This fourth lesson, then, boils down to this: accept the fact that you are positioned toward the bottom of a hierarchy of authority, a hierarchy that will, nonetheless, from time to time, demand acts of great independence and self-reliance from you and sometimes punish you for your success on those occasions of independence.

ANZA LESSON 5

When you have a dedicated enemy higher up in the hierarchy, you are best advised to place your hopes on fate. In 1783, an unpleasant fellow named Felipe de Neve became the Commandante General of the Provincias Internas, or Anza's boss. Neve, as historian Elizabeth John put it, "launched a systematic campaign to oust Anza from the governorship of New Mexico and to wreck his career." Other members of the hierarchy tried to fight Neve, but Neve had the balance of power and influence. Where, then, was Anza's remedy? As Elizabeth John explains, "Luckily for Anza, Neve died in the summer of 1784" and was replaced by a man who supported and admired Anza and tried to undo the damage Neve had done to him.[6] As we saw before, finding lessons in history is very tricky and the results are not always particularly nice. But here is the lesson from the Anza-Neve conflict: If you have a boss who unreasonably stands in your way and works to undermine you, be patient. A fellow with a temperament like that has probably made a mess of his cardiovascular system, and relief may be on the way.

Anza Lesson 6

If you are persuaded that killing is necessary, then kill without regret. When, in 1779, Anza traveled into what is now the state of Colorado, his mission was to invade Comanche territory to strike a military blow that would demoralize the Comanches and eliminate Cuerno Verde, the chief who had led his people on many raids into Spanish territory and killed many Spaniards and Pueblo Indians. In the battle at Greenhorn Mountain, Anza and his men killed Cuerno Verde, as well as his eldest son, the heir to his command, his four leading captains, and his shaman, along with ten more warriors. *One* Spanish soldier was lightly wounded. While Anza is very appropriately known as a maker of peace, it is also true that he was an effective and spirited maker of war. Continuing in the vein of morally unsettling historical lessons, lesson 6 seems to be this: Don't kill people if you don't have to, but if you are convinced that you have to, then kill them wholeheartedly.

Anza Lesson 7

Believe that people can make an instant switch from the status of enemies to the status of allies. Believe, in other words, that bitter memories from the past do not need to set the tone for the present and the future. After the 1779 victory over Cuerno Verde, Anza shifted his attention to peacemaking with the Comanches. In 1786, he took part in the negotiation of the famous treaty establishing peace between the Spanish and the Comanches. When we remember how bitter relations had been between these two groups, when we think of all the raids, murders, and captivities, Anza's ability to believe that a peace treaty was possible appears astonishing. At one point in the treaty negotiations, a Comanche leader expressed the hope for the "entire and mutual forgetfulness of the aggravations and hostilities committed on the part of both [sides] and in the very long period of war."[7] Reading that hope with Iraq or Kosovo or Rwanda on the mind or, for that matter, reading it with a sense of the ethnic resentments that are ongoing in American life, one's inclination is to say, "Dream on." But Anza and a significant number of the Comanches believed that this "forgetfullness" was possible, and as a vindication of that belief, delegations of Comanches were soon traveling amicably among Spanish settlements, settlements that they had very recently been attacking and raiding.

Anza Lesson 8

If you can, get involved in appointing the other group's leader. Play as much of a role as you can selecting the counterpart with whom you will have to deal. Here is a very useful lesson, full of applications for current times. One of the elements of Anza's success in negotiating a peace and in maintaining a peace was the role he played in identifying, supporting, and validating the Comanche leader who would be most cooperative in dealings with the Spanish. Because of Ecueracapa's "talents, natural ascendancy, affection for our government and customs, docility, obedience, disinterestedness, and other estimable qualities," Anza explained to his superiors, he was "the most appropriate instrument that we could desire for the new arrangement of peace, not only to assure the continuance of peace, but also to subject the warlike Comanche nation to the dominion of the king."[8] So Anza encouraged the Comanches to take Ecueracapa as their principal leader, and he gave Ecueracapa everything he could in the way of prestige and rank. Thus, the lesson: it is a lot easier to negotiate productively with your enemies if you get to play a part in picking their leader.

Anza Lesson 9

Participate in rituals gladly and willingly. One of the ways in which Anza bucked up Ecueracapa's standing was to lend him Anza's own ceremonial cane, or staff, of office. On many other occasions, Anza comfortably and wholeheartedly took part in rituals and ceremonies, whether they were Spanish or Indian in design. When the peace treaty was finally arrived at, Anza gave Ecueracapa a banner and a sabre and stood by graciously while the Comanches engaged in their ritual of peace, digging a hole and then ceremoniously filling up the hole, thus burying the war. Perhaps most strikingly, Anza, like Bill Clinton (though this may be their only similarity), was a hugger. Anza embraced Ecueracapa; and on one remarkable occasion, in the midst of the peace negotiations, Anza hugged and was hugged by two hundred Comanche men, in succession. Think about this. It is fairly time-consuming to shake hands with 200 people, but think about *hugging* two hundred men, in a row, and men representing quite a different culture from your own.

Just as striking, when Anza presided over a peace agreement between the Comanches and the Utes, the two sets of leaders acknowledged and celebrated this agreement by exchanging their clothes.[9] There is a ritual worth contemplating: if the Democrats and Republicans had to begin each session of Congress by finding a counterpart and exchanging clothes, wouldn't that have a remarkable impact—albeit an impact that is hard to anticipate—on their conduct thereafter? Anza gives us a very clear lesson here: when offered the chance to back up your political acts with ritual and ceremony, take it.

Anza Lesson 10

In the same spirit as lesson 9, do not skimp on presents. In Anza's diplomacy, the use of gifts was very important. His superiors in the hierarchy usually recognized this and made appropriate allocations. Government spending, in this case, was clearly justified and necessary. The lesson here seems very clear, if also difficult to apply in our times: presents make peace possible.

Anza Lesson 11

Don't cheat at trade. Any short-term advantage you gain will be more than offset by long-term penalties. One of Anza's greatest contributions to the creation of peace between the Spanish and the Comanches came from his willingness to take seriously Comanche complaints about cheating at the trade fairs. Anza listened and, to the best of his ability, acted, trying to raise some prices for the Indians' benefit and trying to persuade the Spanish that the anger that they created by cheating put them at great risk. Indeed, Comanche contentment with the improvement in trading conditions was crucial to the maintenance of the peace. The lesson: Recognize that cheating in commerce works against the cheater's own self-interest.

ANZA LESSON 12

Here we return to lessons of a less-uplifting nature. If you make peace with one group, do so in order to make war more effectively against another group. The desire to create conditions under which the Spanish and the Comanche could combine in their fight against the Apache was fundamental to the motives driving Anza. Everyone involved understood this: the goal of a Comanche-Spanish peace was a more effective and devastating collaborative war against the Apache. Anza was ahead of many other Europeans and Euro-Americans in anticipating the problems that could result from alliances like this: "the governor presented printed cottons and a red badge for each [Comanche], to distinguish them in any affair, and avoid all error if they should become mixed in an affray with the enemies."[10] How or if lesson 12 can be transformed into a positive and uplifting instruction, a building block for a better tomorrow, is a puzzle I leave for others with greater ability to search out the best in human nature.

ANZA LESSON 13

Take advantage of situations where your side does not have the strength of numbers. Surely one of the great advantages that Anza had, in negotiating the Comanche peace, is that the Spanish empire was modest in its population growth. He could make a peace with the Comanches because there was little, virtually nothing, in the way of settler pressure to occupy Comanche lands. He could *not* make a peace with the Apaches, because Spanish settlers were scattered all over Apache territory. So, while many smug Anglos have observed that the Spanish empire was sadly handicapped by its shortage of a colonizing population, Anza's example reminds us that, for certain purposes, a shortage of a colonizing population is quite an advantage, permitting a flexibility and effectiveness in diplomacy that a booming settler population would destroy in an instant. On some occasions, sparse population is a wonderful state of affairs. In other words, there are other ways to measure the success of an empire, other ways besides the measures by which guppies and rabbits do so well.

According to the standard set by this last lesson, Anza did not fare so poorly over the passage of time. George Washington and Abraham Lincoln have Presidents' Day; millions may take holidays on Presidents' Day, but hardly any of them can now identify the exact date of Washington's or Lincoln's birth. It is even less likely that many in those millions can speak concretely, accurately, and with detail about the achievements of Washington and Lincoln. So here, if you make a determined escape from the tyranny of numbers, is the conclusion you reach: Anza Day in Poncha Springs, Colorado, does not have a lot of observers, but it has *quality* observers. Anza Day has participants who actually know a lot about the person whose memory they are ceremonially tending.[11] Shift from quantitative measures to qualitative measures, and Anza carries the day.

II-B

John Sutter:
Prototype for Failure

A few years ago, during a visit to Sacramento, my husband and I took a tour of Sutter's Fort. In one room of the fort, a staff person undertook to instruct us on the subject of John Sutter's personal life. "Sutter had a common-law Hawaiian wife," we were informed, "but he dropped her and brought his Swiss wife to California." Receiving this news, one woman in the group was moved to exclaim, "Men! They never change."

"Men! They never change"—that is one viable interpretation of the meaning of John Sutter for our times. Sutter is often referred to as the "Father of California." If Sutter did not, in literal fact, father California, that failure cannot be blamed on any lack of trying. With his Hawaiian mistress and his many encounters with Indian women and with Indian girls, Sutter did not spend his time cursing his luck for having been born too early for the sexual revolution of the 1960s. In these matters of personal behavior, behavior dampened but not ended by the later arrival of the wife he had abandoned in Switzerland in 1834, Sutter seems distinctly modern.

Over the last century and a half, Americans have used two extremely effective methods to dehumanize the people of the Western past. The more commonly recognized method is to make historical figures seem worse than they were—to cast Indians as brutal savages or Mexicans as cruel *bandidos* or white settlers as uniformly ruthless pillagers of people and places. But there is another, just as effective method that works by the opposite approach. You can dehumanize historical figures just as effectively if you portray them as better than they were. The noble pioneer, selfless servant in the cause of bringing civilization and advancing progress, endurer of hardship in the service of the common good—this is one of the best mechanisms available for taking an extremely interesting human being and making him into a one-dimensional bore.

That was the unhappy fate of John Sutter for decades. He was in life one of the more-interesting human beings on the planet, but he be-came in death a bore. Those who did Sutter this disservice did not, of course, intend to injure him. Moreover, it is important to note that he spent his last years acting as his own nineteenth-century image maker and spin doctor and thereby making his own contribution to this cu-rious campaign to paint a vivid life in dull colors. When the cam-paign succeeded, Sutter's rich and revealing story shrank to a thin, pious parable about a man who stood at the gate of Mexican Cali-fornia, who welcomed Anglo-Americans as they came over the Sier-ras, who sponsored the discovery of gold, and who thereby made California prosper while he watched his own empire disappear in a tidal wave of gold seekers.

Sutter failed, in other words, so that others might succeed.

When it comes to an interest in Western American history, I was a distinctly late bloomer. Born and raised in Banning, between River-side and Palm Springs, I was twenty-two years old and attending graduate school in Connecticut before Western history caught my at-tention. Speaking of the services of historical image makers and spin doctors, I would like to have had a more clear and purposeful per-sonal narrative to tell. I would like to be able to say that I became in-terested in Western American history in earliest childhood. But there are too many witnesses to the contrary. My parents and my big sisters can testify that I did not bounce from the car on family vacations, eager to steep myself in the ambience of Western historical sites. I suspect, though I cannot clearly remember, that we made a stop at Sutter's Fort, but I fear trustworthy memories would recall that I had to be pried from the car like a barnacle from a rock—a barnacle, in this case, protesting that she would really prefer to stay on the rock and read while the others saw the sites.

With this unfortunate personal history, I am in the market for someone to blame. I would like to hold someone responsible for the conviction that held me captive for my first twenty-two years, the conviction that Western history was a very dull business. Searching for a possible villain, the eye falls on Sutter. Not, of course, the real Sutter—the man who abandoned his family in Switzerland; who traveled to Missouri, Santa Fe, Fort Vancouver, Alaska, Hawaii, and California; who exploited Indians in a manner uncompromised by mercy; who womanized and drank and bragged and lied in the grandest manner; who outdid our own historical era's savings and loan managers in financial ineptness; and who lost his empire in a way that does indeed make him a prototype for failure. Like any other normal human being, I find that Sutter quite interesting.

I blame, instead, the fake Sutter, the dehumanized Sutter, the Sutter who had been washed, sanitized, bleached, shrunk to size, and thereby brought into compliance with the dullness standards of material suitable for schoolchildren, for tourists, and for residents of the city of Sacramento, where every imaginable hospital or health service seems to bear the patriarch's name, with "Sutter Psychiatric Services" having the most appealing historical resonance.

What happened to Sutter, of course, happened as well to Western American history: a story of great drama and complexity became a dull and pious parable of a continent mastered and progress advanced, where a few failed so that others might succeed. Reversing that process of infused dullness at first seems impossible; it is a little like restoring circulation to a mummy. But this is where historical figures like Sutter are extremely helpful. Keeping him on a pedestal requires a constant struggle against the facts of his life. To let him off that pedestal and to restore him to full humanity, one simply has to cease to fight the facts and, instead, let the facts speak freely.

Over the last century, the facts of Western history have had, and in some circles still have, a tough time of it. They barely start to speak for themselves when an anxious part of the audience immediately drowns them out with the cry, "How disillusioning! The facts will ruin our most treasured myths." But that is the happy part of life in the 1990s: it is increasingly clear, to the Western public as well as to

Western historians, that we are not fighting a pointless war between Western facts and Western myths. We are, instead, engaged in a campaign to allow Western facts to inspire Western stories that can guide instead of misguiding, stories that can lead instead of misleading.

Let us review the facts of failure in Sutter's case. The common version of his story had him thriving and prospering, presiding over an inland empire of wheat and cattle, when a flood of unprincipled Gold Rushers swept in and stripped him of his property and his power. Sutter's failure, in this model, came completely from the outside. A plague of locusts swept down on him; what was worse, he had been kind and hospitable to these locusts, welcoming Anglo-Americans throughout the 1840s. And then, in a mockery of gratitude, they stole his property and forced him over the edge of failure.

And now the facts.[1] Long before the Gold Rush could push him there, Sutter had taken up permanent residence on the edge of failure. In Switzerland, a family man with five children, he had reached a state of bankruptcy as a merchant. It only added a special note of poignancy to his troubles that his principal creditor appears to have been his unadmiring mother-in-law. He left Switzerland as a debtor, pursued by a warrant for his arrest. In America, he entered the Santa Fe trade and ended up on the losing side of that enterprise. Encouraging several Missouri acquaintances to invest in his venture, Sutter took a load of toys to New Mexico and learned that New Mexicans did not particularly care for toys, nor did his Missouri acquaintances care for any more investment advice.

Arriving in Mexican California in 1839 and securing the governor's encouragement in the planting of an interior colony, Sutter seemed to be off to a genuinely fresh start, with his debts and creditors left far behind. Then, in 1841, he made the curious move of buying Fort Ross on the Northern California coast from the Russians—buying, of course, only the buildings and livestock, because the Russians held no claim to the land. With this purchase, Sutter placed himself heavily in debt. Arrangements to pay off the debt in wheat, needed by the always hungry Russian Alaskan colony in Sitka, only added new occasions for anxiety, as the precarious fortunes of wheat farming left Sutter with disappointing crops in several key years.

The Russians were not the only ones to take over the role once occupied by Sutter's mother-in-law: creditor with good prospects of getting a series of empty promises, and poor prospects of getting any actual repayment. A number of California merchants and ranchers advanced Sutter various goods—livestock, food, tools—and got in return a series of letters explaining why he could not pay them back yet. In these letters, Sutter sometimes played the role of innocent victim; he was injured, he was maligned, by those who said he did not pay his debts. If there had been schools of business and management in the 1840s and if Sutter had been recruited as a professor, they would have made Sutter swear to keep his distance from the financial management courses, except on the one day a semester when he would be brought in as an example of how *not* to manage one's debts.

On the other side, Sutter's courses in labor management would have been sellouts. On this count, as Albert Hurtado has shown, Sutter was a clear success, recruiting, directing, coercing, and manipulating Indian labor.[2] Sutter knew how to get Indians to herd cattle, construct buildings, tan hides, and plant and harvest wheat. But in this area where he demonstrated unmistakable success, the floor has fallen out from under Sutter. This achievement, judged by another set of standards, appears as something of a moral failure. The business colleges of today, one has to hope, would be reluctant to use Sutter as a model of how to get the most out of a labor force.

And what about other spheres of achievement, say, the military? Sutter did succeed in the creation of an Indian militia, and, when he chose to support the cause of one California governing faction against another, Sutter had the occasion to lead his Indian troops, as well as Euro-American troops, in a campaign. But the campaign was almost immediately a mess: the governor whom Sutter chose to support was an uncertain and slow commander, Sutter wasn't much better, the non-Indian troops soon began to desert, and Sutter's military career came to a halt when he surrendered to and became briefly the prisoner of the enemy.

Elbowed aside by John C. Fremont during the Bear Flag Rebellion, Sutter could not be a principal player in the conquest of California. Nonetheless, when he sponsored, indirectly and unintentionally, the discovery of gold in 1848, he seemed to be placed by providence at the center of opportunity, with chances to get in on the ground floor of both mining and merchandising. But Sutter did not seize the opportunity in merchandising, and his ventures into the gold country proved aimless and unproductive. He did, however, make some brief financial progress by turning his financial affairs over to his newly arrived Swiss son, a procedure of questionable legality that nonetheless led to the payment of many of his debts, including his longstanding obligation to the Russians. But then relations with his son declined, and Sutter resumed control of his estate. Trusting the estate to the management of Peter Burnett led to a period when Sutter seemed to be gaining ground financially, but then Sutter removed Burnett as business agent. Submitting to the seductive proposals of speculators and schemers, Sutter, step by step, did himself in.

It did not help, of course, that the United States government confirmed only one of Sutter's two land grants. The New Helvetia grant stood, but his Sobrante Grant was disallowed. Since Sutter had already sold parts of that second grant, he had to make good on those purchases with land from the New Helvetia property, and this further reduced his holdings.

Were his successes, then, domestic and familial? Did the reunion with his wife and surviving children, who joined him at long last in California, permit Sutter at least a domestic variety of success? Abandoned in Switzerland for over fifteen years, his wife did not instantly forgive and forget. Bearing the burden of managing his father's estate, Sutter's eldest son broke mentally under the strain and finally moved to Mexico to escape the burdens of life with his father. Sutter's wife and daughter tried to contain his reckless hospitality, as well as his drinking, while Sutter's second son Emil seemed to have his heart set on being the maddest Sutter of all. When, in 1865, a disgruntled former employee set the Sutters' Hock Farm home on fire and the Sutters decided to move to Washington, D.C., they did not leave a site hallowed by happy family memories.

Why did they move to Washington? In 1865, John Sutter took up his new, and final, career as a lobbyist. Unlike lobbyists who push for wide causes and broad issues, Sutter had one interest to press on Congress: his own. From 1865 to 1880, virtually up to the moment of his death, Sutter pled his case with Congress: he had welcomed Americans to California; his help had, indeed, been crucial to the American takeover, and an ungrateful citizenry had taken his help and left him landless and powerless. A country that honored justice would surely compensate him for his losses.

After several years in Washington, Sutter and his wife moved to a small town in Pennsylvania, but he still traveled to Washington for each session of Congress. With years of practice, Sutter and his champions produced a set piece, a formula, a litany, almost a kind of scripture of Sutter's life. Over a century and a half, many other Westerners have approached life as if it were a great stage drama, in which they were assigned the part of the innocent victims. Miners who intruded into Indian territory and then felt beleaguered and harassed by Indians defending their turf, ambitious fortune hunters who let their own exaggerated hopes lead them into improvident investments and who then denounced the cruel fate that had robbed them of their money—there are hundreds of variations on these Western innocent victims, all of them chanting some variation on the theme, "I only tried to make the most of an opportunity, and now look how unjustly I've been treated."[3]

Sutter had them all beat. Sutter was simply the best at constructing a version of his misfortunes in which everything was *done to him,* a version in which he bore no responsibility—beyond the admirable weakness of trusting and helping people.

It is the final capstone on the theme of failure that even this masterpiece of self-packaging did not work. While he did, for a time, secure a pension of $250 a month from the California State Legislature, Sutter never succeeded in his campaign for congressional compensation. Just hours before he died in 1880, the most recent legislative session ended, and Sutter lost again.

It was this campaign for compensation, with the rhetorical demands it imposed, that drained the life out of Sutter's story. By the mid-1870s, Sutter and his friends had constructed a narrative which, if unsuccessful in moving Congress, was perfectly put together to bore Western schoolchildren for a hundred years to come.

To see what had become of Sutter, to see how a colorful character had become monochrome, we can look at the proceedings of the Associated Pioneers of the Territorial Days of California, a group organized in February 1875, in New York City. The first thing that strikes the reader, in looking at the records of their annual meetings, is that writing speeches to deliver to this crowd was a pretty easy business. Every year, it seems, their speakers and toast makers said what someone had said the year before. To write a toast or speech on the subject of John Sutter, you simply chose from a standard list of phrases and assembled them in the order you preferred.

These were the parts in the speech assembly kit from which the Associated Pioneers chose their words:[4]

> Great fame and services to California and to the Republic
> Good and noble old Pioneer
> pioneer and philanthropist
> mentor and protector of Indians
> hospitable welcome
> courtly gentleman and benefactor
> the benefits which he conferred upon California,
>   our country, and all mankind
> inestimable services for his fellow man
> the great Patriarch of our tribe
> the revered chieftain of our clan
> genial hospitality and unselfish generosity
> pure character and spotless integrity
> kindness and charity
> liberal and generous to a fault
> noble deeds and golden virtues
> honorable and unselfish devotion to humanity
> noblest of men
> noble Patriarch
> the beauty, purity, and bravery of his life
> the nobility of his nature
> The purity and nobleness of his character

The pattern of language and reference here is not a subtle one. When the publication of the Associated Pioneers records the fact, for instance, that "Jos. S. Spinney, Esq. . . . delivered a fervid and beautiful tribute to [Sutter,] the great and good Pioneer, but there is no record of the same, and [it] cannot, after this lapse of time, be reproduced,"[5] one does not feel an overpowering sense of loss. Unless there was more to Jos. S. Spinney, Esq., than we presently realize, it is a pretty sure thing that the words "noble" and "patriarch" figured prominently in Spinney's "fervid and beautiful tribute."

Sutter himself attended some of these meetings. It strikes me as something of a wonder that, in the midst of all these tributes to his integrity, Christian charity, and, of all things, purity, he did not finally exclaim: "This is all extremely kind, but I think you've got the wrong

fellow." But we are, with these tributes, clearly in the presence of ritual belief, belief that Sutter had evidently come to share himself. In
this formulaic story, every other element of Sutter's history disappeared, and only two facts remained: he had welcomed and aided arriving emigrants, and he had sponsored an undertaking, the
construction of a mill, which surprised everyone by turning up gold.
Those two facts gave him indisputable standing as a great agent of the
Manifest Destiny of the United States and thereby made all other facts
dismissible.

Following his death, the San Jose newspaper the *Pioneer* derived
from those two facts a wonderfully improbable summation of Sutter's
career and character: "Truly he was in all respects a Christian, and his
every act through life was that of true Christianity. . . ."[6]

This business of Western mythmaking is indeed a wonderful thing.
Religion, Christian or any other, does not seem to have figured much
in Sutter's life in California, but so what? A man almost constitutionally unable to keep his obligations and pay his debts, a man whose
use and abuse of women remains unsettling and disheartening, such
a man nonetheless can be spruced up and launched on the road to
sainthood, sent out to personify nobility, integrity, purity, and, of all
things, Christianity. Perhaps the height of improbability comes with
the comparison of Sutter to Jesus Christ. Speaking to the Associated
Pioneers in New York, Sutter's friend General H. G. Gibson drew a
remarkable picture of Sutter facing death "with no bitterness or anger
in his heart, only a sorrowful reproach in the spirit of the prayer of the
Divine Master: 'Father! forgive them for they know not what they
do.' "[7] Sutter on his deathbed, Christ on his cross—and yet, by some
miracle, General Gibson finished his speech and was not struck down
by lightning in midsentence.

In a book that is as fascinating as it is maddening, *The Fatal Environment: The Myth of the Frontier in the Age of Industrialization*,
the literary scholar Richard Slotkin applies similar thinking to the
death of George Armstrong Custer. Custer's death, Slotkin argues, fits
the fundamental patterns of Christian thought. Custer's death was, to
white Americans in the 1870s, a sacrifice that redeemed and revitalized his nation; Custer's death thus mirrored Christ's.[8] When I first
read Slotkin's book, I found this analogy unpersuasive. But now,
after a tour of duty with the Associated Pioneers of California, listening to them celebrate Sutter's virtues and lament his many in-

juries, Slotkin's analysis is harder to deny. If nostalgic Americans could cast Sutter as a trusting lamb sacrificed so that others might prosper, then it would be no particular struggle to provide the same intellectual service to Custer, a man who was surely Sutter's equal in saintliness.

"Father! forgive them for they know not what they do" was not a sentiment Sutter expressed in real life. On the contrary, in Sutter's long campaign in Washington, D.C., years in which he became one of the most familiar characters around the Capitol, forgiveness did not figure in what he asked of Congress. Keeping the memory of his injuries alive was his principal cause. This was a man who had learned to treasure his wounds, virtually to savor the contrast between what he was in the past and what he had been reduced to in the present. It is, indeed, important to note that others have been considerably more reduced. As Richard Dillon wrote of Sutter's last years, his "circumstances were comfortable, although he had to pose as a destitute petitioner in his memorials to Congress." He and his wife built a "fine brick home" in Pennsylvania.[9] But fine brick home or not, the contrast between what he had had in the 1840s (or what he would have had in the 1840s if he had ever gotten his empire clear of debts) and his reduced state in the 1870s was so galling that he could not adopt the Christ-like resignation that his eulogist later attributed to him.

Much more effective in capturing his feelings was the statement he made to the historian H. H. Bancroft, a ringing summation of the innocent victim's view of the world:

> I have been robbed and ruined by lawyers and politicians. My men were crushed by the iron heel of civilization; my cattle were driven off by hungry gold-seekers; my fort and mills were deserted and left to decay; my lands were squatted on by overland immigrants; and, finally, I was cheated out of all my property. All Sacramento was once mine. . . .[10]

You will notice here that wonder of human expression, the passive voice verb—by which everything *was done* to Sutter, and Sutter did *nothing* to himself. His failure came upon him like a blow from the sky; his own failures in financial management were gone, erased, stricken from the record by the wretched behavior of the Gold Rushers.

There is nothing particularly surprising in Sutter's choice of historical explanations. One could logically ask Congress for compensation if one's misfortunes stemmed from the cruel and ungrateful acts of others. It would be a lot tougher to ask for compensation on the basis of injury done to oneself *by* oneself, by one's own acts of improvident and misguided management.

No wonder Sutter adopted an innocent victim's formulation of his own history. What might seem considerably more surprising is that his society confirmed and supported him in that creative and selective reading of his experience. But this is only briefly surprising: Sutter's story fit smoothly inside that great, vanity-satisfying myth of American destiny. By pioneering settlement in the California interior, welcoming and aiding American arrivals, he had been on the side of the angels, or, at the least, of the Anglos. He could, therefore, be indulged and supported in his assertion that he was the victim of outsiders, when he should have been the beneficiary of their gratitude.

When I published *The Legacy of Conquest,* I myself committed at least one terrible act of ingratitude. I made absolutely no mention—in text, footnotes, or bibliography—of the name Josiah Royce. Born during the Gold Rush, Josiah Royce grew up in California and went on to become a philosopher at Harvard. At his request, his mother, Sarah Royce, wrote down her memories of the overland trail and of Gold Rush California, and this text reveals her to have been an uncompromisingly moral person. Sarah Royce, a woman who lived every day of her life with religious thoughts in her mind, would have been nonplussed by the notion of John Sutter as an exemplary Christian.

Very much his mother's child, Josiah Royce in 1886 published a study of his home state's history, *California: From the Conquest in 1846 to the Second Vigilance Committee in San Francisco: A Study of American Character.*[11] Note the timing: 1886, seven years before Frederick Jackson Turner would draw on his memories of childhood in Wisconsin to offer his version of Western, or more accurately Midwestern, history, "The Significance of the Frontier in American History." Josiah Royce put forward his model of Western expansion seven years before Turner did. And yet, for reasons that stem mostly from national pride, Turner caught on and became the father of Western history, and Royce, though renowned as a philosopher, held no standing in Western history.[12]

Royce always used the word "conquest" freely and honestly; while something short of a model in his awareness of Indian history, he was fully aware that Hispanic people were established in the Far West long before Anglos arrived. Royce's facing up to the fact of conquest very much influenced me in my younger days; by my older days, I had pushed that influence to the edge of awareness, and I completely failed to include an acknowledgment of my debt to him in *Legacy*. You only hurt the ones you love, I suppose; in any case, I take this opportunity to make up for that sin of omission in *Legacy*.

Josiah Royce is exhibit number 1 in this proposition that what we now call the New Western History has its own distinguished history.[13] Look through Royce's California book, and it is clear that a critical appraisal of Western expansion did not begin in the 1960s.

When Royce wrote his California book, the cult of Sutter was fully developed. If he had wanted to, Royce could have joined the chorus of celebration, acclaiming Sutter as the vital instrument in the civilizing of California. Instead, and very characteristically for Royce, he thought hard about Sutter and then wrote a few brief, but essential sentences:

> In character Sutter was an affable and hospitable visionary, of hazy ideas, with a great liking for popularity, and with a mania for undertaking too much. A heroic figure he was not, although his romantic position as pioneer in the great valley made him seem so to many travelers and historians. When the gold-seekers later came, the ambitious Sutter utterly lost his head and threw away all his truly wonderful opportunities. He, however, also suffered many things from the injustice of the newcomers. He died a few years since in poverty, complaining bitterly of American ingratitude. He should undoubtedly have been better treated by most of our countrymen, but if he was often wronged, he was also often in the wrong, and his fate was the ordinary one of the persistent and unteachable dreamer. He remained to the end a figure more picturesque than manly in our California life.[14]

"A mania for undertaking too much," "utterly lost his head and threw away all his truly wonderful opportunities," "a heroic figure he was not, although his romantic position . . . made him appear so," "if he was often wronged, he was also often in the wrong"—these are all phrases or sentences I would happily have written myself, if Josiah Royce, that annoying and inspirational New Western Historian, born in 1855, had not written them first.

We did not have to wait for Josiah Royce to come along to find nineteenth-century observers who saw the weaknesses in Sutter's claims on paradise. In 1846, the Swiss immigrant Heinrich Lienhard traveled overland to California. Like many other overland travelers, Lienhard saw his arrival at Sutter's Fort as a landmark in his life. But the passage in which he described his arrival is a disturbing one:

> It was one of the happiest moments of my life, as I stood there and gazed at my actual, my final destination. After passing several more adobe corrals, [we] reached the main gate of the fort. There a gruesome sight met my eyes: the long, black hair and skull of an Indian dangling from one of the gateposts.[15]

This display of a defeated enemy was a long-running tradition in the battles that punctuated the invasion and conquest of North America. In this case, the sight echoed an even more long-running tradition in the thought and literature of European civilization—the death's head in the garden, included in many of the classic paintings of Western civilization. *"Et in arcadia ego"* is the announcement Death makes in this tradition; "I, too, am in paradise."

Signing up to work for Sutter, Heinrich Lienhard cultivated a garden. In 1848, when James Marshall had made his gold discovery, Lienhard felt pulled to the mines. But he had devoted himself to his garden, and "finally I abandoned the idea of going to the mines; I did not believe I could be happy away from my plants."[16] So Lienhard stayed and worked in his garden, a type of labor that gave him great pleasure. But then came a return of the *"Et in arcadia ego"* theme, Death's reliable announcement, "I, too, am in paradise." Lienhard wrote,

> By May twentieth, my potatoes were in bloom, and my grain was three or four feet high. That morning when I woke up the air seemed unusually chilly. When I got out of bed to my surprise I found the grass covered with frost. My hopes vanished into thin air. . . .
>
> After the sun was up, I inspected my plants and found that every melon, tomato, bean, and cucumber I had set was dead and black. Potatoes that were in full bloom yesterday were now frozen to within six inches of the ground; tall green grain that was about to ripen had turned into a few shriveled ends. . . . My vines, that had been thick with grapes the size of small bullets, were dropping.[17]

Not a man of excessive sanguinity on any occasion, Lienhard was one of many nineteenth-century Westerners who did not deny the facts of failure. He would not fudge his description of the risk of frost in the theoretically Arcadian environment of California; he would not puff himself up for a windy proclamation announcing that this year's melons, potatoes, and grapes had frozen so that next year's crops might prosper. In the same spirit, Lienhard would not join in the canonization of Sutter. When he first met Sutter, Lienhard was enchanted: "as I listened to his pithy conversation, to his tales so highly colored with romance and adventure, I was spell bound." Sutter was, Lienhard wrote, "an incredibly entertaining talker, and for the time being at least, I believed it all, in spite of myself." Over time, Lienhard learned that a number of Sutter's tales—stories, for instance, of his service in the Swiss-French army—were colorful fibs. Sutter's drinking problems, Sutter's callous treatment of Indians, Sutter's use of Indian women and girls, Sutter's unpaid debts, Sutter's susceptibility to flatterers and swindlers, Sutter's conflicts with his family—Lienhard's portrait included all the details that grounded Sutter as a three-dimensional human being, not an ethereal and dull pioneer saint.[18]

Summing up the pious and sanitized version of Sutter's character, his friend Colonel I. S. Tichenor said this: "it may truly be said: 'A more noble man never lived.'" Lienhard's down-to-earth stories convey an immeasurably greater vitality and interest. Consider the human reality in this encounter with Sutter's vanity: "I owned a pair of black trousers [Sutter] wanted to buy," Lienhard reported, "and I knew I would not have any peace until I complied with his request." Lienhard finally set a high price, and to his surprise, Sutter paid it. "But his hips were larger than mine, and the first day he wore the trousers they split when he sat down and leaned over suddenly."[19]

In his old age, Sutter had erased these embarrassments and failures from his record, and perhaps from his memory. He constructed, instead, a simplified and sanctified version of his character. He created a story of his past in which he was riding on a one-way, nonstop, direct trajectory to success until the Gold Rush threw him off track. "When I settled first in the Sacramento Valley," he wrote in 1879 to a supporter, "then I thought to make me a home for life, and I would have become one of the wealthiest Citizens on the Pacific, but the discovery of the gold, has destroyed all my enterprises and plans and bad designing men, swindlers and thieves, and even the courts treated me very badly & unjust."[20]

If it had not been for the Gold Rush, Sutter said several times, he would have been the richest man in California. Nostalgic imagining aside, before gold ever appeared in the mill traces, Sutter had encountered frustration, disappointment, and failure. He had a world of evidence to tell him that the pursuit of fortune in newly conquered areas is a very uncertain matter, that short-term successes, in these circumstances, have a way of evolving into long-term failures. The conquest of natives and nature was, and is, a risk-filled and precarious operation. Trying to ride westward expansion, Sutter's experience showed, was often enough the prelude to getting bucked by westward expansion. Serving as the host for American colonization, Sutter evidently thought he had this force under control. Later, lost in the contemplation of his own injuries, Sutter could not take the story of his failure, with all its historical lessons, seriously. At long last, thanks to the changing currents of Western American life, we are ready to learn the lessons that Sutter chose to forget. Said so memorably at Sutter's Fort a year or two ago, the proposition "Men! They never change" is now open for rethinking.

II-C

Turnerians All:
The Dream of a Helpful History
in an Intelligible World

> I prefer to believe that man is greater than the dangers
> that menace him; that education and science are power-
> ful forces to change these tendencies and to produce a ra-
> tional solution of the problems of life on a shrinking
> planet.[1]
>
> FREDERICK JACKSON TURNER, 1924

When you enter an essay by Frederick Jackson Turner, you enter an enchanted world. In this world, abstractions are tangible and virtually animate, right on the verge of speaking for themselves. Conditions, forces, ideals, institutions, traits, types, elements, and processes inhabit the Turnerian world like the weightiest and most settled of citizens. If you bump into a social force or a pioneer ideal, it will be you who gets the bruise. You can, of course, try to refuse the impact. "Neither a 'social force' nor a 'pioneer ideal,'" you can declare, with accuracy on your side, "is a real thing. Both are intellectual constructions. Neither should have the power to bruise."

As they have for nearly a century, Turner's conditions, forces, ideals, institutions, traits, types, elements, and processes remain undissolved by such a challenge. You are free to show, at length and in detail, that these concepts exist without the support of much evidence. You will still have to walk around them. After a century of holding their ground, they are not going to disappear in response to the latest frail protest against their power.

Most enduring of all his hardy mental constructions, Frederick

Jackson Turner's Frontier Thesis entered its second century in remarkably good shape. First presented in 1893 as "The Significance of
the Frontier in American History," the thesis has become a historic
relic itself, an important and instructive artifact of the American past.
When John Mack Faragher referred to Turner's 1893 essay as "the
classic expression of the 'frontier thesis,' " his phrasing called to mind
the special provisions many states offer to owners of old cars.[2] At a
certain vintage, aged automobiles receive the title of "classic" and
gain an exemption from emissions tests. In a very similar manner, the
Frontier Thesis has become a classic, exempted from the usual tests of
verification, evidence, and accuracy. While other historical models
are stopped and inspected at every checkpoint and at many sites in between, the Frontier Thesis operates with a different license entirely.

If one doubts the staying power of this historic model, one has
only to remember that it did not lose momentum despite a devastating set of critiques in the 1930s and 1940s.[3] Perhaps most remarkably,
the Frontier Thesis kept running even when it collided with the full
force of Richard Hofstader's critical intelligence, in his book *The Progressive Historians,* in 1968. When Hofstader was through with it, if
the outcome had been governed by the usual set of historiographic
rules, the thesis would have been finished. Consider just a few items
from Hofstader's catalogue of the significant elements of westward expansion that received little or none of Turner's attention in the thesis:

> . . . the careless, wasteful, and exploitative methods of American
> agriculture; . . . the general waste of resources and the desecration of
> natural beauty; the failure of the free lands to produce a society free
> of landless laborers and tenants . . . ; the rapacity and meanness so
> often to be found in the petty capitalism of the new towns; . . . the
> crudeness and disorder, the readiness to commit and willingness to
> tolerate violence; the frequent ruthlessness of the frontier mind, to
> which Indians, Spaniards, and Mexicans could testify and which had
> its repeated reverberations in national policies; the arrogant, flimsy,
> and self-righteous justifications of Manifest Destiny engendered by
> American expansionism. . . .[4]

A model so riddled with holes could explain only a fraction of the
frontier story, and Hofstader did not hold back in sketching the scale
of these omissions. Characteristic of his bluntness and refusal to pull
punches was his appraisal of Turner's casting of Thomas Jefferson as

a typical, democratic product of the frontier. "[A]lmost everything Turner says about Jefferson," Hofstader said, " . . . is either badly nuanced, a misleading half truth, or flatly wrong."[5] After 1968 and the publication of Hofstader's *The Progressive Historians,* there was every reason to recognize that Turner's Frontier Thesis existed in its own bewitched historiographical space, a zone in which critiques and contradictory evidence instantly lost power and force. Fighting the thesis was like fighting the Pillsbury Dough Boy; it bent momentarily to absorb challenges and then instantly resumed its previous shape.

A greater awareness of my predecessors' experience with this less-than-satisfying combat could have saved me considerable time and trouble. I was, at one time, convinced that the revitalization of Western American history began with the recognition that the Frontier Thesis had become entirely irrelevant to the history of the Trans-Mississippi West.[6] But this campaign to reenergize Western history turned out to yield a wonderfully ironic side effect. The New Western History's campaign to declare Turner irrelevant revitalized Turner's reputation. It got the name Frederick Jackson Turner featured in stories in the *Washington Post,* the *New York Times, U. S. News and World Report,* the *New Republic,* and many other newspapers and magazines. It restored his celebrity. It allowed his followers and supporters to say that his argument in "The Significance of the Frontier" must be very worthwhile and important if it was still worth attacking a century later. The more forcefully one said that Turner was wrong, the more one provided in the way of well-publicized opportunities for his admirers to praise him.

In the cause of appraising rather than praising Turner, recent squabbles over Western American historiography become blessedly insignificant. The issue becomes, instead, the much more consequential one of Frederick Jackson Turner's demonstration of the perils and privileges of being an historian. Central to that demonstration is this mystifying fact: in a century of challenges to the 1893 thesis, no historian put forth a more telling challenge than did Frederick Jackson Turner himself.

The author of the Frontier Thesis, in other words, was also the author of the Frontier Antithesis. The two bodies of ideas came with a considerable difference in form of presentation: the thesis appeared in one, dedicated essay, while the antithesis appeared in scattered sentences and paragraphs in essays written and published before and after 1893. It is a telling fact that Turner never brought the antithesis together into one essay. In truth, he never remarked on how thoroughly his own reflections elsewhere had eaten the ground out from under his thesis of 1893. And yet, if one brings together these dispersed remarks, the results reveal the clear outline of a forceful Frontier Antithesis.

An appreciation of the Frontier Antithesis requires a brief review of the characteristics of the thesis itself. In casting the frontier as the most important factor forming American character and democracy, the 1893 essay paid little attention to Indians. It stressed the individualism and self-reliance of the pioneer and had correspondingly little to say about federal aid to expansion. It concentrated on the history of the humid Middle West to the neglect of the arid West beyond the hundredth meridian. Perhaps most consequentially, it provided support for models of American exceptionalism by emphasizing the uniqueness of the American frontier experience. The following paragraphs, a composite of direct quotations with a few interludes of paraphrasing, present Turner's challenges to his own claims from 1893.

THE FRONTIER ANTITHESIS

by
FREDERICK JACKSON TURNER
with the assistance of PATRICIA NELSON LIMERICK

In the history of Indians lies fresh and important territory for exploration. Scholars are now uncovering "evidences of the rise and fall of Indian cultures, the migrations . . . , hinted at in legends and languages, dimly told in the records of mounds and artifacts, but waiting still for complete interpretation." As one indication of the natives' importance, in various areas of North America, "the Indians had burned over large tracts," creating a new landscape before European arrival. The patterns of trade between and among Indians shaped the fur trade between whites and Indians. "It was on the foundation, therefore, of an extensive intertribal trade that the white man built up the forest commerce." "Another set of problems which need study is to be found in the effect of the Indian on our political institutions." "There is needed a study of our relations to the American Indian" because this topic "is an exceedingly important one in the history of American development, and one from which rich results may be expected." "The native populations have . . . been determining factors in our development."[7]

In the Trans-Mississippi West, "the systematic slaughter of millions of buffalo . . . destroyed the economic foundation of the Indians. Henceforth they were dependent on the whites for their food supply." The Far West offered compelling evidence that the pioneers, like the Indians, found themselves in a state of dependence. When "the arid lands and the mineral resources of the Far West were reached, no conquest was possible by the old individual pioneer methods. Here expensive irrigation works must be constructed, cooperative activity was demanded in utilization of the water supply, capital beyond the reach of the small farmer was required." Individual effort and enterprise were no longer sufficient; thus, "the West has been built up with borrowed capital." "Railroads, fostered by government loans and land grants, opened the way for settlement . . . ; [t]he army of the United States pushed back the Indian, rectangular Territories were carved into checkerboard States." States like these did not arise from the usual evolutionary processes of frontier democracy; they were, instead, sudden "creations of the federal government." In many ways, "the later frontiersman leaned on the strong arm of national power." Most recently, "the government has taken to itself great areas of arid land for reclamation by costly irrigation projects. . . . The government supplies the capital for huge irrigation dams and reservoirs and builds them itself." "By the conditions on which [the federal government] disposes of the land and water privileges, it preserves a parental control over the social and economic conditions of the section." In these circumstances, "the pioneer of the arid regions must be both a capitalist and the protege of the government," "adjust[ing] his life to the modern forces of capital and to complex productive processes."[8]

In the Trans-Mississippi West and elsewhere, international forces were clearly at work in the frontier process. American history was shaped by "world-wide forces of reorganization incident to the age of steam production and large-scale industry." In this case and many others, "ideas, commodities even, refuse the bounds of a nation. All are inextricably connected, so that each is needed to explain the others." Despite the claims of antiquarians, "local history can only be understood in the light of the history of the world." The historian is thus obliged to push his inquiries beyond national boundaries. "If, with our own methods of the occupation of the frontier, we should compare those of other countries which have dealt with similar problems—such as Russia, Germany, and the English colonies in Canada, Australia, and Africa—we should undoubtedly find most fruitful results."[9]

In comparison with the assertive style of the 1893 frontier essay, a number of these remarks may sound tentative—less assertions than calls for new studies and new approaches, really more an *invitation* to an antithesis than a presentation of the antithesis itself. And yet each proposition shines a bright light on a central weakness in the 1893 thesis. In the attention to Indians, to federal involvement in Western expansion, to the factor of aridity, and to the desirability of a comparative history that avoided the trap of national exceptionalism, the Turnerian antithesis anticipated many of the major objections to the 1893 thesis.

Thus, the mystery: if Turner had, on his own, identified many of the principal flaws in his earlier position, why did he not say so directly? It would have been a simple matter, and to many an impressive and graceful gesture, for him to have written a later statement like this: "In 1893, nine years before the passage of the Newlands Reclamation Act, I simply did not foresee the expansion of federally subsidized, irrigated agriculture. This, along with my preoccupation with the well-watered Middle West and my personal enthusiasm for the character traits of the frontiersman, led me to underestimate the role of the federal government in Western development, and to underestimate, as well, the differences between the frontier process as it worked in the Mississippi Valley and as it worked in the Far West."

The reflective essay was Turner's favorite genre, and retrospect and reappraisal have always been very compatible with that literary form. Turner had, moreover, laid the groundwork for this kind of reconsideration. "Generalizations . . . upon the West as a whole," Turner once wrote in a statement that seemed to leave wide maneuvering room for hindsight, "are apt to be misleading."[10] In a habit still very much in evidence among present-day practitioners of his profession, Turner built into many of his articles a number of declarations of modesty, tentativeness, and incompleteness:

> Within the limits of this article, treatment of so vast a region, however, can at best afford no more than an outline sketch. . . .[11]

> I have not the temerity to attempt a history of the [Ohio] Valley in the brief compass of this address. Nor am I confident of my ability even to pick out the more important features of its history in our common national life.[12]

And, from the 1893 frontier essay, a firm declaration of its own limits:

> This paper will make no attempt to treat the subject exhaustively; its aim is simply to call attention to the frontier as a fertile field for investigation and to suggest some of the problems which arise in connection with it.[13]

In theory, these statements left their author a free man, free to reconsider and even free to confess error and second thoughts. Since he had never claimed to have figured everything out, Turner was fully licensed to rethink, reappraise, reconsider, and revise his earlier assertions.

In an essay on "The Old West," Turner made the most handsome and quotable of his humble disclaimers: "The present paper," he said, "is rather a reconnaissance than a conquest of the field."[14] The conqueror has to hold his ground and cannot retreat; the man conducting a reconnaissance can always go back, gain new information, and add to or modify the impressions recorded in his initial report. The passage of time offered this particular historical explorer many chances to rethink his earlier impressions. There were opportunities beyond counting for the older Turner to engage in an instructive dialogue with the younger Turner. And yet, except in the brief and indirect suggestions of the Frontier Antithesis, Turner consistently refused those opportunities.

Why? Here we return to Turner's standing as the representative historian, a central player in the routinizing and professionalizing of the academic historian's activities. Turner's life, Richard White has reminded us, is remarkable for the very elements that make it now seem commonplace. In a time in which professional roles were becoming defined and institutionalized, "Turner was an academic historian of middle-class origins and progressive sympathies whose professional career centered on university teaching." White's characterization underplays the degree to which Turner felt himself obligated to speak to public audiences; by Turner's definition of the role, neither the historian nor his ideas were to be locked up within the university. And yet, with a broadened definition of the historian's role, White is right in observing that Turner "never seemed to have aspired to be anything more than a professional historian and a university professor."[15]

Reading this passage evokes an unexpected chord of solidarity. Who, one surprises oneself by thinking, would aspire to more? The ambition to be a professional historian and a university professor seems, to a surprising number of people in the 1990s, still to be an appealing and compelling goal. A walk through the mass interviewing area at the American Historical Association meetings will certainly verify how commonplace Turner's once novel ambitions have become.

Since Turner was, genuinely, a founding father of the profession, the patterns of his life, the working of his mind, and, especially, the pressures and mandates of his ambition carry lessons far beyond the individual. As a young man, Turner wanted to make an impact. His biographers, both Ray Allen Billington and Allan Bogue, make it clear that Turner, as a young man, actively solicited and pursued opportunity and recognition. As John Mack Faragher notes, when the frontier paper appeared in print in 1894, Turner "purchased hundreds of offprints and distributed them widely, not only to colleagues and associates but also to prominent members of the national intellectual elite—a practice he followed with all his publications."[16]

When all those offprints paid off and the Frontier Thesis finally became a pillar—some would say *the* pillar—of American history, Turner was triumphant. But he was also trapped: trapped, in part, by a host of impossible book-writing obligations brought to him by the success of the frontier essay and trapped by the fact that his career and status now rested on his identification with the 1893 thesis. In a letter in 1919, he referred to the relief he felt on learning that another historian (who happened to be Woodrow Wilson) made no claims to the origins of the Frontier Thesis. It would have been "unpleasant," Turner said, "to contend for the parentage of my intellectual firstborn, dear as it is to me, and much as it means for my reputation."[17]

The phrase "much as it means for my reputation" captures the problem. Turner had wanted very much to succeed, and the favorable reception of the Frontier Thesis was a key part of that strategy for success. Its good standing brought many benefits—the presidency of the American Historical Association, a position at Harvard, many followers and devotees, and a happy package of status, prestige, visibility, and name recognition. But the price of success, it turned out, was a significant one: a surrender of the spirit of open-ended inquiry and forceful assertion that had clearly provided Turner with great satisfaction and pleasure as a young man.

The Originator of the Frontier Thesis had evolved into the Defender of the Frontier Thesis, and defending would offer very little of the fun and adventure that came with originating.[18] One of the pleasures now off-limits to Turner was that of pointing out the shortsightedness and mistaken preoccupations of established authority in American history. When one *was* the established authority in one's field, the pleasures of rebellion were considerably diminished. Turner could not frankly discuss the flaws of the 1893 essay because it formed the foundation of his career, his prestige, and his sense of personal achievement.

This set a precedent from which the profession has never fully broken free. Turner was a historian of great influence, and a graceful and dignified reappraisal of his earlier claims would have set a precedent of great value. At a time when the conventions, requirements, rituals, and traditions of being a historian were still fluid and up for definition, his decision to withhold public reconsideration was a consequential choice.

Given Turner's repeated declarations that our understanding of the past must adapt to changes in the present, it was also a deeply ironic choice. In 1891, Turner had published an essay called "The Significance of History," a forceful and earnest declaration of the unbreakable tie between past and present. In a sentence he himself italicized, Turner declared his faith in presentism: *"Each age writes the history of the past anew with reference to the conditions uppermost in its own time."*

> The aim of history, then, is to know the elements of the present by understanding what came into the present from the past. For the present is simply the developing past, the past the undeveloped present. . . . The antiquarian strives to bring back the past for the sake of the past; the historian strives to show the present to itself by revealing its origins from the past. The goal of the antiquarian is the dead past; the goal of the historian is the living present.[19]

The true Turnerians, one could conclude from this memorable passage, were the historians who paid attention to, and put into practice, Turner's 1891 declaration of the need for writers of history to rethink and revise. The Turnerians who stayed loyal, instead, to the 1893 Frontier Thesis observed the letter and defied the spirit of Turnerian history. But there was the puzzle again: by this categorization, Turner was both true Turnerian and so-called Turnerian, at once a person paying attention to his times and insisting that historical models must be constantly remodeled in response to changing conditions, and a person repeating old formulas that could no longer fit those changing times.

"What endures" in Turner's legacy, John Mack Faragher has said, "is Turner's commitment to contemporary knowledge, his understanding that debates about the past are always simultaneously debates about the present. It marks him as America's first truly modern historian."[20] It marks him, in addition, as an innocent. Orienting a historical inquiry in terms of the present, Turner assumed in 1891, added clarity to one's understanding. One could, the theory went, get a grasp on the fundamental patterns of one's own times. Figuring out the present was an undertaking very much like reading the last pages of a novel; one checked to see how the plot one had been following in the earlier pages finally turned out. In examining events in one's time, one applied the same kind of pattern finding to the present that one applied to the past; and when one had identified the outcome, or the past's product, one was in a much-improved position to trace and understand the whole story, primarily because one could now identify the path of significant change, distinguishing the consequential events from the inconsequential. It was as clear and linear a matter as if the movement from the past to the present were a railroad track. Once one had identified and inspected the point of arrival, it was an easy matter to follow the track back to its origin.

But what if this destination proved difficult to identify? What if the present proved unintelligible, turning out to be even more confusing than the past? Here is where Turner's experience becomes most instructive for his successors in this profession. For reasons that every historian can empathize with, Turner betrayed the doctrine of presentism, and, in turn, the doctrine of presentism betrayed him.

How did he betray it? Like all beliefs, presentism confronts its believers with an irritating challenge: once one has declared one's faith, one is supposed to practice it. That seems easy enough, until the passage of time complicates matters. In 1891, at age thirty-one, Turner recorded his faith in presentism. In 1910, at age fifty, in his presidential address to the American Historical Association, he reconfirmed his 1891 declaration, but he referred now to "the familiar doctrine that each age studies its history anew and with interests determined by the spirit of the time."[21] The very phrase "familiar doctrine" should have been its own warning; "familiar doctrine" was, by definition, unlikely to represent a full reckoning with the cutting edge of the present.

In 1891, Turner had been a young Turk, full of vigor, ready to challenge the powers that be. In 1910, he was president of the American Historical Association, fighting off the challenges of the next cycle's crop of young Turks, themselves now ready to challenge the powers of which Turner had become one. *"Each age writes the history of the past anew with reference to conditions uppermost in its own time,"* and 1910 clearly offered a different set of conditions from 1893. It was time for a vigorous reappraisal of the 1893 Frontier Thesis, or so one might have thought if one were not oneself the author of that much-admired and frequently cited "familiar doctrine."

Like many rebels done in by the success of their rebellion, the middle-aged Turner reneged on the proclamations of freshness and innovation he had made as a young man. But this was a two-way betrayal: if Turner had betrayed his declaration of faith in presentism, presentism had also betrayed him. The present, remember, was supposed to illuminate the past, not befog it; the present was supposed to help the historian's undertaking, not frustrate and obstruct it.

The present, however, broke its half of the agreement by proving to be of no help at all in understanding the past. In the first decades of the twentieth century, the present was turning out to be *more* confusing than the past. If one could not figure out the present and if one's project of explaining the past required one to identify the outcome that the past would then explain, then one had landed, definitively, in a muddle.

Turner knew a lot about the present; he had fulfilled his half of the bargain by keeping up with current events. In the pieces and parts of his Frontier Antithesis, Turner referred to post-1890 booms in petroleum, coal, copper, and irrigation, to the concentration of capital, and to capital's struggles with labor in the early-twentieth-century West.

A presentation in 1924 gave an impressive demonstration of his success in keeping up. Speaking at Clark University, Turner gave an overview of the thirty-five years since Clark's founding. "Few epochs in history," he said, "have included such startling changes within a single generation as that between the [1880s] and the present." He called attention to the impact of the movies and radio, of the automobile and the airplane. He remarked on the change in women's work roles produced by the introduction of the typewriter to offices. He mentioned with concern the American distribution of wealth: two percent of the population owning three-fifths of the property, a fact which was "food for reflection on the outcome of the pioneer democracy that sought equality as well as opportunity in the American wilderness." Turner referred to revolutions in scientific understanding, mentioning the Einsteinian revolution of relativity and the exploration of the atom. He noted the shift of American action and attention to the Pacific basin. When he spoke of the problem of the planet's growing human population, he sounded as if he were writing an early draft for a late-twentieth-century Earth Day rally: "Truly a shrinking earth! An earth compelled by irresistible forces to exercise restraint, to associate, agree, and adjust, or to commit suicide."[22]

"Already," Turner wrote in 1925, responding to the most recent statistical information, "the urban population exceeds the rural population of the United States." Fundamentally, Turner knew that the present of the early twentieth century meant urbanization, industrialization, and the consolidation of capital. "The world," Turner said, "has never before seen such huge fortunes exercising complete control over the economic life of a people. . . . " In his favorite region, the Middle West, this transformation was unmistakable: "The world has never seen such a consolidation of capital and so complete a systematization of economic processes."[23]

But how on earth was one to connect decentralized, rural frontier origins to centralized, industrial outcomes? The easiest option, though it removed most of the punch from the narrative, was to assert, and reassert, and assert once again that it was the disappearance of those rural frontier conditions that generated the centralized, industrial outcomes. While this strategy carried some logic, it had the disadvantage of a fractured narrative. The first half of the story was the direct opposite of the second half of the story; the past was the frontier and the present was the factory, and the appearance of the factory coincided with the disappearance of the frontier; Part two followed on part one by canceling Part one out. And yet the Turnerian theory of presentism would have required a narrative that told the origins of the factory, tracking the foreshadowings of the consolidation of capital, noticing the hints and clues of the shift from the agrarian and rural to the industrial and urban. Instead, loyalty to the 1893 thesis bound Turner to a narrative in which the frontier kept its position at center stage, and the factory thus emerged suddenly, unexplained, from the wings.

Another option was simply to assert that these two phases were connected and, somehow or other, mutually illuminating. "Seen from the vantage-ground of present developments," Turner declared with exuberance, "what new light falls upon past events!" "When we recall the titanic industrial power that has centered at Pittsburgh," Turner offered as his illustration, "Braddock's advance to the forks of the Ohio takes on new meaning." Written more logically, the sentence might read, "When we recall the huge industrial power that has centered at Pittsburgh, Braddock's advance to the forks of the Ohio seems oddly irrelevant, strangely unrelated to the manufacturing of steel that has transformed Pittsburgh in our time." But Turner's faith in the connection between past and present required Braddock to have not a new irrelevance but a new meaning. Namely, "[e]ven in defeat, he opened a road to what is now the centre of the world's industrial energy."[24] Braddock, it is clear at this point, had not entirely benefited from the gospel of presentism; he did considerably better for himself when his wilderness battles represented an important prelude to the American Revolution than when he came to serve as the not-very-convincing advance scout for the steel industry.

The problem came to center on one of Turner's most-valued terms, "ideals." The frontier had produced pioneer ideals, and pioneer ideals were the key to American character and democracy. Thus, the often-noted anxiety lodged at the center of the Frontier Thesis: if the frontier had ended, as Turner said it had, then what force could keep those crucially American pioneer ideals alive and vital? "Long after the frontier period of a particular region of the United States has passed away," Turner tried to convince himself, "the conception of society, the ideals and aspirations which it produced, persist in the minds of the people." The conditions, Turner realized, had changed dramatically: "The solitary backwoodsman wielding his ax at the edge of a measureless forest is replaced by companies capitalized at millions, operating railroads, sawmills, and all the enginery of modern machinery." Somehow, the pioneer ideals of the "solitary backwoodsman" were to continue to govern the operations of heavily capitalized factories, providing continuity between two disconnected phases of history.[25]

If the persistence of these ideals, long past the disappearance of the conditions that had produced them, was the good news, the bad news was that these familiar old ideals could work in support of strange new forces. The "masters of industry and capital," Turner said, "came from" frontier society "and still profess its principles." Connecting the frontier past to the industrial present were these improbable latter-day pioneer idealists: John D. Rockefeller, Marcus Hanna, Claus Spreckles, Marshall Field, Andrew Carnegie, and E. H. Harriman. The frontier, Turner had said in 1893, remakes the colonist. "It takes him from the railroad car and puts him in the birch canoe. It strips off the garments of civilization and arrays him in the hunting shirt and the moccasin." "Before long," the transformed pioneer "shouts the war cry and takes the scalp in orthodox Indian fashion." In asserting a continuity of ideals and character between frontier conditions and industrial conditions, Turner was putting Rockefeller, Hanna, Spreckles, Field, Carnegie, and Harriman through a similar process of transformation. The historian had now supplanted the frontier as the force recostuming these pioneers in hunting shirt and moccasin; it was the historian's voice that told his audience to see these magnates of power as fundamentally still shouting "the war cry" and taking "the scalp in orthodox Indian fashion."[26] While the analogy might have made some sense to those who had been run over by Rockefeller and Hanna in their drives to power, both the war cry and scalping technique had changed character considerably as they evolved into the practices of modern industry.

The mandate of presentism was, meanwhile, standing by, ready to release Turner from these interpretative contortions and stretches. "When we look at these matters in the light provided by present conditions, the frontier proved to be less the main trunk line of history, and more a side path through the forest," Turner could, logically, have admitted if he had chosen to follow the precepts he set forth in 1891. "Industry and urbanization are now clearly revealed as the outcome we are obligated to explain. Now we must re-examine the past to find the origins of these crucial forces of our present. *Each age writes the history of the past anew with reference to the conditions uppermost in its own time.* The Frontier Thesis was fine for its time, but now the times demand the Urban/Industrial Thesis. Antiquarians can try to figure out what became of those pioneer ideals, but historians have more urgent obligations." The opportunity to practice as well as preach the gospel of presentism was an open and obvious one, but it was an opportunity with little appeal to Turner.

I write here with absolutely nothing in the way of smug, placid, distanced judgment of Frederick Jackson Turner. On the contrary, it would have to be said that, in matters of presentism, I have come to share Turner's pain. For years, I applauded and quoted with enthusiasm every declaration Turner ever made on behalf of letting our knowledge of the present and our knowledge of the past illuminate each other. In what many have characterized as my rebellion against Turner, the first words that appeared in *The Legacy of Conquest* were the words I have quoted here from "The Significance of History."[27] But, like Turner, I, too, found out that presentism was a faith with an unbreakable and unappealing habit of turning on its believers.

It was not that I wanted my own Frontier Antithesis, *The Legacy of Conquest,* to stand for the ages. The deference shown to Turner by many Western historians had given me an instructive demonstration of the perils of life in a field where one dominant set of ideas overstayed its period of usefulness. I wanted Western American history to have many historians offering, as Turner had, forceful statements and interpretations. If we were lucky, these historians would show a little more flexibility'would show a little more willingness to declare their independence of the matriarchs and patriarchs of the field. Under those terms, the best I could hope for my own model of the West was to see it become a stimulant, a provocation, the equivalent to the side of a swimming pool from which future inquiries could push off to gain momentum.

Swerving around the dilemma of wanting my work to stand for the ages, I was able to bring all the more momentum to my head-on crash with presentism's much more serious dilemma. As Turner knew and as I now know (and it seems to have caught us both equally by surprise), the present turns out to be even more complicated, more muddled, and more maddening than the past. A historian who goes around declaring that an understanding of the present will deepen our understanding of the past is a historian who will eventually have to eat crow.

The 1990s have served me a generous helping of this unattractive substance, a meal which honesty requires me to consume in public. In the mid-1980s, I was quite sure I had figured out the Western American present and equally sure that I knew how to apply that understanding to history. Recent events and trends, I thought, spoke very clearly: the collapse of the most recent boom in oil and coal; the campaign to cut the federal budget and to reduce the subsidies that had supported much of the Western economy; an economic downturn in the classic rural enterprises of farming, ranching, mining, and timber; the inescapable dilemma posed by the accumulation of nuclear contamination at Western weapons production plants; the visibility of a number of politicians willing to talk about the inability of Western resources to support an endlessly expanding population; the reassertion of Indian rights to land, water, religious freedom, and sovereignty; and the upsurge in immigration originating in Latin America and Asia.

With all these changes under way, the pattern of the Western present and future would simply have to be one of intelligent reckoning and reorientation. Great human diversity was an inarguable quality of the Western past and present; white Westerners would now have to face up to this central quality of their region. The limits of resources and the instability of traditional Western rural economies were now crystal clear; Westerners would have to revise their most basic strategies of water use and land use. While Turner had told us that the frontier ended in 1890, nineteenth-century attitudes toward nature and toward people of color had lasted all too vigorously into the twentieth century. But now, one hundred years after that ostensible end of the frontier, the shift was actually happening—away from short-term extraction toward long-term and permanent residence and inhabitation, away from hostile dismissals of minorities toward a recognition that we would all have to live together.

Readers are entitled to think that my effort to write a happy ending to Western history makes Turner's efforts to find pioneer ideals at work in monopolistic industrialists look hardheaded and realistic. Certainly clues began to appear immediately, indicating that presentism was not going to be any kinder to me than it had been to Turner. Of all those clues, the 1994 elections provided the body blow. The hearty vote in favor of California's Proposition 187, denying services and benefits to illegal aliens and their children, suggested that the West was not embarked on a new path of tolerance and amicable coexistence.

Western voters, moreover, seemed to be saying a vigorous *no* to the public lands reforms undertaken by President William Clinton's Secretary of the Interior Bruce Babbitt. Babbitt earnestly pitched into the effort to reduce the powers of the "lords of yesterday," the legal scholar Charles Wilkinson's fine phrase for the federal resource policies created in the late nineteenth century and still governing the West today.[28] Babbitt's efforts provided the best evidence I had for my theory of an approaching big change in the terms of Western life. But voters in the congressional elections of 1994 seemed to take it as a personal mission to expose my failures in prophecy. As the new Congress took office and the reenergized Republicans undertook to reinstall the lords of yesterday as the lords of today and tomorrow, I found my affection for Turner's 1891 essay, "The Significance of History," diminishing daily.

Along with disappointment, however, came relief, and a kind of relief that Turner may not have permitted himself to feel. When I contemplated my failure to figure out the present, I began to wonder how I had ever fallen into the belief that such an achievement was within my reach, or within my job description. And, happily, as disorientation with the present increased, enthusiasm for studying the past grew proportionately. Compared to the inscrutable present, the past was an open book.

Disillusionment with presentism had the happy side effect of restoring a recognition of contingency and improbability to my understanding of history. When I thought I was tracing a direct, clear line between past and present, an unhealthy fatalism crept into my thinking. Event followed event with all the drama, surprise, and spontaneity of the prearranged program of the Rose Parade. Losing control of the pattern of present events thus offered its own form of liberation; it was as if the floats of that regimented parade suddenly started taking inexplicable right, left, and U-turns, as if the General Electric float suddenly slammed into the California Fruit Growers' entry, filling the air with a rainbow of chrysanthemums and marigolds and giving the poor commentators something, at long last, to comment on. History became correspondingly more interesting as it became more chaotic.

Here, too, Turner's struggles proved to be emblematic and precedent setting. Turner, like many of his fellow participants in the founding of his profession, wanted to establish some control over the past. He wanted to persuade the disorderly events and people of history to submit to some kind of order. The agents and devices he used to produce that order were those reified and nearly animate concepts he stayed loyal to all his life: the conditions, forces, ideals, institutions, traits, types, elements, and processes that could translate the chaos of history into patterns of clarity and manageability.

As with Turner's presentism, a familiar form of historian's hopefulness was at work here. With its powers of analysis, Turner thought, the mind could diagram the working parts of human history and then show how the parts fit together. Turner's hunger for the ideas that would hold a fragmented world together was palpable and urgent. Despite his ritual declarations of tentativeness and modesty in his essays, his heart clearly melted when in the company of a rhetorically convincing generalization, in which abstractions and evidence marched together in a pleasant and ordered parade toward the present.

Success in this venture, though, carried a great price: the more effectively Turner identified and arranged the determinants of history, the more he sacrificed drama, as well as realism. The complexity of historical evidence was silenced and squeezed in order to fit into the tight categories Turner built for it. "Each type of industry," Turner had said in one of his best-known passages of fatalistic thinking, "was on the march toward the West, impelled by an irresistible attraction."

> Each passed in successive waves across the continent. Stand at Cumberland Gap and watch the procession of civilization, marching single file—the buffalo following the trail to the salt springs, the Indian, the fur-trader and hunter, the cattle-raiser, the pioneer farmer—and the frontier has passed by.[29]

A historical procession led by a large herbivore in search of salt was unlikely to provide the material for a celebration of the human will and the power of individual choice. And when this parade, in the next sentence, picked itself up and reappeared to march, in identical order, through South Pass in Wyoming, a large share of the contingency, improbability, and interest of historical change seemed to have been surrendered.

Identifying types, forces, and conditions, Turner could write with a tone of certainty that bordered on the theological. In his historical writings, Turner virtually never referred to God. Even his discussion of religion as a factor in history never got beyond the perfunctory. And yet, in his declarations on the patterns of history, Turner nonetheless wrote in a tone of certainty that conveyed a secularized faith in destiny. A controlling and predestining God might not be visible in the picture, but forces, ideals, institutions, traits, types, elements, and processes were ably filling in for Him.

Without an explicitly religious framework of thought, Turner offered a vision of history which nonetheless seemed destined and predetermined. His unrelenting enthusiasm for hydraulic metaphors gave clear and consistent evidence of his susceptibility to deterministic thinking. Telling the story of westward expansion, one of the most dynamic and complicated stories in history, a story much twisted and inflected by variations in individual and group will, Turner habitually used metaphors that eliminated choice and decision from the picture.

People moved in streams, tides, flows, currents, torrents, floods, and inundations. A Southern "stream" from Virginia "flowed into Ohio," while "the main current that sought Indiana came from North Carolina"; "By 1830 the Southern inundation ebbed and a different tide flowed in from the northeast"; "The homestead law increased the tide of settlers."[30] Here, in these hydraulic metaphors, Turnerian determinism was at its clearest. Whatever individual participants in these movements might have thought they were doing, the historian had, with hindsight, detected and labeled the great sweeps and trends that both caused and explained these individual decisions.

And yet, just as Turner himself challenged his Frontier Thesis with a scattered antithesis, here, too, in the matter of determinism, Turner vigorously and persuasively contradicted himself. One particular topic brought out in him a different spirit from the one he showed when tracing the workings of destiny in westward expansion. When he wrote about the contest of empires for the interior of North America, a very different and much more persuasive historian seemed to have taken control of his pen.

In two articles in particular, "The Origin of Genet's Projected Attack on Louisiana and Florida" and "The Policy of France toward the Mississippi Valley in the Period of Washington and Adams," contingency came back to overpower determinism. In truth, without an admission of contingency, without a recognition that events of the past did not proceed on a fated march toward the present, the story of the schemes and plans of various empires to gain control of the interior would have been killingly dull and pointless. Describing the visions of persuasion and territorial acquisition that Edmund-Charles-Edward Genet took with him to North America in 1792, Turner deliberately broke free from determinism:

> A vast and startling project indeed! sweeping into a single system the campaigns of France in Europe, the discontented frontiersmen of the Mississippi Valley, and the revolutionary unrest that was before long to give independence to Spanish America. The historical possibilities of this great design are overwhelming.[31]

With this remark—indeed, simply with the direct and uncharacteristic use of the word "possibilities"—Turner gave Genet's story a license for vitality. He removed, at least for the moment, everyone's hindsight knowledge that the frontiersmen would remain loyal to the new American nation and that Genet's mission would fail. In the same spirit, his article on "The Policy of France toward the Mississippi Valley" restored possibility as well as complexity to the struggles for empire in the American interior. One learns from the record of French maneuverings, Turner noted, "how wide-spread were the forces of intrigue for the Mississippi valley." It was not his intention, in this article, to say that a clear American destiny would render these "forces of intrigue" inconsequential. On the contrary, his last sentence in the article deliberately asserted contingency:

> No one who has studied the evidence of long-continued menace to the connection of the west with the rest of the United States . . . can doubt that the danger was a real one, and that a European power might have arisen along the Mississippi valley and the Gulf of Mexico, dominating the interior by its naval force, and checking, if not preventing, the destiny of the United States as the arbiter of North America and the protector of an American system for the New World.[32]

With the word "destiny" at the end of this passage, Turner returned to the familiar world of a secularized, nationalistic determinism. But for a surprisingly lengthy interlude in his studies of imperial policy, Turner surrendered his usually firm explanatory structure of forces and conditions and contemplated, instead, the muddled, complex, and open-ended possibilities of the past.

Ten years ago, I felt sure that Turner's weaknesses were the weaknesses of the Frontier Thesis. Both his failure to convey the contingency of history, as well as his failure to comprehend his own times and to align his historical narrative with the outcome facing him in those times, I thought, had their sources in the errors and omissions of his Frontier Thesis. Now his failure seems much less distinctive and peculiar to him and much more an early example of the proposition that the present has a way of turning out to be even more bewildering than the past.

Surely the best demonstration of this proposition has appeared in our own times with the dissolution of the Soviet Union and the end of the Cold War. For diplomatic historians and historians of the Soviet Union, the outcome of this plot had been *very* clear: the rise of Marxism, the face-off between communism and capitalism, the struggles of the superpowers. While they might disagree in their interpretations of the historical process that brought us to the present, until 1989 the outcome which historians sought to explain was not in dispute. But with the collapse of Soviet control over Eastern Europe and then with the end of Russian communism itself, the narrative of history took a wild and unexpected turn. Surely the past was still connected to the present, but the connections followed paths that were unexplored and unfamiliar, paths that would lead historians through terrain they had barely noticed in their previous efforts to explain a different, much more intelligible present.

With his faith in his conditions, forces, ideals, institutions, traits, types, elements, and processes, his objective terms of analysis, Frederick Jackson Turner believed in an intelligible world. "[A] generation that does not attempt to consider its recent past," Turner wrote, "is like the merchant who ignores his ledger, the mariner who takes no observations."[33] His assumption, of course, was that the merchant who consulted his ledger and the mariner who took observations would be a merchant and a mariner who would be equipped to decipher their positions in life and who, understanding their recent past, could then make better and more effective plans for their future. Turner believed, as well, in progress, even though the increasingly urban and industrial character of the United States put that belief to a trying test.

By the time I entered graduate school in 1972, the historian's right to a faith in progress was greatly and appropriately constricted. To note just one factor, the wars of the twentieth century had knocked the pins out from under the idea of a world in which people, as time passed, learned the lessons of history and behaved with increasing wisdom and benevolence. In the graduate schools of the late twentieth century, the phrase "Whiggish history" was in common usage, deployed to indicate that the speaker or writer was too well trained to believe in the old fantasy of progress, too sophisticated to believe in a world in which the transition from past to present was a transition of improvement.

Just beneath the surface of those declarations of cynicism (and in some ways, protected and insulated by the official code of cynicism) was a faith that matched that of Frederick Jackson Turner. By this faith, historians could be *useful,* and useful in a way that might actually help to produce progress. "A just public opinion and a statesmanlike treatment of present problems," Turner wrote in 1910, "demand that [those problems] be seen in their historical relations in order that history may hold the lamp for conservative reform."[34] I myself, along with many of my contemporaries, would have preferred to "hold the lamp" for somewhat less cautious reform, but we certainly had no objection to lamp holding per se, no objection to the notion that historical understanding might lead to wiser and more benevolent action in our own time. An effort to mock the hope that Turner invested in this proposition runs, almost immediately, into the uncomfortable recognition that many historians who are now in their forties and fifties have matched Turner in hopefulness.

On some issues, most particularly on issues of race, Turner's ideas were light years away from current thought in American historical circles. Turner was a white American historian who never questioned (indeed, never noticed) the role that his own racial and ethnic identity played in shaping his point of view, and the result was a general flatness of curiosity when it came to the histories of nonwhites. Turner declared in 1904 that "a study of the negro is needed," but he himself made no move in the direction of that study. In fact, the cause of advancing the significance of the frontier seemed to require, in Turner's judgment, the reducing of the significance of slavery. "[W]hen American history comes to be rightly viewed," he said in the 1893 frontier essay, "it will be seen that the slavery question is an incident," and barely even that. His references to slavery were always brief and almost entirely focused on slavery as a factor in American politics, as a source of tension between white Americans. The lived experience of being a slave barely registered in Turner's otherwise omnivorous historical curiosity.[35]

On an issue like race, then, the use of the phrase "Turnerians All" to describe the common and persistent condition of historians would be absurd. Turner had, for instance, a well-established habit of referring to various ethnic and national "stocks": "By [Indian] intermarriages with the French traders the purity of the stock was destroyed and a mixed race produced"; in considering general literacy on the frontier, it was "at its worst where the Mexican stock abounded"; late-nineteenth-century immigration represented "the peaceful conquest of the old stock by an international army of workers."[36] In his use of the word "stock," Turner appears as a relic of a distant era of both history and historiography, relying on a term and a pattern of thought that have little kinship with the views held by most historians writing and teaching today.

And yet, in other matters, especially in definitions of the historian's professional role and in the benefits to society of vigorous historical inquiry, "Turnerians All" is an appropriate form of professional self-description. "The story of the peopling of America has not yet been written," Turner said in one of his most quotable declarations. "We do not understand ourselves."[37] Turner's words carry undiminished, if also differently inflected, force today. Which "selves," after all, were "we" to understand? Turner's "we" in this passage was the "we" of the American people and not the "we" of the historical profession. And yet the self-understanding of historians is an indispensable part of the project of understanding the history of the region, the nation, and the planet. Turner's unwillingness to scrutinize himself and to put his own earlier, career-establishing ideas through a process of critical examination has become a luxury we can no longer afford. Even if it strikes some traditional historians as oddly and unprofessionally self-indulgent, the project of "understanding ourselves" must include historians' self-understanding and self-disclosure.

In a widespread misreading of changes in the field of Western American history, various critics have noted that Turner, as *New York Times* writer Richard Bernstein put it, "has been scrapped," dumped from the historical canon because he was "Eurocentric, making the whites the only genuine historical protagonists."[38] By this misinterpretation, then, the New Western History has eliminated Turner because he seems to be racist in the terms of the late twentieth century. The point here is, actually, quite different. Turner's own race or, more accurately, his society's construction of the value and meaning of his whiteness did shape and direct his historical attention. Being white set stern limits on his empathy and understanding. While he was an impassioned advocate of paying attention to the history of people who were not members of elites, his attention rarely strayed from the social history of white people.

Although there was nothing to stop Turner from reading, for example, W. E. B. DuBois and getting a headstart in these matters, the notion of examining the impact and consequences of his own racial identity was a completely foreign concept to him. Under these circumstances, the point cannot be to chide him for a failure of self-consciousness. The point is to learn from his example and to use it as an occasion to ask ourselves, "What are *our* blind spots? What are the elements of our social identity that limit our vision as sternly as racial assumptions limited Turner's vision?" However we answer these questions, historians of the late twentieth century have not reached a plateau of comfortable self-understanding from which we can look down smugly on Turner's struggles. In truth, a confession of solidarity—"Turnerians All"—is the place where this exploration begins and ends.

Squabbles over the validity of the Frontier Thesis have distracted us from the much more compelling issue raised by Turner's example. Frederick Jackson Turner embodied the idea of historians as public servants, as scholars whose inquiries into the past could contribute directly and concretely to human well-being in the present. The familiar dispute—Was Turner right about the frontier?—has become trivial and arcane. The much less familiar question—Was Turner right about the present-day value of historical understanding?—remains the question of consequence. In the everyday life of the academic historian, that question has been pushed to the edge of our attention by the constant round of activities of the profession, activities rendered normal by the careers of Turner and his contemporaries: class preparing, lecture giving, discussion leading, paper grading, student advising, archive exploring, note taking, book reviewing, manuscript evaluating, article and book writing, job search conducting, convention attending, paper presenting, critic answering, professional association office holding, and turf defending. In the midst of the business and busyness of professional historians, the question of the purpose and goal of these activities—a question from which Turner did not try to hide—awaits our answer.

PART III

—◆—

ENVIRONMENTAL

IMPACTS

The hottest issue in the American West today is land use. Can historical reflection help the partisans in environmental controversies to understand themselves, each other, and their differences of opinion and behavior? Can perspective drawn from the longer haul of time lower the heat on current conflicts?

Perhaps the answer is yes, but waiting for certainty, before trying to be helpful, may well mean waiting too long. In 1996, the Greater Yellowstone Coalition, a hardy and hearty group of environmentalists, invited me to give one of the opening addresses at their annual conference. Personally, I support many environmental causes, but I also wince over some elements of environmentalist practice, perhaps especially the quite remarkable achievement in self-esteem that allows a person to claim to speak for the planet. I was and am grateful for the willingness of the Greater Yellowstone Coalition members to let me speak to them with an honest, critical edge. "Mission to the Environmentalists" is a revised version of that presentation.

The racial exclusiveness of much of the environmental movement is a disturbing feature of its early history. Despite the goodwill of many of its current leaders, the movement's most visible participants are almost entirely white. As a speaker at many events involving issues of environment and natural resources, I have been troubled by the paucity of people of color as speakers or as members of the audience. The pervasiveness of this problem came home to me when I was asked to write an essay on the "discovery of the landscape" as part of the *Journal of American History*'s observation of the quincentennary of Columbus's arrival. When I started in to work on this article, I was alarmed to "discover" that my own knowledge of attitudes toward nature was restricted to the impressions recorded by white Americans. Instead of following the east-to-west movement of familiar figures like Meriwether Lewis, William Clark, and John C. Fremont, I reversed direction and tracked the encounter of Asians and Asian Americans with the landscape of Western America. Of all the essays presented here, researching and writing "Disorientation and Reorientation" taught me the most.

The sesquicentennial of the discovery of gold in California provided a productive opportunity to explore the operations of that archetypal extractive industry, mining. Opening an exhibit on the Gold Rush, the Oakland Museum of California held a symposium on January 24, 1998, the exact anniversary of the discovery. In the 1990s, the American West has been in the midst of a gold boom comparable in scale to the production of California in the 1840s. And yet the current gold rush has a remarkably low profile. Thus, "The Gold Rush and the Shaping of the American West" explores the impact of the discovery in California over space and through time and puzzles over the near invisibility of the contemporary burst of activity in mining.

III-A

Mission to
the Environmentalists

In Western American history, the word "mission" exceeds the weight limit for cultural baggage. In their relationships with Indian people, missionaries were often imperious and interfering, scornful of tribal customs and certain of the superiority of Euro-American ways. And yet, in a few notable cases, missionaries were also useful allies and advocates of native people, standing up for their interests against the pressure of soldiers and settlers and helping to refine and aim their strategies of resistance.

In spite of its historical burdens, the word "mission" comes to mind when I am in the company of environmental activists. Finding myself in uncomfortable kinship with Father Junipero Serra and Narcissa Whitman, I feel irrepressible urges to offer help and redemption. The historical heritage of latter-day nature lovers is so complicated and so well supplied with traps and hazards that the effort to keep silent tests one's patience. Tangled up with contemporary environmental politics, history demands the attention of activists, even though some of its lessons may not strike them as palatable.

What, then, is the big picture of American attitudes about and behavior toward nature in the past? Can historical understanding offer environmentalists practical lessons? When I started graduate school in 1972, the story of American attitudes toward the physical environment was a much easier one to tell than it is today. The story may have lacked something in complexity and intellectual challenge, but it compensated for those weaknesses with the virtues of clarity, directness, and brevity. Here is the three-part story we told in those ancient days, a narrative now a little battered but still of some use.[1]

When English-speaking people first came to North America, they brought with them a habit of thinking by which untouched nature, or wilderness, was a fearful thing. Wilderness was a condition closely associated with the Devil and dark forces in general; untamed nature was as scary for the moral and mental threats it presented as it was for its physical threats. Thus phase one of the Euro-American response to North American nature could best be characterized as a shudder, and a shudder repeated sequentially as Euro-Americans encountered new and disorienting pieces and parts of North American nature. Thus, by the established story we told in the early 1970s, the Euro-American encounter with nature began in fear, which is not the happiest starting point for a long-term relationship.

That fear was a powerful force behind phase two, the struggle for mastery. If phase one was a shudder, phase two was something closer to the clenching and raising of a fist. Feeling overpowered and vulnerable at first, Euro-Americans eventually rallied to the cause and pitched into the mastery of nature. If forests were dark, dangerous, and threatening places, then the trees could be cut, and light could then drive out darkness. Useful animals would be hunted, trapped, and harvested; destructive animals would be eliminated; land would be plowed and cultivated; the force of water would be put to use to drive mills and factories; previously unused resources would provide homes and opportunities for the hardworking.

Phase two was a matter of finding out what was economically useful in nature, but there was a passion in it that went beyond the concerns of economic development. Having had the effrontery to frighten and intimidate Euro-Americans in their first meetings, nature was going to pay for that very costly, very temporary victory. Plowing, tree cutting, hunting, trapping, and damming were not just matters of finding what was economically valuable in nature and putting it to use; vengeance and retribution also drove this frenzy of activity. Having lorded it over humans, nature was going to get lorded over in return.

Then, in a remarkably rapid transition to phase three, disorienting in its suddenness, mastery made an abrupt shift to appreciation. When the shift in power had reached the point where it was unmistakable and irreversible, then it was all right—more important, it was *safe*—to admit that elements of nature were actually quite attractive and appealing. When human beings had clearly won the war and established their dominance over nature, then it was OK for humans to be gracious winners, and even to give up a little ground to the defeated enemy. Now that the need for brutal and clear exertion of power was over, management could take the place of mastery, and nature could be persuaded, coaxed, herded, guided, led, and sometimes even learned from, rather than overpowered.

Twenty-five years ago, this three-phase story, leading from fear to mastery to congenial management, was doing a very good job of persuading both academics and laypeople that it offered a happy—and, even more remarkable than happy, a clearly defined—ending to a tense and conflict-ridden story. Still, even in the terms of this older, simpler story, the power dynamics were unsettling. There are, after all, all sorts of ways of treating a conquered enemy, and there are all sorts of ways, some of them more subtle than others, of reminding the enemy that it lost the war. Appreciation and admiration offer one way of rubbing in the victory with a message that comes close to saying to the subdued party: "Since you have turned out to be no particular threat at all, we now feel free to find you likable and *cute,* cute enough to where we will be spending our vacations with you." But there was a warning message very near to the surface of this phase three attitude, a warning that said, "And just remember, if you don't *want* to be likable and cute, *we can always go back to phase two.*" This was a peace treaty that never required the victor to disarm.

This overview of Euro-American attitudes toward nature was well established in scholarly thinking and also well established in popular thinking. Like any other historical model with such an elevated level of neatness and simplicity, it was going to have some trouble standing up to close examination. As an historical model, it has all the flexibility and variation of a conveyor belt; it gives very little room to variation in groups and individuals or in places and times. More important, it barely recognizes human will and choice. Whatever their setting and location, Euro-Americans had to begin this ride in fear, travel through mastery, and arrive at appreciation and management. What seems most improbable about the widespread acceptance of the conveyor belt model was the willingness to believe that the story reached an ending, and a happy ending at that, with American society's arriving at some sort of consensus and shared understanding about how human beings should live with nature.

This model *does* have value: as a representation of American history, it provides an outline that corresponds to broad and significant patterns of attitude and behavior, especially behavior that shaped federal policy. It certainly has some bearing on that great shift at the end of the nineteenth century and the start of the twentieth century, the shift represented by the creation of national parks and forest reserves and by the growing American enthusiasm for outdoor life and vacations.

But here is the big problem with the three-phase model: phases one, two, and three probably do more in the way of coexisting and coinciding than they do in the way of preceding and following each other in proper numerical and chronological sequence. In fact, the characteristics of these three phases piled up on each other in the same moments in time, refusing to submit to the logic of sequence and succession. Take, for instance, overland travelers in the 1840s and 1850s, who should have been very much in the phase one mode, since they were moving into unfamiliar and disorienting turf on a journey of uncertain success. Indeed, the overland travelers had plenty of occasions when fear dominated their response to nature. Many of them—probably most of them—were sleeping outside a house for the first time in their lives, and finding themselves out on the plains, encountering a fierce thunderstorm, jarred by wild lightning and drenched by relentless rain, protected (if protected is the word) only by a canvas-covered wagon was an encounter likely to test the goodwill even of those who thought of themselves as admirers of nature.

That's the point: quite a number of people who kept diaries on the overland trail, in the mid-nineteenth century, *did* put themselves on record as admirers of nature. A number of them, while crossing through what is now Wyoming, looked at the mountains and wished that they had more time to explore. By the time they reached the Sierras, they were pressed very hard by the demands of the trip, but even there, some of them went on record with an appreciation for nature made all the more extraordinary by the desperation of their circumstances.

Some of these same people were also alert to signs of valuable minerals, and they were certainly attentive to the availability of the resources they needed immediately, like wood and water. They often assessed the value of the soil for farming, as if they were advance agents for the railroads and the land companies, which, in fact, they were. Their imaginations reached forward, into the moment in the future when these areas would be settled, developed, and Americanized. And so, rather than phase one of three sequential phases, we have in these overland trail encounters all three elements going at once: responses of fear, visions of utilitarian mastery, and sentiments of affection and appreciation.

Both in the more distant past and in the present, our three phases coincide and coexist. The attitudes they represent are more braided and intertwined than they are separate and distinct. While we might call this a problem, it is probably better labeled an opportunity or even a liberation. The recognition of how much the phases overlapped and continue to overlap restores considerable maneuvering room to us today. We often act as if attitudes and behavior toward nature are very much *congealed* by now, set in concrete, and determined by the past, but they are a lot more flexible than they seem.

Moreover, the whole, three-phase model rested on a firm and settled belief that the two terms "nature" and "human" were clearly and easily distinguished, standing for two easily identified worlds or arenas. Nature, in this understanding, was a firm, set, stable thing, sitting out there, placed at a safe distance from human beings, offering a pristine vision of what the planet could be like if humans weren't always making a mess of it. One could speak clearly about "human attitudes toward nature," because it was so easy to distinguish the two manifestations of life and matter: human and nature.

In a way of thinking shared by many preservationists, nature offered clear instructions and prescriptions to human beings. When left alone to arrive at its own balance, nature was supposed to be steady, reliable, and inspirational. The harmony and balance of nature, the theory went, could teach profligate, impulsive human beings a good deal if they could clear out the arrogance blocking their channels of perception. If people could push beyond the limits of understanding set by their vanity, untouched nature would give them a clear and orienting glimpse of the creative forces that shaped the earth. With that glimpse, humans could take their bearings and secure their moorings.

But how steady *was* nature? Winds, hurricanes, tornadoes, blizzards, droughts, floods, and earthquakes showed nature in moods other than the tranquil and harmonic. The widely accepted notion that, without human interference, ecosystems reached a climax state, in which the species arranged themselves in the proper numbers, proportions, and relationships, has yielded to a picture of nature always in change and flux. As historian William Cronon puts it, the natural world has been revealed to be "far more dynamic, far more changeable, and far more entangled with human history than popular beliefs about 'the balance of nature' have typically acknowledged." This changed understanding of nature, Cronon writes, "calls into question the familiar modern habit of appealing to nonhuman nature as the objective measure against which human uses of nature should be judged."[2]

In the last few years, a number of people have misunderstood Cronon to be saying that nature does not really exist, that what we call nature is only an insubstantial and shifting substance of social and cultural construction, and, therefore, that there is really no reason to protect or preserve nature. On the contrary, Cronon is quite aware that there *is* stuff out there, generated and sustained independently of the designs and ambitions of humanity. He is also aware and supportive of the good reasons for preserving and protecting much of that stuff out there. But Cronon's point is that there is no escaping the role, power, and consequence of human thinking and human choice. Nature does not legislate; nature does not write policy; nature does not decree what kind of settlement can occur in which place. Nature may, for instance, make available a certain amount of water, but nature does not declare whether that water will be used for agriculture or industry, sugar beet fields or stream flow for wild and scenic rivers. Responding to and interpreting the conditions presented by nature, human beings legislate, write policy, and determine which settlements will occur where and how they will get their water.[3]

Often in their rhetoric and sometimes in their deepest convictions, human beings act as if they are only vehicles and amplifiers for transmitting nature's messages; nature truly does seem to them to decree what human beings can, should, and *must* do in particular places. But this assumption that nature carries political and economic messages and mandates is finally a failure of self-consciousness, a failure of a recognition that humans implant and install the meaning in these messages and mandates. This belief system, moreover, has its limitations as a political strategy: it works wonderfully when one is speaking to fellow converts; it does next to nothing to persuade the unredeemed and the unawakened. William Cronon wants us to look in the mirror and reacquaint ourselves with the fact that our minds play a governing role in determining the meanings we find in nature.

Cronon's argument thus offers its own liberation. It dramatizes the range of movement open to human will; it restores quite a number of variables to human control. It makes it clear that we are more free and more empowered than we thought we were to influence our contemporaries' thought about nature. The future becomes more approachable, more imaginable, more within the reach of our will and decision making.

If we really believed that there was considerable maneuvering room in these matters, what possible actions would come to our minds? I have some nominations, suggestions that demonstrate the exciting possibilities of what I am calling the Applied Humanities, the application of humanities thinking to contemporary dilemmas. I choose the term with a full recognition that, just as Applied Science can lead its practitioners into a number of moral and mental muddles, so the Applied Humanities offer plenty of pitfalls and places for missteps. It is fair warning to say that some of these suggestions from the Applied Humanities may be terrible ideas; they may, in fact, be ideas that have already been tried and rejected. But they are proposals, nonetheless, that try to use historical knowledge in the cause of cutting loose from the worn-out, the familiar, the predictable, the predetermined, the fated.

1. Preservationists could be much more assertive in claiming *their* share of the pioneer heritage. If you are willing to quote a bit selectively (which card-carrying historians are not permitted to do, but they certainly couldn't stop anyone else from trying it), you can create for present-day preservationists an intellectual lineage reaching back to the pioneers. One of the principal intellectual projects going on in the West today is exactly that: the claiming of legitimacy by the

constructing of a line of descent leading from the nineteenth century to the twentieth century and then directly to oneself. The natural resource users have worked this strategy with particular energy. Miners, ranchers, loggers, and farmers are the ones claiming a line of descent—and a line of honor—direct from the pioneers, from the people who built the West. But the pioneers were complicated people and their legacy is equally complicated, and if preservationists were to select and arrange the quotations intelligently, they, too, could be claiming a direct line of descent from the pioneers. It is undeniable that many pioneers felt strong admiration for natural beauty; many held the conviction that the Creation mirrored the glory of the Creator; and, maybe most appealing, many felt a strong curiosity to figure out the origins of the dramatic Western landforms and the workings of striking and unfamiliar Western plants and animals. Given that invocations of the pioneer heritage still carry emotional and political capital, it puzzles me that one side makes such heavy use of such invocations, while the other side seems to forfeit the opportunity.

2. Develop new strategies for rewarding restraint. Encourage the Boy Scouts to give merit badges for *not* camping, for *not* carving initials into trees, for *not* rafting down crowded rivers, for *not* starting fires by rubbing two sticks together. Give merit badges for redirecting the same resources that they might have put into an extensive outing into the improvement of, say, a local park. At the annual meetings of environmental groups, give prizes to people who *didn't* go anywhere, who *didn't* test themselves by climbing any remarkable rock faces, who *didn't* frighten wildlife by cross-country skiing in remote wilderness areas, who *didn't* feel compelled to prove their masculinity (or, in the case of women, their equivalent toughness) by extreme outdoor activity. Give well-publicized prizes, in star-studded and glamorous ceremonies, to residents of the Pacific Coast or the Northeast who did not buy second homes in the Rockies. Encourage these acts of restraint to connect to and correlate with acts of self-education, so that Boy Scouts and yuppies who do not go camping or skiing do something closer to home that provides a focused and immediate version of some lesson they might have learned out in nature. History, as well as current behavior, tells us that the charms of mobility and outdoor action have already been very well promoted, and thus there is every

good reason to manipulate public opinion in order to place a positive and even heroic aura around acts of restraint and refusal of mobility.

3. Remind the public of the overwhelming familiarity, prosaic-ness, taken-for-grantedness, total humdrumness of the arrangements society makes when not everybody can go into a particular space at one and the same time. Step back from the current situation, and it be-comes astonishing to think that the prospect of rationing access to na-tional parks inspires alarm and resistance. Meanwhile, in virtually every other sphere of life, rationing access is so totally normal that it never comes to mind as something either to rebel against or to ap-plaud. You need to see a dentist, you call to see when the dentist is available, and if it turns out that he has a patient scheduled for the time that you wanted, you do not insist on your right to get in the chair anyway; you do not threaten to lie on top of the holder of the pre-viously scheduled appointment. If you want to go to the theater, you want to go somewhere on an airplane, you want to take a popular class, you want to see a football game, or you want to get your car re-paired, you call and find out if there is a slot available, and sometimes you find out that a particular dentist chair, theater performance, air-plane, class, stadium, or garage is already filled up. While you may be frustrated, you do not condemn the whole idea of regulating and lim-iting access to spaces that cannot accommodate everyone at once. Even if some people accelerate when they see a yellow light, and even if a few people go right ahead and run red lights, nearly everyone un-derstands and accepts the principle of stoplights and recognizes that letting everyone have unlimited access to that space in the intersection would be a prescription for disaster. What could explain resistance to this perfectly predictable, perfectly normal practice, resistance that flares up when it is applied to national parks? If people can be grown-ups when it comes to access to dentists, theaters, airplanes, classes, football games, car repair shops, and street intersections, then why do some of them abandon that common wisdom and become self-indulgent tyrants when it comes to access to national parks? The an-swer lies in point 4.

4. Reexamine and rethink ways in which conventional enthusi-asm for nature unthinkingly glorifies individualism and free will. Why *will* people consent to restraint, in the interest of a common good, for

nearly every other activity and then threaten to withdraw that consent when planning a visit to the outdoors? It does not take the Applied Humanities equivalent of a rocket scientist to figure this out. For 150 years, the principal selling pitch for experience in nature and wilderness has hinged on an appeal to individualism, independence, and freedom. From Henry David Thoreau to John Muir to Edward Abbey, the most vigorous, memorable, persuasive, and quotable advocates of outdoor experience have been very independent fellows, if also wonderful writers. They and their many followers have done a great deal to install in American minds the idea that one goes to nature in order to be freely and independently oneself. Thus, applying to natural preserves the same commonsense rationing of access that operates in so many other spheres of American life strikes many as infuriating, intolerable, wrong, contradictory, and a violation of the fundamental *meaning* of the encounter with nature.

Here is a case where all the arguments about the social and cultural construction of nature come to a head. The idea that regulation is intrinsically at odds with immersion in nature is purely and totally a human construction. The good news, then, is this: if an idea like that lives primarily in our own heads, it can also be *changed* primarily in our own heads. Preservationists have put in their time condemning rugged individualism as practiced in the world of competitive capitalism. And yet they have, themselves, unthinkingly ratified and enshrined their own version of rugged individualism, a version which has turned out to be as injurious to their cause as the business variety.

5. Persuade environmental groups to become boosters of towns and cities. Give up the antiurban sentiment that has long been the live-in partner of the enthusiasm for nature that has rallied to the support of the national parks. Give up antiurbanism, because environmentalists can no longer afford such a self-indulgent luxury. Antiurban sentiment, often popularized and distributed *by* nature lovers, has been an enormous force behind the sprawling of American settlement, and the intrusion of houses into open space. People move to suburbs, people move to remote and beautiful sites and hook themselves up to the city by FAXes and E-mail, in large part because the United States has a well-established tradition by which cities are creepy.

Since dense, clustered human settlements relieve the pressure on outlying areas, it becomes the better part of valor for preservationists to swallow hard and celebrate towns and cities, describe their many charms, encourage generous social funding to improve infrastructures and living conditions in cities. Do your antiurban shuddering in private if you cannot stop shuddering entirely, though a recognition of the degree to which healthy towns and cities could improve the health of rural areas may make the shuddering considerably less violent.

6. Channel popular fantasies about nature in the direction you want them to go, and do this through friends and allies if it is too embarrassing to do it yourselves. Recognize, in other words, that the anthropomorphizing of animals and the commodifying of nature in popular culture are going to continue, whether or not the results are judged to be absurd and unjustifiable by wildlife biologists. So, work with wildlife filmmakers, and direct their enterprises toward the best messages, especially toward a recognition of the ways in which human affection and sentiment can get in the way of an animal's well-being. Weirder, still, work with cartoon makers. Think what one could do, for instance, if the medium of the animated film were put to work to dramatize the problems posed by jurisdictions and boundaries in the Greater Yellowstone ecosystem. Why not a cartoon about Emily the Elk, a secure, protected, and contented young animal as long as she stays on one side of the park border, and a legitimate game animal, caught in the crosshairs of a hunter's rifle, in the next moment, on the other side of the border?

After a moment of horrifying tension, *don't kill Emily.* Instead, kill her mother. This is a proven formula for moving and engaging the American public. Show no restraint here: in a hundred cartoons and children stories, kill elk mothers, buffalo mothers, bear mothers, and wolf mothers, martyrs to the arbitrariness of those jurisdictional boundaries. After there has been more matricide than the public can bear, send all the orphans—little Emily Elk, Bobby Bison, Bonnie Bear, and Willie Wolf—to meet with a congressional committee (and be kind when you draw the cartoon images of the representatives and senators; remember whom you're trying to persuade). Have the orphans describe, to a national audience on C-Span, the injuries done to their family life and to American family values in general by these uncoordinated and arbitrary jurisdictional boundaries. In the cartoon, have the senators and representatives weep a little and then dedicate themselves to unthinking these cruel, family-dividing barriers and boundaries.

7. Revive patriotism, and appeal to it often and shamelessly. In the post–Cold War years, patriotism is up for grabs and for redefinition. Even if it is no longer defined by its opposition to Soviet communism, patriotism is still a potent political force. If you don't put it to use, others certainly will. Of course, people of a certain age—more exactly, *my* age—get a little jumpy with this suggestion. We remember Vietnam; we remember Watergate; we remember J. Edgar Hoover; we remember Iran-contra; we remember *plenty* about acts of oppression and injustice either committed by the federal government or with its support. But the United States is still the nation we live in, and the well-being of the nation we live in cannot be a matter for our smug indifference. Moreover, in the early years of the preservation movement, appeals to national pride were an important part of the movement's success. Invocations of patriotism will continue to carry power, and it seems peculiar for environmentalists to forswear the use of this power because people of a certain age are subject to 1960s flashbacks.

8. Consider the comparison made by many between environmentalism and religion, and decide what to do with it. Frequently this comparison is offered with hostility, as when conservative Christian groups say that environmentalism has become a new pantheism, heathenistically exalting nature over both humanity and the Christian God. In truth, the characterization of nature preservation as a religion does not seem entirely without weight and relevance. People who devote themselves to the cause of preserving nature do behave in ways that seem distinctly religious: they have a sense of a higher good, a higher good often defied and defiled by other humans, and sometimes, they sacrifice their own interests for this higher good; they believe that they are following a higher authority; they make heavy use of the terms and ideas of salvation, redemption, and paradise; and— this is the more regrettable part—they sometimes have a tendency to see those who are not fellow believers as heathens, deviants, and

fallen-away sinners. I myself do not know to what degree environmentalism has become a functional equivalent to religion. But a number of things could happen with a reckoning with this question.

One of the most important benefits of thinking through the religious analogy might well be an improved strategy of communication and conversion. In other words, many preservationist believers have had a way of conducting themselves as if they were part of an established church, authorized to distinguish the saved from the fallen and to judge the unredeemed and condemn them far into eternity. But the history of formal, recognized religion shows a number of far more effective strategies of conversion and missionization, strategies which are better aimed to condemn the sin, without scorning and alienating the sinners and thereby sending them off endlessly to repeat their sin.

9. Take advantage of that wonderful, memorable phrase, in the congressional language designating Yellowstone as a national park. It is a phrase that glows and expands as you contemplate it, and the phrase, of course, is "pleasuring ground." What a concept—ground that gives pleasure, ground from which pleasure sprouts and blooms. Congress so rarely speaks in such evocative language, and it seems a shame not to take full advantage of a rare moment of poetic intoxication on Congress's part.

Plus, the time might be ripe for a reconsideration of the assumption that pleasure must be tied to materialism and consumption. To invite people into experiencing a new and better form of pleasure certainly seems a more persuasive strategy than sourly condemning them for pursuing the wrong kind. The human desire for pleasure is part of the species' permanent equipment, and denying its legitimacy seems to fan its flames. Find ways in which that wonderful adjective "pleasuring" could figure much more conspicuously in the modes of presentation of environmentalist causes. In statements of persuasion and recruitment, cut back on guilt and expand on pleasure. If environmentalists do not come up with better ideas of fun, commercial America certainly will.

10. Imagine a full and productive joining of the causes of environmental well-being and racial equity. Sometimes imagined to be a refuge from the troubles and tensions of the rest of the nation, the na-

tional parks are fully tied into the United States's complicated history of race relations. The creation of the parks, just as much as the creation of farms, mines, and cities, required the removal of Indian people. The opportunity for the privileged to enjoy their outings to parks often rested on a familiar racial hierarchy of labor. Many of the early visitors to Yellowstone remarked on the essential roles played by African American servants. Sir Rose Lambart Price found his trip to Yellowstone made much more comfortable by the services of what Sir Price called "my man," a "coloured trooper," "a capital servant" who was "as sympathetic and attentive as a woman." Yellowstone's famed Washburn-Langford-Hedges party of 1870 included "two colored cooks." A visitor in 1896 remarked on "the staff of coloured waiters in the dining room" in a park hotel. The 1874 expedition of the Earl of Dunraven included "Maxwell, a gentleman of colour, who fulfilled the important functions of barber and cook."[4] All of these references to colored servants remind us that Yellowstone, like other parks, has been anything but an escape from the usual American arrangements of power.

Broadening the environmental movement to include the great diversity of the national population requires a full reckoning with this history, a reckoning that involves much more than an occasional invitation for Americans of all backgrounds to consider the national parks part of their collective heritage. As the example of the African American workforce in the early days of Yellowstone National Park shows, the national parks *are* already part of every American's ethnic heritage. But there is a sizable variation, by class as well as ethnicity, in the degree to which involvement with the parks came in the same package as privilege and leisure. Well-intentioned efforts to invite all of the United States's citizens to enjoy their parks must still reckon with the inheritance of inequality.

There are probably many more lessons from the Applied Humanities that might aid the cause of environmentalist self-examination and reorientation. But, mercifully, Mark Twain's memorable story about going to church to hear a visiting missionary comes to mind at this point. For the first few minutes, Twain said, he was so moved that he began to regret having brought so little money for the collection plate, and he resolved to borrow more from a friend. As the sermon wore on and on, Twain said, he began to think that the small amount of money he had would be sufficient. And then, when the missionary finally ended, Twain reported, he was feeling so mean and nasty that he stole a quarter from the collection plate. Equally useful for preachers, professors, and politicians, *that* parable speaks for itself without the interpretative help of the Applied Humanist.

III-B

Disorientation and Reorientation: The American Landscape Discovered from the West

In the month of September, in the year 1972, I traveled from the Pacific Coast to the Atlantic Coast, from southern California to southern New England. To the east of Arizona lay wilderness, and the exotic names of that wilderness both chilled and lured me: Tennessee, Virginia, the District of Columbia, Philadelphia, and most alarming of all, Manhattan. In the course of this journey, I discovered the Eastern United States, an event as consequential to me as it was insignificant to the residents.

As I drove across Oklahoma, crossing what I later learned was the ninety-eighth meridian, discovery joined up with its usual partner, disorientation. The air became humid, clammy, and unpleasant, and the landscape turned distressingly green. The Eastern United States, I learned with every mile, was badly infested by plants. Even where they had been driven back, the bushes, shrubs, and trees gave every sign of anticipating a reconquest. But the even more remarkable fact was this: millions of people lived in this muggy, congested world, and most astonishing of all, they considered it *normal*.

In my transcontinental journey of discovery, gas station attendants across the country had been impressed by the number of books I had managed to fit into a small car. In retrospect, I am more struck by the books that I did not own and had not read. In 1972, my VW Bug did not contain Henry Nash Smith's *Virgin Land* (1950), Hans Huth's *Nature and the American* (1957), Arthur A. Ekirch's *Man and Nature in America* (1963), Leo Marx's *Machine in the Garden* (1964), William H. Goetzmann's *Exploration and Empire* (1966), or Roderick Nash's *Wilderness and the American Mind* (1967).[1]

Had I read them before my journey to the East, the standard scholarly writings on the discovery of the American landscape would have puzzled me as deeply as the landscape of the Eastern United States did and for many of the same reasons. The study of American responses to landscape ran on an east-to-west track, following the physical and mental migrations of white, English-speaking men. In the conventional view, the process of discovery reached completion when the maps had their blank spots filled in and literate white Americans had seen all the places worth seeing. What the discoverers explored was wilderness, a kind of pristine natural landscape in which Indians lived more as symbols than as three-dimensional human beings. In the same spirit, the authors of the reigning texts in this field took for granted a norm of a green, plant-filled landscape, a norm that they shared with nineteenth-century American explorers of the American West.*

In 1972, with these premises locked into place and with the problem of point of view seemingly settled, one could write comfortably and complacently about this subject. In two decades, comfort and complacency have fled the field. Attention to the east-to-west process of exploration now has to compete with a recognition of Indian prior presence, as well as of northward movements from Mexico and eastward movements from Asia. The notion of a pristine wilderness is in well-deserved tatters, and the discoverers now appear as late arrivals in an already fully occupied and much-changed landscape. Thanks to various environmental messes and crises of scarce resources, the celebration of a completed process of discovery, ending in a landscape known, mastered, and put to good use, seems at best silly and at worst dangerous. The assumption that "normal" means green and

---

*The persistent power of this way of thinking is evident in the use of the adjective "green" to characterize environmentalist causes. Many natural environments of the American West would be better described with the adjective "brown" or perhaps "khaki."

well watered has lost credibility; through pollution and overallocation of what once seemed to be abundant supplies, the residents of the Eastern United States have created for themselves a number of the dilemmas in water scarcity long familiar to the West.

The new, improved, "revised standard" orthodoxy on the discovery of landscape thus does not miss a beat in bringing its charges against the old orthodoxy. The conventional studies concentrated wholeheartedly on the thinking of English-speaking, westward-moving, literate, record-keeping middle- and upper-class, pre-twentieth-century, white men. Offered as studies of American attitudes toward landscape, these standard works were in fact investigations into the minds of a minority. In the late twentieth century, such exclusivity in scholarly inquiry is no longer tenable.

And at this point, the current orthodoxy comes to an abrupt halt. Working on this essay led me to a full recognition of how the new assumptions escort one to the edge of one's ignorance and then leave one to contemplate the vacancy. Of course, I recognize that human beings discovered the American landscape from all directions: east to west, from Europe and Africa; south to north, from Mexico and South America; west to east, from Asia and the Pacific Islands; and from a variety of directions, for Indian people whose arrival took place in another time frame entirely.

And yet almost all of what I know on the subject pulls me back into the old framework of the east-to-west movement of white men. If asked to give an impromptu speech on the subject, I could hold forth for hours on the attitudes and experiences of Meriwether Lewis, William Clark, Zebulon Pike, Stephen Long, John C. Fremont, John Wesley Powell, Clarence King, and the other big names of exploration. I could speak at length on the responses of emigrants to the scenery they saw on the overland trail, on the utilitarian appraisals of landscape by miners, cattlemen, farmers, loggers, and city builders, on the development of a tourist industry based on the aesthetic commodification of landscape, and on the rise to visibility of John Muir, Aldo Leopold, Edward Abbey, and the various celebrators of a nonutilitarian value in landscape. At the end of this megalecture, I would have shown how much I remained loyal to a number of the flaws of the old school of landscape studies. White men would still be the principal, virtually the only, players in my story; and my framework would remain stuck on the east-to-west track of perception.

How to do it better? Ranking high in the category of things easier said than done, here is a list of topics that should figure in the study of the discovery of landscape:

1. The geologic, climatic, botanical, and zoological qualities of a particular place
2. The indigenous people's worldviews and the values they invested (and may well continue to invest) in the landscapes of their home
3. The impact of the native people's actions in creating a landscape that was neither purely natural nor wholly human-made
4. The perceptions and actions of intruders, explorers, invaders, colonizers, and conquerors, responding to places that were at once new to them and familiar to the original residents
5. The second-generation experience of those born to the colonizers—the perspective of the invaders' children to whom the new and exotic area had become home
6. The continuing arrival of both new residents and impression-gathering travelers who may well have felt a sense of discovery, whether or not that sense of originality seemed legitimate to the residents who preceded them
7. The ways in which these various groups saw each other—as legitimate residents, illegitimate invaders, enrichers, despoilers, improvers, or devastators of the landscape or as quaint figures or eyesores in the view
8. Change and continuity in the physical components and arrangements of the landscape over time
9. The ongoing process of discovery and rediscovery, as people with different concerns, needs, and assumptions found and find new meaning in landscapes, even when those landscapes, by an earlier judgment composed of equal parts of cheer and gloom, seemed to have been fully discovered, known, mastered, and thereby reduced in interest
10. A reckoning, in the historian's best judgment and with subjectivity fully acknowledged, of what this whole business added up to—a kind of balance sheet of costs and benefits,

gains that can be sustained and gains that prove temporary, injuries and losses where repair and compensation are imaginable and injuries where repair and compensation are beyond
imagination

This is a thorough and sensible model, and it is one that I would
like to be practicing in the early twenty-first century. I am grateful to
other scholars who have already field-tested pieces and parts of this
model.[2] But my own relationship to this handsome, evenly numbered
approach consists mostly of yearning. I simply do not know enough
about the history of any one place to go through the ten elements,
thoroughly and carefully. Instead, for the purposes of this essay, I will
focus on item 4, the perceptions and behavior of recent arrivals responding to landscapes that were new to them. To dramatize the fact
that the east-to-west movement was only one part of the process of
discovery, I will follow the west-to-east vector of exploration. This
will, therefore, be an investigation of the Asian and Asian American
discovery of North American landscapes, a tracking of the responses
of people moving west to east across the Pacific and into the interior.

Why am I still using the word "discovery"? Columbus, we now
say by rote, could not have *discovered* the Western Hemisphere because native people already lived here. How, then, can I say that the
Chinese discovered California in the nineteenth century? What possible sense could it make to refer to the Japanese and Japanese American discovery of the arid interior of the American West, in a coerced
relocation during World War Two?

The problem lies in the assumption that to qualify for true discovery, the explorer must come upon a place that is without previous
occupants. But we now take it as our premise that the European discoverers found people as well as places. For an experience of discovery, the place involved does not have to be new to everyone; it has to
be new to the discoverer. The encounter is, of course, reciprocal; when
Columbus discovered the Indians, the Indians had the chance to discover Columbus. Sometimes, as in my own discovery of the Eastern
United States, the residents can be thoroughly unmoved by the event.

However the natives respond, the person encountering a new place
is having an experience of some significance. This does not mean that
the act of discovery has *introduced* significance into a place where
there was none before; that arrogant assumption was, after all, what

went wrong with the word "discovery." But why not undercut the hubris of the old idea by defining "discovery" simply as a group's first encounter with a place new to them? While this definition may lack the self-dramatization of discovery on the grand and misguided old model, it gives a down-to-earth meaning to a formerly flighty concept.

It was an easy undertaking to resolve to reverse direction and to track the west-to-east discovery of the American landscape. The resolution made, the easy part ended. With no Asian or Asian American equivalents to *Virgin Land, The Machine in the Garden, Exploration and Empire,* and *Wilderness and the American Mind,* disorientation was the next stop on this journey.[3] This was not to be the sort of pleasant intellectual excursion in which one comfortably reviews, appraises, and critiques the work of one's predecessors in a field of inquiry. Under these circumstances, the analogy between literal, geographical discovery and metaphorical, intellectual discovery became instantly too close for comfort. Simply raising the question of Asian and Asian American responses to the American landscape, I was out of my turf, traveling without landmarks, maps, or guidebooks, yearning for the familiar and predictable company of Meriwether Lewis, William Clark, John C. Fremont, and the rest of that gang.

True to the patterns of Euro-American discoverers, I had a language problem, rendering me dependent on the kindness of interpreters and translators. I do not read Chinese or Japanese; an untranslated source is a source marked off-limits to me. Also true to earlier patterns of Euro-American discovery, the territory that seemed so disorienting to me was in fact a territory familiar to others who traveled in it long before my arrival. How did Asians and Asian Americans see the American landscape? In answering that question, hundreds of thousands of Asian and Asian American people, and a number of historians, had a considerable headstart on me.

Neither Chinese nor Japanese immigrants are, in any direct way, my people. The descendant of Danes whose conversion to the Church of Latter-day Saints brought them to Utah, I come from a rather different line of immigration. To the people of the Mormon past, Utah was a promised land, a new Jerusalem, a sacred place. While I and my immediate family have lapsed far from Mormonism, I show some signs of having held onto a vision of the American West as sacred space. The investment of human life and emotion in particular places, I believe, gives those places transcendent meaning. In American life, this way of thinking—and feeling—is most often evoked by battle-fields. At a site where many people gave up their lives, few have to struggle to grasp the idea that the place has been permanently changed, even sanctified, by death. But I would remove the "death in battle" requirement from the definition of sacred ground. Where people have labored, suffered, struggled, or even just survived, they have planted seeds of memory as directly as farmers sow crops, and memory has its roots in the soul.

The landscape thus has a number of layers, all demanding the scholar's attention: rock and soil; plants and animals; humans as a physical presence, manifested in their physical works; *and* humans as an emotional and spiritual presence, manifested in the accumulated stories of their encounter with a place. Our attention and curiosity here cannot be exclusive. One can glimpse the full power of a place only in the full story of human presence there. Thus, exclusive attention to the movements, actions, and impressions of Anglo-Americans is equivalent to the arbitrary editing of a scripture, skipping entire chapters and devoting disproportionate attention to a few featured verses. The complete story of the investment of human consciousness in the American landscape requires attention to the whole set of participants—indigenous people as well as invaders, eastward-moving Asian American people as well as westward-moving Euro-American people. With anything less, the meaning of the landscape is fragmented and truncated.

Take into account a wider range of points of origin and points of view, and the most prosaic and pedestrian landscape lights up with meaning. While I was at work on this project, taking a taxi from the San Francisco Airport and chatting with the cabdriver, I was suddenly knocked into silence by a glimpse of the sign for the Tanforan Race Track in San Bruno. A subdued borrowing from the traditions of Las Vegas signage, the Tanforan sign tries to convey cheer and festivity. The effect on me was exactly the opposite, and yet Tanforan was a name I would not have recognized two months before. Since then, I had read narratives of Japanese American people who were held captive at Tanforan at the start of World War Two, forced to live in stalls and stables recently vacated by horses. They were still near their Bay Area homes, but they were living in a place that bore no resemblance to home. The stories of life at Tanforan capture the misery and injustice of forced relocation. To a person who knows these stories, even a person rushing by on a highway, a glimpse of the Tanforan sign says instantly, "You are near a place where the human soul was tried and tested."

* * *

In 1900, the young Chinese immigrant John Jeong arrived in San Francisco. Riding with others in an open carriage, he was halfway to Chinatown when "some white boys came up and started throwing rocks at us." Welcome by rock throwing was an intense and memorable opening encounter with the social landscape of the West Coast, and it was a lesson reinforced repeatedly after arrival. The "boundaries" of Chinatown, one old man remembered, ran "from Kearny to Powell, and from California to Broadway. If you ever passed them and went out there, the white kids would throw stones at you." Discovery, in these places, came down to learning the boundaries of safety and mapping one's way through a landscape of risk. This risk extended beyond the coastal cities and into the rural interior. In the Sacramento–San Joaquin Delta, except for the all-Chinese town of Locke, the small towns could mirror the dangers of the city: "the whites would attack you with stones when you walked through some of these towns," Bing Fai Chow remembered. "We never dared to walk on the streets alone then—except in Locke. This was our place."[4]

A landscape so sharply divided between safety and danger, refuge and risk, actively discouraged discovery. Just as important, a preoccupation with finding work and doing work drained both mental and physical energy. "I was always at work," Suen Hoon Sum remembered. "I worked all over the place! . . . It was very easy for a year to go by. Year after year you did the same thing—pick fruit and trim fruit trees." At the California placer mines, in railroad construction camps, on farms and orchards, work swallowed time and energy. Looking for work meant constant travel, but it was not the sort of travel that encouraged one to see the sights. Necessity monopolized attention, and the discovery of the landscape took second place to the discovery of the job. "We went everywhere looking for work," Jone Ho Leong told an interviewer, but the responses she felt to the many places that she saw did not register in the interview.[5]

And indeed, why should they? Beginning this essay, it was my operating assumption that the conditions of immigrant, working class life—inadequate housing, uncertain food, constant work, inequitable rewards for that work, racial harassment, and campaigns for exclusion—made a self-conscious aesthetic response to landscape into a luxury few could afford. It made perfect sense to me that the immigrants would appraise, explore, and read the Western American landscape in terms of jobs and income. But this assumption has become more and more doubtful. The proposition that immigrant workers had little response to landscape begins to seem more and more an artifact of my puzzlement at reckoning with unconventional sources, as well as a product of my assumption that because *I* would have been too fatigued to respond to the landscape, all the Asian immigrants would have been in a similar state.

Asking the question, "But what did they *think* of the landscapes they saw?" gets the scholar few direct answers. Denied an answer often enough, one begins to recognize the narrow limits of the intellectual turf and the kinds of sources that have traditionally fallen within the category of the discovery of landscape. The boundaries of this turf have been set by the particular conditions of American national expansion into contiguous territory. In the context of territorial conquest, the discoverers were commissioned agents of their national government, explicitly directed to report on their findings; they could concentrate on discovering landscapes and not on finding jobs, because discovery *was* their job. Agents of territorial conquest, in other words, kept a lot of records, and historians are thus inclined to define those records as the "normal" source for responses to landscape.

Contrary to white fears of "yellow perils" or Asian invasions, neither China nor Japan had much reason to send advance scouts for conquest into North America. Nineteenth-century Chinese immigrants no doubt had interesting mental responses to the coastline, valleys, cities, mountains, and deserts of the United States. But they were not acting as official information gatherers for their home nation; they had no assignment to record their responses in the official public reports that, in the Anglo-American tradition, have made up the literary record of discovery.

"[T]he Chinese themselves left few records of their perceptions and experience," Sucheng Chan notes in *This Bittersweet Soil,* and that fact makes an inquiry into their thinking a guessing game. Moreover, when Chan remarks that "no [Chinese] landowning-literati class established itself in America," one is suddenly made aware of the enormous role of leisure and privilege in creating the possibility of an aesthetic, self-conscious, recorded response to landscape. A "landowning-literati class" is indeed the source of much of the Anglo-American literature of discovery of landscape; even the wilderness-loving John Muir married into a family of orchard-owning Californians. Without a margin of assured subsistence, without the opportunity for contemplation and introspection, without a way to enter one's memories into a permanent, written source, a group's response to a new geography can be close to impossible for posterity to hear.[6]

Rather than an occasion for defeat, this dilemma offers an opportunity to broaden the turf of inquiry, to look for evidence of the experience of discovery, first, in unconventional literary sources and, second, in action and behavior. In the first category, one turns to the walls of the Angel Island immigration facility. Those walls held poems, written by immigrants and recently transcribed and translated by Him Mark Lai, Genny Lim, and Judy Yung. In these poems, one finds ample evidence that a people, who might initially seem inarticulate to the historian, were charged with intense and profound responses to the American landscape. Opened as an immigration station in 1910, Angel Island in San Francisco Bay served as a focal point in the Chinese discovery of the landscape. Many immigrants spent weeks, even months, on the island, enduring prolonged interrogations and inspections.

Many of the Angel Island poems used the landscape as an analogy for the experience of being stranded and kept waiting:

> *Green waters surround a green hill on four sides.*
> *Ascending to a high place, one does not see the shore.*

In this poem, and many others, the writer found in the island setting a direct mirror for emotion:

> *At times I gaze at the cloud- and fog-enshrouded mountain-*
> *   front.*
> *It only deepens my sadness.*

The remoteness and separation of the island mirrored the social reality of exclusion:

The Western styled buildings are lofty;
But I have not the luck to live in them.

Other poems drew a contrast between the landscape of home and the landscape of a remote place of confinement:

I left the village behind me, bade
*   farewell to my father and mother.*
Now I gaze at distant clouds and mountains,
*   tears forming like pearls.*

In these poems, the authors crafted internal feeling and external setting into one experience. The elegance of their readings of the landscape provides us with a useful reminder for the whole subject. On those occasions when it seems to us that Asian immigrants had no response to the landscape, there is a good chance that we are confronting a failure of records and not a failure of response.[7]

Second, the record of action and behavior can speak with considerable clarity about discovery. Consider, for instance, the Chinese role in expanding California agriculture. In a study of the Chinese in the Monterey Bay area, Sandy Lydon gives discovery a gritty, down-to-earth meaning. The Chinese, Lydon writes, "quickly saw the agricultural potential in the marginal lands of the region." They saw resources that Americans and Europeans could not see. Americans looked at mustard plants growing wild in California and saw a nuisance; the Chinese looked at mustard plants and saw the abundant raw material for a valued spice. The Americans saw willows as the sign of a useless swamp; the Chinese saw willows as the sign of fresh water and fertile land, once it was cleared and drained. This "ability to see the potential in the most mundane things," Lydon concludes, "may be the greatest contribution of the Chinese immigrants to the history and development of the Monterey Bay Region—they showed the Yankees and Europeans the infinite *possibilities* that the region offered."[8]

As the word "contribution" suggests, this line of argument has its risks. It is not simply a question of whether an ethnic group reaches its peak of significance when it contributes to the economic growth of the American nation. In the late twentieth century, environmentalism has added another puzzle to the concept of contribution, a puzzle that points directly to the unfortunate distance separating environmental history from ethnic history. Given the recognition of the various ways in which economic development exacted a heavy price from the physical environment, is a group's active role in the reshaping of landscape and the domination of nature still an occasion for congratulations? In most of the texts of Asian American history, the question still waits for recognition.

Until quite recently, environmental historians paid little attention to ethnic history and focused their inquiries on the attitudes and behavior of white men. There may well have been some logic in that choice. If one's principal interest is in the impact of human action on physical places, then it makes sense to track the attitudes and behavior of people in power. The patterns of change in landscape often reflect the choices and preferences of the segment of society that carries economic and political power. Nonetheless, a full study of the human relationship to landscape cannot confine itself to a powerful elite. Workers, often minority workers, provided the essential labor of environmental change, and members of minorities often absorbed a disproportionate share of undesirable environmental impacts, whether in the siting of dumps or the deploying of pesticides. And yet environmental history and ethnic history have been very separate enterprises. The citing of Chinese contributions to the transformation of Western landscapes provides only one among many case studies in the challenge of finding the common ground between these fields.[9]

One can easily understand how the habit of celebrating contributions began. Huang Zunxian was the Chinese consul general in San Francisco in the early 1880s, facing the challenge of the newly passed Chinese Exclusion Act. "When the Chinese first crossed the ocean," Huang Zunxian wrote in a poem, "they were the same as pioneers. . . . Dressed in tatters, they cleared mountain forests." Thanks to their efforts, "wilderness and waste turned into towns and villages." Or as Zhang Yinhuan, Chinese minister to the United States in the late 1880s, put it, the "barren areas around San Francisco" had become "a metropolis" where "[w]onderful structures now reach the clouds." "How," Zhang Yinhuan asked, "could all this have been accomplished without the efforts of the Chinese?"[10]

Celebrations of the Chinese contribution to the economic development of the American landscape originated in a framework of defending the Chinese against their enemies and defamers. This mode of defensive congratulations extended into the writing of history. In California, Jack Chen writes, the Chinese "played a big role in bringing irrigation to a million acres of California farmland by 1890. This was a vital contribution to fruit and vegetable farming." "With bone and muscle," Sylvia Sun Minnick writes of Chinese laborers in the Sacramento–San Joaquin Delta, "they moved the earth, built the levees and rearranged" the delta. And yet, before its transformation into what Minnick calls "an agricultural wonderland," the delta had been a wildlife wonderland. The Chinese, Minnick writes, "transformed the flat [Central Valley] floor into grazing and workable farm land." Before it grew crops, the Central Valley grew carpets of wildflowers that dazzled John Muir and others. Should the loss of wildlife and wildflowers, as well as the costs of imposing intensive, irrigated agriculture in a semiarid landscape, figure in the writing of the history of the Chinese in California?[11]

The Chinese immigrants "tunneled through mountains, cleared forests, reclaimed swamps, and helped to open up the American West for settlement," Shih-Shan Henry Tsai writes. To this proclamation, the environmentally sensitive reader of the late twentieth century may well respond, "Too bad," rather than "Hurrah." This is not only a matter of putting environmental history into some relationship with ethnic history; it also involves the relationship between different categories of ethnic history. A reader of Tsai's sentence might be equally troubled by the impact that the "opening up" of "the American West for settlement" had on Indian people. The question is an enormous one: what place did Asian immigrants occupy in the broadest picture of the conquest of both nature and natives in North America?[12]

If environmental history has now redefined much of this rearranging of the American landscape as disruption and injury, how do we appraise the Chinese contribution to that disruption? Sandy Lydon's story of the building of a railroad across the Santa Cruz Mountains grounds this abstract question in an unsettling reality. Compared to the Sierras, the mountains of the coastal range between Santa Cruz and San Jose are, in Lydon's words, "small and round, covered with redwoods and Douglas fir. On closer inspection, however, the Santa Cruz Mountains are dark, brooding, mean, little mountains, twisted and gnarled by the faults which run their entire length." To cross these mountains, the South Pacific Coast Railroad required a number of tunnels, including a very long tunnel at the summit, and Chinese labor proved essential for that project.[13]

Begun in late 1877, Wrights Tunnel at the summit took two and a half years to complete. In the excavation, the Chinese crews encountered both coal gas and oil, "creating an extremely volatile and dangerous situation." In February of 1879, oil in the tunnel caught fire, and with the tunnel acting "like a huge cannon," an explosion threw workers against the walls. A dozen wounded Chinese men were brought out of the tunnel, and five of them died. The Chinese for a time refused to work in this dreadful place, but when they returned, the problem with gas and oil continued. In November 1879, in another explosion and fire, twenty-four of the Chinese workers in the tunnel "were killed outright and the remaining were badly burned." An observer described the horror of the scene: "The stench of burning flesh, combined with the escaping gas, is almost overpowering anywhere near the portal. The cabins are filled with mutilated Chinamen, some shrieking with the excruciating pain they are undergoing; others praying in their native tongue to their countrymen to kill them and put an end to their sufferings. . . ."[14]

Completed in April 1880, Wrights Tunnel leaves any simple formulation of the Chinese relationship to the American landscape properly and productively muddled. The violence done to the humans surely outweighs the violence done to the Santa Cruz Mountains. And yet any gesture of celebrating the Chinese for this contribution to the growth of the Santa Cruz economy trivializes their sufferings and deaths. This, like many other cases of the impact of Asian labor on the landscape, is a richer story if we see it as a case study in both the domination of nature and the abuse of labor.

With its grueling details and multiple meanings, the story of the tunnel in the Santa Cruz Mountains puts a spotlight on the meaning of the rediscovery of landscape for scholars today. As a college student in Santa Cruz, I crossed over these mountains dozens of times. The landscape struck me as pleasant, pretty, and really quite untouched and natural. The area had, as far as I knew, the usual stories of American pioneers setting up homesteads, founding small towns, cutting down trees, and building roads and railroads. Crossing the mountains near Wrights Tunnel, it never occurred to me that I was in the neighborhood of tragedy. I never knew that I was passing a site where the price of progress had registered in the smell of burnt human flesh.

In our times, the rediscovery of the landscape hinges on just such recognitions as this one. Never the simple, pristine, virgin place of the European imagination, the landscape is now knee-deep in stories, many of them forgotten and ready for rediscovery. Some of the stories, like the construction of Wrights Tunnel, shake the soul.

* * *

In the late nineteenth and early twentieth centuries, the Japanese immigrant encounter with the American landscape matched some of the patterns of the Chinese encounter. Like Chinese immigrants, the Japanese discovered a landscape of restriction—in prohibitions on alien land ownership, in housing segregation, and in episodes of harassment when they crossed certain boundaries of space and behavior. Like Chinese immigrants, the Japanese created urban neighborhoods, and also played a major role in California rural life, both as migrant workers and as independent farmers. Even though they were pressed hard by necessity and work, many Japanese immigrants recorded, often in poetic form, their response to the landscape. In "Tsugiki, a Grafting: A History of a Japanese Pioneer Woman in Washington State," historian Gail Nomura has written a memorable portrait of Teiko Tomita, a woman who lived first in the Yakima Valley and later in the area near Seattle. Working in the fields or working in garment factories, Tomita crafted her experience into tanka, Japanese poems "consisting of thirty-one syllables arranged in five lines of five, seven, five, seven, and seven syllables successively." Tomita's poems leave a vivid record of the experience of farmwork in the hot Yakima Valley summers:

> As we busily pick beans
> Even the breeze stirring
> The weeds at our feet
> Feels hot

The transformation of "desert and sagebrush into fertile fields of alfalfa, onions, tomatoes, beans, and melons" might be a dramatic one, but Tomita recognized "the tenuous hold on success" that those fields represented:

Sagebrush desert to fertile plain
A transformation, I hear,
But when the windy season comes
There's no transforming the sandstorm

Poems like Tomita's were not the artifacts of a literary elite. As Nomura notes, "one did not have to be highly educated or uniquely
gifted to compose" them. And, as literary scholar Stephen Sumida
points out in an essay on localism in Asian American writing, responses like Tomita's, grounded in intense encounter with a particular place, are by no means the exception. There were, and are, a
number of Japanese American community newspapers publishing
poems, and many of those poems concerned the physical and social
landscape of the immigrants' lives. "For the immigrant in Asian American literature," Sumida writes, "definition of the self and identification of her or his actual culture in America depend critically on
locale."[15]

While some Japanese immigrants moved into the Western interior
and encountered its deserts before 1941, the relocation policy of
World War Two forced the Japanese American residents of California,
Oregon, and Washington into a coerced west-to-east movement.
"Eastward I go only by force; westward I go free": those familiar
words of Henry David Thoreau are usually quoted to reinforce the
standing of the American West as a place of openness and freedom.[16]
The relocation of the Japanese and Japanese Americans gives
Thoreau's cheerful words a different and deeper meaning. Moreover,
the oral histories and autobiographical writing that record the experience of the concentration camps provide a rich source of information on the response to landscape. On the matter of the politics of
landscape representation, it is, however, worth noting the sources that
do *not* exist. At the time of evacuation, "by military orders," John
Armor and Peter Wright note in a collection of camp photographs by
Ansel Adams, " 'Japanese' were forbidden even to own cameras."
While some exceptions were made, most photographs of the camps
were taken by *hakujun* (white) photographers.[17]

The pain of forced relocation dramatized the degree to which the
landscapes of the West Coast had been transformed into home both
for first-generation Japanese immigrants (Issei) and their American-

born children (Nisei). "We had bought a house and my husband had been happy just to smell the trees in the garden up until we were evacuated," Kamechiyo Takahashi remembered. " . . . Even mowing weeds gave us pleasure." As her family prepared to leave its home outside Sacramento, Mary Tsukamoto said, "There were tears everywhere; Grandma couldn't leave her flowers, and Grandpa looked at his grape vineyard. We urged him to get into the car and leave." Tsukamato's family took its last look at "the snow-clad Sierra Nevada mountains that we had loved to see so often." Aesthetic ties to landscape came, of course, in the same package as economic ties: "I had already planted seedlings on fifty acres of land," Masao Hirata remembered, "and all our money was invested in the farm." Picked up by the Federal Bureau of Investigation as a "dangerous enemy alien," Hirata "worried about my wife and my six little children whom I had left behind. I also worried about the land already planted with seedlings. You can't imagine how I felt at that time." Seized by the FBI on the evening of December 7, 1941, and held in Missoula, Montana, Yoshiko Uchida's father wrote frequent letters home, asking "often about his garden."[18]

Immigrants or the children of immigrants, Japanese American families had in the space of a few decades transformed the West Coast from a newly encountered landscape to home. When Yoshiko Uchida stood in the mess hall line at the Tanforan Assembly Center and felt "degraded, humiliated, and overwhelmed by a longing for home," she was not yearning for a far-off, ancestral, foreign home in Japan but for a familiar, domestic, residential landscape in Berkeley, California.[19]

As a midpoint between home and the detention camps in the Western interior, most of the Issei and Nisei went first to a set of temporary camps near the coast. Fairgrounds and racetracks were transformed overnight into assembly centers. Stables designed to hold livestock were instantly redefined as dwelling places for humans; stalls for horses became "apartments" for families. "The government moved the horses out and put us in," Osuke Takizawa said. "The stable stunk awfully." Often only linoleum or a thin coat of paint covered the manure-saturated floorboards. "I understand that we are going to live in the horse stalls" at the Santa Anita Race Track, the diarist Charles Kikuchi wrote. "(Move over Seabiscuit!)"[20]

The guards "treated us as if we were a herd of horses or cows," Tome Takatsuki said. "Suddenly you realized," Mary Tsukamoto said, "that human beings were being put behind fences just like on the farm where we had horses and pigs in corrals." When the veterans of relocation said that they had been treated like animals, this was often more fact than metaphor. Consider the fences that framed the landscape at the camps. Deeply associated with the legends of the "frontier" West, barbed wire was originally designed to set boundaries for and to control the movements of cattle. The assembly centers along the coast and the relocation centers in the interior thus twisted both the use and meaning of barbed wire. Deployed, along with guard towers and armed guards, to remind Japanese Americans that they were prisoners, barbed wire became a symbol with new meanings in regional and national history. It was a symbol that the relocatees read clearly and directly. "The barbed wire fence . . . ," Charles Kikuchi wrote, "reminds us that we are on the inside." Mitsuye Yamada masterfully mocked the rationale of the fence in a poem called "Block 4 Barrack 4 'Apt' C":

> The barbed fence
> protected us
> from wildly twisted
> sagebrush.

"Of one thing I was sure," Monica Sone remembered. "The wire fence was real. I no longer had the right to walk out of it."[21]

If we place the relocatees' encounter with the assembly and relocation centers within the category of the discovery of the American landscape, that field gains new relevance, depth, and tragedy. Forced from their homes, the Issei and Nisei did not know their destination; the experience had all the elements of uncertainty and disorientation associated with journeys of discovery. Deposited at the assembly centers, they could read the terms of their immediate future in the landscape: the stables redefined as barracks made the attack on human dignity a fact of daily life, and the barbed wire and guard towers made the suspension of freedom a visible message in the landscape.

In the summer and fall of 1942, the federal government sent the Issei and Nisei on their coerced west-to-east journey of discovery. In some cases, the trip from assembly center to concentration camp took them past their former homes, with an agonizing nearness to a familiar landscape to which they could not return. Ben Takeshita remembered "asking the MP when we got on the train if when we came to San Mateo [Takeshita's home], we could open the shade and look? And he said no, definitely no. I remember him watching to make sure I didn't open the shades." Yearning for home, Takeshita "consciously count[ed] the bells, you know, the railroad crossings, trying to figure out if this was San Mateo and . . . trying to listen to every little thing that might help me identify it."[22]

The guards' insistence on drawn shades, at night and in areas they judged to be sensitive territory, made for a curiously interrupted encounter with the Western landscape, a journey punctuated by blackouts. Transported from Washington to Idaho, Monica Sone passed through "the Hood River region along the Columbia River"; "we all pressed our faces against the windows and drank in the extravagant beauty," admiring the mountains and "the tumbling blue river." The guards then closed the shades. In the morning, "the scenery had changed drastically overnight." Beauty, in Sone's eyes, had vanished. The land was "parched" into "gray-brown wrinkles out of which jagged boulders erupted like warts. Wisps of moldy-looking, gray-green sagebrush dotted the land."[23]

Even with the opportunity to watch the landscape change in stages, the shift from the comparatively green West Coast to the semiarid or arid interior was an unsettling shock for most of the relocatees. "After the lush greenness of the Willamette Valley" in coastal Oregon, Minoru Yasui's party arrived near Twin Falls, Idaho. When they saw "the sterile, dusty desert which was to be our home 'for the duration,'" many sat on the baggage in the middle of nowhere and wept." To the relocatees, the landscape was a study in vacancy: "No houses were in sight, no trees or anything green—only scrubby sagebrush and an occasional low cactus, and mostly dry, baked earth." Except for two camps in Arkansas, all the sites chosen by the War Relocation Authority were in arid or semiarid places: Minidoka, Idaho; Heart Mountain, Wyoming; Amache (or Granada), Colorado; Topaz, Utah; Poston and Gila River, Arizona; Manzanar and Tule Lake, California. Arid places thus brought a response of distress and disorientation at camps all over the West. At Heart Mountain, Amy Uno Ishii remembered, her party "looked up there at the camp that was to be our home," and "most of the people who got off the train shed tears like you've never seen before," facing a landscape with "no trees, nothing green."[24]

Most of the camps were in areas with frequent winds. In building the camps, the land had been recently bulldozed and the original ground cover destroyed. The conditions were thus perfect for blowing sand and dust. "You couldn't open your mouth," Amy Uno Ishii remembered of the Heart Mountain dust storms, "because all the dust would come in. You could just barely see, and the only way to keep your eyes clean was just to cry and . . . let the tears wash your eyes." At Manzanar, California, on the eastern side of the Sierras, Yoriyuki Kikuchi remembered, "[w]hen the wind blew, it was terrible. . . . [E]verybody resented being put in such a place, especially when they were suffocated in sand." George Fukasawa arrived at Manzanar in the middle of one of the "very common" windstorms. The residents he saw "had goggles on to protect their eyes from the dust, so they looked like a bunch of monsters from another world or something. It was a very eerie feeling to get into a place under conditions like that." At the Utah camp ("Topaz: The Jewel of the Desert," according to the masthead of the official camp newspaper), Mine Okuba and Yoshiko Uchida chose the same metaphor to describe the meeting of people with dust: "everyone looked like pieces of flour-dusted pastry"; "we looked as if we had fallen into a flour barrel." Monica Sone summed up the experience of arrival for many people: "We felt as if we were standing in a gigantic sand-mixing machine as the sixty-mile gale lifted the loose earth up into the sky, obliterating everything." When the Sone family found its assigned room, it offered little refuge: "The window panes rattled madly, and the dust poured in through the cracks like smoke."[25]

At these various dust-choked camps, the American landscape was not laid out serenely, passively awaiting and accepting discovery. On the contrary, it was on the offensive, actively intruding into the eyes of the observer, "dust and sand entering nostrils and ears, lodging between teeth, a horrible feeling." Sweeping could be a full-time job, as the poorly constructed barracks walls put up a weak fight against invasion by the landscape. A poem, written by Toyo Suyemoto Kawakami, captures the sense of domestic space invaded:

The floor is carpeted with dust, wind-borne
Dry alkali, patterned by insect feet.
What peace can such a place as this impart?

The dust, the wind, the sky, the heat, and the cold played enormous roles in shaping people's experience of the camp environment. With the impact on the body, mind, and senses of these uncontrollable forces, one has to abandon the idea of the landscape as scenery, experienced primarily through the eyes, and appraised and judged from a reflective, abstract distance.[26]

In the process of dissolving the division separating visual experience from other encounters of the senses, the case study of the relocation camps also invites a recognition of the shifting boundary between natural and human-made landscapes. The dust and wind were certainly natural, but the bulldozing of the ground made the interaction of wind and dirt far more volatile. Similarly, in the eyes of the internees, the rows and rows of barracks made a perfect match in desolation and bleakness to the desert landscape. Walking in the Manzanar camp, Jeanne Wakatsuki Houston saw a view composed of both natural elements and the products of human action: "I would hike past row upon row of black barracks, watching mountains waver through that desert heat." The built landscape could be as disorienting as the geological landscape; at Topaz, for instance, "all the blocks looked alike." Long "after we settled in," Toyo Suyemoto Kawakami remembered, "camp residents would occasionally lose their sense of direction at night and wander into a barracks not their own, much to their embarrassment and that of the occupants." "All residential blocks looked alike," Mine Okubo put it; "people were lost all the time."[27]

Nature and the War Relocation Authority seemed to have joined forces to construct landscapes designed to break the spirits of the prisoners. In these bleak circumstances, the determination of the Issei and Nisei to improve their settings was and is genuinely astonishing. In our times, it has become a set piece to say that people whom we once thought of simply as victims did, in fact, act to shape their own worlds. The efforts of the Issei and Nisei to reshape their landscapes gives that now familiar phrase "acted to shape their own worlds" fresh and vivid meaning.

At the assembly centers and the concentration camps, the residents took the first opportunity to plant gardens of flowers and vegetables. At Manzanar, Jeanne Wakatsuki Houston noted, "[g]ardens had sprung up everywhere, in the firebreaks, between the rows of barracks—rock gardens, vegetable gardens, cactus and flower gardens." At the Tanforan Assembly Center, Yoshiko Uchida wrote, the residents "made good use of the manure-rich soil, cultivating flowers for pleasure and vegetables to supplement their camp diet." Besides individual gardens, the camps also had farms producing many of the vegetables the residents consumed.[28]

Living under conditions at once infuriating, disorienting, and demoralizing, many of the residents nonetheless pitched into the project of discovering and realizing the potential of these grim landscapes. At Topaz, one of the most discouraging desert sites in the country, "[d]espite reports that the alkaline soil was not good for agriculture purposes, in the spring practically everyone set up a victory garden." Watering these gardens was no easy matter. "In the evening," Mine Okuba remarked, "there was the usual bucket brigade from the laundry buildings to the garden."[29]

The gardens were testimony to the powerful work ethic of the Issei and Nisei. They were also, in part, a response to necessity. The food in the mess halls was often unappealing, and sometimes even dangerous; many residents experienced frequent stomach problems from spoiled food. Used to a diet rich in vegetables, the Issei and Nisei found gardening and farming a route to better health. Indeed, this could be a matter of life and death. Mabel Ota's father, a diabetic, "had always raised all kinds of vegetables in the backyard, fresh vegetables," Ota said, "because they were so essential to his diet." Placed at the Gila River camp, he endured a "terrible" diet; "the food," Ota was sure, "was related to my father's death."[30]

The pressures of the work ethic and the demands of health do not, however, explain the gardens. Powerful aesthetic and spiritual motivations, derived directly from Japanese culture, were also at work. At the Tanforan Assembly Center, "[e]veryone knew," Okuba noted, "the camp was not a permanent one." Would the gardeners still be there when the flowers bloomed and the vegetables became ripe? The harvest was clearly not the only point of these gardens. Leaving the Fresno assembly center, Mary Tsukamoto noted that "the whole camp was transformed," with "so many beautiful flowers and vegetables, so lush and green." "Who but Nihonjins (Japanese)," she asked, "would leave a place like that in beauty?"[31]

At Tanforan, "a group of landscape architects decided to build a lake to beautify the camp." Transformed "from a mere wet spot," the site became "a miniature aquatic park, complete with bridge, promenade, and islands." At Manzanar, gardeners "built a small park, with mossy nooks, ponds, waterfalls and curved wooden bridges." Walking in that park, Jeanne Wakatsuki Houston remembered, "[y]ou could face away from the barracks, look past a tiny rapids toward the darkening mountains, and for a while not be a prisoner at all."[32]

A distinctively creative response to the setting went beyond the planting of gardens. At the Amache camp in Colorado, one woman arrived in the midst of the usual sandstorm. Mrs. Ninomiya remembered a traditional art using sand, "the making of miniature landscapes, or *bon-kei.*" Under her guidance, Amache became a center in the creation of remarkable landscapes and seascapes, sculpted in small trays. Residents at various camps hunted *kobu,* "a curious natural wood growth," found, selected, and then hand-rubbed into an often stunning sculpture. At the Minidoka camp in Idaho, the residents adapted traditional flower arranging to sagebrush, the dominant plant in the area. Indeed, "special gardens" of sagebrush "were developed, largely by thinning, and clumps of it were trimmed as decorative features of the landscape." In examples like these, distinctive cultural responses to landscape were at work. The Issei and Nisei found beauty and coaxed it into visibility, in ways seldom seen in Anglo-American responses to arid lands.[33]

And yet, in other ways, Issei and Nisei seemed to match the Anglo-American notion of a desert as an unfortunate landscape in need of major reconstruction by human enterprise. In Idaho, the camp newspaper recorded a familiar determination to master an uncooperative landscape. We can, the Minidoka *Irrigator* said, "have but one resolve; to apply our combined energies to the grim task of conquering the elements and converting a wasteland into an inhabitable community." The familiarity of the phrasing here was fully intended: "Our great adventure is a repetition of the frontier struggle of pioneers against the land and its elements." It is, of course, important to note that the camp newspapers were supervised and sometimes censored by the War Relocation Authority staff. When the *Irrigator* proclaimed the camp's compatibility with white American expansion or when the newspaper at Amache adopted the name the *Pioneer,* one does not know exactly whose ideology is revealed.[34]

A decade ago, writing a book on attitudes toward the Western deserts, I adopted the notion that a distaste for dry places and an urge to remake deserts into gardens were distinctive, perhaps even unique, cultural properties of Anglo-Americans. It was thus a useful surprise for me to find such a similarity of response in the Issei and Nisei. As American citizens and natives, of course, many of the Nisei had adopted American points of view on the use of nature. They had, moreover, grown up with comparatively green settings, irrigated farms or well-watered urban yards. "Most of us were born in this country," Jeanne Wakatsuki Houston reminds us; "we had no other models." Before World War Two, a number of Japanese immigrants had farmed in places like California's Imperial Valley and Washington's Yakima Valley; the camps were not their first encounter with the challenges facing agriculture in arid lands.[35]

And yet the proposition—that some of the Nisei had picked up the Anglo-American ideology of lands conquered by pioneers and deserts made to bloom—only partially explains the camp residents' response to aridity. Like other Asian immigrants, the Issei had their own reasons to be unsettled by deserts and to take up the project of making the landscape green. Most Asian immigrants came from humid places. The prefectures of southern Japan, the place of origin for most immigrants, had an annual rainfall of at least forty inches a year and as much as eighty inches a year. The rainfall for much of southern China, the place of origin for most nineteenth-century immigrants, was close to eighty inches a year. Asian immigrants did not need to borrow their discomfort with arid lands from Anglo-Americans; they had their own reasons to lament the absence of trees, to flinch at the rarity of the color green, to size up the prospects for manipulating the water supply, and to throw themselves into the enterprise of coaxing at least a small part of the desert into becoming a garden.

The "Jeffersonian agrarian dream" is a stock item in the conceptual tool chest of landscape studies. The gardens in the concentration camps, as well as the earlier Chinese and Japanese vegetable gardens and farms throughout California, offered a powerful statement that the term "agrarian dream" could carry the adjectives "Chinese" and "Japanese," as well as "Jeffersonian." Originating in a very different set of historical and cultural circumstances, the Chinese agrarian dream and the Japanese agrarian dream joined up with the American version in bringing an ideal of order and productivity to bear on the "wild" American landscape. But those dreams were tested under very different conditions. Federal legislation gave official support to the American agrarian dream, while the Chinese and Japanese versions had to persist in spite of racial harassment, official obstacles to land ownership, and, for the Japanese, an involuntary relocation.[36]

To recognize the Japanese and Chinese agrarian dreams is not, of course, to claim an essentially agrarian character for these populations. As Sucheng Chan reminds us, "Though the Chinese who came to California [in the nineteenth century] were peasants, they had not come to farm; they took up cultivation because they needed to feed themselves" and because they "discovered . . . that farming could often provide a more steady income than mining for gold." Many Issei and Nisei people saw farming and gardening as, at best, a temporary expedient. "A countless number of times," Akemi Kikumura's mother remembered of her husband, "he wanted to throw away the pruning shears and study." "My occupation is now a gardener," Iwato Itow told an interviewer, "and working the soil is the one thing I wanted to get away from." To the same degree as Anglo-American society, Asian American society was divided into rural and urban groupings, with very different definitions of familiar landscapes characterizing those two groups. When the older residents of a Japanese American farming community in Del Ray, California, remark that they "were *inaka* (country) . . . We enjoyed living out," they remind us that rural consciousness and urban consciousness both cut across ethnic boundaries and offer a not-always-perceived common ground to people who, whatever their national origin, see themselves as "country" or "city" people.[37]

The politics of Asian American agrarianism are complicated in ways that go beyond the problem of an essentialist cultural character. To be rural and to be Asian American can, in the context of an industrializing and urban nation, be a double dose of restricted power and opportunity. The image of the simple, docile, close-to-the-earth farmer can cross cultural boundaries here. Consider the remark of Bess Tuck, "librarian and local historian" of Granada, the Colorado town next to the Amache camp: "The Japanese were really very good about the whole thing [coerced relocation]. They took immediately to farming the camp and did quite a bit of landscaping." Interpreting the gardens from the outside, Bess Tuck and I take opposite paths: she seems to see a symbol of compliance where I see a symbol of defiance, a visible statement of unbroken will. But the topic remains an unsettling one. It is, for instance, a peculiar experience to examine Allen Eaton's book, *Beyond Barbed Wire: The Arts of the Japanese in Our*

War Relocation Camps (1953). The descriptions and photographs of gardens, *kobu,* miniature landscapes, and sculpted sagebrush are stirring and inspirational; the first pages of the book are not. In the foreword, Eleanor Roosevelt praises "the remarkably fine spirit" of "our Japanese Americans," shown in "the gardens—which I can testify were truly beautiful even in camps where the desert surrounded them." Eaton's book, Roosevelt writes, "shows how well the War Relocation Authority did its work, one of the achievements of government administration of which every American citizen can be proud." Allen Eaton concurs, noting his intention "to share with the reader a part of the distinguished record of the War Relocation Authority . . . ; it is one of the finest achievements in American war- and peacetime government administration." By this point, one's response to the gardens, art, sculpture, and crafts of the prisoners is thoroughly muddled: if one admires the gardens, is one inadvertently joining Roosevelt and Eaton in a round of applause for the institution that provided the challenges for the gardeners to meet?[38]

Precisely because of the interpretive complications they present, the camp gardens are an important chapter in the study of the application of agrarian ideals to the landscape. On a number of counts, the study of attitudes and behavior toward the American landscape is deepened and enriched by attention to Asian American history. The friction created when new arrivals arrive with high expectations and confront less-than-ideal places, the appraisal of and behavior toward arid lands, the variations in agrarian dreams, the split in perception and power between rural and urban populations, the necessity for leisure and a comfortable margin of subsistence in the aesthetic appreciation of landscape, the sense among rural Americans that they are losing ground, unable to recruit children to stay on the farms—on these counts and many others, the similarities and differences between Anglo-American and Asian American experiences, not to mention Indian, Mexican American, and African American experiences, present an open range of scholarly opportunity. In all these cases, the encounter with landscape was also a complex and often conflict-ridden encounter with other groups of people. Refought, with the historian's mind serving now as the place of contest, these struggles for the right to shape and to interpret the American landscape give a new life to what was, not long ago, a set and routinized scholarly subject.

"We knew America was huge, but we didn't know it was this

huge," Amy Uno Ishii remembered of her trip to Heart Mountain, Wyoming.[39] Her perception of vast space matches the response of many Euro-Americans to the landscapes of this continent. But her destination—a clump of barracks tightly bounded by barbed wire—reminds us that many racial and ethnic minorities, as well as working class whites, discovered a landscape of restriction, even in the midst of the widest and most open spaces. Under those circumstances, the discovery of possibilities had to alternate with the discovery of injustice and inequity, as indeed it does in the scholarly rediscovery of this issue.

Starting from very different points on the planet's surface, traveling west and traveling east, Anglo-Americans and Asian Americans met and meet in the American landscape. In the eighteenth century, the area along the upper Missouri River was a center of Plains Indian life, as the Mandans planted gardens along the river bottom and as the Lakota moved in from the east. In 1804, in the archetypal Anglo-American voyage of westward discovery, Lewis and Clark camped near a site that would later become the town of Bismarck and the capital of North Dakota. Seventy years after Lewis and Clark's visit, George Armstrong Custer's wife Elizabeth spent the anxious summer of 1876 near Bismarck, at Fort Abraham Lincoln, where she received the news of her husband's death. Sixty-five years later, when the FBI made its first sweeps through the Japanese communities on the West Coast, many of the "dangerous enemy aliens" were separated from their families, taken to North Dakota, and held at Fort Lincoln, now relocated on the other side of the river.

Far from being the middle of nowhere, central North Dakota is now layered with experiences and perceptions, anticipation and anxiety, arrivals and departures. With this layering of history, the area around Bismarck has become a kind of common ground, between the westward-moving participants in conquest and the eastward-moving participants in a coerced relocation, in which both groups appear as unlikely intruders into the land of the Mandan and the Lakota.

In a similar pattern, the Owens Valley in interior California was first the home of the Paiute Indian people. In the 1860s, it was colonized by white farmers and ranchers. Those residents were in turn displaced in a bureaucratic conquest, as the city of Los Angeles and the Bureau of Reclamation acquired land and water rights in the valley and drained its water. When Los Angeles took the water, the community of Manzanar in the Owens Valley was abandoned, leaving the land available for use as a relocation camp in World War Two. Here, too, the layering of experiences creates a site shaped by cycles of conquest and heavily invested with human memory. And yet we have usually fragmented the history of landscapes like this one, telling the story of the Paiutes and their conquest, the white colonization of the valley, the aesthetic responses of writers like Mary Austin, the maneuverings of the water developers, and the creation of the Manzanar concentration camp in very separate volumes.[40]

In 1943, the Chinese anthropologist and sociologist Fei Xiaotong toured the United States and compared what he saw with his childhood in China. In his home, "there were more places for ghosts than for people." Americans lived in another world entirely. "How," he asked, in the United States, "could ghosts gain a foothold . . . ? People move about like the tide, unable to form permanent ties with places." Fei Xiaotong could not, he said, "get used to people today who know only the present moment." Indeed, he confessed to feeling "a little sorry for people raised in a world without ghosts."[41]

In 1992, we can no longer think of the United States as "a world without ghosts." The landscapes of North America are heavily invested with human memories, and the tangle of those memories provided both common and contested ground for the people of various origins whose descendants now populate this nation. Life "melds past, present, and future" into one "multi-layered scene, a three-dimensional body," Fei Xiaotong wrote. "This is what ghosts are."[42] This "multi-layered scene" is what the American landscape now presents for our exploration. That enterprise requires historians to engage in a constant process of disorientation and reorientation, taking part in both the pleasures, the discomforts, and the conflicts of discovery.

III-C

The Gold Rush
and the Shaping
of the American West

The observing of centennials and sesquicentennials might seem a mysterious ritual if it were not such a familiar one. When a number of years has passed since an event occurred, and when the years add up to a multiple of fifty (or ten or twenty-five), then it is time to pause and pay attention to that event; in any other year, the event will have to look out for itself and compete for attention in the general marketplace. The ethnohistorian Greg Dening has coined the phrase "metric moments" for this phenomenon.

Given the array of consequential events taking place in the 1840s and 1890s, Western America has recently been a hotbed for metric memory. Observed with museum exhibits, conferences, reenactments, publications, and newspaper stories, the 150th anniversary of the discovery of gold in California presented a prime opportunity to reflect on the ties between past and present. After the Gold Rush, mining spread through space into the Western interior and through time into the present. But what exactly is the kinship between the miners of the California Gold Rush and the people who are working—and working with great vigor—in gold mining in the American West today? Why does Sutter's Mill have such widespread name recognition, while the phrase "Carlin Trend" leaves nearly everybody looking blank?

By many measures, the California Gold Rush was the most important event in the history of the American West. The assessment offered in *The Legacy of Conquest* still makes sense to me: "Rather than 'settling' the region, mining rushes picked up the American West and gave it a good shaking—and the vibrations have not stopped yet."[1] Let us review the nature of this shaking, as it spread from California throughout the West; as testimony to the possibilities of continued mental vigor into middle age, it is a pleasure to note that most of these observations did not appear in *Legacy*.[2]

First and in many ways most important, mining rushes created the maximum degree of friction with Indians and set in motion the process that would leave them displaced, removed, and relocated. It is hard to imagine a system that could create more in the way of troubles for Indians: the discovery of precious metals and the movement to exploit them followed mandates that paid no attention to the prior negotiation of Indian treaties and land cessions. Mining rushes flung white Americans around the Western landscape, into Indian terrain, in a way that left few areas untouched, and also left few reasons in the minds of the prospectors and miners as to why they should restrain themselves and their ambitions until a better arrangement could be made with the natives. This is not to say that the expansion of farming or ranching had benign and beneficial effects on natives, but it is to say that mining escalated and emphasized the qualities of haste and bitterness in the conquest.

Second, mining, throughout the West as in California, rested on the white American talent for claiming legitimacy. White Americans in mining rushes were clearly, unmistakably newcomers themselves. The recentness of their own arrival did not cause them a moment's hesitation when it came to claiming the status of the legitimate occupants, the people who had the right to claim and use the local resources and to exclude and brand as illegitimate and undeserving people of other nationalities.

Third, mining, throughout the West, meant a rapidly urbanized kind of settlement, with concentrated populations, in quite a contrast to the more-dispersed, rural pattern of settlement in farming and ranching. Given the fact the West has turned out to be the most-urbanized region, the mining pattern of settlement turned out to be the shaping pattern for the regional future.

Fourth, and very closely tied to point three, following on the California pattern, mining was quite a disheartening chapter in the history of physical health in the West. Concentrated populations in thrown-together, instant towns meant something of a horror in public health and sanitation. At a consultants' meeting for the Oakland Museum's major exhibit on the Gold Rush, I proposed that the museum explore a new frontier in exhibition techniques, by including a little booth, into which exhibit visitors could step and *smell* the smells of a mining camp—sewage, rotting food, and a collection of people not overly committed to bathing. All through the West, mining, unhappy sanitation, and poor health coincided. Mining, in other words, presents a conspicuous contrast to an otherwise well-established pattern in the perception of the West: a place where ailing people went to recover and regain their health. From a combination of changed diet and poor sanitation, many Gold Rushers had an experience quite opposite to that ideal of the West as a healthy place that restores and reinvigorates the ailing; they went West and got sick, miserably and sometimes fatally.

Fifth, following on the precedent of the Gold Rush, participants in mining rushes elsewhere in the West were rarely in a position to provide their own food. For all their legendary association with hardy independence, these communities were some of the most dependent human communities imaginable, relying on someone else to feed them.

Sixth, and springing from point five, mining both provided a market for farmers and threatened the working conditions of farmers. The demand for food, in other words, presented such a hearty market that others took up farming and ranching in the area. But here is the paradox: the earliest complaints about the environmental effects of mining came from farmers, who found that hydraulic mining, especially, made a mess of their land and water.

Seventh, in many parts of the West, as in California, mining set up the framework by which Americans would allocate, distribute, litigate over, and squabble about water. This is really quite striking, given that so much of Western water use would end up concentrated in agriculture. And yet prior appropriation ("first in time, first in right") grew out of mining and set the terms for much of the custom and law governing the ownership of Western water.

Eighth, mining settlements, at least in their early phases, had an unusual gender demography: the much-cited numerical dominance of males, as well as the curiously concentrated cultural performance of masculinity that characterized life and social relations in Western mining towns. Paradoxically, this preponderance of males dramatized the significance of women, whether in the various declarations of faith that respectable white women were the necessary pillars and supports for civilized order or in the income to be made off the fact that many white men hated to do their own laundry (should this be in the past tense?) or even their own cooking.

Ninth is nostalgia, that extraordinary alchemy of memory. Many, many participants in the Gold Rush and in later Western mining rushes had, in immediate terms, quite miserable experiences. They suffered from regular old physical sickness and, maybe more depleting, from draining and debilitating homesickness. They worked hard and, oftentimes, ended up with nothing to show in the way of a reward for that labor. They felt quite desperate loneliness as they tried to forge some sort of ties with the collection of strangers in whose company they had landed. Very frequently, they cursed the various sources—newspapers, guidebooks, and rumors—that had worked their expectations up to such heights and left them so bitterly disappointed. And then, after all that endurance, sorrow, and disillusionment, they went home and began telling anyone who would listen what a glorious time they had in the West.

Nostalgia is a remarkably powerful force in the human mind, at work in every sphere of our lives (I myself once wrote an essay conveying nostalgia for graduate school). And yet participation in mining rushes registers right up there with wartime combat, in terms of miserable experiences that come, really quite rapidly, to glow in memory with a charm they never had in their immediacy. History presents few better opportunities to observe and appraise the workings of nostalgia than in the memories generated out of the California Gold Rush and other Western mineral rushes.

And yet there is this puzzle: for all the floods and tides of nostalgia poured forth by veterans of Western mining rushes, the cowboy still won. In the competition for legendary Westerner—star of dime novels, Hollywood films, TV shows, and Marlboro commercials—the prospector and the miner never got out of the starting gate. Maybe there is an obvious explanation for this puzzle. Maybe it vindicates the theory that it was not, in fact, the *cowboy* that the American public found so profoundly attractive and appealing. Maybe it was actually the *horse,* who usually looks, on screen, gorgeous and elementally charged with energy, especially when galloping, in a way that few humans of any occupation or profession can match. The prospector's burdened burro is a pathetic competitor for a cowboy's gloriously galloping horse, and maybe that is where mystery resolves itself. But it still seems peculiar: all those participants invested all that nostalgia in mining, and yet the novelists and the filmmakers generally spurned the miner and lined up to celebrate the cowboy.

Tenth is the factor of abandonment, by which Western mining, following the California model, involved an extraordinary degree of transience and outright, undisguised indifference to the fate of the place undergoing the mining. There is much talk, in the interior West today, about substainability, about how we can build sustainable economies and sustainable societies. Much of the time, it is hard to figure out what, exactly, people mean by this. When I am particularly confused by these exhortations to sustainable lifestyles, often delivered to me by people who have just driven up in their sports utility vehicles, I say to myself, "I'm not entirely sure what they mean, but I *think* they mean the opposite of mining."

The dimensions of abandonment of old mines test the imagination. The *New York Times* has said that there are, in the West, "more than 500,000 abandoned mines," and this may be one of the most doubtful statistics ever to appear in that distinguished newspaper, since there has never been anything like an inventory and accurate counting of these sites, and 500,000 may, in fact, be a significant underestimate.[3] While their operators moved on and forgot these mines, many of them are getting attention today; they not only make for precarious terrain, many of them also leak acid and heavy metals.

While the interior West was very much shaped by these ten California Gold Rush precedents, there were also some significant differences, which can be summed up in two points. First, precious metal ores in the interior, whether gold or silver, usually were more complicated than they had been in California, and that, in turn, meant that the placer phase, in which men could come upon individually accessible windfalls, harvestable with one person's labor, was usually very brief if it happened at all. Thus the emergence of mining as an industrial, capital-intensive, wage-labor-employing endeavor was even more rapid in the interior than it had been in California. And second, precious metal ores in the interior had a way of appearing in territory that was much rougher, both in landforms and in climate, than the California foothills.

Mining shook California and shook the interior West, but how profound was the social impact of that shaking? Consider the moral to the story of Walter Colton's disrupted breakfast.

Walter Colton was the alcalde of the town of Monterey at the time of the discovery of gold. When the word of the gold discovery got to Monterey in the summer of 1848, a lot of the residents departed for the foothills. Among those departing were a number of people who had worked as domestic servants. "The gold fever has reached every servant in Monterey," Colton wrote. "None are to be trusted in their engagement beyond a week; and as for compulsion, it is like attempting to drive fish into a net with the ocean before them."[4]

The departure of the servants for the gold fields soon came to affect the matter of breakfast. Two military officers shared in this dilemma with Colton: Colonel Richard Mason, the military governor of California, and the commander of a navy vessel in port at the time. These three elite gentlemen found, as Colton said, that "our servants have run, one after another, until we are almost in despair." In case we have drifted too far away from the issue of racial subordination in the Gold Rush, it is important to quote Colton's next line about departing servants:

> Even Sambo who we thought would stick by us from laziness, if no other cause, ran last night; and this morning, . . . we had to take to the kitchen, and cook our own breakfast. A general of the United States Army; the commander of a man of war, and the Alcalde of Monterey, in a smoking kitchen, grinding coffee, toasting a herring, and peeling onions! These gold mines are going to upset all the domestic arrangements of society, turning the head to the tail, and the tail to the head. . . . The gold mines have upset all social and domestic arrangements in Monterey; the master has become his own servant, and the servant his own lord.[5]

This is a very classic and memorable statement of the Gold Rush's disruption of the social order, which seems to harmonize with my statement about the shaking given the West by mining. But the moral of the story of Walter Colton's disrupted breakfast now seems to me to be something of the opposite of a seriously shaken social hierarchy. The surprise here is how rapidly the order restored itself, how rapidly hierarchy got back in charge. The interlude of "economic democracy," to use Malcolm Rohrbough's phrase, seems very brief, very passing, and the rapidity by which conventional arrangements of power and privilege reconstituted themselves seems to be the story that emerges for the long haul.[6] So, yes, the West received a shaking from mining, but the hierarchy and distribution of privilege in American society stopped the shaking pretty fast.

And that brings me to the really quite astonishing journey of Western mining from 1848 to 1998. In the mid-1980s, it looked like precious metal mining in the American West was over and done with. The high-grade deposits had been found and worked over; American mining corporations were much more interested in prospecting overseas. *Business Week,* in 1984, published an article called "The Death of Mining," and in 1986, the Western historian Michael Malone published an article called "The Collapse of Western Metal Mining: An Historical Epitaph." He acknowledged that mining had gone through many booms and busts, but "this time," Malone said, "there seems no possibility that metal mining can recover to anything like its former status in the region."[7]

Fortune-tellers and futurists have never had to fear much in the way of competition from historians. I suspect that what happened here, when we all thought that mining had gone into its final slump, was that we were operating with a kind of unimaginative, technologically simplified notion of the idea of depletion. Eventually, we were all inclined to think, if people just kept mining, they would mine out the resource. That would be that.

Well, guess again.

In the mid-1980s, various authorities announced the end of precious metal mining in the West. Right after they announced this, Western gold mining started off on a boom which has equaled the extraordinary productivity of the early 1850s in California. Right after we got these various epitaphs and obituaries for Western gold mining, the industry launched what the *New York Times* called "a new gold boom, the biggest in American history." The Carlin Trend, the *Times* said, is the "most important gold discovery outside South

Africa this century," "the largest known deposit of gold in North America." In terms of production, *High Country News* has called it "the largest gold rush in American history," a gold boom that matches or even "dwarfs any in the history of the West."[8]

The secret, of course, turned out to be low-grade ore—ore with microscopic gold, ore that never causes anyone to exclaim "Eureka!" because no one can see it is there. This is gold that would be perfectly useless if all we had was the methods of the nineteenth century or, for that matter, the methods of much of the twentieth century. The current gold boom relies on the process of open-pit mining, by which a tremendous amount of rock gets dug up and crushed, and the process of cyanide heap leaching, by which a cyanide solution gets poured over the pounded-up ore, and the cyanide captures the gold and positions it where humans can recover it.

The center of this new gold boom has been Nevada, and especially the area around Elko, the forty-mile stretch called the Carlin Trend. But the enthusiasm for microscopic gold, secured by the use of cyanide leaching, has hit lots and lots of places in the interior West, so that the last decade has seen a proliferation of these open pits. An open-pit mine is a hard thing to describe in words. On site, the scale shakes the mind. As a poor substitute, consider the dimensions of American Barrick's Goldstrike mine near Elko: the pit, in 1992, was 2 miles long, 3/4 mile wide, and 1800 feet deep. A reporter taking a plane flight over the mines outside Elko struggled for words and finally could only say, "I am dumbfounded by the scale."[9]

For a few weeks, I asked all sorts of people if they could identify the term "Carlin Trend." While I got a few guesses about the possible influence of George Carlin, I earned mostly blank stares. This has left me with a great curiosity about the workings of public attention. Here we have a gold rush which dwarfs any mining activity in the preceding century, and it has earned, from the public, a great yawn.

Might it be that the 1849 California Gold Rush set a standard for excitement and compelling human drama by which the 1990s gold rush is just unmistakably, unredeemably dull? Is this simply a restatement of a historical pattern by which mining catches the public's attention when it is a small-scale, individualistic operation and loses its attention as it becomes big and capitalized? Is there some sort of governing principle by which entertaining stories get choked out by the increase in scale of an industry? The contrast still seems to me worth a moment's contemplation. In the Gold Rush 150 years ago, record keeping itself underwent an extraordinary boom, with (from the historian's perspective) a glorious burst in the production of diaries, journals, letters, and personal narratives. But if the Carlin Trend, for all its wealth, has generated even one written autobiography or personal narrative, it has been very privately published.

The characters of the California Gold Rush look particularly bright and amusing when placed in contrast to the little-known figures of the 1990s gold rush. Even people who try to keep up with the headlines might struggle to place the name Peter Munk, the Canadian capitalist who heads the gold-mining company American Barrick Resources Corporation (it is named *American* Barrick, though it is a Canadian company). American Barrick is the operator of the astonishingly productive Goldstrike Mine in the Carlin Trend I described above. One of the remarkable contrasts between Western mining in the past and Western mining today involves the American attitude toward foreign enterprise. In the nineteenth century, American hostility toward the presence of miners from France, Australia, Mexico, Chile, and China was chronic and persistent. In the late twentieth century, many of the companies making the profits are owned by Canadians or Europeans, and yet agitation over this flow of wealth out of the United States has been muted, even silent.

If Peter Munk, CEO of American Barrick, wrote his personal narrative, I suspect that people interested in the history of mining would read it more out of obligation than interest. Before he devoted some of his attention to gold, Munk headed a Canadian company that made stereos, and then he formed what became the biggest hotel chain in the Pacific Basin. Most recently, he has been at work on a business-park development in Germany. If we were interested in his work in mining, we would want to use the index of Munk's autobiography pretty strenuously, sparing ourselves the sections on stereos, hotels, and business parks. Even when we came upon the sections on mining, it would not be a surprise if, after a page or two of Peter Munk's personal adventures in finance, we had found ourselves thirsting, once again, for the earthy and grounded company of Alonzo Delano, William Swain, Sarah Royce, and other memorable record keepers of the 1849 Gold Rush. Peter Munk is a fellow who says things like this: gold "is merely a commodity, like cotton or wool."[10] While this proposition is technically true, it is not an observation that conveys much of the passion and excitement we have sometimes seen directed toward gold and its discovery.

There is *one* topic that understandably brings out strong passion in Peter Munk. In the words of his profiler in the *New York Times,* Munk is "a fervent exponent of the philosophy that executive rewards be linked to company performance."[11] With the profitability of his company American Barrick, if Mr. Munk did not become fervent and passionate on *this* subject, it would be important to start checking his pulse.

Perhaps the scarcity of public attention paid to the gold rush of the 1990s is easy enough to explain. And it may be that the most exuberant phase of this mining boom is already winding down, given the fact that gold prices have gone into quite a slump. Still, there is one element of the current gold boom that seems sufficient to awaken a little of our interest, and this is the remarkable way in which the term "reclamation" figures in everyone's discussion. As one mining professional told me recently, everyone in the business realizes that it is now very unlikely that they will get to mine if the local community opposes them. Moreover, in the last few years, companies have been required to post a bond to cover (theoretically, at least) the costs of reclamation if they should go bankrupt and not be around, as a company, at the time of the cleanup. Moreover, a company buying an old mining site, for purposes of remining the tailings or waste rock, now assumes liability for the cleanup of the old mine as well.

All of this attention to reclamation and restoration is quite a break from the patterns of the past. And yet, as we track the journey of Western mining through time and through memory, in other ways the patterns of the past seem quite persistent. As one illustration of the state of affairs in 1998, the *Denver Post* carried an Associated Press story with an unconvincing headline: "California Ready to Mark Anniversary of Gold Rush."[12] I am not exactly sure how you could tell if a group of people had reached, certifiably, a state of readiness to mark an anniversary. But the Associated Press story itself left me pretty well convinced that, whatever defines that state of readiness, California is not there yet.

The discovery of gold in 1848, the reporter told us, "changed California from a pastoral wilderness into the innovative, materialist state of today." California before the discovery, the reporter says further, "had the sleepy flavor of its agriculture-oriented Californios settlers." In reading a line like that, one has to be struck by the proposition that academic historians are getting nowhere when it comes to communications with the public. Historians have been trying hard to counter the notion of California in January 1848 as a pastoral wilderness, a place without history, a place with, at best, insignificant human presence, a place where both nature and people slumbered their time away. Seeing that picture appear in a nationally broadcast, recent story tells us something about just how effective Western historians have been in our efforts to influence public thinking about Western history.

In another, more important way, this story proved useful because it brought to our attention an aspect of the ways in which Americans in 1998 were living with and interpreting the history of mining in the American West. First, remind yourself that one of the central campaigns in Western environmental affairs these days is the effort to cope with abandoned mines, to address the leakage of water freighted with acid and heavy metals from old mines, and to explore the concept of reclamation of mined areas with revegetation, sometimes even the backfilling of old pits. While these efforts are limited and incomplete, they are nonetheless striking, demonstrating a surprisingly well-rooted societal commitment to repair the damage and restore the disrupted sites of mining in the past.

Here is what Robert Elsner, then executive director of California's sesquicentennial planning committee, said to the Associated Press reporter: "We're not going into denial that Native Americans who had lived here for hundreds of years and Mexicans and Chinese and all the others were abused," he said. But then he added: "We're not going to wring our hands. We're going to acknowledge that they were not treated well and they have a part of Gold Rush history. We're saying, 'Commemorate the past; celebrate the future.' "[13]

I am in Mr. Elsner's debt for that remark. Reading it, we have to realize that "wringing our hands"—and, in fact, "wringing our federal and corporate budgets"—is one way of describing the activity that we are pursuing, in response to the environmental damage done by Western mining. This goes beyond rhetorical expressions of concern to efforts to designate Superfund sites, plug acid drainage, remove or cap waste rock and tailings freighted with dangerous heavy metals, and generally clean up the messes made in the past, often with the commitment of substantial funding.

If there is any comparable movement afoot to assess, rehabilitate, restore, reclaim, and repair the damage done to human beings by the various mining rushes in the West, I have yet to hear of it. By the "damage done to human beings" I mean a number of things: the tremendous displacement and relocation of Indian people because of mineral discoveries; the seizure of the property of and the exclusion from the mines of Mexicans or Chinese; and the multiple injuries done to the limbs, lungs, and lives of miners who did the work that provided others with their fortunes. It would seem to me that a space alien or a Rip Van Winkle sort who looked at the United States on this sesquicentennial would have to be *very* struck by the fact that attention and money are directed to the repair of injured nature, while only a cursory acknowledgment of past losses is directed at the injuries done to humans, with a "what's done is done" sort of tone.

Maybe there is an easy way of explaining this paradox. I suppose one could say that the sites of abandoned mines are still *in place,* there to be reckoned with, while the *people* of the past have died and been replaced by descendants who may or may not have a direct involvement in the events of a previous century. Still, it is very striking to see our heightened sensitivities toward nature's misfortunes developing in such an opposite direction from our indifference toward the misfortunes of human beings.

To what degree do attitudes from the Gold Rush continue to shape the American West today? To a very high degree, I used to say, when I was the Continuity Kid, driven by a passion for asserting the ties that connected the nineteenth-century West and the twentieth-century West and denying that supposed watershed of the end of the frontier. In writing *The Legacy of Conquest,* I was wholeheartedly asserting the continuity and persistence of attitudes. "Mining," *Legacy* says, "set a mood that has never disappeared from the West: the attitude of extractive industry—get in, get rich, get out."[14]

Do I buy that anymore? While the question of the persistence of attitudes generated by the Gold Rush is interesting enough, what seems, now, considerably more consequential is the fact that mining itself—the *activity,* not just the attitude—persists on such an enormous scale today. Just as important, it seems to me now that the relationship—really the *kinship*—that we sometimes claim with our historical predecessors and ancestors is much more a matter of strategy and choice than it is a matter of direct and actual inheritance. The way that the Gold Rush's images get invoked to support and defend federal mining law provides one of the world's best examples of this. The nostalgic, romanticized figure of the small miner, the individualistic prospector exercising the right of free access to gold that was established in California, has been put to work on behalf of the power and profits of enormous, international corporations.

We have now a situation in which the resources of the United States's public lands are being mined by companies that are, many of them, foreign corporations—Canadian, northern European, and South African. Thanks to the 1872 Mining Law, these companies do not contribute revenue to the United States Treasury in return for the minerals taken from the public lands. Moreover, mining in the current mode—open pit, cyanide heap leaching—requires millions to get started; it requires equipment of extraordinary scale and expense. This is not an enterprise for the little guy.

Consider, then, these two recent remarks from Senators Malcolm Wallop and Alan Simpson, representing Wyoming, who spoke in opposition to reform of the Mining Law of 1872, the law that provides the framework for corporate profit without federal revenue, the law that, in Charles Wilkinson's words, is characterized by an "utter lack of any provision for environmental protection":

[Reform of the law] would really hurt the small prospector, and believe me, there are a lot of them out there.

This is not about money. We are defending our Western heritage.[15]

Which "Western heritage" did Simpson have in mind? And how much of that heritage, as it was actually played out in the Gold Rush in California, is alive enough to justify its defense?

I conclude with a story from Dan DeQuille, that memorable and effective writer from Nevada's Comstock Lode. A veteran prospector in Virginia City, Old Daniels, was often so drunk that he could not be sure whether he was dead or alive. Practical-joking friends, on one occasion, lifted the drunken old man and carried him to the graveyard, where they placed him next to a dug but not filled grave. When sunrise awoke Old Daniels, he considered his own situation, looked at the surrounding graves and gravestones, and drew the obvious conclusion: It is "the day of resurrection," he said, "and I'm the first son of a gun out of the ground."[16]

The same could be said for Western gold mining, very thoroughly buried and mourned in the mid-1980s and very much out of the ground now. As Frank Marryat wrote in *Mountains and Molehills*, "Like a stone thrown in the water, the effects of a gold country spread from it in widening circles."[17] In ways that do not seem to be grabbing current popular attention, the mining enterprise launched in California a century and a half ago continues to affect the American West.* Whether the proper word for this impact is the "shaping" of the American West, as the title of this essay puts it, or the "shaking" of the American West, as I phrased it ten years ago, is a choice I leave for your contemplation.

---

*Gold prices have now gone into a slump, and this boom may slack off for a time.

PART IV

———◆———

THE HISTORIAN
AS DREAMER:
PREACHING TO
(AND BY)
THE HALF-
CONVERTED

> Historians, like other human beings, are entitled to have their own idea of a desirable future for mankind, to fight for it and to be cheered up if they discover that history seems to be going their way, as it sometimes does.
>
> ERIC HOBSBAWM, *On History*

Since historical study offers a ringside seat for observing the brutality, as well as the pettiness, of human beings, the job of the historian gives optimism a tough challenge. And yet hoping for the best is a persistent human habit, and historians, like human beings of any occupation, have a right to occasional episodes of unreasonable cheer. These essays rest on the exercise of that right.

Much to their credit, the members of the Mormon History Association annually invite—and listen closely to—a plenary speaker who is neither a Mormon nor a specialist in Mormonism. The fact that my father's family were Latter-day Saints places me in a slightly anomalous category, not entirely outsider or insider, while certainly adding to my interest in the subject. Given in 1994 at Park City, Utah, "Peace Initiative: Using the Mormons to Rethink Culture and Ethnicity in American History," provided the opportunity to reappraise the idea of ethnicity and the concept of culture, and to examine their powers both to reduce and to heighten tensions between groups.

Later in 1994, an evening address for the California Historical Society convention offered a similar chance to explore definitions of insider and outsider in group self-perception. "Will
the Real Californian Please Stand Up?" reflects on ethnicity in
the self-understanding of Californians and puts the spotlight on
one of my favorite figures from Western history, the outspoken
Mary Roberts Coolidge, champion of Chinese immigrants at
the turn of the century. The response of the largely white audience to testimony from an unreconstructed white liberal offered
its own interesting piece of evidence: roughly two-thirds rose for
a standing ovation, while the remaining third stayed completely,
wholeheartedly seated.

"The Shadows of Heaven Itself" first appeared in *Atlas of
the New West* (1997), a project of the University of Colorado's
Center of the American West. My assignment was to reflect on
the reasons for the enormous popularity of the interior West in
the late twentieth century and to weigh some of the benefits
and injuries of the current "amenity boom." In the juxtaposition
of privilege to poverty, this migration dramatizes the inequality
of wealth in American society. At the end of the essay, I seized
the opportunity to team up with a Catholic archbishop to invite
empathy for the poor.

In 1996, Ken Burns and Stephen Ives presented a new documentary series called "The West," accompanied by the publication of an illustrated volume written and edited by Geoffrey
Ward. "Believing in the American West," my contribution to
that volume, considers the West's status as the most secular region of the country, in terms of church attendance and church
membership. This fact opens the door to an exploration of the
many shapes and forms that faith can take. Sometimes dismissed
as an artifact of 1960s flashbacks, the desire to transcend racial
prejudice and injustice is a foundation of faith for many Americans, drawing on a much longer heritage of conviction and
commitment.

A bit to my surprise, a yearning for faith and belief runs
through all four of these essays. In the coming era, Francis

Fukuyama predicts, "people will return to religion not necessarily because they accept the truth of revelation but because the absence of community and the transience of social ties in the secular world make them hungry for ritual and cultural tradition."[1] In a manner that surprises their author, the essays in this section show that proposition at work.

IV-A

Peace Initiative: Using the Mormons to Rethink Culture and Ethnicity in American History

In the summer of 1994, a group called the Flight Safety Foundation issued a report on the relationship between pilots and flight attendants. This relationship is often troubled; in some cases, it has been dangerous. In one instance, the foundation said, "the captain reported over the public address system that he had a problem with the *right* engine. Although the attendants . . . could see that [the] fire [was in] the *left* engine, they did nothing as the pilot shut down the wrong engine [my emphasis]." "If the Engine's Burning," the *Washington Post* intelligently headlined this article, "Tell the Pilot." But why on earth would someone *not* tell the pilot? Even though "cabin and flight deck crews share the same goals," the report offered its explanation, "the two crews have evolved into distinct cultures." Here is the most important thing to note in this parable from aviational ethnicity: the writers of the report took it for granted that living in a state of separate cultures meant living in a state of friction and hostility or, at the least, misunderstanding. Describing how these two cultures interact, the report said that pilots and flight attendants "sometimes show animosity toward one another, are often confused as to when to communicate problems, have little awareness of the other's duties in an emergency and sometimes don't even introduce themselves prior to a flight."[1]

The pilot says the right engine is on fire; the flight attendants know that it is the left engine that is on fire; because of cultural differences, the flight attendants do not speak, even though everybody is on the *same airplane*. Whatever this story tells us about the risks we take when we fasten our seat belts on airplanes, it tells us something considerably more important about the urgent need for people in this nation to think about the operations of culture and ethnicity in our times.

The words "culture" and "ethnicity" appear everywhere in the United States today, and they appear in tones ranging from despair and anger to pride and celebration. Perhaps the cheeriest usages appear in the marketplace, where the word "ethnic" in front of the word "restaurant" has a happy effect on both the appetite and the wallet. Mail-order catalogues of women's clothing are also frequent and comfortable deployers of the word "ethnic." One catalogue describes a flowing gauze outfit as "inspired by ethnic influences"; a striped vest, another catalogue says, offers "ethnic dash for any outfit." "Ethnic" in the mail-order catalogues means embroidered or brightly colored or made of abundant, flowing material. "Ethnic," contrary to the shading given the word in newspaper stories about Rwanda, Bosnia, and Kosovo, does not necessarily refer to clothing that one would wear to battle. An "ethnic dash" is not necessarily a flight for life.

American undergraduates are similarly inclined to the breezy and colorful school of ethnicity and culture. Twenty years ago, a curious habit of mind seemed to take over the students. Repeatedly, in midterm and final exams, they would refer to various lifestyles, to the lifestyle of the Pequot Indians or the lifestyle of the Puritans. It did not help me, in my adjustment to the students' fondness for this word, to hear a repeated radio advertisement for a furniture store. The store claimed to offer every kind of furniture you might want, whether, as the ad said, "your lifestyle is colonial or contemporary." It is a wonderful and wild notion to think of someone in the late twentieth century choosing to have a colonial lifestyle, with a few stools, no chairs, a milk churn, a fireplace to cook in, a few pots, and, if privileged, a spoon or two, with life punctuated by an occasional raid or war of conquest, and with a general sense of subordination to a distant empire.

When the word "lifestyle" appeared frequently in history exams, it seemed that we were not doing all we could to help the students see the past as the people of that time saw it themselves. Then, over the years, "lifestyle" seems to have dropped away; "culture" has taken its place and functions as a synonym for "lifestyle." The Plains Indians, for instance, many students writing exams will tell you, fought in the last half of the nineteenth century to "defend their culture" or to "preserve their culture." There stand the Lakota at Little Big Horn, rallying to defend a concept that white anthropologists were barely starting to create, circulate, and popularize. With the word "culture" as their incantation, students ride around through history on a kind of magic carpet of time travel, visiting far-off places made familiar and comfortable by the fact that every group has a culture, and every culture is, in turn, rich and complex, separate and intact, and equally well defined and well defended.

One of the most significant events in the intellectual and social history of the last century was this: academics invented the concept of culture and then completely lost control of it. On other occasions we may complain about the gap between the university and the world at large, but this is *not* one of those occasions. Every group these days has borrowed academic terminology and taken to talking self-consciously, and sometimes self-importantly, about their "culture." In the last thirty years, sociologists, anthropologists, historians, and cultural critics have written a great many articles and books trying to define the concepts of ethnicity and culture. To some degree, this is a matter of scholars struggling with other scholars over the meaning of key terms of inquiry. But it certainly seems that there is another message to be heard in all these publications, a message of academics saying to the general public, "The word culture is *our* word, not yours. You should have asked our permission before you took it; and if you're not careful, you're going to hurt yourselves with it."

And, in truth, people have hurt themselves and hurt their neighbors with these words. "Culture" and "ethnicity" turn out to be very satisfactory verbal weapons. In 1969, the anthropologist Fredrik Barth wrote a very influential and instructive article, arguing that the meaning of ethnicity lies more in its boundaries than in its core. Ethnicity, Barth said, is not a set of defined, consistent characteristics at the center of a group's being; it is much more a matter of negotiations at the group's edges, arrangements made when and where the group borders on other groups.² Matters here have taken a remarkably ironic twist: the very word "ethnicity" can now function in public exchange as a boundary, the kind of boundary usually constructed of barbed wire and glass fragments. In many situations in the United States, statements about one's culture or one's ethnicity prove to be statements that carry an additional message, and that additional message says to outsiders *keep out.*

In theory, historians should have a particular advantage in providing a kind of escort service across and over these discouraging boundaries. We should be able to provide perspective; we should be able to take the long view, the calm view, the "let's not fly off the handle" view. Historians should be able to provide a genuine social service in calm and reflective analysis of ethnicity and its workings. But this is a service we have not yet performed. Sometimes we actually do engage in calm and reflective analysis, but we have a way of writing up the results in a literary style that shuts out laypeople and nonspecialists. We have also bogged ourselves down in charges of political correctness on one side and charges of racism and insensitivity on the other.

Most important, we have backed away from any vision of human common ground. We have, instead, divided the world into a set of experiences—Catholic, Protestant, Jew, Mormon, and Muslim; male and female, heterosexual and homosexual; Indian, Anglo-American, African American, Mexican American, and Asian American. Of course these are consequential categories, but they are also categories that overlap and categories that are themselves internally full of variation and conflict. But we have set these categories off by themselves, and sometimes drawn the conclusion that no doors or openings connect them; men will never understand women's experiences; Anglo-Americans will never understand Mexican American experiences; African Americans will never understand Korean American experiences.

This state of affairs panics me. Of course, we will never understand each other fully; of course, parts of our experiences will always remain hidden from each other. But empathy and understanding still have the power to cross many of these borders. I take considerable inspiration from the words of Cornel West: "We simply cannot enter the twenty-first century," he writes, "at each other's throats." Whatever our ethnicity or religion, "we are at a critical crossroad in the history of this nation—and we either hang together by combating forces that divide and degrade us or we hang separately."[3]

To avoid the prospect of separate hangings, we will have to show considerable courage. And when we look for examples of courage, contemporary Mormon intellectuals should be high on that list. I believe I know something, from firsthand experience, about how it feels to be a historian in the midst of controversy, but there are a number of Mormon historians who know a lot more about this than I do. Reappraising and rethinking the history of the American West can sometimes make me feel that I have wandered into the midst of a battlefield. But I do not think there is any topic that can beat Mormon history for its power to prove the proposition that how we write and interpret history *matters,* and matters to people who may never set foot in a college or university history department.

Controversial changes in the writing of Mormon history, controversial changes in the writing of Western American history, controversial changes in the writing of national history—these changes are in many ways parallel and related. Reckoning with human diversity, with the economic underpinnings of social relationships, with gender, with the moral complexity of many actions that, in earlier writings of history, once seemed simple—that has been the pattern of change across the whole discipline of history. Mormon history and Western American history have thus undergone very similar processes of transformation. Indeed, when I was writing *The Legacy of Conquest,* I saw considerable common ground in the cause of Mormon history and Western American history. Mormon history is one of the most compelling, distinctive, and instructive components of regional history; and yet, under the terms of the old, frontier school of Western American history, Mormon history had to be dismissed and marginalized.

In his Frontier Thesis, Frederick Jackson Turner had argued that the frontier had created a uniquely self-reliant, individualistic American pioneer. The Mormons, with their tightly knit social bonds and communitarian behavior, did not do much to support Turner's argument. Turner thus reserved four words for Mormons in his 1893 "The Significance of the Frontier," and it should tell you something about the relevance of the Turner thesis to Mormonism that two of those four words were "the" and "in." I refer to his very brief reference to the location of the frontier in 1850, which makes a momentary mention to "the settlements in Utah."[4] In the same spirit, Turner's follower Ray Allen Billington told the *story* of Utah in his narrative books, but when it came time to write about the *meaning* of the frontier and the lessons of history, in *America's Frontier Heritage,* Billington followed Turner's lead and left the Mormons out.[5] The Mormons would not fit the Frontier Thesis, and so Turner and Billington stuck by the Frontier Thesis and dismissed the Mormons. It seems to me a much wiser choice to stick by the Mormons and dismiss the Frontier Thesis.

I had and have a personal stake in seeing that the history of Utah and the Latter-day Saints gets proper attention. My father was born and raised in Brigham City, as part of the Danish LDS community there. My mother was raised in Salt Lake City, and though she was a Congregationalist, her life in Utah seems very similar to Wallace Stegner's experience—never a member but still very much involved in Church of the Latter-day Saints youth activities, with many close friendships uninterrupted and undiminished by religious differences. My father left the church and my parents moved to California before I was born, but the story-and-anecdote part of my heritage has a very heavy Utah flavor to it.

In some ways, this background was the root of my conviction that the establishment of the Church of Latter-day Saints had produced a kind of ethnicity. Over the years, Catholic friends would say, "Only a Catholic can really feel guilt," or others would make reference to the drivenness and workaholicness that come with immersion in the Protestant work ethic. I certainly thought I knew something about guilt, and also about a devotion to work. Until I was in my twenties, I had never been in a Catholic church, and I had only rarely been in Protestant churches. Where and how could I have picked up a Catholic sense of guilt or a Protestant work ethic? And if I hadn't picked those items up from the conventional sources, then whose sense of guilt and whose work ethic *did* I have?

I think you can guess my answer.

While I think that there *is* a phenomenon one can call Mormon ethnicity, I know these things are not simple. If I ever thought they were simple, I have had many fine opportunities to get over that presumption. Consider, for instance, the occasion twenty years ago when I had in my Western American history course a Mexican American student from El Paso, a great supporter of Chicano rights. We were two-thirds of the way through the semester when this student came in to talk about his paper topic. I knew that he would want to write something about Spanish colonization of the Southwest or about Chicano history in the twentieth century.

Instead, he said he would like to write about Mormonism.

Mormonism?

This student was, in fact, fourth-generation LDS, with his family converted by Utah families who fled to Mexico during the polygamy persecutions. My first impressions had been right: he was very much a Chicano activist and proud of his Mexican heritage, but he was also very much a devoted member of the Church of Latter-day Saints, persuaded that he and his family had found their rightful place as redeemed Lamanites.[6]

This young man's complex heritage and identity, as well as his justified anger at the treatment of Mexican American people in El Paso, remind us of how complicated matters of ethnicity can be and also how controversial they are. This helps to explain the curious title of this essay, "Peace Initiative." Ethnic conflict is a very troubling element in the world today, and Bosnia and Rwanda are only two visible manifestations of that problem. Even though the United States is an enormous distance away from those two examples, ethnic friction is no small element of our current national experience.

In the project of addressing that friction, the use of the idea of ethnicity will be a key factor in our success or failure. Ethnicity has become our central concept for categorizing the qualities or traits or actions that identify a group of people as a unit, the features that distinguish one group of people from another. "Distinguish" is, of course, by no means a synonym for "divide." Ethnic groups can be distinguished from each other and still be quite compatible, even collaborative and mutually respectful. Ethnicity also provides us with a vital area of overlap between the interests and concerns of historians and the interests and concerns of laypeople. The idea of ethnicity makes everyone, at least momentarily, into a practicing historian. When you ask people what their ethnicity is, they engage themselves with history. They ask themselves questions about origin and causality; they place themselves in the context of the passage of time; they tie their personal identity into currents of change and continuity. Moreover, people asked to identify their ethnicity do not just report historical fact; they also clearly show themselves to be selectors, shapers, and interpreters of those facts.

Consider these examples, from interviews by the sociologist Mary Waters, speaking to Americans of European descent. Waters asked a nineteen-year-old college student named Bill Kerrigan how he would identify himself on a census form:

> A: I would have put Irish.
> Q: Why would you have answered that?
> A: Well, my dad's name is Kerrigan and my mom's name is O'Leary, and I do have some German in me, but if you figure it out, I am about 75 percent Irish, so I say I am Irish.
> Q: You usually don't say German when people ask?
> A: No, no, I never say I am German. My dad just likes being Irish. . . . I don't know, I guess I just never think of myself as being German.
> Q: So your dad's father is the one who immigrated?
> A: Yes. On this side it is Irish for generations. And then my grand-mother's name is Dubois, which is French, partly German, partly French, and then the rest of the family is all Irish.

As Mary Waters sums this up, "in the course of a few questions, Bill labeled himself Irish, admitted to being part German but not identifying with it, and then as an afterthought added that he was also part French."[7]

Or consider a forty-six-year-old Irish-and-Italian woman interviewed by Waters, who gives an even better demonstration of the way in which ethnicity makes regular people into interpretative historians.

> Q: When you were growing up did you consider yourself ethnic?
> A: Yes, I was very strongly Italian, because . . . whenever I was in a bad mood, that was the Irish in me. So I always related the Irish with the bad things and the Italian with all of the good things. . . . I thought all the Irish were hotheads and all the Italians had clean houses and good food.[8]

The facts of this woman's origins say Irish and Italian; but her conditioning casts the Italian side as superior to the Irish. Thus, the inheritor of this legacy, showing a certain measure of self-esteem, settles on the characterization Italian.

Here we have very literal case studies in the idea of the construction of ethnic identity, of Everywoman Her Own Historian, of Every-man His Own Historian. We have, as well, case studies in what is now established thinking about the idea of ethnicity: that ethnicity is much more a matter of construction, choice, consent, and interpretation and much less a matter of literal inheritance, descent, and lineage. The people interviewed by Mary Waters had particularly open turf for choice. As what Waters calls "white ethnics," they could, if they wanted, choose to claim no ethnicity at all: whenever they wanted, they could drop the whole package—Irish, Italian, French, German, Polish—and simply say "American." You can choose nearly anything in America, the famed cultural pluralist Horace Kallen had said, but you cannot choose your grandfather. Now, as historian David Hollinger has observed, even that apparent knockout punch of an aphorism needs some rethinking. If you cannot choose a grandfather entirely from scratch, you can certainly choose *which* of your various grandfather options you will accent. To the people interviewed by Mary Waters, the construction of ethnicity bordered on play: they could add or subtract, accent or deemphasize, the pieces and parts of their ethnic identity without significant social cost. And they could do it with such flexibility and freedom that they looked as if they had agreed to team up with recent cultural theorists and put on a demonstration of the fact that ethnicity is a matter of consent, far more than descent.[9]

Other Americans would have a harder time putting on such a demonstration. We reach now the arena of ethnicity in which choice and consent seem to be much reduced, the arena in which the construction of ethnic identity could hardly be called "play." We come to the matter perhaps best summarized by the sociologist Robert Blauner in 1972: "Many of the ambiguities of American race relations," Blauner said, "stem from the fact that two principles of social division, race and ethnicity, were compressed into one." Or, as David Hollinger put it, "exactly where ethnicity ends and race begins has been much contested in our time."[10] We understand race to be a socially constructed concept itself, of no particular validity as a category of nature and biology. We understand that there are hundreds of possible ways to define, for instance, African American culture and identity. In a fair and just world, African American ethnicity would be just as much a matter of individual free choice as is Irish American ethnicity or Italian American ethnicity.

In the last decade, a veritable cascade of books have testified to exactly the opposite proposition: that, on the contrary, African Americans continue to have the category "black" imposed upon them, whether or not that is their preference. Cornel West's *Race Matters* and Derrick Bell's *Faces at the Bottom of the Well: The Permanence of Racism* are probably the most widely recognized of these books. Jonathan Kozol's *Savage Inequalities: Children in America's Schools* and Alex Kotlowitz's *There Are No Children Here: The Story of Two Boys Growing Up in the Other America* take unflinching looks at the intersection of race and poverty. If one prefers to take one's doses of despair in autobiographical form, Brent Staples's *Parallel Time: Growing Up in Black and White* and Nathan McCall's *Makes Me Wanna Holler: A Young Black Man in America* make it clear how far away we are from a society that does not make blackness a penalty.

You can read some of these books and try to tell yourself that our dilemma is a matter of class lines, poverty, and the inherited injuries of slavery and segregation. With widened economic opportunity and with the passage of decades since the end of slavery and the end of legal segregation, you can begin to hope, the historically inherited categories of black and white have surrendered much of their rigidity. But then you read Ellis Cose's *The Rage of a Privileged Class,* full of stories of the injuries and insults encountered by black professionals, managers, and executives, and differences of social class cease to be a sufficient explanation for white privilege and prejudice.[11]

Even though it is the most impersonal of all these books, *Two Nations: Black and White, Separate, Hostile, Unequal,* by the white political scientist Andrew Hacker, may be the most disheartening. Hacker offers, for instance, a haunting statistical fact: white Americans will stay in a neighborhood as long as the percentage of black residents remains at eight percent or under.[12] The percentage of blacks in the American population is a little more than 12 percent, and so white Americans, even white Americans who say that they want to live in an integrated neighborhood, will begin moving out before the percentage of blacks in the neighborhood even reaches the percentage of blacks in the general population.

In an often-quoted observation, the novelist Ishmael Reed has remarked that if the black novelist Alex Haley had followed his father's line of genealogy in the search for his own origins, then Haley's book

Roots would have been set in Ireland, not Africa. But Americans continue with their traditional and very arbitrary categorizations of African American descent. Any black heritage at all will identify a person as "black." As the historian Barbara J. Fields put it, we hold onto a convention "that considers a white woman capable of giving birth to a black child but denies that a black woman can give birth to a white child."[13]

Repeatedly finding themselves picked up and placed into ethnic categories that might or might not fit them, people of color have had considerable reason to resent the privilege of choice that white Americans have over the matter of their ethnicity.

Mormons and Gentiles; Mexicans and Anglos; white Americans who think that enough, even too much, has been done to help black Americans recover from the injuries of the past, and black Americans who can provide everyday evidence that racial injuries only changed form and did not stop with *Brown v. Board of Education;* representatives of the culture of flight attendants who will not tell representatives of the culture of pilots which engine is on fire—Americans appear to have landed in the soup, *not* in the melting pot, just in a mess of disunited, fragmented, and clashing ethnicities and cultures.

Thus, I turn now to a hopeful paradox: as contested and controversial as the writing of Mormon history can be, we can talk about the idea of Mormon ethnicity in a comparatively calm and peaceful way. Then we can take the idea of ethnicity we develop in a discussion of Mormonism and apply it to other examples of ethnicity in a way that may actually reduce the friction and polarization of the usual discussions on that turf.

Some readers may be puzzling over that remark: could I really think that a discussion of the terms of Mormon history would be calmer and less controversial than a discussion of, say, Mexican American history? I know the story of Leonard Arrington's too-brief term of duty as church historian; I have read Lavina Fielding Anderson's essay in *Dialogue,* "The LDS Intellectual Community and Church Leadership: A Contemporary Chronology"; I have read Paul Toscano's impassioned book, *The Sanctity of Dissent;* I have followed and admired the career of D. Michael Quinn. I have kept track of press coverage of the disagreements between the General Authorities and Mormon intellectuals and of the disciplinary action taken against historians and feminists. And yet I still think that a consideration of Mormon ethnicity provides a more tranquil and tractable way to approach the topic of ethnicity in the United States.[14]

Why? In part, because Mormon ethnicity allows scholars an arena for thinking about ethnicity as it applies to a group which, for most of its history, has had the white skin and European background of the American majority and whose distinctive consciousness was generated by events that occurred in the United States, not in the "old country." In accenting the whiteness of Mormons, I may seem to be forgetting the Mexican American Mormons of El Paso and Juarez, the African American Mormons whose lives were much changed by the 1978 revelation admitting black men to the priesthood, and all the Mormon converts in Polynesia, Asia, Latin America, and Africa. But still the majority of Mormons, through the bulk of the church's history, have been of European ancestry.

When ethnicity is associated with a skin color other than white, ethnicity can become a category so much imposed from the outside that it becomes harder to distinguish the workings of the individual's choice and consciousness. The history of discrimination on the basis of race can heat discussions of ethnicity to the point where it is, in truth, painful to touch them. While we will return to that arena, the fact that the majority of Mormons have been white allows us at least temporarily to cool down the terms of discussion of ethnic identity. And the case study of Mormonism provides us with a crucial reminder that we must examine the category "white" carefully and critically. Whiteness or Anglo-Americanness cannot remain the taken-for-granted definition of normality by which the peculiarity of the other cultures is measured. In their habits and beliefs and customs, white people, heaven knows, can match any other group in the categories of peculiarity, eccentricity, and interest.

Moreover, Mormon ethnicity is *not* at the center of the disagreements between the General Authorities and Mormon historians. It is also a topic on which we already have models of tranquil, uninjurious, reasoned, clarifying disagreement. In the fine collection of essays, *The Mormon Presence in Canada*, two scholars, Armand Mauss and Keith Parry, take opposite sides on this question. Parry argues for the existence of a Mormon ethnicity and Mauss argues against it, and both writers preserve perfect equanimity and fairness of judgment.[15] In fact, very much following in Jan Shipps's footsteps, I will soon argue that the issue of Mormon ethnicity provides a kind of intellectual refuge from the recent contention between the leadership and some of the members. Rather than taking us back into controversy, ethnicity provides a framework for thinking, calmly and reflectively, about the current dilemmas in the church.

Let us try to put this into practice in a discussion of the origins and the shape of Mormon ethnicity in the last 165 years of history. I ask the forbearance of readers here because, for the next few pages, I will be restating some of the most familiar facts about Church of the Latter-day Saints history and echoing a number of statements made better by other writers and analysts.[16]

The building blocks of a Mormon ethnicity are not difficult to locate. From the very beginning of the church, faith in a particular theology was very much accompanied by a willingness to follow Joseph Smith's revelations and advice in day-to-day behavior. Membership in this church was also membership in a community with its own economic, social, and familial patterns. People who joined the church were often cut off from family members who disapproved of their conversion, and geographically separated from their places of origin as well. Even before the murder of Joseph Smith and the departure from the Mississippi Valley, the conditions were close to ideal for the creation of a community in which religious belief laid the foundations for a new worldview, a new pattern of family organization, a new set of ambitions, a new combination of common bonds and obligations, a new definition of a separate peoplehood—all the components, in other words, of what we now call "ethnicity."

To this situation, already rich in possibilities for the creation of a culture or subculture, persecution and the migration to Utah provided the capstone. Framed in a forceful and compelling analogy to the persecution and exodus of the Israelites, the Mormon move to the Great Basin catalyzed the sense of a separate peoplehood. As a shared memory, full of the literal and direct testing of the spirit, the Exodus was exactly the kind of event that would stay with a people over time, the kind of experience that would bind even those born too late to participate in it to a vision of the special identity that comes with a special history. Richard Bennett's book, *Mormons on the Missouri,* offers a particularly telling case study of the impact of migration in the formation of identity, as Winter Quarters provided the site for a crucial refining and testing of Mormon group purpose.[17]

Analogies to Israel went further than the Exodus. As Jan Shipps has explained, by a "rhetorical construction of blood descent," Mormons became Abraham's descendants, even more explicitly defined as a chosen people. And a sense of kinship—a key component of ethnicity—came from other sources besides the vision of the Saints as the "seed of Abraham." Kinship came, as well, from the custom of adoption, with adult Mormons sealed as children to church leaders, and from the proliferating ties of marriage. Plural marriage thus added to the conditions of ethnicity in two ways: as another form of cultural distinctiveness, perhaps the best for dramatizing the Saints' separate status, and as a very effective way of making people into relatives, creating a wonderfully interwoven chain of in-laws and kin.[18]

The idea—really the imperative—of the gathering of the Saints gave great force to the sense of peoplehood, while arrival in Deseret added place and geography to the forces supporting and sustaining ethnicity. As Promised Land, as Zion, the land just beyond the Rockies provided another foundation for identity, as the Saints invested enormous labor in making that land meet their standards for habitability and in building towns and villages and farms that would add up to what many have called a characteristic Mormon landscape.[19]

The years of comparative isolation, with Mormons firmly the majority in most of Utah, southern Idaho, and northern Arizona, allowed group identity to become even more clearly defined, with, for instance, characteristic patterns of Mormon entertainment—dancing and theater going—taking hold. In a time when Protestant Christians feared the danger and temptations of leisure and recreation, Joseph Smith and Brigham Young, as R. Laurence Moore has pointed out, had a "clear advantage": "They had much less to fear in the matter of leisure because they retained effective control over what happened when Mormons socialized with other Mormons."[20] English, German, Danish, Swedish, and Norwegian converts moved very quickly into this common culture. Scandinavian converts, William Mulder told us in *Homeward to Zion*, attended regular, English-speaking ward meetings but also had auxiliary Scandinavian meetings to ease their transition into both the language and the society.[21] Some elements of imported European ethnicity might linger. I have heard from my father that their old horse in Brigham City would stop plowing precisely at 3:30 P.M. and head for the house, demonstrating my Danish grandparents' continued affection for the cultural concept of the coffee break. Thus, it was particularly interesting for me to learn from Mulder that something a bit short of reverence for the Word of Wisdom was quite characteristic of Danish converts. And yet, with a few persistent variations in behavior, the blending of new immigrants into this new Mormon ethnicity seems to have proceeded with remarkable speed. Meanwhile, the practice of plural marriage and the federal government's mounting hostility to polygamy deepened the Mormon sense of distinctiveness and separateness, providing, as well, an unusual historical legacy awaiting the reckoning of future generations of Saints.

The end of polygamy was a major and consequential moment in Mormon history, but Mormons soon found other ways to mark their boundaries and to define their separate identity. The distinctive elements of Mormon theology, the receiving of endowments in the temple and the sealing of marriages for time and eternity; the growing emphasis on the Word of Wisdom; the daily practices of the priesthood; the Relief Society; Mutual, Primary, and the round of activities at the Ward Houses; the General Conferences; the missionary experience of young men; the baptizing of the dead; tithing; the creation of the church welfare system and the fasting funds for the poor; Family Home Evenings; large families to take part in those evenings; and, perhaps more than anything, the told and retold stories of Mormon history made it very unlikely that Mormons would lose their distinctive ethnicity and disappear into a homogeneous, mainstream, American whole.

With considerably greater efficiency than I have shown, Leonard Arrington has summed up the case for regarding Mormons as both an ethnic group *and* a religious group. "Mormons," Arrington writes, "have (or at least used to have) a distinctive vocabulary, shared history, unique theological beliefs, definite in-group boundaries (prohibitions on the use of alcohol, tobacco, tea, and coffee), emphasis on in-group marriage, and a strong sense of peoplehood, which includes the 'brother' and 'sister' terminology."[22] If one thinks back to the "white ethnics" interviewed by Mary Waters, it is clear that people who chose to identify themselves as Mormon in more than religion could bring more clarity and concreteness to the project of identifying their ethnicity than could the people in Waters's examples.

It is, however, important to note Arrington's phrasing: "Mormons," the quotation begins, "have (or at least *used to have*)" these qualities of ethnicity (my emphasis). That "used to have" is the core of the problem. In the last thirty years, the church has grown enormously, and grown internationally. The Mormon Diaspora of the twentieth century has weakened the ties between peoplehood and place considerably. The idea of a Zion or a promised land has to play a much diminished role in Mormon consciousness, when so many Mormons live so far from Utah. Moreover, many Mormons in the last few decades have ended up living in places where they are by no means a majority and where most of their working life is spent in the company of people who cannot—except, perhaps, by their indifference—reinforce any notion of Mormon identity. This can no longer be the story of ethnicity by immersion that characterized the life of converts in the nineteenth century. Moreover, the spread of Mormonism into many nations and many cultures stretches the persuasive powers and influences of any one cultural system. Simply adjusting styles of greeting and personal friendship, ways of contracting marriages, or forms of expressing deference to accommodate all the world's cultures is a puzzle of the greatest magnitude.[23]

It does not take much in the way of predictive powers to guess that this would prove to be a situation of considerable anxiety and tension. Thus it seems more than possible, twenty or thirty years from now, that historians of Mormonism may adopt exactly the interpretative framework of ethnicity to explain the pattern of events in the church in the last half of the twentieth century. I can, in other words, imagine scholarly articles or books that would put what are, to us, puzzling and unsettling recent events into an explanatory framework in which ethnicity was central. Historians of the future may write statements like the ones that I imagine in these next three paragraphs:

> For 125 years, Mormon religious belief was securely supported by Mormon cultural practice. To be a Mormon was as much a matter of ethnic self-definition as it was a matter of membership in a religious denomination, and those two dimensions of Mormonism reliably reinforced each other. Mormon ethnicity drew its strength from sources that did not require much in the way of official supervision or control; in the Saints' ties to the places of Utah, Idaho, and Arizona, in their well-rehearsed understanding of their common history, and in their complicated network of kinship and descent, the Mormons did not need church strictures to find plenty of reminders of their peoplehood.

In the last four decades of the twentieth century, however, these well-settled conditions began to change. Membership in the church expanded enormously. With the idea of a geographical gathering no longer tenable, there was simply no quick way to match conversion to the Church of Latter-day Saints with a parallel conversion to Mormon ethnicity. Feeling understandable concern about this course of events, the General Authorities undertook to standardize Mormon thought and practice; the Correlation Committee was only one part of a larger process of response to the overstretching and decline of Mormon ethnic identity. In the nineteenth century, as Stanley Kimball remarked in his biography of Heber Kimball, "speculative theology was practiced in the Church."[24] Standardization of that theology came considerably later. Moreover, nineteenth-century Mormonism, as a group of women scholars argued in the collection of essays *Sisters in Spirit*, gave a considerably wider range of options to Mormon women; many activities, particularly in rituals of healing, which would later be confined to the practice of a male priesthood, were once open to women.[25]

Thus, in the 1980s and 1990s, when the church tried to address the loss of Mormon ethnicity with a greater centralization of control over Mormon thought, this was not a restoration of early Mormonism or a return to tradition. It was, in fact, a campaign of standardization that, ironically, in the effort to hold Mormons more tightly together, retreated from the distinctive elements of Mormonism, accenting instead the church's similarity to conventional Christianity. Profoundly disturbing to Mormon intellectuals, and perhaps especially to Mormon historians, this campaign for standardization was in fact an understandable response to unsettling change in the church's position in the world at large.

What I cannot write is a fourth paragraph which says what happened next. But as to the existence of a Mormon cultural identity, something that looked like, functioned like, was experienced like ethnicity, of that proposition, I feel quite certain.

Indeed, on some counts, this idea of Mormon ethnicity as a fading force, as a vestige and relic of a different time, is a puzzling one. If Mormon ethnicity is fading, why is the late twentieth century seeing such a remarkable and impressive flowering of Mormon literature? Anyone troubled by the prospect of a disappearing ethnic identity should read the Mormon creative writers—Mormon novelists, Mormon short-story writers, Mormon poets, Mormon essayists.[26] In their work, a clear cultural identity thrives, and thrives in a way identifiable to any reader. When, in other words, you pick up a collection with the subtitle "Contemporary Mormon Short Stories," you do not become puzzled as to why it would carry that subtitle. The common cultural elements, along with a familiar and distinctive vocabulary of wards, temples, stake presidents, bishops, missions, testaments, Nephites, priesthood, Relief Society, and holidays on April 6 and July 24, tell you that you are reading literature rooted in a particular ethnicity, though also, of course, literature that speaks to a broad set of human concerns. The groundedness of the short stories, the novels, and the essays persuade the reader that obituaries for Mormon ethnicity are decidedly premature.

Reading this literature, one's imagination begins to play with the prospect of what might happen if the church were to spend less time enforcing intellectual conformity and more time distributing and discussing this rich Mormon literature and (if we truly are living in a postliterate, postprint age) translating it into plays, movies, music videos, and Web pages. This technique would allow stories to do what stories have always done best: convey the real meaning and appeal of life within a particular cultural tradition.

There may be some who would argue that when an ethnicity becomes the basis of a thriving literary tradition, it is already on the ropes, already on its way to status as the property of a small group of self-conscious intellectuals and no longer just the lived reality of regular folk. And that takes us back to the lessons of Mormon ethnicity for all of American history.

We are living, in the late twentieth century, in very self-conscious times. When we use any of these terms for people of the past— "lifestyle," "culture," or "ethnicity"—we impose concepts that would have seemed peculiar and alien to them. These terms are not, therefore, off-limits, but there is a huge question of consciousness and choice raised here. I do not think that Latter-day Saints of the nineteenth century thought of themselves as having an ethnicity, but I think we are still entitled to look at the sum of their thinking and behavior and to use the word "ethnicity" to describe the common patterns of their lives. Nineteenth-century Latter-day Saints, one could say, had an ethnicity precisely *because* they did not have to think in those terms. They thought in terms of being a chosen people, the seed of Abraham, but mostly they behaved in ways that demonstrated their common habits and their shared worldview. In the immediacy of that behavior, they never had to draw back to inquire whether they were or were not being certifiably "ethnic."

In truth, one can find something to envy in the un-self-consciousness of the past. The current theoretical literature on ethnicity so strongly stresses the role of choice, of consent, of construction that the idea of authenticity, of immediacy, of simply being who you are, without having to endure repeated bouts of strained and awkward self-definition, has moved out of our reach. It is a rare group today that can escape the curious and oddly nerve-wracking experience of researching, describing, defining, asserting, clarifying, recreating, and overhauling their identity. Not only does every group and every subgroup have to have these discussions, the members of each group also have to go forward with the results, standing before the public, before federal agencies, before academic audiences, explaining the process, method, and assumptions by which it arrived at its ethnic identity. It is a peculiar state of affairs, but it is a state of affairs made even more trying by the enormous emotional, psychological, and even spiritual freight that the idea of ethnicity now has to carry.

In 1994, my colleague at the University of Colorado, Steven Epstein, gave a presentation with me at the National Endowment for the Humanities; I spoke on "New Directions in Western American History" and he spoke on "New Directions in Medieval History," and to the astonishment of the audience, he persuaded them and me that there really *are* new directions in his well-established field. But one direction of inquiry, he suggested, remained both old and new. Medieval history was one field where no historian could ever neglect religious history; at every moment of medieval history, the historian is in the presence of faith, as well as the practical and material consequences of faith. I have thought frequently about that remark in reading Mormon history, because everything that Epstein said about medieval history is equally true of Mormon history.[27]

If one is not a Mormon historian but takes an excursion into this field, then one returns to one's own territory asking oneself a big question. If religious faith is an unavoidable and central factor in Mormon history, then where did it go in Western American history in general? The notion of non-Mormon Westerners living in a fully secularized world, a world in which human consciousness inhabits a thoroughly and complacently material universe and never asks questions about the origins of life, the inescapability of death, and the purpose of existence—after a visit to Mormon history, this idea of a fully secularized modern American consciousness seems deeply improbable.

Religious belief is a well-established current in most phases of human history. It is hard to believe that, for many twentieth-century Americans, it was a current that just stopped. If one holds this mystery in one's mind and then turns back to the public discussion of ethnicity in our times, a curious but inescapable idea comes to mind. In the fervor, defensiveness, and ardor of contemporary assertions of ethnic identity, something more than a polarized social science seems to be at work. I am not saying that assertions of ethnic identity are the exact equivalent of assertions of religious belief. But I am saying that assertions of ethnic identity partake of much of the same mental, even spiritual, energy of assertions of religious belief. By defining and claiming an ethnic identity, individuals try to place themselves in larger currents of life, try to find a sense of destiny and purpose, try to get out, at least momentarily, from under the burden of being isolated individuals responsible for their own self-definition and direction at every moment.

The effort to locate and to rest on an identity, grounded in a context bigger than the individual, structures the search for religious belief. The same effort structures the current search for ethnicity. We have been in the habit of writing about definitions of ethnicity as if we were exploring the mental equivalent of a club house or a political headquarters. And yet, when we explore modern ethnicity, we are in terrain quite a bit closer to a church. The Latter-day Saint movement, Dean May reminds us, "began with a clear purpose—to build an enclave of order, a refuge from the increasingly diverse and individualistic world that modern liberalism had spawned." If the world created by liberalism was disorienting in the 1830s, the disorientation has by no means diminished over time, and the search for ethnic roots is surely a response to that persistent disorientation.

The words that Joseph Smith used to express concern over the distressing world he encountered—"no small stir and division," "great confusion and bad feeling," "strife of words . . . and contest about opinions"—have not lost their resonance or relevance today.[28] Our daily opportunities for disorientation explain the common response many of us have when we hear of an ethnicity that might be threatened, an identity that might be about to yield to geographical dispersal or to the homogenizing forces of the mass media and market. Even though we know how fruitful in friction and division ethnicity can be, when we hear of a fading ethnic identity, many of us respond with an instinctive, "Too bad!" and instantly hope that something can be done to stop this loss of distinctiveness. This remains an unsettling and unmoored world, and one cannot cheer when one familiar form of anchorage ceases to hold.

"Ethnicity is, above all, a form of commitment," Orlando Patterson wrote in his eccentric but thought-provoking book *Ethnic Chauvinism;* "it is an ideology, or more properly, a faith; one that is often secular, but is also frequently a secular faith layered on a more profound religious faith."[29] The advantage of studying Mormon history is that ethnicity and religion were never separable. The reminder thus offered to scholars in all fields of ethnicity is that they are required to proceed with care, respect, and an awareness of the dignity of the people they study. When they write about ethnicity, scholars are exploring turf close to the human soul.

Mormonism, Susan Hendricks Swetman concluded in her study of Mormon pioneers' life-story writing in Idaho, "is a *live* culture, a culture facing difficult and integral challenges, rather than a homogenized set of unthinking conformists."[30] Mormon poet Marden J. Clark made a similar point in his poem "Wasatch." Clark traced the geological origins of the Wasatch range in the movements of faults, tectonic plates, ancient seas, and rising mountains. "What refuge here," Clark asked, "For us as we look up in awe / And love to these high peaks?" "Whose fault," he asked at the end, "If now these plates again should stir?"[31]

In human history, there is no "if" about it. The mountains remain but the conditions change. The context alters. The refuge shifts. The plates stir. The changing patterns of Mormon ethnicity and the current struggles over Mormon identity both set Latter-day Saints apart and bind them to the rest of humanity. In our understanding of ethnicity, in our distinctive and parallel searches for refuge, we either deny our common ground or find it.

IV-B

Will the Real Californian
Please Stand Up?

In the old game show "To Tell the Truth," a panel of four people—
or, as they are usually called, personalities—would listen to the
brief biography of an interesting and unusual person. Then they
would try to decide which of three contestants was really that person.
They would make their guesses, and then the *real* individual would be
asked to stand up. There would be a certain amount of bobbing and
chair adjusting, and then the real person would stand up and the two
frauds would remain seated.

They called the show "To Tell the *Truth*," and yet two out of
three people were lying. But at least the truth, and a shared agreement
on standards for judging truth, did take hold at the end of the show.
When the real individual stood up, the others remained seated and
tacitly admitted that they were imposters.

That is where my question follows a different format. There is no
agreement for deciding who is a real Californian in the present or
who has been one in the past, and this fact has been a source of enormous contention in California's past and present. But here historians
have an advantage: they live with a mandate for inclusiveness that is

imposed on few others. Historians of California have to pay attention to all the individuals who lived in this state and influenced its events. Historians cannot impose narrow definitions of real Californianness without fracturing and simplifying a complex story, and that mandate for inclusiveness requires a generosity of spirit and attention that could be an important and happy influence in contemporary public life.

Even under more narrow definitions of authenticity, I have some claims to being a real Californian, though these are not claims that I am eager to advertise in Colorado today. My birthplace meets one common requirement: I was born and raised in Banning, in the San Gorgonio Pass. With the exception of a couple of trips to my parents' home territory in Utah and to the Grand Canyon, I never left the state for my first twenty-one years. When I did leave, I made a big and awful leap and went to graduate school in New Haven, Connecticut, driving to the East Coast in a state of complete terror. I left early on a Sunday morning. When I crossed the border and entered Arizona, I tried to find a radio station, to pass the time. The one I found was a religious station, and the radio minister was saying, just as I tuned in, "We have a letter here from a young lady in New Haven, Connecticut, who is having some tough times. She wants to know if the Lord is in New Haven, and yes, young lady, the Lord is *even* in New Haven, Connecticut."

Well, maybe so. But leaving California was still a very big problem, and "disorientation" was too mild a term for this problem. At Santa Cruz in the late 1960s, to take one example, I had been much admired for the ease and frequency with which I wept. No one had said, "Oh why don't you grow up and stop being such a crybaby?" On the contrary, the response had been much closer to "How I admire the freedom and honesty of your emotions; how wonderful to be so in touch with your feelings." This California doctrine in support of the free and beneficial flow of tears had not, however, made many inroads at Yale. When I lived up to my role as a faucet in New Haven, people responded with something closer to horror and fear, rather than admiration and envy.

I will not prolong the misery of these stories of regional misunderstanding much longer, but I do have to cap them with the story of the Champagne Social. Early in the school year, we got invitations for a Graduate Student Champagne Social. I was, at first, mystified by this. At Santa Cruz, from 1968 to 1972, while we had plenty of so-cial events, none of them had been called a Champagne Social. But we did have plenty of costume parties and masquerades. Thus, I thought, I had broken the code. This was not a *real* Champagne Social; no one would imagine doing such a thing *seriously* in 1972. On the contrary, this was a clever and good-humored joke. We were to come, as we would have if we had received such an invitation in Santa Cruz; we were to come *as if* we were going to a Champagne Social.

Now I was on familiar turf. I went to Goodwill and got elbow-length gloves, a pillbox hat, and a curious dress with rows of purple taffeta. A friend (I think it was a friend) lent me the remains of an an-imal—something that had once been a mink or a fox or a weasel—to wear around my shoulders. I put my hair in a bun, and I put on heavy rouge and lipstick. Now I was ready for the Champagne Social.

When I entered the Champagne Social, I saw fifty or sixty Yale graduate students who were wearing campus casuals, sweaters and matching slacks or skirts. I was the only one with a pillbox hat, the only one with elbow-length gloves, and this list, of course, goes on. For the brief time I lasted at this party, I learned an interesting pattern of human behavior. In situations like this, humans very badly want to stare, but they do not want you to catch them staring, because of the obvious fear that if they inadvertently made eye contact with you, you might go over and *talk* to them.

In a number of ways in 1972, I struck not just fellow graduate stu-dents but the members of the Yale faculty as a very peculiar person. There were, I learned later, quite a number of concerned remarks made about me. So what saved me from dismissal? How was I able to do everything wrong and still end up with a Yale degree?

Yale gave me an unusual measure of tolerance because I had the extreme good luck to be born and raised in California. "Well, she is certainly odd," became the standard refrain, "but then again, you know she is from California."

Even in the midst of things, I was not entirely sure if this was a fair advantage. Was my eccentricity correlated in any particular way to my point of origin? It does seem likely that if we were to compile a list of the most peculiar Americans of the last 150 years, a remarkable per-centage of them would prove to have some tie with California, from William Walker to Richard Nixon, from Aimee Semple McPherson to Shirley Temple Black, from John Sutter to Walt Disney. I do not know if California was the source of their—and my—peculiarity, but I do know that a widespread association of California with eccentricity worked wonderfully to my advantage twenty-five years ago. Being perceived as a real Californian measurably improved the quality of my life; indeed, it made my career possible.

And that makes my present situation in these matters all the more awkward. Wherever you go today in the interior West, you hear hostile remarks about an invasion of Californians. The *Denver Post* reports regularly on the number of Californians applying for Colorado drivers' licenses, and the tone of these reports is not one of cheer. "Californians," the articles usually begin, "continue to flee their state in large numbers." The word "flee," which invariably appears in the first paragraph, brings to mind wonderfully vivid images and a certain set of historical precedents. You recall Emma Lazarus's words from the Statue of Liberty, words that do not, as far as I know, appear in any place where a major highway, originating in California, crosses the Colorado state border:

> *Give me your tired, your poor,*
> *Your huddled masses yearning to breathe free,*
> *The wretched refuse of your teeming shore,*
> *Send these, the homeless, tempest-tossed, to me.*

With a little rewriting—essentially, changing "Give me your tired, your poor," to "Give me your tired, your tasteless, your *rich*"—Miss Lazarus's words could appear on the letterhead of any number of Colorado home builder and land development companies. Heaven knows, the shore of California *is* "teeming"; and "tempest-tossed" could be easily changed, with an economy of syllables, to "earthquake-tossed." "Wretched refuse," of course, has never been the most flattering of characterizations, but it does give Californians some advance warning of the opinion in which they are held by quite a number of Coloradans.

And so there I am, in Boulder, Colorado, trying to draw attention away from my unfortunate pedigree: born and raised in Banning, a town sadly positioned in the San Gorgonio Pass between Sodom and Gomorrah, or between Los Angeles and Palm Springs. When people ask, "Are you from the West originally?" I am sometimes at a loss, because I know many of them are ready to respond, "You are not from the West; you are from *California.*" Maybe this would be the more effective answer: "I am, in fact, from the West, but I am from the illegitimate West, the fallen and degraded West. Still, I was only a baby when it happened, and no one consulted me."

My Western pedigree gets a lot better in the preceding generation; my father is from Brigham City, Utah, and my mother from Salt Lake. Sometimes, particularly when speaking in Ogden, Logan, Provo, and Salt Lake, I have clutched at this lineage, and tried to pull it, like a veil, over my Californianness.

In the states of the Colorado River Basin, California has for a long time held the role of the rapacious parasite draining the resources of the interior. This hostility has been intense for a long time, and it seems to be getting more intense. A few years ago, I served as a summing-up commentator at a big water conference in Arizona, and in between sessions, I composed this unfortunate limerick, which, I regret to tell you, effectively summarizes the feelings of many residents of the interior West:

When California falls into the sea,
Its neighbors will shout out with glee,
"That state was our bane,
"Causing trouble and pain,
"And now that it's gone, we are free."

More likely, if California left the scene, then states like Arizona, Nevada, Utah, and Colorado would lose one of their favorite scapegoats and have to face up to how much of their "trouble and pain," how much of the problems of growth, smog, and the overallocation of water, is of their own creation, or at least inflicted on them with their full cooperation and complicity. If California falls into the sea, the glee will be pretty short lived, as residents of the interior West discover how few of their problems really can be blamed on the Golden State.

It is hard to be a real Californian living in the Rockies these days, and that is no doubt why I have taken some comfort in deciding that maybe I no longer hold that status; maybe my license has expired. I haven't lived in California since 1972, and surely the decision to live in a state in adulthood should carry more weight in these matters than the accident of birth. But then, when I remember how passing myself off as a real Californian got me through graduate school, my rejection of a Californian identity seems distinctly ungrateful. And there is this more important fact: when residents of the interior West cringe and shudder over California, they are often cringing and shuddering over the challenges California faces in ethnic diversity. When residents of the interior try to edit California out of the West, they are, I think, trying to imagine a West without ethnic friction, without urban poverty, without smog, and without water overallocation.

But Denver, for instance, has ethnic friction and urban poverty, and it certainly has smog, and Denver would have all that with or without the inclusion of California in the boundaries of the West. In truth, especially in terms of water use, Denver is perceived by—and resented by—the Western Slope of Colorado in terms very reminiscent of the way in which the state of California is perceived by—and resented by—interior Westerners. It is not simply that the real Rocky Mountain West is, like California, very urbanized; it is also that the real California has enormous rural areas and extensive public lands, and thus struggles with many of the same issues that now preoccupy the interior West.

The story of my muddled personal identity as a Californian has considerable relevance because it is a miniversion of a larger regional puzzle, a puzzle that I think is one of the most significant, historically created challenges we face today. The American West is a region that came into being through a process of invasion and conquest. There were indigenous people living here, and then, in several cycles of conquest, Europeans and Euro-Americans came into the region and struggled with each other and with the natives. In a society that rested on a foundation of invasion and conquest, the matter of legitimacy was up for grabs, and it remained up for grabs as a large sector of the population continued to be migrants from other regions and nations.

Who, under these circumstances of constant population change, could qualify as a *real* Westerner, either born to Westernness or grown into Westernness, entitled to claim the right to make decisions about Western resources and to profit from those resources? Indian people have an obvious claim based on duration, as well as treaty rights. But the rest of us are all comparatively late arrivals or the descendants of late arrivals, and we are having a hell of a time dealing with this puzzling legacy of history. We often try to use chronology as our solution, trying to draw a line in time before which migrants into the West were legitimate and thoroughly deserving of the right to make use of Western resources and after which migrants into the West became illegitimate and undeserving, aliens and intruders. This is the well-known "close the door right after me" script, usually performed by people who do not seem to be aware of how extremely arbitrary and self-interested they are being in their setting of these deadlines. There is also no avoiding the fact that many of these efforts to close the door, throughout the Western past, have had race and racial prejudice as their determinants. Anyone in the late twentieth century who wants to engage in this exercise of distinguishing legitimate Westerners from illegitimate Westerners had better be prepared to deal, frankly and directly, with this heritage of racism, and of thin and brittle self-interest masquerading as high-minded principle.

In the late twentieth century, many white Americans claim to feel aggrieved and embattled, encountering what they call "reverse discrimination" stemming from efforts to help minorities. If the mandate resting on the California historians is inclusiveness of inquiry and understanding, then we are also under an obligation to inquire into and to try to understand that resentment. A couple of years ago, a white teacher in Oakland told me one story that helped me get a better understanding of these matters, especially of these moments in which our present constructions of ethnicity and identity work equally well at denying the humanity and individuality of that group wearing the label "white." The teacher was attending a panel discussion where the phrase "people of color" or "person of color" was used repeatedly. Thus, when an African American panelist wanted to refer to a white person, the phrase "person of color" was still hanging in the air, leading the speaker to refer to the white individual as a "nonperson of color." This newly coined phrase did not make the white people in the room feel particularly cheerful. I suppose the other option would have been to refer to whites as "colorless people," but that seems even more hurtful.

White people in California history have actually been quite colorful people, not nonpeople and not colorless; they have been very diverse and varied in their opinions, judgments, and behavior and often very much at odds with each other, rarely maintaining a unified wall of hostility toward others. On the matter of hostility between and within Western groups, my thoughts return to one of the rides at Disneyland in Anaheim: the ride in which multicolored dolls danced, bobbed, and sang, in penetrating tones, "It's a small, small world." I have not taken that cheerful ride in years, but it is impossible not to remember it and impossible not to resent it. When one thinks of that ride, one feels overdosed on sweetness, in deep need of a dill pickle or a spoonful of vinegar. The image of human life without conflict or friction, with everyone chirping away at the same squeaky song, drives one to imagine a more realistic counterride. In this ride, the dolls would dance, bob, and take an occasional swipe at one another. "It's a small, small world," the dolls would sing, "but it's a mean one."

For quite a long time, my understanding of the American West tilted toward the spirit of Disney's ride and away from the spirit of the counterride I propose here. In the preface to *The Legacy of Conquest,* I admitted that I was closer to Eleanor Roosevelt than to Angela Davis in my point of view. In the last lines of *The Legacy of Conquest,* I came as close to singing, "It's a small, small world" as a historian can:

> Indians, Hispanics, Asians, blacks, Anglos, businesspeople, workers, politicians, bureaucrats, natives, and newcomers, we share the same region and its history, but we wait to be introduced. The serious exploration of the process that made us neighbors provides that introduction.

One might well imagine that the person who wrote those lines is a person who observes National Brotherhood Week as her favorite annual holiday. And yet, against all probability, some imaginative readers have persuaded themselves that they find in *Legacy* a dark and grim version of the West, a story centered on misery and oppression. In fact, the good-hearted, earnest faith recorded in that book pushes past the edges of probability, all the way to the edge of the proposition that regional identity could give Westerners a bridge across the canyons of ethnic and gender inequality and hostility. In its furthest reaches of hopefulness, *The Legacy of Conquest* walked along the edge of this remarkable proposition: if people from backgrounds of privilege took seriously the history of people from backgrounds of scarcity, then the privileged people would redistribute their wealth, pay equitable wages, and forswear economic advantage.

There have been plenty of good reasons for this vision to unravel in the last few years: the bitterness of recent fights over Western resource use, the 1992 uprising in South Central Los Angeles, the dramatic gap between the lives led by privileged Westerners and the lives led by poor Westerners. Should I recant my earlier excesses of cheer and optimism? Does history offer any support for the hope that human beings will find reasons to be nicer to each other? Is there any prospect for thinking that things might be better than they used to be? Would a realistic view of conflict in the past make us feel better about conditions in the present?

However much scorn is being directed at contemporary Californians these days by residents of the interior West, it is probably dwarfed by the scorn that residents of the state of California have, over a century and a half, heaped on each other. When it comes to scorning and deprecating each other, people in California have been self-sufficient, self-reliant, and independent; they have not needed to import contempt; they have not had to ask for any help from outsiders to develop and train their skills in insulting each other.

The history of internal Californian friction is a rich one: the condescension and violence directed at the Indians by Spanish colonizers; the contempt and violence directed, in turn, at Mexicans *and* Indians, by Anglo invaders; early opposition to the presence of free blacks; the hostility and violence directed at Chinese immigrants, Japanese immigrants, and Filipino immigrants; the hatred of Okies; the scapegoating of Mexican immigrants; the exclusion of African Americans from jobs and housing; the viciousness of the Red Scare and Cold War in Hollywood; and, on a less injurious but still irritating level, the haughtiness of northern Californians peering down at southern Californians. You could write a thorough and coherent history of the peopling of California, and you could title your book: *California: A State of Scorn.* Californians took to wars over legitimacy like ducks to water, constantly questioning each other's right to occupy space in this state. The project of questioning each other's right to residence, questioning each other's status as real Californians, has been something close to the state sport.

Consider, for instance, the well-known but still stunning act of arrogance involved in the Foreign Miners' Taxes of the 1850s. California belonged to Mexico in 1848. In a matter of close timing that probably sent Cortez and Coronado tossing in their graves, James Marshall came upon gold in California just before the negotiators in Mexico City signed their treaty, transferring ownership of the Southwest to the United States. Anglo-Americans rushed into California, a territory in which they had been very sparsely represented, and instantly labeled the other guys "foreigners"—not only labeled them "foreigners" but designed, wrote, and imposed special taxes on these instant "foreigners" to keep them from competing with these instant legitimate Californians. The real Californians, this story reminds us, may well be the Californians who control the legislature, while the rest of us, no matter how distinguished our pedigree, scale down from each other in degrees of illegitimacy.

There is no question that the power to act on, implement, and enforce one's scorn makes that scorn a great deal more consequential. But it would be foolish and inaccurate to imagine that a lack of power revokes or even lessens the capacity for scorn. Consider, for instance, remarks made about immigrants by a San Francisco newspaper in the 1860s. This was what the African American newspaper, the *Elevator,* said about the Chinese in California:

> We have enough—and more—of them here now, eating out our substance, polluting the atmosphere with their filth, and the mind with their licentiousness.

The *Elevator,* historian Douglas Daniels tells us, "also held a low opinion of the European newcomers who caused [San Francisco's] population to swell." California, the editor of the paper felt, "should avoid the mistake of the eastern states, which erred by inviting 'the discontented and vicious of all Europe to their shores.' " African Americans hostile to immigrants drew on solid economic resentment, certain that all these others ranked above native-born blacks in access to jobs and opportunities: "The half idiotic and scrofulous peasant of the Swiss mountains," the *Elevator* said in the 1860s, "the lazzaroni of Italy, the bandit of Spain, the ignorant and unprincipled Greaser, the brutalized denizen of the English mines, the escaped convict from the penal settlements of Australia, all, all have been preferred to the man of color—native to the soil, and to the manner born."[1]

This passage is an essential reminder that the idea of the solidarity of the oppressed is a hell of a principle to put into practice. No wonder African Americans did not set themselves to building bridges of goodwill to the Chinese; the immediate logic of resentment made a lot more sense than the abstract sentiment of joining forces against a common oppressor. Much more recently, the tensions between and among African Americans, Latinos, and Asian Americans, brought to

public display in the Rodney King riots, offer an even more disturbing reminder that occasions when the oppressed transcend their differences are rare and wonderful moments of grace in Western history
but never moments to take for granted.

Another demonstration of the jumbled ties between tolerance and
scorn comes from a woman who has begun to emerge as my favorite
Californian, the much-underrecognized Mary Roberts Coolidge.
Coolidge's pedigree, as a Californian, is flawed: she was born in Indiana in 1860 and spent much of her youth in Ithaca, where her father taught agriculture at Cornell. After several years of
schoolteaching, she got a Ph.D. in 1896 at Stanford and was an assistant and associate professor of sociology at Stanford. She was af-
filiated with the Carnegie Institute in Washington for a time and
worked at a settlement house in San Francisco. In 1918, she became
a professor at Mills College in California. Married to a writer, she
lived in Berkeley until her death in 1945. Again, her pedigree by na-
tivity is not good, but if Mary Roberts Coolidge is not a real Californian, then we are all in real trouble.

At Stanford, Coolidge began working on a book about Chinese
immigration, a book finally published in 1909. This is, of course, a
topic on which passions ran high, and ran highest in the state of California. In twenty-four very detailed, very carefully researched chapters, Mary Roberts Coolidge laid out the history of the Chinese in
California and the rise of anti-Chinese sentiment. Her approach was
remarkably clearheaded and critical. When, for instance, she discussed
the Foreign Miners' Tax, she noted that the law targeted only foreigners of dark skin and "*not* Germans, Irish, and Englishmen, although many of *them*," as she said, "were not naturalized, and had
far less right in the country than the native Indians and Spaniards."
Coolidge was unrelenting in her exploration of the opportunism of
California politicians, noting the direct and constant correlation between elections and cycles of anti-Chinese fervor. When she examined
the California Senate Memorial of 1877, asking the United States
Congress for legislation that would exclude the Chinese, she found it
to be a "desperate resort to misrepresentation [and] falsehood," "explained by the fact that nobody who ever expected to hold office
dared to say a word in favor of the Chinese." When white working-
men began to blame all their troubles on the Chinese, Coolidge was
direct and careful in examining the causes of the depression in Cali-

fornia economic life, a state of affairs that the Chinese could not possibly have caused.[2]

Coolidge's legislative history of the 1882 Chinese Exclusion Law remains one of the best available, and she was typically clear in her judgment of the law, noting that it committed "the United States to a race discrimination at variance with our professed theories of government." She noted how the exclusion law separated Chinese families; without the free immigration of women, Chinese men could hardly create a normal society. In the absence of Chinese women, some Chinese men married Indian, Mexican, or Anglo women. In an era in which many whites abhorred miscegenation, Coolidge was very much on her own track of opinion. The children of these mixed marriages, she said, "so far from being the 'monstrosities' predicted by early Californians, are superior, both physically and mentally." Even if one does not know what provided her evidence for this assertion of superiority, one still has to admire the generosity and tolerance of that assertion.[3]

Coolidge denied that the Chinese refused to assimilate; "it does indeed," she said, "take two to assimilate." The alleged Chinese stubbornness in resisting change was "the least convincing of arguments," she said, "when it comes from the mouths of those who have not permitted them to assimilate." The Chinese had been excluded because of "their virtues, not their vices"—excluded because they were "industrious, thrifty and shrewd," and thus seen as a menace to the monopoly of jobs by white workers. The exclusion of the Chinese arose from an "arrogant and narrow-minded temper bred by pioneer conditions, monopolistic spirit, and the lack of sanity and justice." "Injustice" on that scale, Mrs. Coolidge proclaimed, "brings retribution in the degradation of those who practise it," and California had badly damaged itself with its "lawlessness, class hatred, and incapacity for cooperation."[4]

Now we get back to the matter of consistency in tolerance. Mrs. Coolidge's determination to defend the Chinese meant that she sometimes took a good, solid swipe at European immigrants. "Every charge brought against the Chinese," she wrote, "can be brought with greater force against many of the Europeans who now constitute the bulk of immigration at the Atlantic ports." Coolidge did not sit around waiting for others to suggest what those charges might be. "To bring the comparison nearer home," she said, it is perfectly well-known that the Italian quarter of San Francisco is unsanitary and immoral; that the Italians are clannish and very slow to speak English; that some of them are drunken, violent, even murderous; that only those of the better class assimilate in the first generation and that their children leave school early and are by no means always cleanly or intelligent. It is common knowledge that the Italian has a very low standard of living, that he accepts a low wage, that he is not easily "unionized," and that he pays an infinitesimal part of the state revenue. Yet no one in California proposes that the Italian should go, for two reasons: because he is a Caucasian and because he has a useful vote.

I begin to suspect that Italian Americans living in California will not be joining me in the campaign to make Mary Roberts Coolidge a California hero. I fear I will not do a lot better in recruiting the support of Irish Americans: "In California," Coolidge wrote,

> although [the Irish] constitute only 5 to 7% of the total population, they constitute forty per cent of the almshouse inmates and nearly half of the arrests for drunkenness.[5]

"Oh my goodness, Mrs. Coolidge," one finds oneself thinking, "does the cause of standing up for the Chinese really require you to knock down the Italians and the Irish? Isn't there a way in which you could stand up for the recognition of the Chinese as real, legitimate, deserving Californians, without suggesting that Irish people incline toward madness and alcoholism? Can't one stand up for the rights of the Chinese without having to imply that the Italians are scum?"

These are interesting moments for me, these occasions when I try, and try quite hard, to strike up a conversation with someone from the past. I would very much like to have this conversation about consistency in tolerance with Coolidge, with the African American editor of the newspaper the *Elevator,* and also with Frederick Law Olmsted. Olmsted spent two years trying to manage the estate at Mariposa from 1863 to 1865. In general, Olmsted thought that life in California was a mess: "Everything is as it must be," he said, "where men don't live but merely camp." Olmsted was quite good at designing urban parks, but he was even better when it came to wielding scorn and contempt. John C. Fremont, his predecessor at Mariposa, for instance, was, as Olmsted put it, "a selfish, treacherous, unmitigated scoundrel." Olmsted, in other words, did not like Fremont.[6]

Olmsted was so good at scorn that one's patience with him can run short. The United States, he thought, was "peopled by the weaker, the poorer, the more vagrant; the least valuable, the least civilized." The good, in other words, stayed home. "I hate barbarism and like civilization in all its forms," Olmsted wrote. "I wish I could live in England."[7] When one reads this snooty line, this classic statement of the conviction that the grass is always greener on the eastern side of the fence, one feels inclined to say, "Why don't just you do that, Mr. Olmsted? Try living in England, and see what that does to your comparative understanding of barbarism."

For all his snootiness, Olmsted wrote tolerantly, if also patronizingly, of the Chinese; in comparison with the whites, he said, the Chinese were "the more industrious, peaceable, temperate, and altogether respectable and civilized." But here, too, California tolerance came in skips and starts. The same person who wrote with some openmindedness on the Chinese offered this judgment of another group of people: "After a few generations," Olmsted said of the gradual process of uplift of the degraded, "even the Irish may adopt the habits of a progressive civilization."[8]

My point, with Olmsted, Coolidge, and many other similar case studies, is that it is damned hard to find consistent, clear, coherent examples of tolerance. Saying nice things about one group seems to induce a powerful urge to say something contemptuous about another group. But my point is also that we very badly need heroes of tolerance and empathy these days, and we simply cannot wait around, hoping for purity and consistency in these matters. By the time we find a hero of unquestioned clarity, purity, and consistency, we will have torn each other apart. Making our peace with the muddled state of our moral heroes might, in truth, allow us more room for moral heroism in our own muddled times. An example of pure and consistent nobility, if we could find such a thing, would be useless. As flawed creatures ourselves, we find better, truer, and certainly more practical inspiration in flawed heroes.

In that spirit, I turn to one of the most frustrating of these California case studies in impure and complex empathy. In 1983, a book came out called *Famous All Over Town,* by a fellow named Danny Santiago. I was living in Cambridge, Massachusetts, and I was wild for the opportunity to read stories from the West. I got a copy right away and became, as a lot of reviewers did as well, an instant fan of

Danny Santiago. What a great book, I told a number of people; this is a great portrait of Mexican American life in East Los Angeles, written with a vernacular voice that obviously has some relation to Huck Finn but that has its own distinctive descendant-of-Mexican-immigrants style.

Who was this Danny Santiago?

Who, indeed?

A year passed, and I had enthusiastically recommended this book to a number of people. I had moved from Cambridge, Massachusetts, to Boulder, and a certain lingering form of East Coast dependence had kept me on the subscriber list for the *New York Review of Books*. So I was one of the first to get the word, when an article appeared there in 1984, with the answer to my question, "Who *was* Danny Santiago?"

Danny Santiago proved to be not a young Chicano writer but an elderly white man named Dan James; of course, James translates to Santiago in Spanish. Dan James was from a wealthy white family in Kansas City, Missouri, a family with a second home in Carmel. In the 1930s and the 1940s, he worked in Hollywood and joined the Communist Party. In 1951, three years after he left the party, he and his wife were called before the House Committee on Un-American Activities. Dan James was blacklisted. Writing under his own name became impossible.

While they lived in Los Angeles, Dan and Lillith James spent a great deal of time in the Mexican American community in East Los Angeles. For fifteen years they worked with youth groups. They made many friends and became compadres—godparents—in a number of families. As Dan James wrote his friend John Gregory Dunne:

> Our closest *compadre* was Lalo Rios and it was his family and his wife Connie's that we knew best. We baptized Lalo's Ruben and five years later shared 24 hour watches as Ruben died of leukemia. We baptized their third son Tomas and in '74 we buried Lalo who we thought would one day bury us. . . . And now we stay with his widow when we're in LA. . . . you can say that over the past 35 years we've known four generations of Mexicanos in their best and worst of times. . . .

In the 1960s, Dan James began writing stories about a Mexican American community in Los Angeles, stories that appeared under the name Danny Santiago. James could not, John Gregory Dunne said, "write under his own name both because of the blacklist and because he had lost confidence in his own ability." Danny, Dan James told Dunne, is "so much freer than I am myself."[9]

John Gregory Dunne revealed this hidden story in August of 1984. *Famous All Over Town* had received very favorable reviews, some of them from Chicano reviewers. When the news about Dan James came out, everyone was flummoxed. The young Chicano writer we had admired so much had proven to be an old white man. Over the last ten years, we stayed flummoxed. I myself stopped recommending the book, put it on a shelf, and did not dare look at it, on the chance that it might turn out that I still liked it. But alas, I reread it recently, and I still like it. After more than a decade of being flummoxed by this curious and unsettling event in California identity, it is time to reckon with it.

Henry Louis Gates has called our attention to the issues raised by *Famous All Over Town*. " 'Passing' and 'impersonation,' " Gates writes, "may sound like quaint terms of a bygone era of ethnic thinking, but they continue to inform the way we read. Our literary judgments, in short, remain hostage to the ideology of authenticity." The result is that we treat American authors a bit as we would treat show dogs or show cats; we want to know their pedigree; we want to see their papers; we want proof of their line of descent. When someone like Dan James presents the wrong papers, we travel through disorientation and arrive rapidly at disappointment and disillusionment. "Start interrogating the notion of cultural authenticity," Gates says, "and our most trusted critical categories come into question. Maybe Danny Santiago's *Famous All Over Town*," Gates writes, "can usefully be considered a work of Chicano literature."[10]

Maybe. But it can certainly be considered an essential artifact for thinking about ethnicity and identity in our times. After the House Un-American Activities Committee split James's Hollywood community into the informers and the informed-upon and after the blacklist took away his chances to write under his own name, Dan James became a socially unmoored, unanchored person. He found an anchor in a Mexican American neighborhood in East Los Angeles. American historians have a standard way of handling this kind of story. This becomes another case study, to be matched with the stories of people like George Catlin, Charles Fletcher Lummis, Mary Austin, John Collier, and many others, case studies in antimodernism, case studies in romantic racialism, case studies of white people rendered uncomfortable by their own society who sought, in the company of people of color, an imagined, warmhearted, vital alternative to the coldness of life in a modern, industrial, urban nation-state.

I do not think that is a satisfactory framework for Dan James. Dan James did not *imagine* that life in his modern nation-state was cold and unsatisfying. It is, on the contrary, hard to imagine a more cold and unsatisfying treatment than the one he got during the McCarthy era. The Mexican American people he turned to were *not* a timeless alternative to life in a modern, urban, industrial nation-state; they were themselves fully a part of that modern, industrial, urban nation-state life, just as fully participants in modern life as the congressmen who put Dan James through his grilling in 1951.

"Yes, Virginia, there is a Danny Santiago," Henry Louis Gates concludes his reflections on authenticity. In Danny Santiago, there is a compelling reminder that the quest for ethnic identity is as much spiritual as it is political. When we confront the fact that Dan James could write as Danny and could *not* write as his Anglo–Kansas City, elite, post–Communist Party Dan James self, we are on the turf of cultural politics, but we are also on turf that lies close to the soul. Whatever that maddening term "authenticity" might mean, there was authenticity and real urgency in Dan James's search for a set of relationships more trustworthy than the company of the informers and ideologues of Cold War Hollywood. If we describe James's relationship to Mexican American ethnicity purely in terms of trendy antimodernism, romantic racialism, or even a kinder, gentler cultural imperialism, we give a deep story a shallow meaning.

What is, to me, most terrifying about the present state of American race relations is the evidence that many white Americans are indifferent to, ignorant of, or even bored by the dilemmas faced by nonwhites. Whatever else Dan James signifies, he signifies a response to ethnicity that is radically different from that chilling lack of empathy. "No human culture," Henry Louis Gates tells us, "is inaccessible to someone who makes the effort to understand, to learn. . . ." And that conclusion, one has to hope, is the conclusion we might reach in our inquiries into California history.[11]

In 1855, the African American minister Darius Stokes offered his own statement about who registered as a real Californian, and it is one of the most memorable passages of prose in this state's records. "The white man came," Reverend Stokes said,

> and we came with him; and by the blessing of God we will stay with him side by side; wherever he goes will we go; and should another Sutter discover another El Dorado, be it where it may . . . no sooner shall the white man's foot be firmly planted there than looking over his shoulder he will see the black man, like his shadow, by his side.[12]

Reverend Stokes not only had the gift of language, he also had the gift of prophecy. What he said would happen is what *has* happened: wherever white people have gone in this state, black people have also gone, and gone in the company of Indian, Latino, and Asian people as well. The history of California may not have matched the ride at Disneyland in its cheeriness, but California has proven to be, as Reverend Stokes realized, a small world. We are not escaping each other's company. African American, Indian, Latino, Asian American, Anglo-American—we are all real Californians, and our stories will not be detached from each other. What Stokes predicted is realized truth. And yet it is my guess that most white people who have read Darius Stokes's remarkable statement have reacted to it as an ominous, disturbing, and unsettling prophecy. Remember those words: "No sooner shall the white man's foot be firmly planted than, looking over his shoulder, he shall see the black man, like a shadow, by his side." I suspect most whites who have read this statement have responded with something closer to "Oh dear" than "Thank heavens." Even if I stand convicted as a unreformed believer in the "small, small world" vision of cross-cultural harmony, I go on record with my belief that real California historians live under a mandate for inclusiveness, a mandate that makes "Thank heavens" as viable, logical, and persuasive a response as "Oh dear."

IV-C

The Shadows of Heaven Itself: The Demanding Dreams of the American West

> The shadows of the Rockies which fall across the Front Range every evening are more than a picturesque backdrop to our daily routine; they are the shadows of heaven itself.
>
> Archbishop FRANCIS STAFFORD
> Pastoral Letter, November 24, 1994

> Reliable information concerning the New West is of so recent date that the mass of the people in the East are not posted as to the actual facts. . . . Were some well-posted citizen of the New West to present the actual facts about that domain to the inhabitants of the Eastern States, a multitude would denounce him as a liar, or pity him for possessing more imagination than judgment. . . . This book does not contain all the marvels of the New West, by any means.
>
> WILLIAM THAYER
> *Marvels of the New West*, 1890

THE NEWEST NEW WEST

The "New West" is a phrase with a history. In 1869, excited by opportunities presented by the completion of the transcontinental railroad, the reporter Samuel Bowles called his book *Our New West.* "Nature, weary of repetitions," Bowles wrote, "has, in the New West, created originally, freshly, uniquely, majestically. . . . Nowhere are broader and higher mountains; nowhere, climates more propitious; nowhere broods an atmosphere so pure and exhilarating."[1]

Nineteenth- and twentieth-century observers of their respective New Wests share an exhilaration brought to life by the novelty and power of Western nature. But twentieth-century writers have an advantage: they have every opportunity to recognize that human nature, in its dreams, visions, and ambitions, has turned out to be just as "weary of repetition," just as original, just as astonishing, as anything nature itself ever cooked up.

Consider Denver's winter Stock Show. One of the oldest and biggest livestock markets and rodeos in the West, this annual event, a bastion of tradition, celebrates Old Western rural values. Men— briefly—ride bucking horses and bulls; merchandisers sell corral equipment and bull semen; and even apparent novelties, like the blow-dryers used to primp cattle, serve the traditional goal of securing the best price possible for protein on the hoof. And yet, for all the weight of the past, the Stock Show shows the passage of time in a thousand ways.

In January of 1996, the *New York Times* carried a story about the Stock Show. The reporter called me. What did I think about the rise of Western ranches devoted to emus and ostriches, llamas and alpacas? I said that the history of the West has hinged on the introduction of exotic species; in that sense, the ostrich and the emu were just the latest successors to cows and horses. But another comment, quoted in the article, sticks more firmly in the mind: "There is a dignity in the words 'cowboys' and 'cattlemen'—it's just not there with 'ostrich people' and 'emu people.' "[2]

The newest New West calls itself to our attention in all sorts of ways, though this particular occasion of recognition is my favorite. It raises one's hopes for a new brand of Western literature, in which tall, silent ostrichboys, with their characteristic stiff-legged gait, face off against each other in showdowns on Main Street and then rejoin their Montessori schoolmarms for a debriefing and a capuccino, while the townspeople gather to watch anxiously from the mountain bike stores and the aromatherapist shop. At the turn of the century, Owen Wister published *The Virginian* and created the archetypal Westerner, despite his oddly Southern name. The 1990s present a comparable opportunity, for an ambitious writer to make her authorial reputation with the publication of *The Californian*, symbol of the New West of emus and ostriches, espressos and utility vehicles.

"The rapid increase of [the New West's] population is as great a marvel as a cañon," William Thayer wrote in 1890.[3] To Thayer and his contemporaries, population growth was a wonderful phenomenon, an occasion for celebration. A century later, while some still celebrate growth, many others respond with laments and resistance. One thinks that one has seen all the possible variations on the injuries, costs, and disadvantages of uncontrolled human settlement, and reliably, one turns out to be wrong.

"Growth Hard on Rodents," announced a 1996 headline in the *Denver Post*. In the long-running battle pitting American enterprise against prairie dogs, the rodents had picked up unexpected allies. "Hated, hunted, and otherwise disposed of by ranchers and farmers, who considered them a menace to crops and livestock," prairie dogs now had advocates who recognized that the rodents provide food "vital to numerous animals," including eagles. Others simply found the animals "cute." The collision between expanding human settlements and established prairie dog villages had thus become a "public relations nightmare for developers, businesses, or cities."[4]

What to do? Another headline hinted at the answer. "Dream Led to Prairie-Dog Vacuum": a man named Gay Balfour, in desperate circumstances, received inspiration in a dream. He "saw an enormous yellow truck with a green hose sticking out it, sucking prairie dogs out of the ground." A few days later, he came upon a yellow truck, used for suctioning out sewers, and, at a supply store, he found green hoses of exactly the right diameter. The dream took concrete form: a vacuum called "Dog-Gone." Inserted into a hole, Dog-Gone pulled out the rodent, rocketed it through the tube, and shot it out, "into a big tank on the back of the truck, slamming it into a wall of thick foam rubber," where it dropped onto a similarly padded floor.[5]

The rapid pace of change in this region has made a lot of its longtime residents feel that they have been on the equivalent of the prairie dog's trip through the Dog-Gone, though without the benefit of the foam-rubber landing. Dreams drove the New West of the nineteenth century, and though they have taken a beating, dreams persist—even thrive—in our New West, familiar dreams of a new beginning in a new place, new dreams of humane vacuums for prairie dogs or of open ranges of ostriches. Human nature has met and matched nature in wildness and novelty. William Thayer's phrase of 1890 has new resonance: "This book does not contain all the marvels of the New West, by any means."[6]

THE WEST AS REMEDY

Once there was a fellow in Missouri whose health reached a point of collapse. "I can't do anything more for you," his doctor told him. "Your only hope is to move as soon as you can to a place with a healthier climate."

Racing against frailty, the man packed up and left for Santa Fe. But the opportunity to breathe dry, pure air came too late, and his decline continued. In a matter of weeks, his body was returned for burial in Missouri. At the funeral, two of his pals stood contemplating the attractively presented corpse.

"Don't he look nice?" one of them said.

"He sure does," the other said. "It looks like Santa Fe done him a world of good."[7]

Square at the center of the dreams directed at the American West has been the hope that the West will prove therapeutic, medicinal, restorative, and reinvigorating. Name the affliction, and the West seems to offer the remedy: dry air to cure respiratory problems, open spaces to relieve the pressures that weigh down the soul in teeming cities, freedom and independence to provide a restorative alternative to mass society's regimentation and standardization. As the story of the Missouri old-timer indicates, the American West has defaulted as often as it has delivered on its promise to cure. And yet the belief in the West as remedy persists. We stand currently on another one of its peaks.

In the nineteenth century, finding themselves afflicted with ill-defined diseases, a variety of influential Americans convinced themselves that their road to recovery ran westward. From Francis Parkman to Theodore Roosevelt, these men wrote vividly of their experiences, formalizing and codifying an image of the West as a place where purity of air, inspiring landscapes, and general vigor and heartiness brought weakened men back to strength. For a number of these health seekers, luckier in their timing than the late-arriving fellow from Missouri, the American West did indeed do them a world of good, and they were ardent in passing on the news.

By the late nineteenth century, the West had a well-established reputation as an open-air pharmacy stocked with antidotes for the afflictions of conventional life. A century later, the faith that defines the West as remedy for the malaise of conventional life claims a multitude of believers. Life in the centers of power—in New York, in Los Angeles, in Washington, D.C.—wears down the soul; the spirit of rebellion flares. The powers that be need not, however, tremble. Before malaise can even begin to whisper the call to resist or rebel, the West will provide a remedy: a vacation, a second home, a skiing trip, an Indian painting, a New Age workshop, a sculpture of a coyote, a visit to a dude ranch. The movie *City Slickers* provided the best recent example of the pattern: the discontented businessman can't take the city and the rat race anymore; he and his friends head West to a ranch where they take a herd on the trail and find inner strength and peace; the businessman returns, in good spirits, to take up his burdens in the city. The West works him over and sends him back to the rat race, a restored and revitalized rat.

In the late twentieth century, the West is very popular indeed: popular as a remedy for social and personal discontent; popular as a setting for movies, documentaries, novels, essays, and memoirs; popular as a source of imagery for commercially appealing clothing, jewelry, furniture, buildings, and interiors; popular as a place of inspiration for seekers after spiritual connection in a disconnected world; and, perhaps most consequentially, popular as a residential sanctuary for prosperous emigrants from the East and West Coasts.

This is a heavy burden to bear. Consider what effort it takes for the city of Santa Fe to remain properly quaint. In the late nineteenth century, Santa Fe's buildings represented a range of building types. Emotionally drawn to the style of Pueblo and Spanish colonial buildings, an Anglo elite in the city pushed for adobe construction. They encouraged use of the Santa Fe Style, even if that meant covering brick or wooden buildings with a veneer of adobe-simulating stucco. In 1957, a city ordinance expanded the means of persuasion, beyond exhortation to mandate.[8]

Today's visitors to Santa Fe may feel themselves in the company of the spirits of the distant Indian and Spanish past. They are, however, in more direct contact with the spirits of a group of twentieth-century Anglo boosters, determined to make Santa Fe look right. Santa Fe *would* fulfill the newcomers' dreams, even if it took a considerable exercise of regulatory power to bring the town into compliance. Santa Fe became one of a number of settings designed and built to convince visitors that they were having an authentic and genuine Western experience.

The processing and refining of Western places into marketable commodities is an old and established custom. The impact of television and movies surely added wagonloads of grist to this mill. All through the West, businesses and entire towns offer tourists the chance to visit the "Real West." Viewed with detachment, the popularity of these places seems profoundly silly. In P. T. Barnum's times, there was a sucker born every minute, and the birth rate in this particular sector of the population has certainly not declined. These prove, moreover, to be very-consenting suckers who regard any effort to rescue them from error as an attack on a deeply held faith. Any effort to point out the fakeness of the "Real West" will unleash from its enthusiasts many cries of injury. Try to write realistically about the Old West, and what you write will be condemned as gloomy or disillusioning.

Is there anything surprising in this? Remember the West's emotional role as the antidote, the remedy, the painkiller, the refuge, the space where the soul recuperates from a multitude of injuries. At the end of the last century, John Muir referred to his treasured places in the Sierras as "temples," sacred places that commerce would desecrate and dishonor. At the end of this century, Muir's extension of the religious metaphor has kicked off the traces and run wild. Belief bordering on religious faith has been heavily invested in the most unlikely sites and situations. Commerce still devotes some of its time to its old habits of invading and trashing Muir's sacred natural settings. But commerce has also created a range of new Western sites, icons, and images that are, to their believers, equally sacred concerns. Among its other marvels and wonders, the New West offers shrines to the Old West, places where faith and profit making prosper together.

BABY BOOMERS HOME ALONE

[*American Demographics*] reports that, as the baby-boomers turn 50, publications targeted at older readers are using such euphemisms as "mature" and "prime" and coming up with upbeat titles such as "Looking Forward," "New Horizons," "Now Is the Time," and "Young at Heart."

Denver Post, December 1996

People blame New York when their relationships don't work out. They think if they just lived someplace else it

would be better. But they don't want to go to Iowa. They
want to go to Colorado. . . . It's so beautiful. It's like
Shangri-La. It's a place to go where people never age.
> Interview with CANDACE BUSHNELL,
> author of *Sex and the City*,
> *Denver Post*, September 1996

Why is the West currently so popular? What is it about the 1990s
that brought Western dreaming to one of its all-time peaks?

There are any number of good answers. The most paradoxical of
them rests on the fact that the 1990s are a time when so many
things—entertainment, public debate, political conventions, commercial products—seem manipulated and manufactured. When reality appears in a state so unmistakably simulated, designed, and
virtual, the Old West gains heightened appeal as the place where people who have had enough of falsity go to find authenticity—even if
that Old Western authenticity is itself a theme-park creation.

These are, moreover, times in which no one wants to cast herself—or admit herself to be—an insider to power. Everyone running
for office, for instance, struggles to claim the image of the outsider,
free of the taint of Washington Beltway insiderness. There is no better stage set on which to play the role of the rugged outsider than the
American West. Here, of course, is another sizable paradox: because
the West is very much associated with individualism, it thereby attracts floods and herds and hordes of people sharing the identical
ambition to play the part of rugged individualists, too.

Anxiety about gender is also at stake here. The enthusiasm for nature and for the Old West in the 1990s bears a noticeable correlation
to a rejection of and retreat from the transformed gender roles of our
times, whether in the presence of women in occupational areas formerly forbidden to them or in the androgynous self-presentation of
stars like Michael Jackson. In peculiar times like these, some enthusiasts may well be thinking, best to retreat to the mythic region where
men are men, and women recognize and celebrate the maleness of men.

If this seems an overstretched interpretation, think of Edward
Abbey, one of the New West's most popular writers, the writer frequently celebrated as representing—indeed, launching—a whole new
attitude toward Western nature. There is reason to be moderate in
finding originality or novelty in Abbey's thinking. Although Abbey is
"usually portrayed as an outrageous iconoclast," the historian Elliott

West has noted, Abbey's "refrain would ring familiar and true to thousands before him." Many European and Euro-American men before Abbey "have pictured themselves standing alone in the West's big spaces." Quite the opposite of a radical break in American attitudes toward nature, "nothing could be more traditional—more hidebound—than Abbey's old, longing dream." In West's memorable phrase, Abbey was the "the modern master of the adolescent male escape fantasy."[9] However different their constituencies of fans may have been in politics and in attitudes toward extractive industries, John Wayne and Edward Abbey stood united in their warm feelings toward masculinity.

The environmental movement has, of course, done a great deal to persuade the American public that life lived in the presence of nature is life with a heightened opportunity for balance and sanity. Here, too, paradox works with a heavy hand: environmentalists spoke so persuasively of the attractions of nature that they recruited many visitors and new residents, who then, by their sheer numbers, jeopardized the natural attractions that the environmentalists had set out to protect in the first place.

White flight has also been a powerful factor in this story. Along with traffic, congestion, pollution, an uneven economy, and high real estate taxes, the racial and ethnic complexity of the West Coast and the East Coast was one of the principal "push" factors recruiting new arrivals to the interior; in much of the Rocky Mountain West, whites were an undisputed majority. It was no coincidence that environmentalists like Edward Abbey and former Colorado governor Richard Lamm have been fierce in their condemnations of Mexican immigration. We should meet the immigrants at the border, Abbey was given to saying, "and then arm them. They can go back to Mexico and start their own revolution."[10]

When environmentalists targeted Mexican immigrants, strong emotion was giving reason a run for its money. Claiming that their concern is the overuse of natural resources and an excessively heavy human impact on the land, Western environmentalists who take up the cause of immigration restriction target Mexican immigrants, the people who are in the weakest position as consumers, the least likely to crowd into the national parks or into the newest subdivision. While the human diversity of the interior West is considerable, for white Americans troubled by the ethnic complexity that is unmistakable and unavoidable on the East and West Coasts, areas like the Northern Rockies can still look like the place of remedy and refuge. When Los Angeles Police Department officer Mark Fuhrman, the man who, thanks to the O. J. Simpson trial, was for a time America's most famous racist, chose to relocate to northern Idaho, it was an unhappy reminder of the degree to which the 1990s enthusiasm for things Western coincides with a white retreat from other races.[11]

An equally important and much more frequently addressed explanation for the West's popularity involves technology: the emergence of the FAX machines and computers and Internet ties that make it possible to detach the workers from the office and let the workers choose their place of residence by its amenities and attractions, especially its scenic appeal. As telecommuters in places like Telluride report, their working day is invigorated and enriched by the chance to punctuate it with snowboarding or a hike. "It's great," reported one young woman, a writer of reports on focus groups, describing the pleasant working experiences she and her boss were able to achieve: "We ride up the chairlift with our red pens and edit reports."[12]

Popular attitudes and tax policies of the 1980s are another important determinant. The 1980s took many of the restraints off the accumulation of wealth, wealth which would then head off in search of novel and satisfying ways to exercise purchasing power. One target of that quest would be real estate in handsome Western settings. And that real estate would carry particular attractions precisely because of the conglomeration of factors that had reduced its attractions in earlier times—isolation, aridity, altitude, heavy snow, or general ruggedness, particularly if there was a good airport a short distance away.

These answers are all surely clues to a puzzle that may be too immediate for solution in our times. But the answer that impresses me as the most important of all comes, compactly, in one word, and the word is "baby boomers."[13]

In the middle of the twentieth century, when baby boomers were babies and toddlers, two trends of influence coincided: the rise of television and the popularity of Roy Rogers, Gene Autry, and Hopalong Cassidy. Hoppy was a particular marketing success. "Every product that adopted his name (at a fat fee to Hoppy)," *Time* magazine reported, "was sucked instantly into the maw of an insatiable demand." Badgered by their resourceful children, the parents of the baby boomers invested heavily in Hoppy items. Hoppy was a good guy who nonetheless wore black clothes (though symbol systems could only be stretched so far, and so he held on to his white hat). In one year during Hoppy's glory days, so many children wanted clothes modeled on his that the United States ran short of black dye.[14]

In regular television episodes, Hopalong behaved admirably, with impeccable bravery, and reliably and regularly brought bad guys to justice. Hoppy's fictional virtue proved to be a powerful force in actuality. William Boyd, the actor who played the part, had been a profligate and unsteady fellow; after a year or two in the job, swept away by the admiration of his youthful fans, Boyd got his own life in order, refusing to let Hopalong be tainted by his impersonator's flaws. William Boyd had been transformed into a good guy by his role as white-hatted Hoppy; he cut back on drinking, he stayed away from wild parties, and he is reported to have stayed faithful to his final wife.[15] As in all things Western, image and reality traveled, not as distant strangers, but as close companions and certainly as business partners.

William Boyd took to talking about himself—which is to say, about Hoppy—in the third person. "Look at the way those crowds act," he said. "They all want to touch Hoppy. . . . Crowds never pull at Hoppy or try to tear his clothing. If they start pushing I just say, 'Now kids . . . be good kids'—I call them all kids, grown-ups and all—and they settle down." Under his powerful influence, "children with impressively styled cap guns and bejeweled double holsters . . . were so commonplace that those without them seemed a little underdressed, and those who still carried such outmoded armament as X-ray Guns or Atomic Disintegrators, hopelessly old-fashioned."[16]

Roy Rogers matched and even exceeded Hopalong Cassidy's marketing energy. At his peak, Jane and Michael Stern have written, "the only celebrity name on more things than Roy's was Walt Disney." Consider a partial listing from a recent collector's inventory of Roy Rogers memorabilia: alarm clocks, archery sets, badges, bandannas, savings banks, basketballs, beds, bedspreads, belts, binoculars, boots, briefs, bubble gum, calendars, cameras, canteens, card games, cereal bowls, chaps, charm bracelets, chinaware, clay-modeling sets, coats, coloring sets, combs, cups, curtains, dartboards, dolls, flashlights, footballs, furniture, milk glasses (marked, at different stages of emptiness, tenderfoot, posse leader, deputy, sheriff), gloves, guitars, guns, harmonicas, hats, holster outfits, rocking horses, horseshoes, jackets, jeans, jewelry, key cases, chains, and rings, knifes, lamps, lanterns, lariats, lassos, lunch box sets, masks, mittens, moccasins, mugs, napkins, outfits, pajamas, pants, pens and pencils, pistols, plates, playing cards, playsuits, puppets, puzzles, raincoats, ranch sets, rifles, rings, robes, saddles, scarves, school bags, scrapbooks, shirts, shoes, shorts, slacks, sleepers, slippers, soap, socks, spurs, suits, suspenders, sweaters, sweatshirts, swim trunks, T-shirts, tables, writing tablets, telephones, telescopes, tents, ties, toothbrushes, tops, Trigger toys, V chairs, vests, view masters, wall plaques, wallets, washclothes, watches, watercolor sets, and yoyos, as well as toy buckboards, chuck wagons, covered wagons, horse wagons, jeeps, and stagecoaches. Roy Rogers's own children tested the products he endorsed, and thus they spent their childhood carrying items emblazoned with their father's name and face. Years later, Dusty (Roy, Jr.) poignantly "confided" that "one of his fondest dreams was to have a Gene Autry or Hopalong Cassidy lunchbox."[17]

While one might, appropriately, accent the ways in which the TV cowboys shaped the consuming habits of the baby boomers, the influences may have been, at least temporarily, moral and political as well. The cowboys, as Jane and Michael Stern put it, "provided young baby boomers with unconfusing heroes and a clear sense of right and wrong." Everyone knows that a significant percentage of the people coming of age in the 1960s were driven by a hope for racial justice, effective social welfare policies, and meaningful individual action. Contemplate, then, a few items from the various creeds or rules or statements of belief offered by the 1950s Western TV heroes to guide and sustain their loyal fans. Here lies one point of origin for the activism of the 1960s in the picture of little 1950s cowboys and cowgirls pledging their faith to these various declarations of true Western behavior.

> I believe that all men are created equal and that everyone has within himself the power to make a better world. *(The Lone Ranger's Creed)*

> [The cowboy] must not advocate or possess racially intolerant ideas. He must help people in distress. *(Gene Autry's Cowboys' Code)*

> Protect the weak and help them. *(Roy Rogers Riders Club Rules to Live By)*

No one knows what might or might not connect the cowboys' creeds to the Port Huron Statement of the Students for a Democratic Society and other inspirational statements of the 1960s New Left, but there is no question that the cowboy stars of the 1950s were very much aware of the particular bonds tying them to a certain demographic segment of baby boomer kids.[18]

"What you have to understand, about Westerns and the people who were part of them," Gene Autry said, "is that it was a great way not to grow up." An interviewer of Hopalong Cassidy (speaking, as usual, through William Boyd) reported that Hoppy "seems to feel that he has retapped the same deep vein of American character which made the Old West, and that it is both his fate and his duty to strengthen the fiber of U.S. youth." "We were put in a position to be role models for many American boys and girls," Roy Rogers said, "and believe me, we have taken that job seriously." "It always happens," Rogers said of his encounters with middle-aged fans: "when people see me, they become kids again. I think some of them would crawl right into my lap if I let them." "I believed then, as I do now," testified one fan of mature years, "that if Roy Rogers knew that I needed him, he would come."[19]

Cowboys were at their peak of popularity in the movies and on TV in the 1950s and early 1960s. Those years were the formative years for the hearts and minds of the baby boomers. Put those two facts together, and it is easy to see the New West coming. As children, a significant percentage of the baby boomers imprinted on the heroes of the open range. Cowboys trained them in consumerism; cowboys gave them purchasing desires that left them with two choices: buy or be miserable (in which case, make sure your parents hear plenty about, and finally come to share in, your misery).

As adults, reaching the peak of their spending power and reaching the midpoint of their lives, assessing their achievements and assessing their disappointments, planning their vacations and planning their retirements, furnishing their homes and furnishing their clothes closets, buying movie tickets and buying novels, many of the more prosperous among the baby boomers would, predictably, be drawn back to the landscapes of their childhood yearnings, back to the mountains, deserts, and grasslands where Hopalong Cassidy and Roy Rogers and Gene Autry once rode free. With goals as clear and hands as steady as their one-time heroes, the baby boomers would reach for and draw their checkbooks and credit cards, and the New West would be the result. They no longer had to ask their parents; without having to waste time in pleading and wheedling, they could go direct to spending.

In the outdoor sports of the New West, the dreams of baby boomer childhood and the dreams of baby boomer middle age coincide. Performed in the landscape associated with televised Western adventure, the vigorous outdoor exercise associated with the New West seemed to promise a postponement of aging and an extension of life itself. In a pattern familiar to several thousands of generations before them, the baby boomers have been getting clues that aging is itself a rough ride. This lesson, however, comes as a particular shock to the cohort of people who had the bad judgment to coin a slogan like "Don't trust anyone over thirty," a slogan that would not, over the long haul, be conducive to self-esteem. Thus, even if their years are going to add up anyway, baby boomers hold on to the option of *behaving* as if they are not over thirty, an option for which the New West provides an essential setting to play hide-and-seek with time. As much as they provide the center of the New West's economy, hiking, mountain biking, skiing, rock climbing, and rafting provide the rituals by which people of a certain age have been putting up a determined battle against aging.

For New Western baby boomers, *Mad Magazine's* Alfred E. Newman's "What, me worry?" had been translated into "What, me age?" The very term "New West" remains a baby boomer's dream come true. It is, elsewhere, pretty much the pattern that the passage of time transforms young things into old things. Years pass, and a young tree becomes an old tree; a new town becomes an old town; a young person becomes an old person. But the West has received a special dispensation, an option to reverse the rules of the universe. Time passes, ordinary logic reverses, and the Old West *ages* into the New West. This, any baby boomer would have to agree, is a heck of a good deal.

SALVATION BY SAGE

On one count, the basic pattern behind the New West is very old: the late twentieth century provides another chapter in the long story of Americans wanting the West to be a remedy, a cure, and a restorative, wanting the West to make them feel young, vigorous, clean, and re-plenished again. And yet other patterns at work here make quite a break from the past.

If you want a contrast between the nineteenth-century West and the twentieth-century West, consider attitudes toward sagebrush. White people in the West in the mid-nineteenth century hated sage-brush. Mark Twain spoke for many of his fellow white Americans when he described the botanical setting of Carson City. In this "in-fernal soil nothing but the fag-end of vegetable creation, 'sage-brush,' ventures to grow." Since few writers have directed more strong emo-tion at a plant, Twain is worth quoting at length:

> If you will, take a lilliputian cedar tree for a model; and build a dozen imitations of it with the stiffest article of telegraph wire—set them one foot apart and then try to walk through them, [and] you'll understand (provided the floor is covered twelve inches deep with sand) what it is to wander through a sage-brush desert. When crushed, sage-brush emits an odor which isn't exactly magnolia, and isn't exactly polecat, but a sort of compromise between the two. It looks a good deal like greasewood, and is the ugliest plant that was ever conceived of.[20]

Twain, in other words, would have preferred a plant in a softer and greener model, a model which the deserts and plains of the West did not have in stock.

In the 1860s, the famed British traveler Richard Burton crossed the plains and matched Twain's feelings. He called sagebrush "this hideous growth," and that was one of his kinder remarks. "When used for cooking," Burton said, "it taints the food with a taste be-tween camphor and turpentine." In its "gnarled, crooked, rough-barked deformity," sagebrush has "no pretensions to beauty," and "its constant presence in the worst and most desert tracks teaches one to regard it . . . with aversion."[21] Here we have the judgment of the nineteenth century: other, better-favored areas of the earth have trees and forests, and much of the West, in a draw of cosmic, botan-ical bad luck, got sagebrush.

Now try this act of the imagination: place Twain and Burton, in a time machine and deposit them in Santa Fe, at the New Age fair and festival held there each summer. Before bewilderment can overwhelm them entirely, introduce the two time travelers to Wendy Whiteman, author of the pamphlet, *Sacred Sage: How It Heals,* on sale at the New Age fair.

In occupational terms, Whiteman describes herself as a "Wounded Healer," a term that asks for wide adoption and application: "Wounded Stockbroker," "Wounded Software Designer," "Wounded Professor." In the 1980s, unaware of the full scale of her psychic injuries, Whiteman seemed to have everything she could want: a "secure, comfortable" East Coast world of "cadillacs, fine jewelry, marriage, tennis, and society." But contentment moved out of her reach. "A still, small voice inside" was beginning to make itself heard, crying, " 'Hear me, find me, heal me. . . .' " The voice, she knew, was her "very own soul," and ignoring its call left her "listless and unmotivated." And then, "like a snake shedding layer after layer of skin," she left her marriage and her business and launched an uncertain effort to respond to the inner voice's urgings.[22]

"By 1988," Whiteman reported, "Divine Grace saw that I needed some extra help to get grounded on my newfound path, and batted me to Second Base—the American West." When she arrived in Taos, New Mexico, "a remembrance eons old opened up within—I *knew* Taos, though I had never previously seen or heard of it." She had arrived, like so many drawn to the New West, at *home.* Walking in the Sangre de Cristo Mountains, Whiteman had her full epiphany. She was "introduced" to the "Spirit of the sagebrush": "I respectfully asked the Spirit of the sage to share its knowledge of healing with me when the time was right."[23]

Now imagine Mark Twain and Richard Burton listening to Wendy Whiteman speak in praise of that "hideous growth," that "fag-end of botanical creation." The smoke of burning sage, Whiteman believes, offers a means of "cleansing energy fields." "Our bodies," she explained, "can have astral entities 'sticking' to them."

> Have you ever had people come into and out of your space, and afterwards had it feel like they've left something behind? They could have dumped something on you: low emotions, illness, astral garbage.

What to do if you find yourself in the role of astral garbage dump? Smudging or smoking with sage proves to be the way to remove "unwanted astral beings" and "dead orgone energy" both from rooms and from people. When smudging people, it is important to pay "special attention to the chakra areas," or "the parts of humans and animals that are maximum energy intakers."[24]

You would have had to cover Mark Twain's and Richard Burton's chakras with clouds of sage smoke to remove all of their unwanted astral beings and bring them to an understanding of Wendy Whiteman's vision of the West as a place of distinctive spiritual advantages. As the source of supply for sagebrush and as the location of many land formations judged sacred by New Age practitioners, the old theme of the West as remedy has taken a curious new twist. The New Agers' celebration of sagebrush finds value where previous Westerners found only irritation. Conversely, many of the West's present emigrants reject the traditional forms of economic development that, for quite a long time, fueled and directed the West's development.

At its most disorienting, this rejection of earlier practices manifests itself as a direct and clear intention to reverse history, a determination to take the West and swing it around in an abrupt U-turn. Take, as one concrete example, what one might call the West's changeover in Turners. For many years, the famed historian Frederick Jackson Turner dominated interpretations of the American West, thanks to his influential 1893 essay, "The Significance of the Frontier in American History." Turner was also the author of a book called *The Rise of the New West*. Lest this title seem prophetic, note the dates of this particular "New West" in the full title: *1819–1829*. Add 180 years to the dates, though, and it is easy to imagine *The Rise of the New West* with an author of the same surname.[25]

The West of the 1990s is, more than ever, a Turnerian West, but "Ted" has replaced "Frederick Jackson." As one of the bellwether moments in the coming of the New West, media mogul Ted Turner bought a ranch in Montana and then flummoxed local ranchers by announcing that he was going to sell off the cattle on his range and replace them with buffalo. He wanted to make this change, first, because the buffalo were the emblematic animals of the Old West and especially of the days before the white American conquest (he was going to turn the clock back at the ranch, he said, "nearly two hundred years"), and second, because cattle prices were falling and buffalo prices were rising ("I also intend," Turner told his neighbors, "to make twice as much from bison as you would make from cattle."). And the custom of casting the West as remedy was surely at work here: "In case I don't like being Vice Chairman of Time Warner," Turner said, "I can always come back here." By 1996, Turner owned nearly 1.3 million acres of Western ranch land, and owned it with a "total control," which meant, in contrast to the more congested world of broadcasting, he "never has to make compromises."[26]

Of all the people who could bear vivid witness to the changing times in the West, surely one of the best pieces of testimony would come from Bud Griffith, who had been manager of the Turner's main ranch. After thirty years of managing a cattle ranch, Griffith found himself instructed by his new boss to oversee the "removal of all the outbuildings, corrals, cattle pens, and barbed wire fences that Griffith himself had put up over the past three decades," while also eliminating all the overhead power lines and utility poles.[27] The achievements of the Old West had become the obstacles and impediments of the New West; the reversed direction of Ranch Manager Griffith's tasks embodied this surprising about-face. In one era, Griffith built corrals and fences, and in the next era, he demolishes corrals and fences; while it does seem to add up to full employment for ranch managers, it also seems as if Griffith's life is some sort of regional capsule version of the alienated labor of the army private who digs holes in order to fill them up.

The combination of sentiment and romance (Turner's dream of the lost West, restored) with economic ambition (Turner's recognition of the pleasant rise in buffalo prices) characterizes the New West. As Ted Turner once said, "If I want to save the West, I'll have to buy it."[28] Far from states of opposition, commerce and sentiment weave between and around each other in a maypole dance, with the Western landscape playing the role of the maypole. Consider, for instance, the Arizona town of Sedona and its two namesake magazines. Located in handsome redrock country, with mountains and deserts in a riveting landscape dialogue, Sedona is one of the principal boom towns of the New West, with recreationists, retirees, and New Age seekers increasing the population dramatically.

One of the magazines named *Sedona* celebrates the town's abundant offerings in real estate deals, tourist entertainment, art galleries, and clothing and jewelry shops. This very glossy magazine, by all appearances, does not struggle against a shortage of advertising income. Housing developments in handsome redrock landscapes dominate the pages. "In the shadow of ruins from ancient Native American civilizations," to cite the description of one typical development, Enchantment Resort "combine[s] the tranquility of nature with all the amenities of sophisticated living." Mystic Hills is "Sedona's most beautiful and environmentally sensitive master planned residential community"—"so desirable that a great many of Mystic Hills homesite owners are Presidents or CEOs of Leading Corporations."[29]

All this is very familiar, classic Western boosterism cast into a modern lingo. And then one turns to the second magazine named *Sedona*. This one, as a clue to its distinctiveness, carries the subtitle *Journal of Emergence!*. If real estate dominates the other *Sedona*, somewhat less real states are the topic here. The cover promises "Past Lives of a Being from Neptune! Channeling from YHWH, Zoosh, Lazaris, Ramtha, Vywamus, Hilarion and Others! Features on Crop Circles, Mayan Calendar, Reincarnation, Healing and Astrology! Predictions on Earth Changes, the Weather, Human Energy, and More!" As a literary journal, *Sedona: Journal of Emergence!* has a very distinctive feature. Most of the articles are, one might say, coauthored, by a regular human being and a cosmic being in channeling partnership: "How Your Thought Affects Every Living Thing," by YHWH through Arthur Fanning; "You Are Creating the Changes," by Ramses through Brent Powell; "July Predictions," by Peter and the Beings of Light through Ruth Ryden; "The Great Infusion," by Archangel Michael through Ronna Herman; "Empowering Your Imagination," by Lazaris through Jack Pursel. In one of the few variations from the norm of cross-entity collaboration, the author of "Cosmic Astrology," Scott Amun of Cottonwood, Arizona, "writes through his present self," though lest this seem too conventional, note that he does this by "resonating from his past in ancient Sumeria."[30]

A picture of the channeler, though never of the coauthor, accompanies each article, and the most astonishing element of the whole periodical is the utterly normal appearance of these people. They are the neighbors next door; they appear to be more likely voices for Tupperware and Avon products than for celestial beings. And yet they have struck up very comfortable partnerships with ancient and alien beings. "It is a pleasure to be connecting with you once again," Lazaris remarks to us through Jack Pursel, sounding as much at ease as a luncheon speaker at a Rotary or Elks Club meeting.[31]

The "End-Time Historian" Zoosh and his channeler, Sedona resident Robert Shapiro, are a particularly comfortable and prolific pair.

Shapiro "grew up with the experience of ET contact. Throughout his life there have been communications with beings from several star systems and dimensions." A "professional channel for over sixteen years," Shapiro "can channel almost anyone or anything with an exceptionally clear and profound connection," but "he most often channels Zoosh." Zoosh and Shapiro are now at work on the third volume of *The Explorer Race,* immersed in a writing process quite different from more terrestrial forms of composition. Every Tuesday night in Sedona, Zoosh dictates through Shapiro; for a $10 admission fee, one can "be a part of this historic process as Zoosh goes deeper into the history and the future of the Explorer Race—the human race."[32]

Thus, we have two seemingly very different, actually very compatible *Sedona* magazines. Neither magazine is, finally, any more or less commercial than the other. Both are full of advertisements and hearty and earnest suggestions for the spending of money. However much time channelers might spend in the company of the extraterrestrials, they remain themselves material beings, with material desires and needs. Thus, books and tapes and workshops and healing sessions come with an appropriate fee schedule. Sedona is, in New Age belief, a vortex—a place where cosmic energies accumulate. Places where cosmic energies congregate are, in the 1990s, places where real estate agents congregate. More often than not, these two congregations prove capable of interfaith services.

HOME ON THE PAGE

Once upon a time, there was a region whose stories fell into a trap. While life was as varied in this region as it was anywhere else on the planet, writers found themselves stuck with two choices. By the first choice, they could write stories about white men riding horses in wide-open spaces and sometimes shooting at each other. These stories would sell, but they would be recognized by everyone as unoriginal and formulaic Westerns. Or, by the second choice, they could write stories that reflected the actual human complexity of the region— stories about towns and cities, mines and boarding houses, ethnic barrios and Indian reservations, missile silos and sheep ranches. These stories would probably not sell well, and might not even get published; moreover, by virtue of the absence of white men on horse-

back, they would be disqualified from the category of Western literature.

This was a disheartening pair of choices. For a time, only a few
writers gave the second choice a try, and even those who succeeded received only stingy praise and recognition. Western American literature
had been backed into a corner: ride with the cowboys, or don't ride
at all. In the 1970s, Norman Maclean tried to find a publisher for his
Montana stories; the publishers found them commercially unpromis-
ing and told Maclean no. "These stories have trees in them," one editor explained his decision. About the same time, twelve publishers
said an equally emphatic no to Ivan Doig and his Montana memoir.
They liked his writing, but they were certain that the manuscript had
no commercial appeal.[33]

And then the fairy-tale moment in this story about stories arrived.
The ugly duckling turned into a swan; the prince proposed to Cin-
derella; the University of Chicago Press published Maclean's *A River
Runs Through It* and sold thousands and thousands of copies; the
thirteenth publisher took Doig's *This House of Sky*, with comparable
success. The more trees—and mesas and mountains and arroyos and
streams and canyons—that one could get into a book, the better the
chance of its publication. As peak moments go in the annals of regional vengeance and vindication, no one ever topped Norman
Maclean's on a certain day in 1981.

The letter he wrote was published twelve years later in *Harpers*,
under the very apt title, "A Grudge Runs Through it." Maclean had
been corresponding with an editor at Alfred A. Knopf about the
prospect of publishing his second book, *Young Men and Fire*. He
abruptly remembered that "Alfred A. Knopf turned down [the soon-
to-be-bestselling *A River Runs Through It*] after playing games with
it, or at least the game of cat's-paw, now rolling it over and saying they
were going to publish it and then rolling it on its back when the president of the company announced it wouldn't sell." And now Knopf
had expressed interest in his next book. Finding it likely that some of
the "finest fuck-you prose in the English language" had been written
under similar circumstances, Maclean added a memorable entry: "if
the situation ever arose when Alfred A. Knopf was the only publishing house remaining in the world and I was the sole surviving author,
that would mark the end of the world of books. Very sincerely, Norman Maclean."[34]

The spillways were open, and a great flood of Western books poured through. Readers, who had found keeping up with Western American literature to be one of the easier projects in the literary world, were inundated. Norman Maclean, Ivan Doig, William Kittredge, James Welch, Mary Clearman Blew, Simon Ortiz, Rudolfo Anaya, Teresa Jordan, Leslie Marmon Silko, N. Scott Momaday, Terry Tempest Williams, Sherman Alexie, Judith Freeman, Levi Peterson, Luci Tapahanso, Dierdre McNamer, Linda Hogan, Barbara Kingsolver, Joy Harjo, C. L. Rawlins—the bookshelves began bending under the weight of their work.

Many of the reasons for the general popularity of the West worked equally well as explanations for this regional literary bonanza. But there was an added dimension here, one connected to the fact that many of these writers were born and raised in the West and now spoke explicitly of writing about "home." For more than a century, the pattern of the most influential writing about the West had been of the "visit from outside" tradition. Easterners or Europeans traveled to the West and found it exotic and unsettling; their perception of Western difference set their writings in the vein of discovery and surprise. In the late twentieth century, writing about the West underwent a basic reorientation; instead of unsettled outsiders writing from their position as strangers, literature about the West was, more and more, the product of people who had grown up in the West, who did not see it as exotic but as home. While Indian people were leading participants in the Western literary renaissance, many of those now claiming status as insiders were the descendants of the white invaders.

Having so many people who were born and raised in the West writing well-received novels, short stories, poems, essays, and memoirs has been tremendously beneficial. Their writing has improved our chances for regional self-understanding; it has given interested non-Westerners a much more grounded and complicated picture of the West to contemplate; it has done a great deal to lessen the regional inferiority complex that has, for so long, been an element of the Western intellectual scene.

And yet, in the 1990s, one began to wonder about some aspects of this celebration of the nativeness of white writers. Isn't there a good chance that this will, in the judgment of future historians, register as a predictable phase for a settler society? Begin with a place occupied by aboriginal people; they may have migrated and shifted location, but they were native to North America over centuries and millennia. Then an invading population appears on the scene and takes control of the place, generating all the moral discomfort and unease that comes with conquest. At a certain point, the descendants of those invaders could be expected to make a great show of settling down, nestling in, cocooning, declaring and demonstrating their credentials as indigenous folk, referring to their places of origin as home. It is a movement in which I was an enthusiastic participant, and it was exactly the movement that one would expect from a settler society now entering into its fifth or sixth generation. Whatever might be in the minds of individual writers, the audience enthusiasm for this school of writing suggests that the idea of whites at home in the West relieves some of the inherited tensions of conquest. Tired of being the invaders and the intruders, whites now find a way of claiming a pedigree, a line of descent, a status of legitimacy.

The struggle to claim legitimacy is, of course, the oldest story in the region: one group of people gets settled in, then another group of people appears on the scene and challenges the standing and power of the group who arrived earlier, and then everyone struggles and pushes and shoves to try to get possession of the title "Legitimate and Authentic Resident of the West." Sometimes the locals, who are defending themselves ardently against the newest wave of emigrants and settlers, are people who only established their own standing as locals in the very recent past. Thus, the movement among writers to claim the West as home and to stake their claims to the status of Western insiders, natives, and indigenes becomes the most recent episode in a long-running contest to claim legitimacy, a contest for which there have never been any agreed-on ground rules.

Have we gone overboard in celebrating the insights of insiders? Have we, by sanctifying line or descent or birthplace or pedigree, mystified the process of understanding a place and condemned new arrivals to a permanent condition of folly and ignorance? Have we, at the same time, discounted the value of the insights and impressions that newcomers, outsiders, and visitors have been known to have from time to time? While the knowledge that comes from being at home is often deep and valuable, the observations of visitors do not, by that recognition, surrender their value. One thinks of the pleasure and surprise still triggered by a reading of Meriwether Lewis's and William Clark's journals; one thinks of the heightened appreciation of one's home territory to be gained by reading travelers like Isabella Bird; one thinks, especially, of Lord James Bryce's observations in *The American Commonwealth*. Touring the West in the 1880s, the British aristocrat and ultimate outsider found the behavior of Western boosters to be a marvel and puzzle. In his book, Bryce wrote down a speech he wished he had the occasion to give to Western men. These remarks carry undiminished relevance for the New West, and they also reawaken respect for outsiders as interpreters of the West:

> Gentlemen, why in heaven's name this haste? You have time enough. No enemy threatens you. No volcano will rise from beneath you. Ages and ages lie before you. Why sacrifice the present to the future, fancying that you will be happier when your fields teem with wealth and your cities with people? In Europe we have cities wealthier and more populous than yours, and we are not happy. You dream of your posterity, but your posterity will look back to yours as the golden age, and envy those who first burst into this silent splendid Nature, who first lifted up their axes upon these tall trees. . . . Why, then, seek to complete in a few decades what the other nations of the world took thousands of years over in the older continents? Why do things rudely and ill which need to be done well, seeing that the welfare of your descendants may turn upon them? Why in your hurry to subdue and utilize Nature, squander her splendid gifts? . . . Why hasten the advent of that threatening day when the vacant spaces of the continent shall have been filled, and the poverty or discontent of the older States shall find no outlet? You have opportunities such as mankind has never had before, and may never have again. Your work is great and noble; it is done for a future longer and vaster than our conceptions can embrace. Why not make its outlines and beginnings worthy of these destinies the thought of which gilds your hopes and elevates your purposes?[35]

Why not, indeed?

REGION, HEAL THYSELF

In the 1990s, the idea of the West as the remedy for individual and national ills was running head on into a visible and unmistakable fact: the West was badly in need of remedies itself. The social conflicts over growth, the wounds inflicted by the decline of rural enterprises, the overstretched infrastructure of roads and water systems, and the very familiar American dilemmas of inequality by race and class all served as reminders that the West's shelf life as a remedy was reaching its expiration date.

Most compelling—and most expensive—of the situations calling for remedy were the nuclear weapons production and testing sites, places like Hanford, Rocky Flats, and the Nevada Test Site. In the 1980s, reporters and community groups dug out the hidden stories of these places, stories of shortcuts, expedient and risky waste disposal, compromises on safety, and knowingly misleading reassurances to the public. The terrible paradox finally came to light: during the years of the Cold War, American atomic weapons were never used to injure an enemy population; the only people whose well-being was jeopardized by these weapons were American citizens—uranium miners working in unventilated mines in the Four Corners region, production plant workers exposed to worrisome doses of radiation, people living downwind from the Nevada Test Site and downwind and downriver from the Hanford Nuclear Reservation.

The end of the Cold War made these revelations all the more unsettling, since the unraveling of the Soviet Union carried a particular blow for the American West. Without an evil empire to oppose, the mandate for preparedness in defense lost much of its punch. Base closing, downsizing, and the termination of weapons production shook many local Western economies. Without an evil empire of Communism to serve as external threat, the West lost one of its principal claims on federal money. The Cold War had provided the reason to continue the defense-spending party begun in World War Two; indeed, the party went on so long it gained the status of a normal, taken-for-granted, and even reliable element of regional prosperity. Western towns and cities with military bases as neighbors benefited most directly; patriotism merged pleasantly with the advantages flowing from the presence of a larger workforce with paychecks to spend.

Thus, there were double, even triple, reasons for a Western sense of resentment at the end of the Cold War. Lost access to federal money was the clearest and most direct inspiration for injury. Tangled together with that was the recognition of the Cold War's legacy to the West of radioactivity and toxic chemicals. Muddling this already complicated situation was the ideological disorientation brought on by the loss of the Soviet Union. The Cold War had established a mandate for a patriotic telling of Western American history. The struggle with

Communism required the United States to be the innocent and honorable party; with American identity so thoroughly tied to the images of the frontier, the cowboy, and the pioneer, Western American history was the perfect piece of turf for a tug-of-war between those who insisted on American innocence and honor and those who saw human nature, wherever it operated, as complex and mixed. With the end of the Cold War, the rope pulling for a patriotic and proud version of the development of the American West suddenly snapped. The pattern presented by this tug-of-war is a common one: when the rope on one side breaks, the forces on both sides lose their footing; no one knows quite which way to pull; and thus the pulls come from all directions at once, in a pattern almost beyond discerning.

The question at issue was an impossible one: How had the West turned out? No one could deny that the development of Western resources had exacted high social and environmental costs. But was the outcome nonetheless one to be celebrated? Assessing the degree, direction, and quality of recent change in the West has not been an easy task for anyone. The national press has not been of great help in the task.

Various Western states observed their statehood centennials in 1989, and *Newsweek* used that occasion to appraise the condition of Wyoming, Montana, Idaho, Washington, and North and South Dakota. Rhetorically, this article was its own marvel of writing about the West, a high achievement in prose drenched with doom and gloom. "America's Outback," the article was called: "Amid scarcity and broken dreams, six Western states mark 100 hard years at the end of the cracked whip." A flood of "d" words—decline, destitution, desolation, desperation—cast the hundred-year birthday party for these states in shades of black: "the commemoration," *Newsweek* said, "is pocked by scarcity and stillborn dreams." Thus was the curtain drawn down on the West: "the frontier's precious vein of promise and possibility is running out." The Rocky Mountain West—or at least its northern half—was a battered, smashed, wrecked, and ruined place. If there were a Dr. Jack Kevorkian for regions, it was time to get the number for his pager and lodge an urgent request.[36]

And then a few years passed.

Now it was *Time* magazine weighing in for an appraisal, and it took a keen eye to recognize the dilapidated and drained region of four years before. "Boom Time in The Rockies," the cover of *Time* said: "More jobs and fewer hassles have Americans heading for the hills." "These are sustainable economies, absolutely," *Time* quoted former Colorado governor Richard Lamm, belying his nickname "Governor Gloom": "It's not just another cycle but a permanent, historic shift." With a series of portraits of refugees fleeing from both coasts, *Time* declared the states from Montana to New Mexico to be "the good news-belt," with a higher growth rate and a lower unemployment rate than any other region of the country.[37]

For a reader trying to be attentive to these various expert reports, bewilderment was the only sensible response. When was the West in a bust and when was it in a boom, and how on earth was one to tell the difference? If the national media at one moment told you that you were living in a moribund region and at the next moment told you that you were living in one of the most vital regions of the nation, in what sort of region did you actually live? If one sector—the traditional rural, extractive industries—of a local economy was declining sadly, and another sector—recreation and the relocation of prosperous, amenity-seeking settlers—was growing exuberantly, was the economy in a boom or a bust? And, if the prosperity, cheer, comfort, and good times of the privileged rested on the hard work and low pay of the poor, how widely distributed was the "good" in this "good news-belt"?

On Thanksgiving Day, 1994, one of the most powerful statements on the dilemmas of the New West appeared. "The Heights of the Mountains Are His: The Development of God's Country" was a pastoral letter from J. Francis Stafford, archbishop of Denver. If the New Agers devoted any thought or attention to the distribution of wealth in the New West, such concern seldom worked its way into magazines, books, newsletters, leaflets, or transcripts of channeling. In contrast to New Age comfort and complacency, in this remarkable pastoral letter, the Catholic Church took readers on an unsettling journey to the foundation of the New West.

Colorado's Front Range is in the midst of a boom, the archbishop's letter noted, and a parallel boom, focused on recreation, is under way in Colorado's mountain communities. This episode of growth exposes these small towns to particular peril:

> In the last century the Western Slope functioned as a resource colony for timber and mining interests. Those scars will be with us for gen-

erations. We cannot afford to stand by now as the culture of a leisure colony, like the walled communities which dominate so many American suburbs, takes its place.

Resort communities rely on the labor of women and men who cannot afford to live in these islands of privilege; they are forced to live at some distance, often in trailers or tents, enduring "long commutes on highways that, especially during the winter months, cannot safely or adequately handle the traffic flow." Confronted with the needs of the working poor, "the basic social infrastructure is simply being overwhelmed," with churches, public schools, utilities, courts, and social services swamped by more demands than they can handle.[38]

"The New West's Servant Economy," *High Country News* headlined an article in 1995. Among the preparers and servers of food and the cleaners of rooms, the writer Ray Ring found "all sorts of people who came a long way to earn treadmill wages here and get tucked away in the trailer-park ghettos or low-income apartments or behind some pretty mountain, where their problems are mostly invisible to the skiers and vacation-homesteaders." Ring even found a group of West African immigrants, dispatched by an employment agency in New York to Colorado, where they made a daily 120-mile commute from Kremmling to their jobs at the Breckenridge Hilton.[39]

As an Immigration and Naturalization Service raid in Jackson, Wyoming, in 1996 showed, Mexican immigrants are an increasingly important part of the New West labor force. That pre-Labor Day raid seized 120 undocumented Mexican workers and sent them home; a little over a week later, 116 had returned. As working class residents were squeezed out of the mountain boom towns, as ski bums aged and sought more-rewarding jobs, "into this vacuum came the Latinos." "El Nuevo West," *High Country News* labeled the situation in late 1996, pointing out the continuity between the past and the present: "The gruntwork in the West has always been done by the foreign born. El Nuevo West is also the Old West."[40]

These stark differences in wealth and privilege in the New West, the archbishop's pastoral letter said, must be understood "in the wider moral ecology of our lives." "We are moral as well as economic creatures"; "authentic growth can never be merely economic; it is always primarily moral." Thus, in New Western towns where the privileged ignore the dilemmas of the poor, "we may legitimately speak of economic 'structures of sin,' constructed stone by stone from many acts of indifference and other personal sins over time."[41]

In the most memorable warning in the pastoral letter, Archbishop Stafford spoke to the biggest social, economic, moral, and cultural problem of the New West: "What we risk creating, then, is a theme-park 'alternative reality' for those who have the money to purchase entrance. Around this Rocky Mountain theme park will sprawl a growing buffer zone of the working poor."[42] The dreams of people of privilege would design the theme park, and the hopes of the poor would recruit the work force to build and maintain it.

The dream is unending, even if it changes its shape like Proteus. Through sagebrush smoke or affordable real estate, through novel workplaces or novel vacations, through every variation on the theme of newness, the West will make us whole. It will separate us from the familiar and the wearying; it will return us to bedrock; it will reassure us that we are people who matter. In a region so dominated by mountains, the West lies, as the archbishop's pastoral letter said, in the "shadows of heaven itself." Heaven's shade both shelters and darkens our lives.

IV-D

Believing in
the American West

GROWING UP POST-MORMON

My father and I are not Mormons. This fact is true of many other people in the American West, but it is particularly true of us. My father was raised Mormon in Brigham City, Utah. Although it is common for fallen-away members of the Church of Jesus Christ of Latter-day Saints to become fervent believers in other churches, my father took a different path. When he cut his ties to the Mormon Church and moved to California, he turned away from all organized religion.

My sisters and I thus grew up with a particular opportunity to drive our father batty. Here was our distinctive and very gratifying channel of rebellion: we could insist on our First Amendment right to freedom of religion, get dressed up for church, and demand that Father drive us there. The peak of this soul-satisfying mutiny came in asking him for money to put in the collection plate. And, since Mother was (and is) a non-church-attending Congregationalist and thus nearly as vulnerable as Father to the abrasive powers of our piety, there was also considerable pleasure to be gained from coming home from church, sitting down to Sunday dinner, and delivering an earnest prayer on behalf of our parents' redemption.

Such rebellion, however, came at a cost. For me, the cost was repeated exposure to the misery of the unbaptized heathen. Churched or not, our parents had installed into our thinking a great devotion to justice and fairness. And so the dilemma of the poor souls in Africa and Asia, living and dying and heading off to hell without the opportunity to hear the Christian gospel, weighed heavily on me. If God really had decided to let salvation hinge on the basis of the arbitrary facts of place of birth (a fact that He, in His omnipotence, had determined), then God seemed to be following rather questionable values Himself, showing a tenuous understanding of the concept of fairness.

The pleasures of bugging my father were, therefore, already wearing thin on a memorable day in 1962 at the First Baptist Church in Banning, the day on which my rebellion ended. The membership of the First Baptist Church was entirely white. On this Sunday, a black woman, new in town, came to church. I happened to be behind her in the line, waiting to shake hands with the minister. We had spent some time in Sunday School singing about Jesus's transcendence of racial prejudice:

Red and yellow, black and white,
They're all sacred in His sight.
Jesus loves the little children of the world.

This song was not easy to reconcile with the dilemma of the unbaptized heathen, and our minister had, himself, not gotten very far in reconciling Jesus's sentiments with his own. When the black woman shook hands with him, the minister told her that *her* church was on the other side of town.

Since that Sunday, I have learned more about the ways in which race relations in the American West came to bear an unhappy resemblance to race relations in the rest of the country. In religious terms, it was not simply a matter of segregation in Western churches, it was often a matter of the active use of the church as a social institution to maintain racial separation and inequality. The minister of the First Baptist Church not only gave me a memorable introduction to this topic, he also persuaded me that my rebellion against my father had gone far enough. Since then I have taken the path leading away from organized religion and toward what I will call disorganized religion. My father and I remain post-Mormon and unchurched but nonetheless driven by convictions about right and wrong.

For decades, I thought that Father and I had placed ourselves on the margins of conventional religious behavior. But, like so many other Westerners who treasured a picture of themselves as odd birds, we have turned out to be birds positioned right at the center of the flock. "[P]oor church attendance is characteristic of westerners generally," historian Michael Quinn has written. Here lies the West's principal claim to distinctiveness in religious terms: it is the region with the lowest rates of church participation, in both the nineteenth and the twentieth centuries. In the nation as a whole, "the West as a region has the lowest attendance (36 percent) in church or synagogue." The West thus holds the status of the nation's "Unchurched Belt."[1] In this region, participants in disorganized religion have held and hold a considerable numerical advantage over participants in organized religion.

My father and I turn out to be not rebels and eccentrics but representative Westerners. Still, without official papers of membership, we and our many disaffiliated comrades are not likely to register in the records of Western religious history. Contemplating the prospect of one's invisibility, one finds good reason to question how much the fact of church membership reveals about a matter as subjective and private as religious belief. Churches are, of course, the places where *records* of official religious performance accumulate. Historians of religion, oriented to written documents, have had good reason to place churches and their members at the center of their inquiry, in the manner of labor historians who, for a time, hinged their history of the working class on the much more narrow topic of membership in unions.

"In comparison with Whites in the United States today," the anthropologist Harold Driver once wrote, "the Indians [of the past] were at least ten times as religious."[2] Of all the improbable proclamations of academics made over the last forty years, this one is my personal favorite, an example of confident, social-scientific thinking at its goofiest. And yet, whatever Harold Driver meant by this memorable assertion, one suspects that he did *not* mean that Indians were ten times as religious because they were ten times more likely to join formally chartered and organized churches. On the contrary, Driver thought (and he shared this conviction with many others) that Indian people were more religious because they unmistakably and consistently demonstrated their faith, observing little separation between the secular and the spiritual. They did not need to join churches and attend formal services, because they lived virtually every moment in a religious way. By contrast, in Driver's equally widely shared but considerably more questionable assumption, modern white American people have been a very secular group, driven primarily by economic motives. For a group of people holding their souls on such a tight leash, religious conviction could only appear in official membership in an institutional church, with even that level of religious commitment often confined to attendance at Sunday services, cresting at Easter and Christmas.

Consider, by contrast, the state of affairs in mid-nineteenth-century rural Oregon. True to the Western pattern, church membership there was very limited. But a low percentage of church attendance, historian Dean May has argued, "does not imply . . . an absence of religious sentiment and feelings." The settlers' religious practice was local, often within households, "involving them rarely, if at all, in any broader community." They had Bibles in their homes, and recorded significant family events in those Bibles. "Blessings on food, prayers, prayer meetings, hymn singing, and exhortation were held in home and schoolhouse for gatherings of families and close neighbors." Preachers sent by home missionary societies found Oregon's "seeming incoherence of religious organization" both puzzling and frustrating. In a curious convergence of opinion, historians would come to share the judgment of the preachers: "religion in any setting other than an established congregation was to them hardly religion at all."[3]

Few of the people of the Oregon settlements were joining churches, but they gave many other signs of religiousness. The pattern of Oregon may well be the pattern of the Western United States. "[E]xcept in Mormon territory, the majority of far westerners have cared little about traditional religious institutions and practices," the historian Eldon G. Ernst put it. "They form the most secular society in the United States if gauged by church membership statistics, yet when questioned they claim to be religiously concerned and find religion to be important in their personal lives."[4]

We return to the common difficulty faced by anyone exploring this topic: in its subjectivity and privacy, religious belief is very hard to track. A few groups—Indians, missionaries, and Mormons—have made the task easier: for all their differences, these groups were believers who consistently and visibly demonstrated their faith in frequent public rituals, steering by religious principles in everyday activities. Whether the ritual was a dance, a hymn, or a ward house meeting, whether the consecrated activity was hunting, teaching, or irrigated farming, Indians, missionaries, and Mormons placed their faith front and center, where no one could miss it. Thus, Western historians fell into a perfectly logical habit of confining the explicit discussion of religion to topics where it simply could not be avoided. For all the other Westerners—for the sizable numbers who were *not* Indians, *not* missionaries, and *not* Mormons, the most resolutely secular history is all they seemed to deserve and generally all they got.

The fact that American westward expansion was so strongly governed by economic motives reinforced the apparent wisdom of this strategy of reserving religious history for the few and leaving secular history for the majority. The experience of overland travel during the Gold Rush had many of the qualities of a sacred pilgrimage, testing determination and persistence in a thousand ways. But a journey undertaken as a tribute to Mammon surrendered its credentials as pilgrimage. Fervent participation in mineral rushes and land rushes, in timber booms and cattle speculation deepened the impression that the determination of white Americans to develop the West's natural resources left very little room for the development of their souls. Often invoked in support of these expanding commercial enterprises, God's name looked as if it had become little more than another product endorsement.

Consider, as a striking example of this linkage of religion with commerce, the memorable song, "The Cowboy's Prayer":

Lord, please help me, lend me Thine ear,
The prayer of a troubled cowman to hear.
No doubt my prayer to you may seem strange,
But I want you to bless my cattle range. . . .

> *As you O Lord my fine herds behold.*
> *They represent a sack of pure gold.*
> *I think that at least five cents on the pound*
> *Would be a good price for beef the year round.*[5]

When God was asked to intervene on behalf of rising cattle prices, the theological seemed to have made a full surrender to the secular. But then again, when whites asked God to bless their economic undertakings, was this *entirely* different from an Indian hunter's hope that the right gestures of respect would recruit the spirits as the sponsors of a successful hunt? Didn't both practices serve as examples of a people's refusal to draw a hard line between the spiritual and the worldly? If God wanted the best for His Chosen People, wouldn't He *want* them to prosper in the cattle market?

In 1973, my husband and I were driving west, crossing the country on yet another secular pilgrimage. Through the journey, we had invested a great deal in the services of auto mechanics, purchasing, among other things, an entire replacement engine for our VW Bug. We were not entirely sure that we had enough money left to get to California. On a Sunday morning, we turned on the radio and found an evangelist in the middle of a prayer that spoke directly to our dilemma: "Lord," the evangelist asked, "Heal our families; heal our hearts; and heal our finances." When my father wired us money in Laramie, we felt that prayer had been heard.

WESTWARD THE COURSE OF CHAOS TAKES ITS WAY

The year after I parted with the First Baptist Church, a remarkable event occurred in the demography of Banning, California. A bunch of kids appeared out of nowhere. Banning was a town of eight or nine thousand people, and I thought I knew most of them; I certainly knew the ones around my own age. But when we left the sixth grade at Central Elementary School and moved on to the seventh grade at Susan B. Coombs Junior High School, some fifteen or twenty strangers joined us. Had a large caravan of families moved to town over the summer? On the contrary, and very mysteriously, the strangers claimed that they had lived in Banning most, sometimes all, of their lives. But where had they been? How had they stayed hidden all those years?

The strangers were, it turned out, Catholics. They had been hidden in parochial school, but parochial school—whatever that was—ended in sixth grade, and so now they were out of hiding. The term "Mormon," I understood, but "Catholic"? Or, even more puzzling, "Jew"? In the First Baptist Sunday School, our education on that particular topic had been *very* brief. One of the children had said to the Sunday School teacher, "We keep seeing the word 'Jew' in the Bible, but we don't know what it means." The teacher looked unhappy and then seized on her way out. "You all know Jeff," she said, pointing to one member of the class. "Jeff used to be a Jew, but now he's a Baptist."

The extent of my Sunday School teacher's—and my—ignorance in these matters was at a cosmic scale and quite surprising, given the West's great history of religious diversity. This diversity represented the realization of the worst fears of many Protestants in the nineteenth-century West. Protestant clergy in the West confronted a region in which every moment in daily life told them that they were working against a great disadvantage. White American Protestants in the nineteenth-century West knew that they were outnumbered. They knew that they had before them a long struggle to find a permanent place in a society in which neither Episcopalians nor Baptists, Presbyterians nor Congregationalists could be numerically dominant.

In many Western areas, Catholics and Mormons had gotten the jump in timing, as well as in membership, on Protestants of any denomination. Jews were early arrivals in many Western settlements. At the same time, American Indian religions and the Buddhism, Taoism, and Confucianism of Asian immigrants stretched the categories of faith along an extraordinarily wide continuum. In the nineteenth-century West, as historian Ferenc Szasz has written, the mainline Protestant groups "confronted the greatest challenge of their day: dealing with religious diversity." Several decades before their counterparts in the Eastern United States would come to face a comparable challenge, Western Protestant ministers "dealt with pluralism on a daily basis." In religious terms, the West was the American future.[6]

For many of those getting an advance look at this future, religious pluralism proved to be fruitful soil for discomfort and doubt. Where we might see an extraordinary and fascinating mosaic of religious practice, the Protestant ministers were more inclined to see chaos, and dangerous chaos at that. Take the concerns and worries recorded by the Reverend Josiah Strong. After two years' service as a Congregationalist minister in Cheyenne, Wyoming, Reverend Strong came down with a pronounced case of Western Protestant anxiety. The West, he wrote in his book *Our Country* (1886) was "peculiarly exposed" to the principal "dangers" of the times: "Mammonism, materialism, luxuriousness, and the centralization of wealth."[7] The region was particularly burdened, as well, with the threats posed by socialism, the saloon, Mormonism, Catholicism, and foreign immigration. Not only were the dangers greatest in the West, the Protestant churches were at their weakest, ill equipped to respond to any of these challenges.

If this was a region in which all its enemies ganged up on Protestant Christianity, might the good news be that the region's sparse population rendered its religious condition irrelevant to the nation's well-being? On the contrary, in Reverend Josiah Strong's judgment, the West determined the national future. With its vast resources, ready to support an equally sizable population, the West "is to dominate the East"; in the near future, "the West will direct the policy of the Government, and by virtue of her preponderating population and influence will determine our national character and, therefore, destiny."[8]

If Protestant Christianity could not save the West, then nothing could save the nation. And the stakes went considerably beyond the national. In Reverend Strong's vision, the settling of the American West would be only one test of the Anglo-Saxon's "instinct or genius for colonizing," a genius that would finally work its way around the entire planet "in *the final competition of races, for which the Anglo-Saxon is being schooled* [his emphasis]." Through the religious challenge posed by the American West, "God was training the Anglo-Saxon race for an hour sure to come in the world's future."[9]

Full of distrust for European immigrants, for Mormons, and for New Mexican Hispanics, Reverend Strong nonetheless reserved his greatest distrust for the actions and beliefs of his fellow Anglo-Saxons, those "church-members who seem to have left their religion behind when they crossed the Missouri."[10] Of course, Reverend Strong would worry about all those others, but it is, at first, a surprise to see how doubtful he was about the religious reliability of his fellow whites.

Given the continued status of the West as the nation's unchurched region, he was right to be worried. My father and I, and our many disaffiliated fellow Westerners, are Reverend Strong's worst nightmare come true.

In the intervening century, few writers have been able to produce texts that can match *Our Country* in its remarkable mixture of confidence and doubt. In the space of a few pages, Reverend Josiah Strong could shift from a cosmic confidence in Anglo-Saxon destiny to rule the world and to install God's kingdom in the process, to a dark vision of a West soon to collapse before the pressures of evil and disorder. How could he be at once so confident and so anxious? The paradox here was a great one. On the ground level the American West had the greatest religious diversity of any part of the nation, and the heightened anxiety of the nineteenth-century Protestant clergy testified to the challenge posed by that diversity. And yet, in the broader sweep of history, expansion into the American West seemed to have shown white American religious belief at its most homogeneous, combining a Christian sense of mission with patriotism to form a virtual state religion. Faith in the United States's Manifest Destiny had long ago melted the division between the sacred and the secular. And yet, by a considerable irony, when Protestant fervor merged into national policy, it ended up producing the region in which Protestant denominations had their weakest hold.

Whites had an indisputable claim on the West, Senator Thomas Hart Benton had said, because they used the land "according to the intentions of the CREATOR." As historian Albert Weinberg observed, "[T]heological literature was scarcely more abundant in reference to Providence than was the literature of expansionism." To one typical expansionist during the Mexican-American War, "war was the religious execution of our country's glorious mission, under the direction of Divine Providence, to civilize and christianize, and raise up from anarchy and degradation a most ignorant, indolent, wicked and unhappy people." And yet one outcome of this enterprise was not the redemption of the Mexican people but the slide into religious "anarchy and degradation" of many of the Americans who were supposed to be the agents of the West's redemption. As William Jennings Bryan put it after the start of the Philippine insurrection, " 'Destiny' is not as manifest as it was" a while ago.[11]

THE *KIVA* IN MY SOUL

In New Mexico, it was never possible to draw a firm border between the secular and the sacred. For centuries, Indian religious belief erased any line between faith and worldly activity. In the Spanish colonization of the sixteenth and seventeenth centuries, missionaries played a role in conquest as important, if not more important, than the role of soldiers. For the Spanish, religious motives came interwoven with economic and political motives; even when governors fought with friars for the control of colonies, those struggles dramatized the central role that religion played in the whole undertaking. In the nineteenth century, when white Americans entered the scene, Protestant disapproval of Catholicism added to the contest over land and labor and to the frictions of nationality and race. In the history unrolling in New Mexico, religious belief has been everywhere, shaping and being shaped by even the most secular elements of human thought and behavior.

In the summer of 1992, Santa Fe—the town called "Holy Faith"—permitted me a memorable visit to the blurred border between the secular and the sacred. I was meeting with a group of international scholars studying American regionalism. From Senegal to Thailand, from Belgium to the Philippines, all of my companions had grown up watching Western movies, and watching them with feelings that bordered on reverence. No conventionally religious mission society, one learned from the testimony of these visitors, has ever come close to matching the achievements of the Hollywood Western in global proselytizing and conversion.

On our last day of class, the participants were having a competition to see who had been the most influenced or tainted by the Wild West myth. We had heard a number of eloquent statements from men whose childhoods had included frequent visits to "Old West" tourist towns in Germany and Austria, where they had cheerfully fired away at the Indian targets in shooting galleries. Then a woman from Poland suddenly and urgently announced her candidacy as the most mythically influenced. "The first thing I can remember," she told us, "is my father reading to me from Karl May's Western novels. As soon as I could read, I read them for myself. I loved old Shatterhand, and even after I saw a movie with a fat Frenchman playing his part, my love for him did not change. You may tell me they are factually wrong, but Karl May's novels are . . ." Here she paused and searched for the right word, seizing on a term she had learned the day before during a tour of a pueblo. "Karl May's novels," she ended, with the right word firmly in hand, "are the *kiva* in my soul."

Here was yet another piece of testimony from Santa Fe, reminding me of the hopelessness of trying to separate faith from worldly fact in Western America. Once again, Santa Fe offered a reminder that of all the places on the planet where the sacred and the secular meet, the American West is one of the hot spots. One could argue (as indeed one had, and at length) that the vision of the West as a romantic place, where strong and good men went down to Main Street or out to the wilderness to take their courageous stands, held little connection to historical fact. And yet, if Karl May's Western fantasies had provided a spiritual and emotional sanctuary for a young woman growing up in Poland in tough times, then we were clearly talking about a realm of belief out of reach of historical fact checking.

Trained in movie theaters in Senegal or Thailand, New York City or Denver, the human spirit has developed the conditioned response of soaring when it confronts certain images: horses galloping across open spaces, wagon trains moving through a landscape of mesas and mountains, cruel enemies and agents of disorder defeated by handsome white men with nerves of steel and tremendous—and justified—self-esteem. And when the human spirit undertakes to soar, it is not necessarily the obligation of the historian to act as air traffic controller and force the spirit down for a landing. Improbable as it may seem to the prosaic historian, an imagined and factually unsubstantiated version of Western American history has become, for many believers, a sacred story. For those believers, a challenge to that story can count as sacrilege.

In American life today, lots of groups have made a heavy emotional investment in the proposition that history is a sacred, not a secular, tale. The best and clearest example of this comes from the Mormons. In the last few years, historians who are Mormon believers but who try to write searchingly and critically about Mormon history have had a rough time. Some of them have been excommunicated for their failure to write what the church's General Authorities call faith-affirming history.

The pattern seen among the Mormons appears everywhere. Consider, for instance, how similar the Mormon call for faith-affirming history is to the Afrocentic call for a history of African American people that consistently praises their accomplishments and affirms their self-esteem. Or consider the desire, on the part of some American Indian people, for a writing of Indian history that enshrines Indian people as ecological and environmental saints and traces an unbroken line of nobility and solidarity among tribal people. When white politicians condemn "revisionist" or "multicultural" history and call for a narrative of the past that affirms the achievements and virtues of white Americans, those politicians show a striking kinship to the Afrocentric intellectuals and to the General Authorities of the Mormon Church. *Everyone* wants faith-affirming history; the disagreement is just a question of which faith any particular individual wants to see affirmed. Each group wants history to provide guidance, legitimacy, justification, and direction for their particular chosen people.

These contests over history, often focused on the West, resemble and echo more familiar contests over religious faith. Different versions of history have become creation stories or origin stories for the people who treasure them, and, with so much feeling at stake, the clash between these sacred tales grows increasingly bitter. And yet, while these separate and contesting claims on history proliferate, more and more evidence emerges from the historical record to counter these assertions of exclusivity. Explorations of Western American history reveal many examples of unexpected kinship, mixed heritage, cultural trading, syncretism, and borrowing. It is not simply a matter of the blending of the West's people through intermarriage, though this is certainly an enormous part of the region's story. It is also a matter of reciprocal influence and mutual assimilation. The various peoples of the American West have been bumping into each other for an awfully long time, and it cannot be a surprise to discover that their habits and beliefs have rubbed off on each other.

Indian religious movements—from the Ghost Dance to the Native American Church with its use of peyote—show many Christian elements. Perhaps the best example of this complexity in religious identity is the Lakota religious leader Black Elk. Thanks to the writer John G. Neihardt's telling of his life story in *Black Elk Speaks,* Black Elk came to stand for the most traditional practice of Indian religion, a practice brought to a tragic end by conquest. But his daughter, Lucy Black Elk Looks Twice, hoped to correct and deepen the standing image of her father, and, working with the anthropologist Michael Steltencamp, Lucy told the postconquest story of Nicholas Black Elk, who became a leading Catholic convert and cathechist on his reservation. This was not a matter of Black Elk's selling out, or betraying his traditional beliefs; this was a matter of sincere religious conviction responding to new beliefs in new times.[12]

In the nineteenth-century West, white Americans had denounced the religions of the others, labeling other systems of belief as paganism, heathenism, superstition, barbarism, or savagery and struggling to convert American Indians and Asian immigrants to Protestant Christianity. In the late-twentieth-century West, the tide seems to be reversing, as a number of white Americans have developed an enthusiasm for tribal religions, as well as for the varieties of Asian Buddhism. Particularly well represented in the West, New Age religion has appropriated pieces and parts of American Indian religions, with both Indian and white claimants to enlightenment, in the familiar area of overlap between commerce and religion, cashing in on the opportunities so presented. Reverend Josiah Strong and his colleagues were presumably tossing in their graves, but all over the West, the lines dividing the vision quest from communion, the *kiva* from the church, were shifting and wavering.

"DREAM OTHER DREAMS, AND BETTER"

To many white Americans in our times, belief in the mythic Old West has come to resemble belief in more conventional religious doctrines. For these believers, the Old Frontier is the nation's creation story, the place where the virtues and values of the nation were formed. And yet, for all the faith now invested in it, the mythic version of the Old West had little room for ministers and pastors, congregations and parishes. In a story full of cowboys, sheriffs, saloon girls, outlaws, gunfighters, prospectors, and stagecoach drivers, the church was, at best, the place where the frightened townspeople gathered to sing hymns and await rescue by the all-too-worldly hero. The church, after all, was aligned with the forces of respectability, the forces that would eventually tame the Wild West and end all the fun and adventure of the glory days. If one went in search of the classic heroes in the mythic turf of the Old West, one would not bother to look among the clergy.

In the quest for Western heroes, there is good reason now to look in unexpected, less-explored places. The old heroes are a pretty battered and discredited lot, with their character flaws on permanent display. The examples they provide often affirm the wrong faith entirely—the faith in guns and violence—or serve solely as individual examples of courage and determination, attached to no particular principle. Driven by the values of conquest and domination, or purely by the goal of personal fortune seeking, the old heroes are looking pretty tired—depleted, exhausted, and ready for retirement. In truth, they deserve a rest.

And yet, when the critics of academic historians say that we have discredited the old heroes and failed to replace them with any new ones, they are right. But this is not because we lack the resources. We have all the material we need to put forward a better team, people whose examples affirm a faith of considerably greater promise. It is time for a different kind of Western hero: the sustainable hero who can replace the old, exhausted, and depleted Western heroes. As Wallace Stegner said of the old Western myths, "dream other dreams, and better."

Sustainability in a hero means, very concretely, providing inspiration that sustains the spirit and the soul. While inconsistency can disqualify a conventional hero, a degree of inconsistency is one of the essential qualifications of a sustainable hero. Models of sustainable heroism are drawn from the record of people doing the right thing *some of the time*—people practicing heroism at a level that we can actually aspire to match. The fact that these people fell, periodically, off the high ground of heroism but then determinedly climbed back, even if only in order to fall again, is exactly what makes their heroism sustainable. Because it is uneven and broken, this kind of heroism is resilient, credible, possible, reachable. Sustainable heroism comes only in moments and glimpses, but they are moments and glimpses in which the universe lights up.

Assigned in 1867 to preside over the vast district of Montana, Idaho, and Utah, Bishop Daniel Tuttle "traveled more than forty thousand miles" by stagecoach. "Most times I enjoyed that mode of traveling," he remembered, "many times I grimly endured it, a few times I was rendered miserable by it." Think about what it meant to ride with strangers for hours and hours, jammed into an inflexible, jostling container, and the fact that Bishop Tuttle kept his temper and most of the time enjoyed the ride is its own measure of sustainable heroism.[13]

While misery most often derived from the rough road conditions or the inadequacy of stagecoach shock protection, fellow passengers could sometimes match the bumps in the road in their power to annoy. In one case, a fellow passenger "by manner and act was insulting to a colored woman in the coach." Bishop Tuttle firmly "reproved him." When words proved insufficient and the passenger "repeated the offense," Tuttle reported, "I shook him soundly." If this demonstration of muscular Christianity failed to produce a conversion, it still made for a happier ride. "At the next station," the offender "got out and slunk entirely away from our sight."[14]

Bishop Tuttle was a complicated man, full of self-righteous disapproval in his appraisal of Mormon belief and earnestly committed to the growth of his denomination. But when Bishop Tuttle took his stand on behalf of the right of African American women to travel with dignity, he offered a memorable demonstration of sustainable heroism, an episode in faith-affirming history for those trying to hold onto a belief in an American commitment to justice and fairness.

And then there is the remarkable example of heroism set by Reverend Howard Thurman. An African American man who was the chaplain at Howard University, Reverend Thurman headed west to team up with a white man as copastor of a new and courageous church. As a young child, he had attended his father's funeral and listened to a preacher condemn his father as an example of an unredeemed, unchurched sinner. Ever since then, Thurman had been on a campaign against exclusivity in Christian practice, fighting the exclusivity of the smugly saved as persistently as he fought the exclusivity of race. When he learned of an effort to form a church in San Francisco uniting people of all races and backgrounds, Reverend Thurman felt called. The year was 1943, more than ten years before the Montgomery, Alabama, bus boycott.

The location and the timing were both crucial. "Segregation of the races," Reverend Thurman wrote, "was a part of the mores, and of the social behavior of the country." "San Francisco with its varied nationalities, its rich intercultural heritages, and its face resolutely fixed toward the Orient" was the ideal place to undertake a trial run toward a better future in American race relations. War work had brought a much-increased black population to San Francisco and heightened the prospects of community friction. Responding to these challenges, an interracial group had decided to form the Church for the Fellowship of All Peoples, and Reverend Thurman joined them, following his quest to find out "whether or not it is true that experiences of spiritual unity and fellowship are more compelling than the fears and dogmas and prejudices that separate men." There was considerable risk, financial and otherwise, in the "mission" that brought Reverend Thurman and his family "three thousand miles across the continent." And there were constant tests of the spirit, as the Fellowship Church and Reverend Thurman faced the prospects of sponsoring interracial marriage and other challenges to the social order. Simply visiting a member of the congregation in the hospital could prove to be a test of Reverend Thurman's spirit; hospital staffs repeatedly stumbled over and resisted the notion that a white believer could be in the care of a black pastor.[15]

Fellowship Church under Reverend Thurman's leadership proved to be a great success, navigating its way through the difficult divisions between denominations as well as those between races. In God's presence, Reverend Thurman always insisted, "the worshiper is neither male nor female, black nor white, Protestant nor Catholic nor Buddhist nor Hindu, but a human spirit laid bare." "Religious experience," he believed, and he had lived this gospel, "must unite rather than divide men."[16]

The examples set by heroes like Bishop Tuttle and Reverend Thurman encourage me to believe in the real American West, a place—in the past and in the present—of dazzling human and natural possibility. Believing in the other West, the mythic and imagined West, has never been much of an option for me. Instead, the very notion of investing any faith in a simple, romantic, glorified West always brought to mind the verse that I learned from my father when I was very young:

> With this bright, believing band,
> I have no claim to be.
> What seems so true to them,
> Seems fantasy to me.

This verse has kept me on course in the company of those who have fallen head over heels in love with a Western illusion; and yet, in the presence of more traditional religious believers, it gives me much less comfort. The company of people secure in their faith, whether that faith is a tribal religion, Catholicism, Judaism, Mormonism, or a Protestant denomination, can make me melt with envy. But then the verse "With this bright, believing band, I have no claim to be" comes to mind and interrupts the melting. I remain a member of a battered, disorganized, but still pretty bright, believing band of my own, churched and unchurched, composed of all races and backgrounds— people who hold onto a faith that fairness and justice might some day prevail in this region and in this nation. That faith, the faith of my father and my mother, of Bishop Tuttle and Reverend Thurman, is the *kiva* in my soul.

PART V

———◆———

EPILOGUE

I want professors to make their understandings accessible to public audiences. Many of the tricks I now know about writing and speaking for wider audiences were matters about which, fifteen years ago, I did not have a clue. These are learned, rather than inherited, talents, and so I have compiled my best understandings of technique and strategy into a new essay, "A How-to Guide for the Academic Going Public."

The Association of American University Presses invited me to give a talk, "Saving Professors from Themselves and Detoxifying Academic Prose," and the *New York Times Book Review* printed a version of that speech in October 1993. "Dancing with Professors: The Trouble with Academic Prose" has had a wonderful life in department photocopying machines on campuses around the country. Fifteenth- or sixteenth-generation photocopies were beginning to get pretty faint, so this essay is reprinted here.

Lamentations over professorial and student writing styles are set pieces. Is there any remedy for these afflictions? For years, I have held the conviction that salvation lies in thinking of words as three-dimensional, sentient beings. Words are creatures in a dynamic but highly dependent relationship to writers. When misplaced and mistreated, words are miserable. When rescued from these painful situations, words—unlike people—instantly forgive. The last piece in this section, "Limerick's Laws of Verbal Etiquette," has also enjoyed quite a lively existence in photocopy machines. On the chance that they might offer some redemption to those who are inadvertently torturing words and readers, the laws are reprinted here.

V-A

A How-to Guide for the Academic Going Public

By an unfortunate theory, only a few academics can communicate with a broad audience. Rare individuals may speak with energy, charm, and clarity, but most professors are best left in peace in their preferred habitat, exchanging their findings with other specialists and lecturing students, who are enduring what they need to endure to secure a college degree.

While it has many believers, the theory is almost entirely nonsense. Student impatience with dull lectures is a palpable force in today's classroom; professors whose speaking styles mimic the dull droning of a hive of bees teach to nearly empty rooms. Students used to the peppy pacing of Sesame Street and MTV have pushed many of us into developing far more engaging and interactive styles of expression; no longer can we, with impunity, read from yellowed lecture notes. The skills we have developed for our classrooms can, in a number of ways, carry over to public audiences.

More important, effective communication with the public is an acquired, not an inherited, skill. Ten years ago, when the invitations to speak to nonacademic audiences started coming to me, I had no idea how to seize these opportunities. Over those years, partly through observations of others and partly through my own experiments (both successful and unsuccessful!), I have developed a set of strategies, techniques, and even tricks that work a lot more often than they fail. Anything in this list can be adapted, expanded, or discarded to fit personal style.

1. Early on, ask for copies of the agency's or organization's newsletters; if that is not an option, have an extensive conversation with a long-term member of the group. Read the newsletters or other printed material from the organization closely and thoughtfully, as if you were getting ready to write an ethnography of this interesting group. What are the group's preoccupations? Worries? Enthusiasms? Characteristic phrasings? Most often used acronyms? In what ways is the group confronting unsettling change? (In these times, there is *no* chance of finding a group for whom that question does not apply.) How does the group feel misrepresented or misunderstood by the media or the rest of society? This background investigation gives you what you need to pitch your remarks to the strike zone of your audience. Wonderfully, the audience will often have forgotten that so much information about them is available in the public record, and thus they will find it almost miraculous that you understand them so well. Sounding unexpectedly like an insider (or at least like someone who has spent time in bars or coffee shops with insiders), you gain considerable credibility. Comfortably deploying a few of the group's characteristic acronyms, in a manner that suggests that these are terms that come up from time to time in your own casual conversation, has quite a happy way of advancing the impression that you are among friends.

2. Express sympathy for your audience's dilemma. It is, again, guaranteed that they *have* a dilemma. At the turn of this millennium, everyone feels pressed and faced with too many demands. Regardless of profession or ideology, Americans feel that they are being asked to keep doing what they were already doing, and also to keep up with a bunch of new developments and challenges. Since professors certainly feel that this has happened in their own professional lives, this provides fruitful territory for empathy. While it would, of course, be a mistake to dwell on the excessive demands placed on professors,

thinking of the ways in which you yourself feel stretched and over-committed offers an effective method-acting technique for relating to an audience living with a similar sense of pressure.

3. Bow to the audience's expertise; the members of the audience, after all, live the experiences that you read about. Express anticipatory gratitude for the things that they know, things that you will soon benefit from learning (while this is in part a gesture of politeness, it is also a matter of substance, since you are in the happy position of an invited participant-observer among people whose testimony really will instruct you). Remark on the fact they know the subject under discussion in ways that are far more direct than your more distant knowledge. Though seemingly modest, this is also a prelude to demonstrating the value of distance in a perspective.

4. Take every opportunity to shuck off the academic stereotype that has surely preceded you. After the gestures of deference recommended in point 3, it will be very difficult for anyone to cast you as one of those know-it-all experts from the university. That stereotype anchors audience resistance to academics, and when you remove it from the tool kit, it can be pretty difficult to rebuild the walls of defensiveness and dismissal. Don't try to win the audience over with your own performance of academic bashing; they have already been supplied with everything they need along that line. Direct criticism of professors should not exceed a moment or two of gentle mockery of your people; most of the countering of the stereotype should occur not in direct and spoken challenge but in behavior that calls standard images of academics into question.

5. Surrender unnecessary dignity and claims on authority. On the Overland Trail in 1849, many travelers overpacked, and the weight of their baggage depleted the strength of their draft animals. In an almost exactly similar way, vanity and arrogance can only weigh you down and jeopardize your journey as a public intellectual. Of course, this recognition comes with some pain. All the time and trouble of getting a Ph.D. can create a conviction that you are entitled to immediate and sustained respect, and often people are very generous in humoring you in that conviction. And yet, while the practice of the

strategies recommended here will reduce the likelihood of attacks, you still have to be ready to absorb some direct verbal blows. If you protest the injustice of these blows, in any way that suggests that, as a Ph.D.-carrying expert, you are entitled to a protected status, you will sound shrill and thin skinned. In this case, a little suffering in silence can pay off.

Of course, by the tenets of academic freedom, you are free to say whatever you want to whomever you like. There are, however, good reasons to invoke academic freedom only when every other option is gone. Most people have few of the protections available to academics. In many forms of employment, jobholders have to spend a lot of their time calculating what they can and cannot say in front of the boss and fearing penalties if they miscalculate. For individuals who live with those restrictions, academic freedom of expression can provoke considerable resentment, particularly because it is resentment rooted in envy. Thus, being a good sport proves to be a substantially better strategy than shrilly asserting your untrammeled right to speak your mind. When facing a stiff challenge in front of an audience, breathe deeply and try to respond in a tone in which you will seem the personification of reason and tolerance, forcing your opponent to struggle to regain the high ground and match you in goodwill. A soft answer may or may not turn away wrath, but it certainly makes wrath look bad.

6. Seize the moment when you make a mistake or inadvertently convey ignorance. Handled right, a moment of this sort can be so disarming that it would almost be worth erring on purpose. Fortunately, venturing into the world of other people's lives and occupations makes it unnecessary to err intentionally; for sure, you'll get something wrong. The attraction of error is this: when the audience points out your mistake, you have a wonderful opportunity to pursue the agenda of point 4, by *thanking* them.

7. Whenever the opportunity comes up to change your mind in public, take it. Demonstrate what it looks like when a reasonable person listens to evidence and a reasonable argument and says, in response, "I recognize the reasons for your position, and I will rethink my own." Americans are *hungry* for demonstrations of this ability to listen and to respond, since they rarely, if ever, get to see it at work in

the national political scene. One of the most successful exchanges I have taken part in involved a debate on affirmative action with a conservative businessman. He and I agreed to argue on each other's behalf. We met several times and attended closely to each other's position; at the event, we presented each other's side as thoughtfully as we could, and we then returned to our actual positions for a period of reflection on what we had learned from each other. When we began our planning, we both thought we would perish from the discomfort of this exercise, but this fear proved ungrounded. Our audience seemed extremely relieved and pleased to see two people discuss a contentious subject with the goal of reciprocal understanding and not mutually assured destruction.

8. If you are having a tough time and meeting direct hostility, think of this experience in terms of rodeo. The rodeo riders' scores depend on the defiance of the animals they ride; however skilled the riders might be, no one will see those skills unless they are tested. When a rodeo rider draws a docile, sweet-tempered animal, perfectly eager to be ridden, why show up for the competition? By analogy, there is no point in selecting audiences that you expect to agree with you. The wilder the ride, the higher your score; the wilder the ride, the greater adventure and achievement. Moreover, verbal injuries are immeasurably to be preferred over the physical dangers of rodeo. What an enviable situation! On our worst days, we end up insulted and miffed, but not fractured.

9. Make your peace with the fact that journalists control your access to a wider audience. Your fate as a public intellectual rests in large part on the goodwill of reporters. But there is no avoiding the fact that journalists work under tight mandates to write *fast* and to present complicated matters in simple terms. Thus, when a writer quotes you weirdly or the quotation is accurate but madly out of context and when you thereby register on the public record as a certified idiot, then you can only be a good sport and find this *funny*. Almost certainly, the journalist didn't intend to destroy your reputation, and even if she did, she still controls the medium; any effort on your part to demand apology or correction will prove as unsatisfying as mud wrestling. Best to have a good laugh and resolve to speak a little more carefully next time.

10. Deploy your pronouns in wily and strategic ways. Pronouns are so short and seemingly characterless that they can sneak across borders and infiltrate opposing camps without anyone's noticing. If you are discussing a controversial subject, you can get a lot of mileage out of the use of "we," as in "we who stand in the middle," "we who are trying to understand all sides of this question." "We" can work like a butterfly net, thrown inclusively over your audience before they quite realize what is happening.

The pronoun "you" can be equally effective and reorienting. In talking to a largely white audience of university administrators, for instance, I have told stories about the dilemmas encountered by minority students. One African American student, from a pretty impoverished background, was filling out an application to be a dormitory resident assistant when she encountered the question: "Have you ever spent much time in the company of people from backgrounds different from your own?" At what time in the day, on our mostly white campus, was she not having this experience? As I said to the administrators, this question gave the student one of those moments when the universe says to you, "There *is* a norm, and *you* are not it." Note: the "you" in the reference was a young black woman, while the "you" addressed was largely white males, who are, more often than not, permitted to believe they *are* the norm. In theory, the disparity in the "yous" should have made this story ineffective, maybe even unintelligible. In fact, in this case and others, the bending and twisting of the pronoun "you" can sneak in a sense of empathy, community, loyalty, and shared experience that would probably encounter resistance if the speaker asked for it directly.

11. Do not "go subtle" when it comes to making your points or drawing your lessons. Audiences are much more attentive when you declare, "I see five—or eight or ten—principal issues here." They are reassured that you'll get on with it; the reputation of academics for "going on" is widespread, and the very idea that you are aware of the passage of time and are heading to a conclusion can lift their spirits. Moreover, planning a presentation in this way encourages you to make sure that each of your punch lines is marked and noticeable. Once you have declared your number of salient observations, you dare not change plans; this device triggers vestigial habits of note tak-

ing in many, and if you decide to leave out point 6 in a list of ten, you will distress a significant percentage of the audience.

12. Celebrate the value of distance in a perspective. Years ago, in New Haven, our parked car was hit by another vehicle skidding on ice. The sorrowful result of this incident was a fender jammed up against the tire, thus preventing our car from moving. What to do? A pleasant person from a repair shop arrived with a device which, inched into place, then expanded to push the fender back away from the tire (thus permitting us to drive the car into the shop to find out how badly rearranged the wheel alignment now was). This wonderful service has stuck in my mind and provided the best analogy for the good work that a visiting academic can do in matters of public controversy. People in the midst of the fray have little room to *think*, and thoughtful, detached commentary on their situation can provide a wonderful respite, putting some space between the tire and the fender and restoring the possibility of *movement*.

13. Go to church, watch how preachers use parables, and imitate them. Tell stories, and then reflect on the stories, very much in the manner of a minister wrestling over the meaning of the Parable of the Talents or of Peter's Denials While the Cock Crowed Thrice. Stories will last in the memory long after declarations of abstract truths are gone. Selecting and polishing your best parables for public audiences is labor that carries over nicely to enrich your classroom presentations, your papers delivered at academic conferences, and your conversation at cocktail and dinner parties.

14. Every ten minutes, do something to bring more oxygen to the listeners' brains. If you are comfortable with humor, then give them the occasion to laugh. If using strategically timed humor makes you feel that you are painfully trying to be funny or, worse, trivializing a serious matter, do something else—ask the audience a question that allows them to respond audibly, yes or no, up or down, right or left; to raise their hands; to look out the window or at the ceiling; or to turn and ask their neighbors something. Even those not stupefied by television, cinema, and web surfing can still get drowsy or find their attention wandering after a prolonged spell of listening. A small

stimulus to take a deep breath and reoxygenate their brain cells will go a long way, in Reverend Jesse Jackson's words, to keep hope alive.

15. Hang out, and do *not* depart for the airport right after your talk. Stay for dinner; sit in the lobby of the convention hotel; hang around the hospitality suites; go on the field trips. These are wonderful opportunities for participant-observer work, but, more important, the self-important "rush to the waiting airplane" will undermine everything you have worked to achieve in your presentation.

For professors who take up this line of work, there are plenty of rewards, but a few actions will make it more likely that the rewards get delivered to the right address. If you can remember, ask someone from your host agency or organization to write a letter to your university administrators, testifying to the value of your service; make it clear to presidents, chancellors, and deans that you are doing good work in making friends and recruiting support for higher education. At some rapidly approaching moment, universities will have to reconsider their reward structure, which at present gives the most niggardly recognition for the category "service." At a meeting of Colorado county commissioners, one commissioner asked me how my university values my participation in gatherings like the one we were attending. I changed the subject, preferring not to let him know that, under my current department procedures for awarding merit points, speaking to public officials would register at something like one-twentieth of a point (in contrast, publishing an article in a scholarly journal delivers eight full points). This system shouts out for its own reform.

And yet there is no necessary tug-of-war between activities as a public intellectual and activities as a scholar. When you speak to a public audience, you operate under a healthful and restorative mandate to escape specialization and think big. In truth, every academic field desperately needs synthesis; every topic lies buried under a flood of specialized studies. Speaking to a nonacademic audience puts you in the Noah role; while everyone else disappears in the flood, you make your selection of ark mates and sail off safely. When you return to Mt. Ararat, or the academic world, you have taken the journey that will give you the perspective to put the details of academic studies into a larger picture. Gaining practice in confident but thoughtful generalization in your travels outside the university, you can come up with ideas that will advance your career as an academic.

Like players in any competitive sport, professors like prizes, and prizes can be effective incentives for altering behavior. Thus, I end with a few proposals for new prizes, designed to give status and standing to achievements that could play a big part in the redemption of higher education. Professional organizations, philanthropic foundations, or charitable individuals—all who seek to encourage greater engagement between academics and the broader community are urged to make these ideas their own, with no constraints of intellectual property.

THE PRIZE FOR THE MOST DRAMATIC ESCAPE FROM ACADEMIC SPECIALIZATION AND JARGON

Candidates would submit before and after samples: first, the candidate's work when timidity most tightly tied her into a narrow field of inquiry; second, the candidate's work when courage returned, and she felt free to draw the most enterprising conclusions from her knowledge and to state those conclusions in the clearest language. This prize would celebrate a willingness to take chances and to think hard about both forests and trees.

THE PRIZE FOR THE MOST FORTHRIGHT AND GRACEFUL CONFESSION OF ERROR

Before this prize can be awarded, scholarly journals will have to create a new feature, one guaranteed to please readers. Before the articles, the abstracts, the book reviews, the list of dissertation topics will come the section called "Errors Admitted, Omissions Acknowledged, Oversights Recognized, Debts of Gratitude Belatedly Confessed." It is almost guaranteed that this section will be the first one readers turn to; checking it out will be an important way of keeping up with the field, while also carrying considerable human interest. (I myself come well supplied with examples to get things started: the author of *The Legacy of Conquest* witlessly forgot to remark on her indebtedness to a number of her most-valued predecessors—Josiah Royce, Angie

Debo, Bernard DeVoto, Wallace Stegner, and especially Carey McWilliams. In a similarly goofy move, she left cities out of her portrait of Western American history, even though the West is the most urbanized of regions.) Once these sections are in place in the journals, then it will be easy to institute the prize. The judges, who are themselves certified for their grace and good humor in admitting error, review the confessions of error and select, as the winning entry, the most moving, the most honest, the most telling.

The Prize for the Best Demonstration That Communication Is a Two-Way Street

This award goes to the academic who goes out into the world to give a speech and returns to the university having learned something consequential from the people he met. The material thus acquired must appear somewhere—in classroom lectures, in published writing—as proof that this communication went beyond the exchange of pleasantries and an honorarium.

The public intellectual, like any human being, is entitled to dreams, and I conclude with my wildest one. At the start of every football game at the University of Colorado, our mascot—a real, live buffalo named Ralphie—thunders out onto the field and runs in a grand, madly energetic circle, accompanied by student handlers in prime condition. Thus, I imagine a herd of professors pouring out of the university, unleashed from timidity, jargon, snobbery, and an exaggerated sense of purity. Students run alongside, enjoying the exercise, while enthusiasm for the university—for the students, the professors, and for the communities that benefit from their company—swells into a roar of applause.

V-B

Dancing with Professors: The Trouble with Academic Prose

In ordinary life, when a listener cannot understand what someone has said, this is the usual exchange:

Listener: I cannot understand what you are saying.
Speaker: Let me try to say it more clearly.

But in scholarly writing in the late twentieth century, other rules apply. This is the implicit exchange:

Reader: I cannot understand what you are saying.
Academic Writer: Too bad. The problem is that you are an unsophisticated and untrained reader. If you were smarter, you would understand me.

The exchange remains implicit, because no one wants to say, "This doesn't make any sense," for fear that the response, "It would, if you were smarter" might actually be true.

While we waste our time fighting over ideological conformity in the scholarly world, horrible writing remains a far more important problem. For all their differences, most right-wing scholars and most left-wing scholars share a common allegiance to a cult of obscurity. Left, right, and center all hide behind the idea that unintelligible prose indicates a sophisticated mind. The politically correct and the politically incorrect come together in the violence they commit against the English language.

University presses have certainly filled their quota every year, in dreary monographs, tangled paragraphs, and impenetrable sentences. But trade publishers have also violated the trust of innocent and hopeful readers. As a prime example of unprovoked assaults on innocent words, consider the verbal behavior of Allan Bloom in *The Closing of the American Mind,* published by a large mainstream press. Here is a sample:

> If openness means to 'go with the flow,' it is necessarily an accommodation to the present. That present is so closed to doubt about so many things impeding the progress of its principles that unqualified openness to it would mean forgetting the despised alternatives to it, knowledge of which makes us aware of what is doubtful in it.

Is there a reader so full of blind courage as to claim to know what this passage means? Remember, the book in which this remark appeared was a lamentation over the failings of today's *students,* a call to arms to return to tradition and standards in education. And yet, in twenty years of paper grading, I do not recall many sentences that asked, so pathetically, to be put out of their misery.

Jump to the opposite side of the political spectrum from Allan Bloom, and literary grace makes no notable gains. Contemplate this breathless, indefatigable sentence from the geographer Allan Pred, and Mr. Pred and Mr. Bloom seem, if only in literary style, to be soul mates:

> If what is at stake is an understanding of the geographical and historical variations in the sexual division of productive and reproductive labor of contemporary local and regional variations in female wage labor and women's work outside the formal economy, of on-the-ground variations in the everyday context of women's lives, inside and outside of their families, then it must be recognized that, at some nontrivial level, none of the corporal practices associated with these variations can be severed from spatially and temporally specific linguistic practices, from languages that not only enable to con-

veyance of instructions, commands, role depictions, and operating rules, but that also regulate and control, that normalize and spell out the limits of the permissible through the conveyance of disapproval, ridicule and reproach.

In this example, 124 words, along with many ideas, find themselves crammed into one sentence. In their company, one starts to get panicky. "Throw open the windows; bring in the oxygen tanks!" one wants to shout. "These words and ideas are nearly suffocated. Get them air!" And yet the condition of this desperately packed and crowded sentence is a perfectly familiar one to readers of academic writing, readers who have simply learned to suppress the panic.

Everyone knows that today's college students cannot write, but few seem willing to admit that the professors who denounce them are not doing much better. The problem is so blatant that there are signs that students are catching on. In my American history survey course last semester, I presented a few writing rules that I intended to enforce inflexibly. The students looked more and more peevish; they looked as if they were about to run down the hall, find a telephone, place an urgent call, and demand that someone from the American Civil Liberties Union rush up to campus to sue me for interfering with their First Amendment rights to compose unintelligible, misshapen sentences.

Finally one aggrieved student raised her hand and said, "You are telling *us* not to write long, dull sentences, but most of our assigned reading is *full* of long, dull sentences."

As this student was beginning to recognize, when professors undertake to appraise and improve student writing, the blind are leading the blind. It is, in truth, difficult to persuade students to write well when they find so few good examples in their assigned reading.

The current social and political context for higher education makes this whole issue pressing. In Colorado, as in most states, the legislators are convinced that the university is neglecting students and wasting state resources on pointless research. Under those circumstances, the miserable writing habits of professors pose a direct and concrete danger to higher education. Rather than going to the state legislature, proudly presenting stacks of the faculty's compelling and engaging publications, you end up hoping that the lawmakers stay out of the library and stay away, especially, from the periodical room, with its piles of academic journals. The habits of academic writers lend powerful support to the impression that research is a waste of the writers' time and of the public's money.

Why do so many professors write bad prose?

Ten years ago, I heard a classics professor say the single most important thing—in my opinion—that anyone has said about professors: "We must remember," he declared, "that professors are the ones nobody wanted to dance with in high school."

This is an insight that lights up the universe, or at least the university. It is a proposition that every entering freshman should be told, and it is certainly a proposition that helps to explain the problem of academic writing. What one sees in professors, repeatedly, is exactly the manner that anyone would adopt after a couple of sad evenings sidelined under the crepe-paper streamers in the gym, sitting on a folding chair while everyone else danced. Dignity, for professors, perches precariously on how well they can convey this message: "I am immersed in some very important thoughts, which unsophisticated people could not even begin to understand. Thus, I would not *want* to dance, even if one of you unsophisticated people were to ask me."

Think of this, then, the next time you look at an unintelligible academic text. "I would not *want* the attention of a wide reading audience, even if a wide audience were to *ask* me." Isn't that exactly what the pompous and pedantic tone of the classically academic writer conveys?

Professors are often shy, timid, and even fearful people, and under those circumstances, dull, difficult prose can function as a kind of protective camouflage. When you write typical academic prose, it is nearly impossible to make a strong, clear statement. The benefit here is that no one can attack your position, say you are wrong, or even raise questions about the accuracy of what you said if they cannot *tell* what you have said. In those terms, awful, indecipherable prose is its own form of armor, protecting the fragile, sensitive thoughts of timid souls.

The best texts for helping us understand the academic world are, of course, Lewis Carroll's *Alice's Adventures in Wonderland* and *Through the Looking-Glass*. Just as devotees of Carroll would expect, he has provided us with the best analogy for understanding the origin and function of bad academic writing. Tweedledee and Tweedledum have quite a heated argument over a rattle. They become so angry that they decide to fight. But before they fight, they go off to gather various devices of padding and protection: "bolsters, blankets, hearthrugs, tablecloths, dish covers, and coal scuttles." Then, with Alice's help in tying and fastening, they transform these household items into armor. Alice is not impressed: " 'Really, they'll be more like bundles of old clothes than anything else, by the time they're ready!' she said to herself, as she arranged a bolster round the neck of Tweedledee, 'to keep his head from being cut off,' as he said." Why this precaution? Because, as Tweedledee explains, "it's one of the most serious things that can possibly happen to one in battle—to get one's head cut off."

Here, in the brothers' anxieties and fears, we have an exact analogy for the problems of academic writing. The next time you look at a classically professorial sentence—long, tangled, obscure, jargonized, polysyllabic—think of Tweedledum and Tweedledee dressed for battle and see if those timid little thoughts, concealed under layers of clauses and phrases, do not remind you of those agitated but cautious brothers, arrayed in their bolsters, blankets, dish covers, and coal scuttles. The motive, too, is similar. Tweedledum and Tweedledee were in terror of being hurt, and so they padded themselves so thoroughly that they could not be hurt; nor, for that matter, could they move. A properly dreary, inert sentence has exactly the same benefit; it protects its writer from sharp disagreement, while it also protects him from movement.

Why choose camouflage and insulation over clarity and directness? Tweedledee, of course, spoke for everyone, academic or not, when he confessed his fear. It is, indeed, as he said, "one of the most serious things that can possibly happen to one in a battle—to get one's head cut off." Under those circumstances, logic says tie the bolster around the neck and add a protective hearthrug or two. Pack in another qualifying clause or two. Hide behind the passive-voice verb. Preface any assertion with a phrase like "it could be argued" or "a case could be made." Protecting one's neck does seem to be the way to keep one's head from being cut off.

Graduate school implants in many people the belief that there are terrible penalties to be paid for writing clearly, especially writing clearly in ways that challenge established thinking in the field. And yet, in academic warfare (and I speak as a veteran), your head and your neck are rarely in serious danger. You can remove the bolster and the hearthrug. Your opponents will try to whack at you, but they seldom, if ever, land a blow—in large part because they are themselves so wrapped in protective camouflage and insulation that they lose both mobility and accuracy.

So we have a widespread pattern of professors' protecting themselves from injury by wrapping their ideas in dull prose, and yet the danger they try to fend off is not a genuine danger. Express yourself clearly, and it is unlikely that either your head—or, more important, your tenure—will be cut off.

How, then, do we save professors from themselves? Fearful people are not made courageous by scolding; they need to be coaxed and encouraged. But how do we do that, especially when this particular form of fearfulness masks itself as pomposity, aloofness, and an assumed air of superiority?

Fortunately, we have available the world's most important and illuminating story on the difficulty of persuading people to break out of habits of timidity, caution, and unnecessary fear. I borrow the story from Larry McMurtry, one of my rivals in the interpreting of the American West, though I am putting this story to a use that Mr. McMurtry did not intend.

In a collection of his essays, *In a Narrow Grave,* Mr. McMurtry wrote about the weird process of watching his book, *Horseman, Pass By* being turned into the movie *Hud.* He arrived at the Texas Panhandle a week or so after filming had started, and he was particularly anxious to learn how the buzzard scene had gone. In that scene, Paul Newman was to ride up and discover a dead cow, look up at a tree branch lined with buzzards and, in his distress over the loss of the cow, fire his gun at one of the buzzards. At that moment, all the other buzzards were supposed to fly away into the blue Panhandle sky.

But when Mr. McMurtry asked people how the buzzard scene had gone, all he got, he said, were "stricken looks."

The first problem, it turned out, had to do with the quality of the available local buzzards, who proved to be an excessively scruffy group. So more appealing, more photogenic buzzards had to be flown in from some distance and at considerable expense.

But then came the second problem: how to keep the buzzards sitting on the tree branch until it was time for their cue to fly.

That seemed easy. Wire their feet to the branch, and then, after

Paul Newman fires his shot, pull the wire, releasing their feet, thus allowing them to take off.

But, as Mr. McMurtry said in an important and memorable phrase, the film makers had not reckoned with the "mentality of buzzards." With their feet wired, the buzzards did not have enough mobility to fly. But they did have enough mobility to pitch forward.

So that's what they did: with their feet wired, they tried to fly, pitched forward, and hung upside down from the dead branch, with their wings flapping.

I had the good fortune a couple of years ago to meet a woman who had been an extra for this movie, and she added a detail that Mr. McMurtry left out of his essay: namely, the buzzard circulatory system does not work upside down, and so, after a moment or two of flapping, the buzzards passed out.

Twelve buzzards hanging upside down from a tree branch: this was not what Hollywood wanted from the West, but that's what Hollywood had produced.

And then we get to the second stage of buzzard psychology. After six or seven episodes of pitching forward, passing out, being revived, being replaced on the branch, and pitching forward again, the buzzards gave up. Now, when you pulled the wire and released their feet, they sat there, saying in clear, nonverbal terms: "We *tried* that before. It did not work. We are not going to try it again." Now the filmmakers had to fly in a high-powered animal trainer to restore buzzard self-esteem. It was a big mess; Larry McMurtry got a wonderful story out of it; and we, in turn, get the best possible parable of the workings of habit and timidity.

How does the parable apply? In any and all disciplines, you go to graduate school to have your feet wired to the branch. There is nothing inherently wrong with that: scholars should have some common ground, share some background assumptions, hold some similar habits of mind. This gives you, quite literally, your footing. And yet, in the process of getting your feet wired, you have some awkward moments, including the intellectual equivalent of pitching forward and hanging upside down. That experience—especially if you do it in a public place like a graduate seminar—provides no pleasure. One or two rounds of that humiliation, and the world begins to seem like a very treacherous place. Under those circumstances, it does indeed seem to be the choice of wisdom *to sit quietly on the branch,* to sit without even the *thought* of flying, since even the thought might be sufficient to tilt the balance and set off another round of flapping, fainting, and embarrassment.

Yet when scholars get out of graduate school and get Ph.D.s, and, even more important, when scholars get tenure, the wire is truly pulled. Their feet are free. They can fly wherever and whenever they like. Yet by then the second stage of buzzard psychology has taken hold, and they refuse to fly. The wire is pulled and yet the buzzards sit there, hunched and grumpy. If they teach in a graduate program, they actively instruct young buzzards in the necessity of keeping their youthful feet on the branch.

This is a very well established pattern, and it is the ruination of scholarly activity in the modern world. Many professors who teach graduate students think that one of their principal duties is to train the students in the convention of academic writing.

I do not believe that professors enforce a standard of dull writing on graduate students to be cruel. They demand dreariness because they think that dreariness is in the students' best interests. Professors believe that a dull writing style is an academic survival skill because they think that is what editors want, both editors of academic journals *and* editors of university presses. What we have here is a chain of misinformation and misunderstanding, where everyone thinks that the other guy is the one who demands dull, impersonal prose.

Let me say again what is at stake here: universities and colleges are currently embattled, distrusted by the public and state funding institutions. As distressing as this situation is, it provides the perfect setting and the perfect timing for declaring an end to scholarly publication as a series of guarded conversations between professors.

The redemption of the university, especially in terms of the public's appraisal of the value of research and publication, requires all the writers who have something they want to publish to ask themselves the question: Does this have to be a closed communication, shutting out all but specialists willing to fight their way through thickets of academic jargon? Or can this be an open communication, engaging specialists with new information and new thinking, but also offering an invitation to nonspecialists to learn from this study, to grasp its importance, and, by extension, to find concrete reasons to see value in the work of the university?

This is a country desperately in need of wisdom and of clearly reasoned conviction and vision. And that, at the bedrock, is the reason behind this campaign to save professors from themselves and detoxify academic prose. The context is a bit different, but the statement that Willy Loman made to his sons in *Death of a Salesman* keeps coming to mind: "The woods are burning, boys, the woods are burning." In a society confronted by racial and ethnic conflicts, a growing gap between the rich and the poor, and environmental dilemmas, "the woods are burning," and since we so urgently need everyone's contribution in putting some of those fires out, there is no reason to indulge professorial vanity or timidity.

Ego is, of course, the key obstacle here. As badly as most of them write, professors are nonetheless proud and sensitive writers, resistant to criticism. But even the most desperate cases can be redeemed and persuaded to think of writing as a challenging craft, not as existential trauma. A few years ago, I began to look at carpenters and other artisans as the emotional model for writers. A carpenter, let us say, makes a door for a cabinet. If the door does not hang straight, the carpenter does not say, "I will *not* change that door; it is an expression of my individuality; who cares if it will not close?" Instead, the carpenter removes the door and works on it until it fits. That attitude, applied to writing, could be our salvation. If we thought more like carpenters, academic writers could find a route out of the trap of ego and vanity. Escaped from that trap, we could simply work on successive drafts until what we have to say is clear.

Colleges and universities are filled with knowledgeable, thoughtful people who have been effectively silenced by an awful writing style, a style with its flaws concealed behind a smokescreen of sophistication and professionalism. A coalition of academic writers, graduate advisers, journal editors, university press editors, and trade publishers can seize this moment *and pull the wire*. The buzzards *can* be set free—free to leave that dead tree branch, free to regain their confidence, free to soar.

V-C

Limerick's
Rules of Verbal Etiquette

Words are our friends, and people should not put their friends in awkward positions. When an author mistreats them, words and sentences feel discomfort, even pain, and certainly resentment. And yet, unlike human beings, words have no capacity to hold a grudge. As soon as the writer relieves their misery, words and sentences will work wholeheartedly for the writer's cause. The empathy, commitment, and attention that produce good relationships among people match, exactly, the qualities that build friendship between writers and words.

1. Weak subjects and verbs tremble and strain to hold up under the weight of important content. Kindness often requires their author to relieve them of this impossible task and replace them with strong subjects and strong verbs.

2. When the passive-voice verb tries to drain the energy from your sentences, you must rescue the sentences and bring them back to life with active verbs.

3. Sentences want to be limber, flexible, sleek, and agile. Often, this means they want to be small and manageable in size. They do not want to be bulky, awkward, and overweight, nor do they want to be overloaded or overdressed. They especially resent having to carry around an excess of prepositional phrases and polysyllables.

4. A sentence fragment knows and resents the fact that no one is going to listen to it or have any respect for it. Kindness requires the writer to make a sentence fragment into a whole sentence.

5. Words hate it when you ask them to convey unclear thoughts or no thoughts at all. They are very uncomfortable when readers ask them, "What on earth are you trying to say?" and they have no answer to give. They feel, in those moments, all the misery of a person who has been introduced to give a speech and who does not, in fact, have a speech to give. The good news is this: if you place your words in sentences with clear and direct content, they will gratefully do everything they can to help you out. But if you ask a word to take its place in a confusing sentence and you do not give it a clear message to convey, it is going to look you in the eyes and say, "Why did you do this to me?"

6. When you ask a group of sentences to form a paragraph, they expect to arrive in the paragraph and find that they have a lot in common. They expect, moreover, to find that one sentence is in charge of the paragraph (the topic sentence), and ready to introduce the other sentences to each other and remind them why they have all gotten together in the same paragraph. When, instead, they show up in the paragraph and discover that they have nothing in common and no one to introduce them, they are as uncomfortable and lonely as people who have arrived at a party where they know no one.

Notes

INTRODUCTION: SOMETHING IN THE SOIL

1. Of all the articles interpreting the New Western History, Gerry Kearns, "The Virtuous Circle of Facts and Values in the New Western History," *Annals of the Association of American Geographers* 88, no. 3 (September 1998): 377–409, makes the most sense, while the essays by Jerome Risk and Forrest G. Robinson, in *The New Western History: The Territory Ahead,* ed. Forrest G. Robinson (Tucson: University of Arizona Press, 1997), make the least.
2. Robert Utley, foreword to *The Old West,* by the editors of Time-Life Books (Englewood Cliffs, N.J.: Prentice-Hall, 1990), 6–7.
3. Joseph Wood Krutch, *More Lives than One* (New York: Sloane, 1962), 210–211.
4. "Calling 'Dances with Wolves' Fantasy, a Historian Sounds a Charge Against the Mythic Past of the American West," *People* 35, no. 15 (April 22, 1991). The first three "c"s appeared in this article explicitly, while the fourth "c" was implicit.

I-A HAUNTED AMERICA

1. Note 115 in *Black Hawk: An Autobiography,* ed. Donald Jackson (Urbana: University of Illinois Press, 1964), 138–139.
2. For this story, I am very much in debt to Keith A. Murray, *The Modocs and Their War* (Norman: University of Oklahoma Press, 1959), Richard Dillon, *Burnt-Out Fires* (Englewood Cliffs, N.J.: Prentice-Hall, 1973), and Francis S. Landrum, comp., *Guardhouse, Gallows and Graves: The Trial and Execution of*

Indian Prisoners of the Modoc Indian War by the U.S. Army (Klamath Falls, Oreg.: Klamath County Museum, 1988).

3. Dillon, *Burnt-Out Fires,* 157.

4. Murray, *The Modocs and Their War,* 105.

5. Dillon, *Burnt-Out Fires,* 158.

6. "Proceedings of a Military Commission Convened at Fort Klamath, Oregon, for the Trial of Modoc Prisoners," Appendix B, in *Guardhouse, Gallows, and Graves,* Landrum, 126, 128.

7. Murray, *The Modocs and Their War,* 125, 238.

8. Ibid., 231, 236.

9. Ibid., 237, 241.

10. Dillon, *Burnt-Out Fires,* 260.

11. Murray, *The Modocs and Their War,* 277.

12. Dillon, *Burnt-Out Fires,* 178.

13. Mae T. Parry, "Massacre at Boa Ogoi," Appendix B, in *The Shoshoni Frontier and the Bear River Massacre,* Brigham D. Madsen (Salt Lake City: University of Utah Press, 1985), 235.

14. "Proceedings," in *Guardhouse, Gallows, and Graves,* Landrum, 86, 95, 125.

15. Murray, *The Modocs and Their War,* 301.

16. Ibid., 309.

17. Ibid., 274.

18. Juanita Brooks, *The Mountain Meadows Massacre* (Norman: University of Oklahoma Press, 1964), xviii.

19. James Kirby Martin, Randy Roberts, Steven Mintz, Linda O. McMurry, and James H. Jones, *America and Its People* (Glenview, Ill.: Scott, Foresman, 1989), 282.

20. Murray, *The Modocs and the War,* 313–316.

21. Dillon, *Burnt-Out Fires,* vii.

22. *Bookworld* 5 (December 5, 1971).

23. *Booklist* 68 (April 1972): 663–664.

24. *Newsweek* 78 (December 27, 1971): 57.

25. *Newsweek* 77 (February 1, 1971): 69.

26. Peter Farb, "Indian Corn," *New York Review of Books* 17 (December 16, 1971): 36–38.

27. *Life* 70 (April 2, 1971): 9.

28. Thomas A. Bailey and David M. Kennedy, *The American Pageant: a History of the Republic,* 9th ed. (Lexington, Mass.: Heath, 1991), 588.

29. Alan Brinkley, Richard N. Current, Frank Freidel, and T. Harry Williams, *American History: A Survey,* 8th ed. (New York: McGraw-Hill, 1991), 501, 504.

30. James A. Henretta, W. Elliott Brownlee, David Brody, and Susan Ware, *America's History* (Chicago: Dorsey, 1987), 597.

31. John A. Garraty, *The American Nation: A History of the United States,* 7th ed. (New York: HarperCollins, 1991), 489.

32. R. Jackson Wilson, James Gilbert, Stephen Nissenbaum, Karen Ordahl Kupperman, and Donald Scott, *The Pursuit of Liberty: A History of the American People,* 2d ed. (Belmont, Calif.: Wadsworth, 1990), 682, 688.

33. Robert A. Divine, T. H. Bran, George M. Fredrickson, and R. Hal Williams, *America: Past and Present,* vol. 2, 3d ed. (New York: HarperCollins, 1991), 502–504.

34. Martin et al., *America and Its People,* 503.
35. Robert Hine, *The American West: A Interpretive History,* 2d ed. (Boston: Little, Brown, 1984), 212.
36. Tad Szulc, "The Greatest Danger We Face," *Parade,* July 25, 1993, 4–7.
37. Dee Brown, *Bury My Heart at Wounded Knee: An Indian History of the American West* (New York: Holt, Rinehart & Winston, 1971) and *The Gentle Tamers: Women of the Old Wild West* (1958); Lincoln: University of Nebraska Press, 1968).
38. Antonia I. Castaneda, "Women of Color and the Rewriting of Western History: The Discourse, Politics, and Decolonization of History," *Pacific Historical Review* 61, no. 4 (November 1992): 520–521.
39. Henry James, *Hawthorne* (1887; reprint, New York: AMS Press, 1968), 3, 12, 13.

I-B THE ADVENTURES OF THE FRONTIER IN THE TWENTIETH CENTURY

1. "Velcro: The Final Frontier," *Discover,* May 1988.
2. Frederick Jackson Turner, *The Frontier in American History* (1920; reprint, Tucson: University of Arizona Press, 1986), 2.
3. David M. Wrobel, *The End of American Exceptionalism: Frontier Anxiety from the Old West to the New Deal* (Lawrence: University Press of Kansas, 1993), 145.
4. Robert Cahn, "The Intrepid Kids of Disneyland," *Saturday Evening Post,* June 18, 1958, 22–23.
5. Ibid., 120.
6. Ibid., 119.
7. Ira Wolfert, "Walt Disney's Magic Kingdom," *Reader's Digest,* April 1960, 147.
8. Ibid.
9. John M. Findlay, *Magic Lands: Western Cityscapes and American Culture after 1940* (Berkeley: University of California Press, 1992), 93–94.
10. Change seems to have been as dramatic in Disney thinking about Indians. In 1993, the Walt Disney Company announced plans for a new American history theme park in Virginia. The section called "Native America," one company representative said, would now display "the sophisticated, intelligent societies that existed here before European settlers came, and in fact wiped out their societies." Michael Wines, "Disney Will 'Recreate' U.S. History Next to a Place Where It Was Made," *New York Times,* November 12, 1993.
11. See Jack D. Forbes, "Frontiers in American History," *Journal of the West* 1, nos. 1, 2 (1962): 63–74, and "Frontiers in American History and the Role of the Frontier Historian," *Ethnohistory* 15 (Spring 1968): 203–235; Howard Lamar and Leonard Thompson, eds., *The Frontier in History: North America and Southern Africa Compared* (New Haven, Conn.: Yale University Press, 1981), 3–13; William Cronon, George Miles, and Jay Gitlin, "Becoming West: Toward a New Meaning for Western History," in *Under an Open Sky: Rethinking America's Western Past,* eds. Cronon, Miles, and Gitlin (New York: Norton, 1992), 3–27; and Stephen Aron, "Lessons in Conquest: Towards a Greater Western History," *Pacific Historical Review,* February 1994.
12. Theodore C. Sorensen, ed., *"Let the Word Go Forth": The Speeches, Statements, and Writings of John F. Kennedy,* (New York: Delacorte, 1988), 100–102.

13. For a wide-ranging discussion of this assumption, see Wrobel, *The End of American Exceptionalism.*

14. Sorensen, *"Let the Word Go Forth"*, 100–102.

15. "President Very Much at Home on Ranch," *Denver Post*, August 23, 1986 (originally *Washington Post*).

16. United Press International, "Complete text of President Reagan's remarks," July 5, 1982.

17. "Transcript of Second Inaugural Address by Reagan," *New York Times*, January 22, 1985.

18. William Safire, "Grading the Speech," *New York Times*, January 24, 1985.

19. "Text of the President's State of the Union Address to Congress," *New York Times*, February 7, 1985.

20. Dukakis borrowed this phrase from Robert B. Reich's influential book, *The Last American Frontier: A Provocative Program for Economic Renewal* (1983; reprint, New York: Penguin, 1984). Reich himself subscribed to a modified safety valve image of the nineteenth-century frontier:

> During the years when the foundations of America's culture were being fixed, avoiding social conflict was far easier than settling it. The vastness of America's territories enabled generations of Americans to solve social problems by escaping from them, instead of working to change them. So long as the frontier beckoned, the sensible way to settle disputes was not painful negotiation, but simply putting some distance between the disputants. American notions of civic virtue came to center less on cooperating with neighbors than on leaving them alone. (p. 7)

21. "The Basic Speech/Michael Dukakis: A Call to Meet the Challenges of 'the Next American Frontier,' " *New York Times*, January 4, 1988.

22. Headlines are from the Boulder *Daily Camera* and the *Denver Post* for August 1986; the final one, "Frontier Legacy Lives," is from the *Denver Post*, August 5, 1991.

23. Molly O'Neill, "Eating to Heal: The New Frontiers," *New York Times*, February 7, 1990; "Edward Louie Is Dead, Cookie Pioneer was 69," Associated Press, May 31, 1990; "Two Cinnamon Roll Pioneers Are Spicing Up Product Line," *Nation's Restaurant News*, June 6, 1988; Cecilia Deck, "Fast-Food Pioneer A&W Survives to Map Comeback," *Chicago Tribune*, November 19, 1989; Berkley Hudson, "Laura Scudder Was More Than a Name; Monterey Park Will Honor 'Pioneer, Instigator, Doer' Who Helped Create Snack-Food Industry," *Los Angeles Times*, April 9, 1989; Marcia Dunn, "Pioneer in Natural Foods; Organic Farm Founder Had 50-Year Head Start," *Los Angeles Times*, January 15, 1989; Felicia Gressette, "Pioneer Vegetarian Fests Gets '90s Update," *Miami Herald*, February 18, 1993; Judith Sims, "A Walk in the Garden with Pioneer of Edible Landscape," *Los Angeles Times*, February 25, 1989; Andrew Gumbel, "Pasta Pioneers," *Chicago Tribune*, December 15, 1988; "Potato Pioneer Dead at 73," United Press International, June 20, 1989; Russell Mitchell, "Golden Valley Needs a Side of Fries; A Pioneer in Microwave Popcorn," *Business Week*, November 7, 1988; and Andy Wallace, "Antoinette Iannelli, Restauranteur and Pioneer of the South Philadelphia Hoagie," *Philadelphia Inquirer*, April 8, 1992.

24. Mary Rowland, "The Passionate Pioneer of Fitness Franchising," *Working Woman*, November 1988; Joe Ditler, "Surfing Pioneer Donald Takayama is Chairman of the Board Again," *Los Angeles Times*, May 3, 1990; Steve Morse,

"A Psychedelic Pioneer Remembered," *Boston Globe,* June 16, 1989; Marianne Meyer, "New Age Pioneers," *Marketing and Media Decisions,* February, 1988; Eric Lichtblau, "Sex-Change Pioneer Sues a Mission Viejo Hospital for Damages," *Los Angeles Times,* December 2, 1988, and "Sex-Change Pioneer Jorgensen," Associated Press, May 4, 1989; John Johnson and Michael Connelly, "A Porn Pioneer Still Baffles Police, Peers," *Los Angeles Times,* August 20, 1989; Pete Bowles, "A Drug 'Pioneer' Gets Life—Pioneer in the City's Crack Business," *Newsday,* December 2, 1989; Michael Kilian, "Frederick's: Peekaboo Pioneer," *Chicago Tribune,* June 6, 1990; "Underwear Pioneers Targeting Men," *Chicago Tribune,* December 24, 1989; Michael Arndt, "Amoco Spins a Reward for Polyester Pioneer," *Chicago Tribune,* May 4, 1989; "Inventor of Lexan (R), Resin and Plastics Pioneer Dies," PR Newswire, February 17, 1989; and Lisa Ann Casey, "Stainless Steel Cookware Pioneer," *Weekly Home Furnishings Newspaper,* April 17, 1989.

25. "Pioneer in Root Canal Dentistry," *Los Angeles Times,* March 29, 1988; and David Hancock, "Sleeper-Sofa Pioneer Bernard Castro Dies," *Miami Herald,* August 25, 1991.

26. Franklin D. Roosevelt letter reprinted in *Science—The Endless Frontier: A Report to the President on a Program for Postwar Scientific Research,* Vannevar Bush (Washington, D.C.: National Science Foundation, 1945; reprint 1960), 3–4.

27. Ibid., 8.

28. *Pioneering the Space Frontier: The Report of the National Commission on Space* (New York: Bantam Books, 1986), 3–4. See also Gerard K. O'Neill, *The High Frontier: Human Colonies in Space* (Princeton, N.J.: Space Studies Institute Press, 1989), and Harry L. Shipman, *Humans in Space: 21st Century Frontiers* (New York: Plenum, 1989). Shipman's remark—"Americans, in particular, value exploration in and of itself because of the importance of the frontier in our history" (p. 27)—typifies the space boosters' understanding of the history of westward expansion. For a more extensive discussion of the cultural psychology of the space program, see Patricia Nelson Limerick, "Imagined Frontiers: Westward Expansion and the Future of the Space Program," in *Space Policy Alternatives,* ed. Radford Byerly, Jr. (Boulder, Col.: Westview, 1992).

29. See Oscar J. Martinez, *Troublesome Border* (Tucson: University of Arizona Press, 1986), Mario Garcia, "La Frontera: The Border as Symbol and Reality in Mexican-American Thought," *Mexican Studies,* Summer 1985, 195–225, Alan Weisman and Jay Dusard, *La Frontera: The United States Border with Mexico* (Tucson: University of Arizona Press, 1986), and Tom Miller, *On the Border: Portraits of America's Southwestern Frontier* (New York: Harper & Row, 1981).

30. Gloria Anzaldua, *Borderlands/La Frontera: The New Mestiza* (San Francisco: Aunt Lute, 1987), 3.

31. Ibid., 4.

32. See Luis Alberto Urrea, *Across the Wire: Life and Hard Times on the Mexican Border* (New York: Doubleday, 1993).

33. Anzaldua, *Borderlands/La Frontera,* 63.

34. "Thousands Form Human Chain across Romania-Bulgaria Frontier," Reuters, June 8, 1990; "Palestinian Guerrilla is Killed at Lebanese-Israeli Frontier," *New York Times,* September 6, 1989; "Algeria and Morocco Reopen their Frontier," Reuters, June 5, 1988; and Jim Bodgener, "Turkey Will Close its Frontier with Bulgaria Today," *Financial Times,* August 22, 1989.

35. David Maraniss, "Memories in Black and White; Desegregation's Pioneers," *Washington Post*, June 6, 1990; "Genevieve Stuttaford Reviews *A. Philip Randolph: Pioneer of the Civil Rights Movement*," *Publishers Weekly*, May 11, 1990; "Rights Pioneer Parks Hospitalized," *Los Angeles Times*, February 2, 1989; "City in Ohio Honors Civil Rights Pioneer (Rosa Parks)," *Chicago Tribune*, May 11, 1990; Tanya Barrientos, "Civil Rights Pioneer Julian Bond Perplexed by Persistence of Racism," *Philadelphia Inquirer*, May 9, 1992; David Treadwell, "She is the First Black to Give Commencement Address: Integration Pioneer Returns to Speak at U. of Georgia (Charlayne Hunter-Gault)," *Los Angeles Times*, June 12, 1988; "Thelma Cowans, Pioneer Black Professional Golfer, Dies," United Press International, February 7, 1990; Rosemary L. Bray, "Renaissance for a Pioneer of Black Pride," *New York Times*, February 4, 1990; G. D. Clay, "First, There Was Fritz; Long before Art Shell, Pollard was NFL's Pioneer Black Coach," *Newsday*, December 20, 1989; "Didi Daniels Peter; Pioneer Black Producer," *Los Angeles Times*, March 2, 1989; Joseph W. Bostic: Pioneer Black Announcer," *Los Angeles Times*, June 2, 1988; Charles Fountain, "A Baseball Historian Goes to Bat for Some Negro League Greats: Blackball Stars: Negro League Pioneers," *Christian Science Monitor*, April 15, 1988; C. Gerald Fraser, "J. Saunders Redding, 81, Is Dead; Pioneer Black Ivy League Teacher," *New York Times*, March 5, 1988; David Mills, "Tuned In to Jockey Jack; Tribute to a Black Radio Pioneer," *Washington Post*, June 23, 1990; "Clifton R. Wharton Sr. Dies; Foreign Service Pioneer," *Jet*, May 14, 1990; "Pioneer Black L.A. Judge Edwin Jefferson Dies at 84," *Jet*, September 18, 1989; "Pioneer Black Journalist Albert J. Dunsmore, 73, Praised at Detroit Rites," *Jet*, February 20, 1989; Tia Swanson, "A Pioneer in World of Black Film," *Philadelphia Inquirer*, June 4, 1992; "Black Oscar Nominees Gala Celebrates Movie Talents (Sidney Poitier wins Pioneer Award)," *Jet*, April 17, 1989; Gene Siskel, "Poitier the Pioneer: He's Back on Screen—and Taking a Second Look at a Life Full of Firsts," *Chicago Tribune*, January 31, 1988; and Nick Jesdanun, " 'Pioneer' Futures," *Newsday*, June 24, 1989.

36. "NL President Plays Down 'Pioneer' Talk," *Chicago Tribune*, May 16, 1989. See also "NL Boss Won't Wear Pioneer Tag," *USA Today*, May 16, 1989.

37. The first efforts at including African Americans within Western American history left the framework of traditional frontier history unchallenged. In the introduction to the first edition of *The Black West* (reprint) (Seattle, Wash.: Open Hand, 1987), William Loren Katz remarked, "When historian Frederick Jackson Turner told how the frontier shaped American democracy, he ignored the black experience—not because it challenged his central thesis, but because he wrote in a tradition that had denied the existence of black people" (p. xii).

By the time of a later edition, Katz was developing a more critical approach; consider this remark from the 1987 introduction: "A U.S. Army that treated its Buffalo Soldiers shabbily and cynically buried their military record, has accepted an image rehabilitation and trumpeted black heroism the better to recruit despairing, unemployed black youths. Will it, in the name of troopers who battled Apaches, Sioux and Commanches, train dark young men to stem Third World liberation forces? This would be a tragic misuse of the past" (p. xi). See also William Leckie, *The Buffalo Soldiers*. The recent issuing of a United States Post Office stamp, commemorating the Buffalo Soldiers, puts an unintended spotlight on the question of the African American role in conquest; see "Part of

America's Past Becomes a Stamp of Tomorrow," *New York Times,* December 8, 1993.

38. Don Terry, "A Graver Jackson's Cry: Overcome the Violence!" *New York Times,* November 11, 1993.

39. Arthur Schlesinger, Jr., *The Disuniting of America: Reflections on a Multicultural Society* (New York: Whittle, 1991) is usually cited as the exemplar of this concern, but Schlesinger's position is more complicated than most of his critics have recognized.

40. These impressions come from a number of speaking engagements with United States Information Agency tour groups, where international scholars have told me about their early encounters with the American frontier myth.

I-C THE CASE OF THE PREMATURE DEPARTURE

1. Robert A. Divine, T. H. Breen, George M. Frederickson, and R. Hal Williams, *America: Past and Present,* vol. 2, 3d ed. (New York: HarperCollins, 1991), 763.

2. Irwin Unger, *These United States: The Questions of Our Past,* 4th ed. (Englewood Cliffs, N.J.: Prentice-Hall, 1989), 504; and R. Jackson Wilson, James Gilbert, Stephen Nissenbaum, Karen Ordahl Kupperman, and Donald Scott, *The Pursuit of Liberty: A History of the American People,* vol. 2, 2d ed. (Belmont, Calif.: Wadsworth, 1990), 677. Unger also drops the number of soldiers killed with Fetterman from eighty to eight.

3. Wilson et al., *The Pursuit of Liberty,* vol. 1, x.

4. In most of the books, the Western fur, mining, cattle, and farming businesses are all frontiers, even though the patterns of their development seem very different indeed. In Mary Beth Norton, David M. Katzman, et al., *A People and a Nation* (Boston: Houghton Miflin, 1990), the South after the Civil War is also a frontier (p. 467). In Thomas A. Bailey and David M. Kennedy, *The American Pageant: A History of the Republic,* 9th ed. (Lexington, Mass.: Heath, 1991), cities in the late nineteenth century are an urban frontier (p. 554) and the typewriter is a new frontier for women (p. 749), while in John M. Blum, William S. McFeely, Edmund S. Morgan, Arthur M. Schlesinger, Jr., Kenneth M. Stampp, and C. Vann Woodward, *The National Experience: A History of the United States,* 7th ed. (San Diego, Calif.: Harcourt Brace Jovanovich, 1989), outer space offers itself as "an endless frontier" (p. 844).

The reader, tracking these—and more—usages, struggles for a coherent definition of what a number of Western historians have taken to calling the "f-word." Consider one sentence from George R. Tindall, *America: A Narrative,* vol. 2, 2d ed. (New York: Norton, 1988): "The miners' frontier was in fact not so much a frontier as a scattering of settlements in parts unsuitable for farming, such as steep mountainsides, remote highlands, and barren deserts" (p. 758). Since, in other usages, a scattering of settlements seems to be precisely the meaning of "frontier," this attempt at definition does more to heighten than to dispel the confusion.

5. The term "Mexican-American War" has not caught on in any of the textbooks; the term remains "Mexican War." A moment contemplating the prospect of asking Mexican citizens what they think of "the Mexican War" (to the obvious response, *"which* Mexican war?"*) demonstrates the problem with the term. Norton has modified the usual term "Spanish-American War" to include all the

parties (the Spanish-American-Cuban-Filipino War, p. 647), but no comparable rethinking of "Mexican War" has occurred.

6. Gary B. Nash, Julie Roy Jeffrey, John R. Howe, Allen F. Davis, Peter Frederick, and Allan M. Winkler, *The American People: Creating a Nation and a Society*, 2d ed. (New York: Harper & Row, 1990), is unusual in noting the Trans-Mississippi dimensions of the Civil War (p. 516). Alvin M. Josephy, Jr., *The Civil War in the American West* (New York: Knopf, 1991), would be of use to any author or teacher wanting to rethink the idea of "the War in the West."

7. The phrase "folding frontier" comes from Bailey and Kennedy, *The American Pageant*, p. 601; "the final phase" is from James A. Henretta, W. Elliott Brownlee, David Brody, and Susan Ware, *America's History* (Chicago, Ill.: Dorsey, 1987), 617.

8. While Geronimo and the Apaches, as well as Chief Joseph and the Nez Perce, make occasional appearances, textbooks concentrate on the nomadic Indians of the northern Plains, and especially on the Sioux. In *The American Nation: a History of the United States*, 7th ed. (New York: HarperCollins, 1991), John Garraty calls the Plains Indians "by far the most important" (p. 487); in *An American History*, 4th ed. (New York: Knopf, 1985), Rebecca Gruver remarks that the Plains Indians were the "most important" (p. 460). This seems to be a judgment where significance is set, first, by numbers (the Plains Indians were "the most numerous," in *American History*, 8th ed., Alan Brinkley, Richard N. Current, Frank Freidel, and T. Harry Williams [New York: McGraw-Hill, 1991], 500) and by celebrity status (the Plains Indians are called the "best known" in *America and Its People*, James Kirby Martin, Randy Roberts, Steven Mintz, Linda O. McMurry, and James H. Jones [Glenview, Ill.: Scott, Foresman, 1989], 377). Perhaps the most curious assertion of their significance is in *These United States*, Unger: "The Plains Indians were the classic 'Indians' of American frontier legend: tall, bronzed, with straight black hair, high cheekbones, and prominent curved noses" (p. 500).

9. It is a rare textbook that does not include a picture of the Populist leader Mary E. Lease; Wilson et al.'s *Pursuit of Liberty* is one conspicuous exception. With a focus on Plains farming comparable to the focus on Plains Indians, other varieties of Western farming risk invisibility. A few books do make an effort to discuss Western farming beyond the Plains: see Divine et al., *America*, vol. 2, 520; Henretta et al., *America's History*, 773; Nash et al., *The American People*, 585–586; and Unger, *These United States*, 520–521.

10. Tindall, in *America*, vol. 2, concludes the chapter on the West with Turner's words, without any commentary or reappraisal: " 'the frontier has gone and its going has closed the first period of American history' " (p. 774). A few authors note the possibility that the closing of the frontier may be a bit overstated, but despite that observation, the West vanishes as completely as it does with a definitively closed frontier. See Brinkley et al., *American History*: "In fact, Turner's forebodings were premature. A vast public domain still existed in the 1890s, and during the forty years thereafter the government was to give away many more acres that it had given as homesteads in the past" (p. 500); Bailey and Kennedy, *The American Pageant*: "The frontier survived its 'death' by several decades" (p. 601); and Norton, *A People and a Nation*: "The fading of the frontier, though of great symbolic importance, had little direct impact on people's behavior, because vast stretches of land remained unsettled" (p. 468).

11. The index of Blum et al., *The National Experience,* has, under "Frontier, American," "see West" (p. 905); the index of Brinkley et al., *American History,* has, under "Frontier," "see Far West (Index p. 1xi)"; and the index of Divine et al., *America,* has, under "Frontier," "See West" (vol. 1, p. I-5, and vol. 2, p. I-6). By retitling Frederick Jackson Turner's famed speech, "The Significance of the Frontier in American History," as " 'The Significance of the West in American History,' " Henretta et al. demonstrate how strong the notion of "West" and "frontier" as synonyms can be (*America's History,* p. 255).

12. Henretta et al., *America's History,* lxiv; and Nash et al., *The American People,* I-32.

13. In every book, the only prolonged discussion of the oil business involves John D. Rockefeller and Standard Oil. The Trans-Mississippi oil business receives no comparable attention. Blum et al., *The National Experience,* make a brief mention of alarm over oil spills (p. 842), as do Brinkley et al., *American History* (p. 985) and Henretta et al., *America's History* (p. 966); Paul S. Boyer, Clifford E. Clark, Jr., Joseph F. Kett, Thomas L. Purvis, Harvard Sitkoff, and Nancy Woloch, *The Enduring Vision: A History of the American People* (Lexington, Mass.: Heath, 1990), has a two-page insert on Houston's recent boom and bust with the energy business (vol. 2, pp. 1129a–1129b); Gruver, *An American History,* makes a very brief mention of contemporary conflicts over oil leasing (p. 477); Bailey and Kennedy, *The American Pageant,* refer quickly to the rise of a Western "oil frontier" which was also an "industrial frontier" (p. 745); Martin et al., *America and Its People,* briefly mention the oil boom at Spindletop (p. 515); and Norton, *A People and a Nation,* briefly foreshadows the twentieth-century Western oil business (p. 474).

14. Besides the usual post-1890 references to the Dust Bowl, Hollywood, Japanese American relocation, and other Western events of certified significance, *The Enduring Vision,* Boyer et al., uses Butte, Montana, as an example of a specialized city (p. 643); puts forward Omaha, Nebraska, as an example of a city with a rapidly shifting population (p. 645); includes Hispanics in Los Angeles and Chinese in San Francisco as examples of ghettoized populations in the 1890s (p. 651); uses a case study of a Great Plains childhood as an example of family work roles (p. 682); demonstrates urban ethnic culture with a reference to the saloons of Denver (p. 691); illustrates a discussion of the late-nineteenth-century commitment to education with a picture of a San Diego schoolhouse (p. 705); uses a picture of San Francisco children saluting the National Recovery Administration Blue Eagle insignia (p. 880); features a special insert on the Los Angeles barrio in the 1930s (pp. 909a–909b); refers to the Texan restoration of the Alamo as an example of 1930s patriotism (p. 919); dramatizes the relief at the end of World War Two with descriptions of celebrations in San Francisco, Salt Lake City, and San Diego, not just Boston and Chicago (p. 935); and uses Orange County as an example of explosive suburbanization and the development of Chavez Ravine in Los Angeles as an example of invasive urban redevelopment (pp. 1023, 1034).

15. Textbooks usually confine the problem of Western water scarcity to a discussion of the nineteenth-century Plains farming frontier or a mention of the Mormons' adoption of irrigation. (On that subject, Henretta et al., in *America's History,* make the statement that the Mormons "developed innovative principles of communal water rights that the federal government and all the states of the semiarid

West later adopted" [p. 383], giving Western water law an improbable uniformity.) The general impression is that Western water scarcity posed a problem for nineteenth-century Plains farmers, but aridity was somehow transcended in the twentieth century. What George Tindall in *America* calls "the unchangeable fact of aridity" (vol. 2, p. 771)" is also, in the texts, the disappearing fact of aridity.

Most strikingly, in the many descriptions of the Sunbelt, only Gruver, in *An American History*, notes that some of the Sunbelt states faced "a shortage of water" (p. 913). Otherwise the question of the water supply's ability to support growth remains one among many unmentioned matters of Western environmental history. The only prolonged discussion of water development occurs in one of William Cronon's environmental essays in Brinkley et al. ("The Flow of Water," pp. 405–409), though it concerns the use of water and water power in the Eastern United States. *The American People*, Nash et al., makes a remark that surely deserves to be extended to the West beyond California: "The value of much of California's agricultural land, especially the southern half of the Central Valley, depended on water" (p. 585). Very influential, if also controversial, in Western historical circles, Donald Worster's *Rivers of Empire: Water, Aridity, and the Growth of the American West* (New York: Pantheon, 1985) appears to have made no impact on the textbooks.

16. Divine et al., *America*, vol. 2, 495; Henretta et al., *America's History*, inside front cover, 589; Bailey and Kennedy, *The American Pageant*, inside back cover; Martin et al., *America and Its People*, inside front cover; and Norton, *A People and a Nation*, inside front cover.

17. For maps showing a nineteenth-century, Trans-Mississippi pattern of settlement that would test anyone's ability to mark the frontier, see Brinkley et al., *American History*, 372; Gruver, *An American History*, 288; Nash et al., *The American People*, 457; and Norton, *A People and a Nation*, 258.

18. For maps with large areas of "blank" space, see Blum et al., *The National Experience*, 496; Boyer et al., *The Enduring Vision*, 587; Divine et al., *America*, 521; Henretta et al., *America's History*, 596; and Wilson et al., *The Pursuit of Liberty*, vol. 2, 674.

19. Other Western events or people seem on their way to achieving permanent place in the canon and, if permitted, to enriching the standard version of Western history: the Western Federation of Miners; the Coeur d'Alene and Ludlow strikes; the first McDonalds in San Bernardino, California; Henry Kaiser; Allan Bakke; James Watt; Henry Cisneros; and Sandra Day O'Connor.

20. Brinkley et al., *American History*, 976.

21. For maps showing recent population growth in the South and the West, see Bailey and Kennedy, *The American Pageant*, 872; Brinkley et al., *American History*, 978; Divine et al., *America*, vol. 2, 952; Henretta et al., *America's History*, 973; Nash et al., *The American People*, 1031; and Norton, *A People and a Nation*, 887, 989. Garraty, *The American Nation*, is one of the few books without a discussion of the rise of the Sunbelt.

22. In some books, the chapters on Manifest Destiny and post–Civil War expansion carry a marked tone of fatalism, often quite different from the open and flexible appraisal of causality that characterizes other parts of the text.

The framework of inevitability is at its most pronounced in Unger's *The United States*. The American "expansionist impulse," Unger tells students, was "almost a physical law." Confronting an "almost empty" West, the movement of Anglo-Americans was like "the rush of air into a vacuum." The war against Mexico was thus "an inevitable event" (p. 277). See also Martin et al., *America and Its People* ("The underlying cause of the Mexican War was the inexorable movement of American pioneers into the Far West. . . . inevitably Mexican and American interests clashed" [p. 392]), and Henretta et al., *America's History* ("The Plains Indians inevitably tried to hold on to their way of life. Their subjection was equally inevitable" [p. 597]). As teachers of the American history survey course know, undergraduates are already all too receptive to the concept of inevitability. When a textbook writer places the concept of inevitability in their hands, everything from the arrival of the Pilgrims to the election of Ronald Reagan is on its way to becoming a matter of predetermined fate and physical law.

23. Presently the balance of attention goes overwhelmingly toward the British Atlantic colonies, with, at most, a few paragraphs on the Spanish colonies in the American interior. The Spanish colonies are sometimes discussed in the chapter on Manifest Destiny, isolated from any possible comparison with the British colonies. Even when the Spanish and British examples are closer to each other in the text, the process of comparison is at best cursory.

For instance, Boyer et al., in *The Enduring Vision*, compare British behavior toward Indians with Spanish and French behavior, at the risk of some loss of complexity for all three groups: The French and Spanish empires, "spread thin, depended heavily on Indian goodwill or acquiescence. In contrast, British North America was compact, aggressively expansionist, and usually antagonistic toward the native Americans" (p. 95); Brinkley et al., in *American History*, compare the Spanish empire to the British, though with no particular application to the northern borderlands (where "the surface riches" and "easy wealth" [p. 13] of other parts of the Spanish empire were simply not a factor) and without raising the question of whether the English matched the Spanish in their "remarkable brutality and greed" (p. 11); Martin et al., in *America and Its People*, observe that "the people of New Spain were more tolerant of racial differences than were the English" (pp. 20–21); and Nash et al., in *The American People*, note that "racial intermixture and social fluidity were more extensive than in the English colonies" (p. 101).

The assumption that the English colonies are the true subject of colonial history can be seen graphically in several maps: consider Boyer et al., *The Enduring Vision*, "European Settlements in North America, 1525–1625" (p. 34), a map that only covers the Atlantic Coast (and seems, as well, to reveal some confusion about whether Mexico is in North America; see similar references to a Mexico-free North America in Wilson et al., *The Pursuit of Liberty*, 32, and Bailey and Kennedy, *The American Pageant*, 6); see also maps of what will become the Eastern United States in Blum et al., *The National Experience*, "The Extension of Settlement, 1660–1760" (p. 49); in Gruver, *An American History*, "Colonial Settlement by Nationalities" (p. 72); Norton, *A People and a Nation*, "The American Colonies in the Early Eighteenth Century" (p. 44); and Unger, *These United States*, "Colonial Settlement, 1650–1770" (p. 44).

It is easy to imagine how a broader definition of "colonial" would enrich chapters like these, presently devoted to the British colonies: Bailey and Kennedy, *The American Pageant*, chap. 3, "American Life in the Seventeenth Century" (pp. 44–61), Blum et al., *The National Experience*, chaps. 2 and 3, "The Pattern of Empire" and "The First American Way of Life" (pp. 29–77); Brinkley et al.,

American History, chap. 3, "Life in Provincial America" (pp. 59–91); Divine et al., *America,* chaps. 3 and 4, "Putting Down Roots: Colonists in an Empire" and "Expanding Horizons: Eighteenth Century America" (pp. 65–123); Garraty, *The American Nation,* chap. 2, "American Society in the Making" (pp. 30–61); Gruver, *An American History,* chap. 3, "Shaping an Identity" (pp. 60–93); Henretta et al., *America's History,* chaps. 3 and 4, "The Creation of the American Political System and Economy" and "Cultures of Pre-Industrial America" (pp. 62–115); Martin et al., *America and Its People,* chaps. 2 and 3, "Plantations and Cities Upon a HIll" and "Provincial America in Upheaval" (pp. 36–101); Nash et al., *The American People,* chaps. 2 and 3, "Colonizing a Continent" and "Mastering the New World" (pp. 34–91); Norton, *A People and a Nation,* chap. 3, "Growth and Diversity" (pp. 73–101); and Unger, *These United States,* chap. 3, "Colonial Society: How Did Old World Culture Change in the Wilderness?" (pp. 52–81).

24. Brinkley et al., *American History,* 976.

25. How and where to incorporate Asian Americans into the narrative is a puzzle no textbook has solved. The problem is most conspicuous in what is a well-established three-part litany on the position of minorities: African Americans, Mexican Americans, and Native Americans—in the Depression, in World War Two, in the 1960s, in our times. In this litany, the absence of the fourth group, Asian Americans, persists until the section on our own times. Asian Americans thus make brief appearances for the building of the Central Pacific Railroad, the Chinese Exclusion Act, the Japanese American relocation camps, and the upsurge in Asian immigration in the last twenty-five years. Many of the books cite the fact that Chinese Americans and Japanese Americans now have considerable educational achievement and family incomes higher than whites. The combination of success with persistent anti-Asian stereotyping and prejudice is too great a variation from the "normal" pattern of minority history to allow an easy inclusion of Asian Americans in the usual African American, Mexican American, and Native American sequence.

This is obviously a sensitive and difficult issue; there may be understandable reasons why the forces behind Asian American success in the wake of fierce discrimination, as well as the question of how widely distributed that success may be among the various Asian nationalities, currently receive little discussion. In *The American People,* for instance, Nash et al. note Asian American educational success (p. 1032) and, a page or two later, in a section called "The Continuing Struggle for Equality," list only "women, blacks, Hispanics, and Native Americans" as participants in that struggle (p. 1036), giving the impression that Asian American success is now complete and unobstructed.

26. Henretta et al., *America's History,* 935. For similar suggestions that black protest inspired, perhaps even caused, Hispanic and Indian protest, see also Boyer et al., *The Enduring Vision,* 1066: "The black movement inspired other minority groups to mobilize and aggressively press their claims"; Brinkley et al., *American History,* 923: "[B]lack protest . . . encouraged other minorities to assert themselves and demand redress of their grievances"; Divine et al., *America,* 923: "Other groups quickly emulated the African-American phenomenon"; Garraty, *The American Nation,* 895: "The struggles of black people for equal treatment in the 1950s and 1960s radicalized many Indians"; Martin et al., *America and Its People,* 969: "The struggles of black Americans for racial justice inspired a

host of other groups to seek full equality," and 983, "The example of the civil rights movement inspired other groups to press for equal opportunity"; Nash et al., *The American People,* 1008; "Hispanics, like women, followed the example of blacks in the struggle for equality"; and Unger, *These United States,* 817: "Among ethnic minorities, the example of the black civil rights movement inspired Mexican-Americans . . . and Indian-Americans (Native Americans) to organize movements to fight for political recognition and an end to discrimination."

   In the same spirit, various writers see the movement of blacks out of the South as the process that spread the problem of race relations, a notion that simply cancels out the long history of Western American racial discrimination and friction. See Henretta et al., *America's History,* 923: "The black exodus from the South made civil rights a national, not a sectional, issue," as well as Bailey et al., *The American Pageant,* 844: In World War Two, "some 1.6 million blacks left the land of their ancient enslavement to seek jobs in the war plants of the West and North. Forever after, race relations constituted a national, not a regional, issue."

27. A very different picture emerges from books like Mario Garcia, *Mexican-Americans* (New Haven, Conn.: Yale University Press, 1990), Juan Gomez-Quinones, *Chicano Politics: Reality and Promise, 1940–1990* (Albuquerque: University of New Mexico Press, 1990), and Emilio Zamora, *The World of the Mexican Worker in Texas* (College Station: Texas A & M University Press, 1993). In contrast to those studies of Mexican-American self-assertion, see Garraty's assertion in *The American Nation:* "Spanish-speaking residents of the Southwest . . . tended to accept their fate with resignation, to mind their own business, to make little trouble" (p. 894). The problem of including Asian Americans is particularly notable in this connection: African American, Mexican American, and Native American activists, as well as feminists and gay and lesbian activists, earn attention, but the Asian American movement never registers in the texts. William Wei's study of Asian American activism (Philadelphia: Temple University Press, 1992) should prove helpful on this count.

28. Brinkley et al.'s *American History* takes a notable step in the inclusion of environmental history, with seven effective essays by William Cronon on "The American Environment." Only one essay, "Dust Bowl," has a particular application to the Trans-Mississippi West.

29. In *The National Experience,* for instance, Blum et al. mention the Sagebrush Rebellion's campaign against "federal supervision of the public lands" (p. 813). And yet there is almost nothing in the preceding pages, beyond two paragraphs on Theodore Roosevelt and Gifford Pinchot (p. 513), to tell the students what the public lands might be and why federal supervision of them would be controversial. In *American History,* Brinkley et al. include a helpful map on the "Establishment of National Parks and Forests" (p. 647), but, like all the other authors, they do not say what kind of entity national parks might be or how they originated or how their definition and management might have changed over the twentieth century.

   While a number of textbooks make a quick reference to the 1902 Newlands Reclamation Act, none of them follow up on the paradoxes and conflicts built into a kind of conservation, particularly directed at the arid West, which is also a kind of development. In *The American Pageant,* on the subject of reclamation,

Bailey et al. stick to congratulations: "Thanks to this epochal legislation, dozens of dams were thrown across virtually every major western river in the ensuring decades" (p. 680), claiming, as well, that "settlers repaid the cost of reclamation from their now-productive soil" (p. 679), though they often did not. Consider the difficulty of distinguishing between "development" and "exploitation" in Garraty's remarks, in *The American Nation,* on New Deal conservation: "Government public power projects, such as the giant Bonneville and Grand Coulee dams in the Pacific Northwest were only the most spectacular part of a comprehensive New Deal program to develop the nation's natural resources. Exploitation of the natural resources of the West was checked. . . ." (p. 784). To say, as Gruver does in *An American History,* that Theodore Roosevelt "established a national policy [in conservation] that would endure for generations to come" (pp. 630–631), is to throw a blanket of consensus over what remains a very contentious set of economic and governmental issues.

30. Gruver, *An American History,* 476; and Norton, *A People and a Nation,* 487.

31. Most of the books make very brief references to the wartime work at Los Alamos and sometimes to the test at Alamogordo; only Divine et al., in *America,* refers by name to the Hanford Reservation, the most polluted site in the United States, ("Scientists . . . worked at the University of Chicago; Oak Ridge, Tennessee; Hanford, Washington; and a remote laboratory in Los Alamos, New Mexico, to perfect this deadly new weapon" [p. 825].) In *The Enduring Vision,* Boyer et al. mention the risks of fallout from the Pacific nuclear tests (p. 1005) and Nash et al., in *The American People,* print a photograph of what seems to be a Pacific atomic test, but neither refers to any comparable, domestic risk from the use of the Nevada Test Site. In *A Nation and a People* (p. 877), Norton cites Howard Ball's *Justice Downwind* (a study of the people affected by fallout from the Nevada Test Site) but does not mention the downwinders in the text itself. Wilson et al., in *The Pursuit of Liberty,* print a picture that seems to be of the Nevada Test Site (vol. 2, p. 943), but it is not identified by name, and the significance of its location—on Western terrain left suitable for bombing by virtue of aridity and federal ownership—is not discussed. Henretta et al., in *America's History,* use a photograph of soldiers exposed to a test in Nevada (p. 899); the discussion of the topic is confined to the caption.

32. One can see this reliance on a dated version of Western history most conspicuously in the frequent citations of Ray Allen Billington. The most-determined upholder of the propositions that "West" and "frontier" are synonyms and that both ended in the 1890s, Billington is almost universally cited and often cited first in the recommended reading sections; even the rare books that fail to mention him still follow his basic plot. The "approval rating" for Billington's version of Western history often goes several steps beyond including his name. "The best overview of expansion to the Pacific" (p. 365), Divine et al. call Billington's *The Far Western Frontier* (1956), while Billington's *Westward Expansion* (1967) is "the best general account of the movement west" (p. 522). Unger offers a similar appraisal: in *The Far Western Frontier,* "Billington deals with all of the important aspects of the Trans-Missouri westward movement" (p. 299). For an exploration of reasons why Billington is not the final word in Western history, see Patricia Nelson Limerick, "Persistent Traits and the Persistent Historian: The American Frontier and Ray Allen Billington," in *Writing Western History,* ed. Richard Etulain (Albuquerque: University of New Mexico Press, 1991).

33. In *America and Its People,* for instance, Martin et al. bring the Santa Fe Trail to New Mexico and then "back up" for the story of the Spanish settlements (pp. 372–376); Gruver, in *An American History,* follows the same strategy of supplying the information on Spanish colonization under the topic heading of the United States's "Further Westward Expansion" (p. 352).
34. Unger, *These United States,* 498.

II-A HISTORICAL LESSONS ON ANZA DAY

1. Charles Neider, ed., *The Complete Short Stories of Mark Twain* (New York: Bantam, 1971), 619.
2. The following have biographical information on Anza: Herbert E. Bolton, ed., *Anza's California Expeditions,* 5 vols. (Berkeley: University of California Press, 1930); Herbert E. Bolton, *Outpost of Empire: The Story of the Founding of San Francisco* (New York: Knopf, 1931); Elizabeth A. H. John, *Storms Brewed in Other Men's Worlds: The Confrontation of Indians, Spanish, and French in the Southwest, 1540–1795* (College Station: Texas A & M Press, 1975); and Alfred Barnaby Thomas, ed. and trans., *Forgotten Frontiers: A Study of the Spanish Indian Policy of Don Juan Bautista de Anza, Governor of New Mexico, 1777–1787* (Norman: University of Oklahoma Press, 1932).
3. Emmett C. Murphy with Michael Snell, *The Genius of Sitting Bull: 13 Heroic Strategies for Today's Business Leader* (Englewood, N.J.: Prentice-Hall, 1993), xxi.
4. Ibid., 119, 122.
5. Consider Anza's understated observation from his diary: "On this day frost and cold as though it were the months appropriate to this weather" (Thomas, *Forgotten Frontiers,* 125).
6. John, *Storms Brewed in Other Men's Worlds,* 609–610.
7. Thomas, *Forgotten Frontiers,* 303–304.
8. Ibid., 317.
9. Ibid., 301–305.
10. Ibid., 317.
11. In addition to Poncha Springs's Anza Day, a group of Anza enthusiasts, registering higher in quality than in quantity, hold an annual conference, alternating between Mexican and United States locations.

II-B JOHN SUTTER: PROTOTYPE FOR FAILURE

1. Sutter's biography is available in Richard Dillon, *Fool's Gold: The Decline and Fall of Captain John Sutter of California* (New York: Coward-McCann, 1967).
2. Albert Hurtado, "John Sutter and the Indian Business" in *John Sutter and a Wider West,* ed. Kenneth Owens (Lincoln: University of Nebraska Press, 1994).
3. Chapter 1 in Limerick, *The Legacy of Conquest* (New York: Norton, 1987) takes up this theme. Regrettably I did not think to include Sutter, despite his perfect fit.
4. Associated Pioneers of the Territorial Days of California, *A Nation's Benefactor: Gen'l John A. Sutter: Memorial of His Life and Public Services, and an Appeal to Congress, to Citizens of California, and the People of the United States, by his Fellow Pioneers of California* (New York: Polydore Barnes, printer, 1880).

5. Ibid., 12.
6. Reprinted ibid., 24.
7. Ibid., 13.
8. Richard Slotkin, *The Fatal Environment: The Myth of the Frontier in the Age of Industrialization, 1800–1890* (New York: Atheneum, 1985).
9. Dillon, *Fool's Gold,* 346.
10. Quoted in Dillon, *Fool's Gold,* 347.
11. Josiah Royce, *California: From the Conquest in 1846 to the Second Vigilance Committee in San Francisco: A Study of American Character* (1886; reprint, Santa Barbara and Salt Lake City: Peregrine, 1970).
12. In *Josiah Royce* (Norman: University of Oklahoma Press, 1991), Robert Hine at long last gives Royce his proper consideration as a Western intellectual.
13. For an exploration of the New Western History, see Patricia Nelson Limerick, Clyde Milner, and Charles Rankin, eds., *Trails: Toward a New Western History* (Lawrence: University Press of Kansas, 1991).
14. Royce, *California,* 34.
15. Heinrich Lienhard, *A Pioneer at Sutter's Fort, 1846–1850,* ed. Marguerite Eyer Wilbur (Los Angeles: Califia Society, 1941), 3.
16. Ibid., 122.
17. Ibid., 123.
18. Ibid., 5, 9, 67, 74–75, 154–155, 68, 75–76, 84, 93–94, 110, 159, 148–152, 198.
19. Colonel Tichenor to Annie Bidwell, July 13, 1880, in *John A. Sutter's Last Days: The Bidwell Letters* (Sacramento: Sacramento Book Collectors Club, 1986), 47; and Lienhard, *A Pioneer,* 79.
20. Sutter to Smith Rudd, December 26, 1879, Rudd mss., Lilly Library, Indiana University, Bloomington, Indiana.

II-C Turnerians All: The Dream of a Helpful History in an Intelligible World

1. Frederick Jackson Turner, "Since the Foundation [of Clark University]," in *The Significance of Sections in American History* (1932; reprint, Gloucester, Mass.: Peter Smith, 1959), 234.
2. Edited with commentary by John Mack Faragher, *Rereading Frederick Jackson Turner,* (New York: Holt, 1994), 1.
3. See Stephen C. Sturgeon, "Where Seldom Is Heard a Discouraging Word: The Failure of the First Anti-Turner Rebellion, 1930–1945," unpublished manuscript.
4. Richard Hofstader, *The Progressive Historians: Turner, Beard, Parrington* (New York: Knopf, 1968), 147–148.
5. Ibid., 133. See also Richard Hofstader, "Turner and the Frontier Myth," *American Scholar* 18 (1949): 433–443.
6. Patricia Nelson Limerick, *The Legacy of Conquest: The Unbroken Past of the American West* (New York: Norton, 1987); Patricia Nelson Limerick, Clyde A. Milner II, and Charles E. Rankin, *Trails: Toward a New Western History* (Lawrence: University Press of Kansas, 1991); Richard White, *"It's Your Misfortune and None of My Own": A New History of the American West* (Norman: University of Oklahoma Press, 1991); and James Grossman, ed., *The Frontier in*

American Culture: Essays by Richard White and Patricia Nelson Limerick (Berkeley: University of California Press, 1994).

7. Frederick Jackson Turner, "The Significance of the Mississippi Valley in American History," in *The Frontier in American History* (Tucson: University of Arizona Press, 1986), 179, 89, "The Indian Trade in Wisconsin," in *The Early Writings of Frederick Jackson Turner,* comp. Everett E. Edwards (Madison: University of Wisconsin Press, 1938), 93, "Problems in American History," (1892) in *Early Writings,* 77, "Problems in American History," (1904) in *Sections,* 18, and "Problems in American History," (1892) *Early Writings,* 75–76.

8. Turner, "The Middle West," in *Frontier,* 144, "Contributions of the West to American Democracy," in *Frontier,* 258, "The Problem of the West," in *Frontier,* 219, 218, "Pioneer Ideals and the State University," in *Frontier,* 278, "Is Sectionalism Dying Away?" in *Sections,* 310, and "Pioneer Ideals," in *Frontier,* 279, 276.

9. Frederick Jackson Turner, "Social Forces in American History," *American Historical Review* 16, no. 2 (January 1911): 217, "The Significance of History," in *Early Writings,* 57, and "Problems in American History," in *Sections,* 18–19.

10. Turner, "The West—1876 and 1926," in *Sections,* 236.

11. Turner, "The Middle West," in *Frontier,* 127.

12. Turner, "The Ohio Valley in American History," in *Frontier,* 160.

13. Turner, "The Significance of the Frontier in American History," in *Frontier,* 3.

14. Turner, "The Old West," in *Frontier,* 69.

15. Richard White, "Frederick Jackson Turner," in *Historians of the American Frontier: A Bio-Bibliographical Source,* ed. John R. Wunder (New York: Greenwood, 1988), 660. White draws this characterization from the telling description of Turner's role in the professionalization of history in Ray Allen Billington, *Frederick Jackson Turner: Historian, Scholar, Teacher* (New York: Oxford University Press, 1973).

16. Faragher, *Rereading Turner,* 3.

17. Frederick Jackson Turner to William E. Dodd, October 7, 1919, in *The Genesis of the Frontier Thesis: A Study in Historical Creativity,* ed. Ray Allen Billington (San Marino, Calif.: Huntington Library, 1971), 190.

18. The use of the word "originating" here should not be understood as an assertion the Turner thesis's originality is a cultural artifact. For what remains the best survey of the ways in which Turner incorporated preexisting ideas, see Henry Nash Smith, *Virgin Land: The American West as Myth and Symbol* (Cambridge, Mass.: Harvard University Press, 1950).

19. Turner, "The Significance of History," in *Early Writings,* 52–53.

20. Faragher, *Rereading Turner,* 4.

21. Turner, "Social Forces," *American Historical Review,* 16, 225.

22. Turner, "Since the Foundation," in *Sections,* 207, 220–221, 234.

23. Turner, "The Significance of Sections in American History," in *Sections,* p. 35, "Social Forces," *American Historical Review,* 16, 222, and "The Middle West," in *Frontier,* 153.

24. Turner, "Social Forces," *American Historical Review,* 16, 226.

25. Turner, "Contributions," in *Frontier,* 264, and "Pioneer Ideals," in *Frontier,* 280. See David M. Wrobel, *The End of American Exceptionalism: Frontier Anxiety from the Old West to the New Deal* (Lawrence: University Press of Kansas, 1993).

26. Turner, "Contributions," in *Frontier,* 264, and "The Significance of the Frontier," in *Frontier,* 4.
27. See Limerick, *The Legacy of Conquest,* 17.
28. Charles F. Wilkinson, *Crossing the Next Meridian: Land, Water, and the Future of the West* (Washington, D.C.: Island, 1992).
29. Turner, "The Significance of the Frontier," in *Frontier,* p. 12.
30. Turner, "Dominant Forces in Western Life," in *Frontier,* 224, "Middle Western Pioneer Democracy," in *Frontier,* 346, and "Pioneer Ideals," in *Frontier,* 276.
31. Turner, "The Origin of Genet's Projected Attack on Louisiana and the Floridas," *American Historical Review* 3 (October 1897–July 1898): 655.
32. Turner, "The Policy of France toward the Mississippi Valley in the Period of Washington and Adams," *American Historical Review* 10, no. 2 (January 1905): 273, 279.
33. Frederick Jackson Turner, "Since the Foundation," in *Sections,* 208.
34. Turner, "Social Forces," *American Historical Review,* 16, 226.
35. Turner, "Problems in American History," (1904) in *Sections,* 18, and "The Significance of the Frontier," in *Frontier,* 24.
36. Turner, "The Fur Trade," in *Early Writings,* 167, "The West—1876 and 1920," in *Sections,* 252, and "Since the Foundation," in *Sections,* 211–212.
37. Turner, "The Significance of History," in *Early Writings,* 64.
38. Richard Bernstein, *Dictatorship of Virtue: Multiculturalism and the Battle for America's Future* (New York: Knopf, 1994), 48.

III-A Mission to the Environmentalists

1. The principal studies available at the time were Hans Huth, *Nature and the American: Three Centuries of Changing Attitudes* (Berkeley: University of California Press, 1957), Arthur A. Ekirch, Jr., *Man and Nature in America* (New York: Columbia University Press, 1963), and Roderick Nash, *Wilderness and the American Mind* (New Haven, Conn.: Yale University Press, 1967).
2. William Cronon, *Uncommon Ground: Toward Reinventing Nature* (New York: Norton, 1995), 24–25.
3. For an important example of this, see the map on the proportions of Western agricultural and industrial water use in *The Atlas of the New West,* ed. William Riebsame (New York: Norton, 1997), 83.
4. Sir Lambart Price, *A Summer on the Rockies* (London: Sampson, Low, Marston, 1898), 125–126; Hiram Martin Chittenden, *The Yellowstone National Park* (Cincinnati, Ohio: Clarke, 1903), 74; *John L. Stoddard's Lectures* (Boston: Balch, 1903), vol. 10, 215; and Windham Thomas Wyndham-Quin (Earl of Dunraven), *The Great Divide: Travels in the Upper Yellowstone in the Summer of 1874* (1876; reprint, Lincoln: University of Nebraska Press, 1967), 32.

III-B Disorientation and Reorientation

1. Henry Nash Smith, *Virgin Land: The American West as Symbol and Myth* (Cambridge, Mass.: Harvard University Press, 1950); Hans Huth, *Nature and the American: Three Centuries of Changing Attitudes* (Berkeley: University of California Press, 1957); Arthur A. Ekirch, Jr., *Man and Nature in America* (New York: Columbia University Press, 1963); Leo Marx, *The Machine in the Garden:*

Technology and the Pastoral Ideal in America (New York: Oxford University Press, 1964); William H. Goetzmann, *Exploration and Empire: The Explorer and the Scientist in the Winning of the American West* (New York: Knopf, 1966); and Roderick Nash, *Wilderness and the American Mind* (New Haven, Conn.: Yale University Press, 1967). It does seem important to note that another book on the discovery of landscape, published considerably after 1972, matched these books in its exclusive attention to the east-to-west movements of white men: Patricia Nelson Limerick, *Desert Passages: Encounters with the American Desert* (Albuquerque: University of New Mexico, 1985).

2. The books that come closest to matching this model are William Cronon, *Changes in the Land: Indians, Colonists, and the Ecology of New England* (New York: Hill & Wang, 1983), William deBuys, *Enchantment and Exploitation: The Life and Hard Times of a New Mexico Mountain Range* (Albuquerque: University of New Mexico Press, 1986), and Richard White, *Land Use, Environment, and Social Change: The Shaping of Island County, Washington* (Seattle: University of Washington Press, 1980).

3. Of the various surveys of Asian American history, only Ronald Takaki, in *Strangers from a Different Shore: A History of Asian Americans* (New York: Little, Brown, 1989), makes repeated references to perceptions of landscape; those references are, however, scattered through the text and not pulled together in a systematic discussion of the issue. The issue of landscape is rarely mentioned in Roger Daniels, *Asian America: Chinese and Japanese in the United States since 1850* (Seattle: University of Washington Press, 1988), or Sucheng Chan, *Asian Americans: An Interpretive History* (Boston: Twayne, 1991). Lucy M. Cohen, *Chinese in the Post-Civil War South: A People Without a History* (Baton Rouge: Louisiana State University Press, 1984), and Robert Seto Quan, *Lotus among the Magnolias: The Mississippi Chinese* (Jackson: University Press of Mississippi, 1982), for instance, make virtually no mention of the immigrants' response to the Southern landscape. Noting these absences, one's first response is the typical one associated with mainstream scholars looking at ethnic history: "Perhaps there is so little written about this topic because there are no sources." And yet even when one confines oneself to published primary and secondary sources, there proves to be a considerable amount of material.

4. John Jeong, quoted in *Longtime Californ': A Documentary Study of an American Chinatown,* Victor G. and Brett de Bary Nee (1972; reprint, Boston: Pantheon, 1974), 73; Wei Bat Liu, quoted ibid., 60; and Bing Fai Chow, quoted in *Bitter Melon: Stories from the Last Rural Chinese Town in America,* Jeff Gillenkirk and James Motlow (Seattle: University of Washington Press, 1987), 64.

5. Suen Hoon Sum, quoted in *Bitter Melon,* Gillenkirk and Motlow, 56–59; and Jone Ho Leong, quoted ibid., 102.

6. Sucheng Chan, *This Bittersweet Soil* (Berkeley: University of California Press, 1986), xx, 369.

7. Him Mark Lai, Genny Lim, and Judy Yung, *Island: Poetry and History of Chinese Immigrants on Angel Island, 1910–1940* (San Francisco: San Francisco Study Center, 1980), 122, 54, 40, 92. See also Marlon K. Hom, *Songs of Gold Mountain: Cantonese Rhymes from San Francisco's Chinatown* (Berkeley: University of California Press, 1987).

8. Sandy Lydon, *Chinese Gold: The Chinese in the Monterey Bay Region* (Capitola,

Calif.: Capitola, 1985), 22–24. Italics in the original. Why were the Chinese able to discover values in landscapes Europeans and Americans found useless? Lydon fits the Chinese into a familiar model of colonization in which immigrants chose landscapes that reminded them of home and then, as much as possible, transferred skills developed at home to these new but still familiar places. In a study of the Chinese in the San Joaquin Valley, Sylvia Sun Minnick is even more certain of this trans-Pacific continuity in landscape preference. She sees the similarities between the Sacramento Delta and the Pearl River Delta, where many of the immigrants originated, as clinching the argument: "Instinctively, [the immigrants] realized that the [Sacramento] Delta region was as close as they could come to finding conditions and climate similar to those of their native homeland" Sylvia Sun Minnick, Samfow: The San Joaquin Chinese Legacy (Fresno, Calif.: Panorama West, 1988), 23. This claim seems convincing until one reads Sucheng Chan's compelling counterargument:

> It would add a romantic touch to our story were it possible to claim that Chinese immigrants came to farm in the Delta because it reminded them of home—the Pearl River Delta of Kwangtung Province, where most of them had lived. Such a case cannot be made, however, because though the Chinese no doubt saw the deltaic marshlands as they rode steamers up the Sacramento River on their way to the mining regions, they did not enter the Delta to farm on their own initiative. They first went to work in the area when white landowners recruited them to do reclamation work. Only after they became aware of the extraordinary fertility of Delta soil did they lease land to grow crops. Chan, *This Bittersweet Soil*, 159.

Even if the Chinese had wanted to live in a landscape that resembled their homes, they would still have had to subordinate this preference to other concerns. The ability to choose to live in a particular place hinges, after all, on economic power. Even in a place that looked familiar and comfortable, the unavailability of a job or income would drain the comfort out of the experience.

9. The overlap between environmental issues and racial and ethnic issues is getting much more attention recently; see, especially, Robert D. Bullard, *Dumping in Dixie: Race, Class, and Environmental Quality* (Boulder, Colo.: Westview, 1990).

10. Huang Zunxian, "Expulsion of the Immigrants," in *Land without Ghosts: Chinese Impressions of America from the Mid-Nineteenth Century to the Present*, eds. R. David Arkush and Leo O. Lee (Berkeley: University of California Press, 1989), 62; and Zhang Yinhuan, "Chinese in America," ibid., 73.

11. Jack Chen, *The Chinese of America: From the Beginnings to the Present* (San Francisco: Harper & Row, 1981), 89; and Minnick, *Samfow*, 25, 53.

12. Shih-Shan Henry Tsai, *The Chinese Experience in America* (Bloomington: Indiana University Press, 1986), xi.

13. Lydon, *Chinese Gold*, 93.

14. Ibid., 95–99.

15. Gail M. Nomura, *"Tsugiki,* a Grafting: A History of a Japanese Pioneer Woman in Washington State," in *Women in Pacific Northwest History: An Anthology,* ed. Karen J. Blair (Seattle: University of Washington Press, 1988), 208, 213, 207; and Stephen H. Sumida, "Hawaii, the Northwest, and Asia: Localism and Local Literary Developments in the Creation of an Asian Immigrants' Sensibility," *Blue Funnel Line (Seattle Review)* 11, no. 1 (Spring-Summer 1988): 10.

16. Henry David Thoreau, "Walking," in *Walden and Other Writings,* ed. Brooks Atkinson, (New York: Modern Library, 1950), 607.

17. John Armor and Peter Wright, *Manzanar* (New York: Times Books, 1988), xviii–xx. Forbidden to photograph certain features of the camp, Adams found creative ways of fudging. He was not permitted to take photographs of the guard towers, and so he took a photograph *from* that vantage point, entitling it, "Manzanar from Guard Tower: Summer Heat." See *Manzanar,* 154.

18. Kamechiyo Takahashi, in *The Issei: Portrait of a Pioneer, an Oral History,* ed. Eileen Sunada Sarasohn (Palo Alto, Calif.: Pacific Books, 1983), 181–182; Mary Tsukamoto, in *And Justice for All: An Oral History of the Japanese American Detention Camps,* John Tateishi (New York: Random House, 1984), 11–12; Masao Hirata, in *The Issei,* Sarasohn, 162–163; and Yoshiko Uchida, *Desert Exile: The Uprooting of a Japanese American Family* (Seattle: University of Washington Press, 1982), 50.

19. Uchida, *Desert Exile,* 71.

20. Osuke Takizawa in *The Issei,* Sarasohn, 183; and John Modell, ed., *The Kikuchi Diary* (Urbana: University of Illinois Press, 1973), 49, 51.

21. Tome Takatsuki, in *The Issei,* Sarasohn, 199; Mary Tsukamoto, in *And Justice for All,* Tateishi, 12; Modell, *The Kikuchi Diary,* 156; Mitsuye Yamada, *Camp Notes and Other Poems* (Berkeley: Shameless Hussy, 1976), 27; and Monica Sone, *Nisei Daughter* (1953; reprint, Seattle: University of Washington Press, 1979), 177.

22. Ben Takeshita in *And Justice for All,* Tateishi, 244. See also Uchida, *Desert Exile,* 103.

23. Sone, *Nisei Daughter,* 190–191.

24. Minoru Yasui in *And Justice for All,* Tateishi, 76; and Amy Uno Ishii in *Japanese American World War II Evacuation Oral History Project, Part I: Internees,* ed. Arthur A. Hansen (Westport, Conn.: Meckler, 1991), 80, 67.

25. Amy Uno Ishii in *Oral History Project,* Hansen, 67; Yoriyuki Kikuchi, ibid., 206; George Fukasawa, ibid., 236–237; Uchida, *Desert Exile,* 109; Mine Okuba, *Citizen 13660* (1946; reprint, Seattle: University of Washington Press, 1983), 123; and Sone, *Nisei Daughter,* 192.

26. Amy Uno Ishii, in *Oral History Project,* Hansen, 67; and Toyo Suyemoto Kawakami, "Camp Memories: Rough and Broken Shards," in *Japanese Americans: From Relocation to Redress,* eds. Roger Daniels, Sandra C. Taylor, and Harry H. L. Kitano (Salt Lake City: University of Utah Press, 1986), 28.

27. Jeanne Wakatsuki Houston and James D. Houston, *Farewell to Manzanar* (Boston: Houghton Mifflin, 1973), 31; Toyo Suyemoto Kawakami, in *Japanese Americans,* eds. Daniels et al. 27; and Okubo, *Citizen 13660,* 136.

28. Houston, *Farewell to Manzanar,* 72; and Uchida, *Desert Exile,* 87. While the gardens were the most visible, outdoor sign of this effort to recreate normality, a similar campaign went on indoors, in the building of furniture and the partitioning and reshaping of the barracks rooms.

29. Okuba, *Citizen 13660,* 192–193.

30. Mabel Ota in *And Justice for All,* Tateishi, 111.

31. Okuba, *Citizen 13660,* 98; and Mary Tsukamoto in *And Justice for All,* Tateishi, 14.

32. Okuba, *Citizen 13660,* 98–99; and Houston, *Farewell to Manzanar,* 72.

33. Allen H. Eaton, *Beauty Behind Barbed Wire: The Arts of the Japanese in Our War Relocation Camps* (New York: Harper, 1952), 16–19, 32–35. Eaton also provides descriptions and photographs of gardens; see 24–25, 50–53, 56–57, 74–75, 92–95.

34. *Irrigator,* quoted in "Japanese Americans in Idaho," Robert C. Sims, in *Japanese Americans,* Daniels et al., 107.

35. Limerick, *Desert Passages;* and Houston, *Farewell to Manzanar,* 72. Despite different cultural origins, Anglo-American teachers and anthropologists at the camp sites were equally repelled by the setting. Rosalie Wax described the landscape she saw near the Gila River camp: "It looked like the skin of some cosmic reptile, an ocean of coarse grit, studded at repulsively regular intervals with regularly shaped projections. . . . Every stone, every piece of cactus, looked bleached and tired." Arrived at the camp, Wax remembered, "I washed my face and told myself I would feel better the next day. I was wrong." Rosalie H. Wax, *Doing Fieldwork: Warnings and Advice* (Chicago: University of Chicago Press, 1971), 67–68.

A teacher at Topaz, Eleanor Gerard Sekerak, remarked on one part of their required curriculum addressing the theme of "Adaptation of Our Socioeconomic Arrangements to the Control and Direction of Technological Development." "We were provided with illustrations," Sekerak remembered, "of how to adapt this theme to the various grades, e.g., in grade one, 'How can the yard at school be made more useful and beautiful?' In reality, the yard was dust (or mud) with huge piles of coal, and not a leaf could be coaxed from that alkali soil." Sekerak, "A Teacher at Topaz," in *Japanese Americans,* Daniels et al., 40. All of these responses are, of course, quite at odds with my own definitions of an arid norm in 1972. City or country, the areas of California from which the Japanese and Japanese Americans (and a number of the Anglo-American teachers and anthropologists) departed were, by the 1940s, very much remade—and turned green—by large-scale development. In contrast, my own place of origin—Banning, California—had a set of lawns and parks, but these green areas were limited in scale. The surrounding setting of the desert was always visible and thus shaped my definition of normality.

36. On the Japanese and Japanese American agrarian dream, see Valerie J. Matsumoto, *Farming the Home Place: A Japanese-American Community in California, 1919–1982* (Ithaca, N.Y.: Cornell University Press, 1994), and David Masumoto, *Country Voices: The Oral History of a Japanese American Family Farm Community* (Del Ray, Calif.: Inaka Countryside Publication, 1987).

37. Chan, *This Bittersweet Soil,* 79; Akemi Kikumura, *Through Harsh Winters: The Life of a Japanese Immigrant Woman* (Novato, Calif.: Chandler & Sharp, 1981), 49; Iwato Itow in *And Justice for All,* Tateishi, 145; and Masumoto, *Country Voices,* 81. See also Gillenkirk and Motlow, *Bitter Melon,* 44, 56, 74, especially the remarks of Wong Yow: "I had just finished learning to be a carpenter in China, so I was ready for that. Instead, I went to work in the orchards, picking pears and trimming trees. . . . There was plenty of work to do if you were interested in doing farmwork. . . . I never did get to use my carpentry skills. It just wasn't done. . . . [Chinese people] weren't expected—I guess allowed—to do anything else" (p. 44).

38. Bess Tuck, quoted in "Return to Amache," *Denver Magazine* 12, no. 6 (May 1982), George Lurie: 36; and Eaton, *Beauty Beyond Barbed Wire,* xi–xii, xiii. The question of the gardens also returns us to the unsettled border territory be-

tween environmental history and ethnic history. In works like Donald Worster, *Rivers of Empire: Water, Aridity, and the Growth of the American West* (New York: Pantheon, 1985), and James Earl Sherow, *Watering the Valley: Development Along the High Plains Arkansas River, 1870–1950* (Lawrence: University Press of Kansas, 1990), environmental historians offer a quite stern judgment of the unintended consequences and the inappropriateness of irrigated agriculture in deserts. Should that appraisal apply to the camp gardens, or do the smallness of scale and injustice of the circumstances mitigate the judgment?

39. Amy Uno Ishii in *Oral History Project,* Hansen, 67.

40. John Walton, *Western Times and Water Wars* (Berkeley: University of California Press, 1992) is the first to come close to a united narrative of this sort.

41. Fei Xiaotong, "The Shallowness of Cultural Tradition," in *Land without Ghosts,* Arkush and Lee, 177–180.

42. Ibid., 178.

III-C THE GOLD RUSH AND
THE SHAPING OF THE AMERICAN WEST

1. Patricia Nelson Limerick, *The Legacy of Conquest: The Unbroken Past of the American West* (New York: Norton, 1987), 100.

2. For overviews of Western mining, see Rodman Paul, *Mining Frontiers of the Far West, 1848–1880* (Albuquerque: University of New Mexico Press, 1963), and Duane Smith, *Mining America: The Industry and the Environment* (Lawrence: University Press of Kansas, 1987). For recent, innovative studies of mining communities, see work by Yvette Huginnie, Elizabeth Jameson, Susan Johnson, and Mary Murphy.

3. Timothy Egan, "Billions at Stake in Debate on a Gold Rush," first article in "Who Owns the West?" a periodic series, *New York Times,* August 14, 1994.

4. Walter Colton, *Three Years in California* (New York: Barnes, 1854), 247.

5. Ibid., 248.

6. Malcolm J. Rohrbough, *Days of Gold: The California Gold Rush and the American Nation* (Berkeley: University of California Press, 1997), 2.

7. "The Death of Mining: America Is Losing One of its Most Basic Industries," *Business Week,* December 17, 1984; and Michael Malone, "The Collapse of Metal Mining: An Historical Epitaph," *Pacific Historical Review* 55 (August 1986): 455–464, reprinted in *Major Problems in the History of the American West,* ed. Clyde A. Milner (Lexington, Mass.: Heath, 1989). Quotation is from Milner, *Major Problems,* 647.

8. Egan, "Billions at Stake," *New York Times;* "Gold Mining Agreement Set," *New York Times,* January 30, 1992; Jim Robbins, "Gripped by Gold Fever," *New York Times,* December 4, 1988; Jon Christensen, "Two Nevadans in Search of Mining Reform," *High Country News,* October 4, 1993; and Steve Hinchman, "A Tenacious Law May Lose Its Grip," *High Country News,* June 4, 1990.

9. Charles Wilkinson, *Crossing the Next Meridian: Land, Water, and the Future of the West* (Washington, D.C.: Island Press, 1992), 28; and "Mining Reform: Searching for Common Ground," *High Country News,* October 4, 1993.

10. Clyde H. Farnsworth, "Peter Munk—Lucky Gold Strike and Wise Hedging Help Keep His Shareholders Smiling," *New York Times,* May 30, 1993.

11. Ibid.

12. Jennifer Kerr, "California Ready to Mark Anniversary of Gold Rush," *Denver Post,* January 22, 1998.

13. Ibid.

14. Limerick, *The Legacy of Conquest,* 100.

15. Wilkinson, *Crossing the Next Meridian,* 49; and Malcolm Wallop and Alan Simpson quoted in Egan, "Billions at Stake," *New York Times.*

16. William Wright (Dan DeQuille), *The Big Bonanza* (1876; reprint, New York: T. Y. Crowell, 1947), 280–281.

17. Frederick Marryat, *Mountains and Molehills* (London: Longman, Brown, Green, & Longmans, 1855), 321.

Part IV The Historian as Dreamer

1. Francis Fukuyama, "The Great Disruption: Human Nature and the Reconstruction of Social Order," *Atlantic Monthly,* May 1999, 80.

IV-A Peace Initiative: Using the Mormons to Rethink Culture and Ethnicity in American History

1. Don Phillips, "If the Engine's Burning, Tell the Pilot: A Report Faults a Sometimes Fatal Failure to Communicate," *Washington Post,* weekly edition, June 6–12, 1994, 32.

2. Fredrik Barth, "Introduction," in *Ethnic Groups and Boundaries: The Social Organization of Cultural Difference,* ed. Fredrik Barth (Boston: Little, Brown, 1969).

3. Cornel West, *Race Matters* (New York: Random House, 1994), 159.

4. Frederick Jackson Turner, "The Significance of the Frontier in American History," in *The Frontier in American History* (1947; reprint, Tucson: University of Arizona Press, 1986), 8.

5. Ray Allen Billington, *America's Frontier Heritage* (New York: Holt, Rinehart & Winston, 1966). The index contains neither the word "Utah" nor the word "Mormonism."

6. F. LaMond Tullis, *Mormons in Mexico: The Dynamics of Faith and Culture* (Logan: Utah State University Press, 1987).

7. Mary C. Waters, *Ethnic Options: Choosing Identities in America* (Berkeley: University of California Press, 1990), 24.

8. Ibid., 25.

9. David A. Hollinger, "Postethnic America," *Contention* 2, no. 1 (Fall 1992): 84. See particularly Herbert J. Gans, "Symbolic Ethnicity: The Future of Ethnic Groups and Cultures in America," *Ethnic and Racial Studies* 2, no. 1 (January 1979): 1–20, and Werner Sollors, *Beyond Ethnicity: Consent and Descent in American Culture* (New York: Oxford University Press, 1986).

10. Robert Blauner, *Racial Oppression in America* (New York: Harper & Row, 1972), 117; and Hollinger, "Postethnic America," 86.

11. Derrick Bell, *Faces at the Bottom of the Well: The Permanence of Racism* (New York: Basic Books, 1992); Jonathan Kozol, *Savage Inequalities: Children in America's Schools* (New York: Crown, 1991); Alex Kotlowitz, *There Are No*

Children Here: The Story of Two Boys Growing Up in the Other America (New York: Doubleday, 1991); Brent Staples, *Parallel Time: Growing Up in Black and White* (New York: Pantheon, 1994); Nathan McCall, *Makes Me Wanna Holler: A Young Black Man in America* (New York: Random House, 1994); and Ellis Cose, *The Rage of a Privileged Class* (New York: HarperCollins, 1993).

12. Andrew Hacker, *Two Nations: Black and White, Separate, Hostile, Unequal* (New York: Scribner's, 1992), 36.

13. Ishmael Reed, in "Is Ethnicity Obsolete?" a panel discussion in *The Invention of Ethnicity*, ed. Werner Sollors (New York: Oxford University Press, 1989), 227; and Barbara J. Fields, "Ideology and Race in American History," in *Region, Race, and Reconstruction*, eds. J. Morgan Kousser and James M. McPherson (New York: Oxford University Press, 1982), 149.

14. Leonard Arrington, "The Founding of the LDS Church Historical Department, 1972," *Journal of Mormon History* 18, no. 2; Lavina Fielding Anderson, "The LDS Intellectual Community and Church Leadership: A Contemporary Chronology," *Dialogue* 26, no. 1, 7–64; Paul James Toscano, *The Sanctity of Dissent* (Salt Lake City, Utah: Signature Books, 1994); D. Michael Quinn, "On Being a Mormon Historian (And Its Aftermath)," in *Faithful History: Essays on Writing Mormon History*, ed. George D. Smith (Salt Lake City, Utah: Signature Books, 1992), 69–111; and Quinn, "Dilemmas of Feminists and Intellectuals in the Contemporary LDS Church," *Sunstone* 17, no. 1 (June 1994): 67–73. See also D. Michael Quinn, ed., *The New Mormon History: Revisionist Essays on the Past* (Salt Lake City, Utah: Signature Books, 1992).

15. Armand L. Mauss, "Mormons as Ethnics: Variable Historical and International Implications of an Appealing Concept," and Keith Parry, "Mormons as Ethnics: A Canadian Perspective," in *The Mormon Presence in Canada*, eds. Brigham Y. Card, Herbert C. Northcutt, John E. Foster, Howard Palmer, and George K. Jarvis (Logan: University State University Press, 1990), 329–365.

16. The next few pages are drawn from Thomas Alexander, *Mormonism in Transition: A History of the Latter-day Saints, 1890–1930* (Urbana: University of Illinois Press, 1986), Leonard Arrington and Davis Bitton, *The Mormon Experience: A History of the Latter-day Saints* (New York: Knopf, 1985), Lawrence Foster, *Religion and Sexuality: The Shakers, the Mormons, and the Oneida Community* (New York: Oxford University Press, 1981), Klaus Hansen, *Mormonism and the American Experience* (Chicago: University of Chicago Press, 1981), Marvin S. Hill, *The Mormon Flight from American Pluralism* (Salt Lake City, Signature Books, 1989), Mark Leone, *Roots of Modern Mormonism* (Cambridge, Mass.: Harvard University Press, 1981), Armand L. Mauss, *The Angel and the Beehive: The Mormon Struggle with Assimilation* (Urbana: University of Illinois Press, 1994), Dean L. May, "Mormons," in *The Harvard Encyclopedia of Ethnic Groups* (Cambridge: Belknap Press, 1980), 720–731, Thomas F. O'Dea, *The Mormons* (Chicago: University of Chicago Press, 1957), and Jan Shipps, *Mormonism: The Story of a New Religious Tradition* (Urbana: University of Illinois Press, 1985), "Making Saints: In the Early Days and the Latter Days," and "Change, Change, and More Change: The Latter-day Saints Since WWII."

17. Richard E. Bennett, *Mormons at the Missouri: 1846–1852: "And Should We Die"* (Norman: University of Oklahoma Press, 1987).

18. Jan Shipps, "Making Saints," in *Mormonism,* 69–70.

19. Richard Francavaglia, *The Mormon Landscape: Existance, Creation, and Perception of a Unique Image in the American West* (New York: AMS Press, 1978).

20. R. Laurence Moore, "Learning to Play: The Mormon Way and the Way of Other Americans," *Journal of Mormon History* 16, 89–106.

21. William Mulder, *Homeward to Zion: The Mormon Migration from Scandinavia* (Minneapolis: University of Minnesota Press, 1957). For another illuminating case study of the relation between European ethnicity and Mormonism, see Frederick Stewart Buchanan, *A Good Time Coming: Mormon Letters to Scotland* (Salt Lake City: University of Utah Press, 1988).

22. Leonard Arrington, *History of Idaho,* vol. 2 (Moscow: University of Idaho Press, 1994), 268.

23. See F. LaMond Tullis, ed., *Mormonism: A Faith for All Cultures* (Provo, Utah: Brigham Young University Press, 1978).

24. Stanley B. Kimball, *Heber C. Kimball: Mormon Patriarch and Pioneer* (Urbana: University of Illinois Press, 1981), 268.

25. Maureen Ursenbach Beecher and Lavina Fielding Anderson, eds., *Sisters in Spirit: Mormon Women in Historical and Cultural Perspective* (Urbana: University of Illinois Press, 1987). See also Maxine Hanks, ed., *Women and Authority: Re-Emerging Mormon Feminism* (Salt Lake City, Utah: Signature Books, 1992).

26. Phyllis Barber, *And the Desert Shall Blossom* (Salt Lake City, Utah: Signature Books, 1993); Eugene England, ed., *Bright Angels and Familiars: Contemporary Mormon Stories* (Salt Lake City, Utah: Signature Books, 1992); Eugene England and Dennis Clark, eds., *Harvest: Contemporary Mormon Poems* (Salt Lake City, Utah: Signature Books, 1989); Lewis B. Horne, *What Do Ducks Do in Winter? and Other Western Stories* (Salt Lake City, Utah: Signature Books, 1993); Levi S. Peterson, *The Canyons of Grace* (Urbana: University of Illinois Press, 1982), *Backslider* (Salt Lake City, Utah: Signature Books, 1990), and *Night Soil* (Salt Lake City, Utah: Signature Books, 1990), and ed., *Greening Wheat: Fifteen Mormon Short Stories* (Midvale, Utah: Orion, 1983); Douglas H. Thayer, *Under the Cottonwoods and Other Mormon Stories* (Midvale, Utah: Orion, 1977); and Terry Tempest Williams, *Refuge: An Unnatural History of Family and Place* (New York: Pantheon, 1991) and *An Unspoken Hunger: Stories from the Field* (New York: Pantheon, 1994). See also studies of Mormon folklore: Hector Lee, *The Three Nephites: The Substance and Significance of the Legend in Folklore* (Albuquerque: University of New Mexico Press, 1949); Austin and Alta Fife, *Saints of Sage and Saddle: Folklore Among the Mormons* (1956; reprint, Salt Lake City: University of Utah Press, 1980); Susan Hendricks Swetnam, *Lives of the Saints in Southeast Idaho: An Introduction to Mormon Pioneer Life Story Writing* (Moscow: University of Idaho Press, 1991); and Barre Toelken, "Folklore in the American West," in *A Literary History of the American West* (Fort Worth: Texas Christian University Press, 1987), 29–67.

27. Steven Epstein, "New Directions in Medieval History," unpublished manuscript presented at the National Endowment for the Humanities, April 1994. For contemporary applications of this theme, see Stephen L. Carter, *The Culture of Disbelief: How American Law and Politics Trivialize Religious Devotion* (New York: Basic Books, 1993).

28. Dean L. May, "Writing from Within as a Mormon," unpublished paper presented at the American Historical Association, San Francisco, January 1994, 4.

29. Orlando Patterson, *Ethnic Chauvinism: The Reactionary Impulse* (New York: Stein & Day, 1977), 10.
30. Swetnam, *Lives of the Saints*, 120.
31. Marden J. Clark, "Wasatch," in *Harvest*, England and Clark, 19.

IV-B WILL THE REAL CALIFORNIAN PLEASE STAND UP?

1. Douglas Henry Daniels, *Pioneer Urbanites: A Social and Cultural History of Black San Francisco* (Philadelphia: Temple University Press, 1980), 32–33.
2. Mary Roberts Coolidge, *Chinese Immigration* (New York: Holt, 1909), 20, 95.
3. Ibid., 182, 441.
4. Ibid., 458, 489, 495–496.
5. Ibid., 456, 457.
6. Victoria Post Ranney, Gerard F. Rauluk, and Carolyn F. Hoffman, eds., *The Papers of Frederick Law Olmsted: The California Frontier, 1863–1865,* vol. 5 (Baltimore: Johns Hopkins University Press, 1990), 100, 220.
7. Ibid., 679, 207.
8. Ibid., 263, 753.
9. John Gregory Dunne, "The Secret Life of Danny Santiago," *New York Review of Books,* August 16, 1984, 17–20, 22, 24–27. Quotations are from p. 25. The book under discussion is Danny Santiago, *Famous All Over Town* (New York: Simon & Schuster, 1983).
10. Henry Louis Gates, Jr., " 'Authenticity,' or the Lesson of Little Tree," *New York Times Book Review,* November 24, 1991, 1, 30.
11. Ibid., 30.
12. Darius Stokes, at the First State Convention of the Colored Citizens of California, 1855, quoted in *Pioneer Urbanites,* Daniels, 25.

IV-C THE SHADOWS OF HEAVEN ITSELF:
THE DEMANDING DREAMS OF THE AMERICAN WEST

1. Samuel Bowles, *Our New West* (Hartford, Conn.: Hartford, 1869), 1.
2. James Brooke, "Cattle-Poor Ranchers Turn to Elk," *New York Times,* January 29, 1996.
3. William M. Thayer, *Marvels of the New West* (Norwich, Conn.: Henry Bill, 1890), xxxi.
4. Renate Robey, "Growth Hard on Rodents" and "Survey: Rodents Bad Neighbors," *Denver Post,* September 9, 1996.
5. Julia Prodis, Associated Press, "Dream Led to Prairie-Dog Vacuum," *Daily Camera,* September 9, 1996.
6. Thayer, *Marvels,* xxxv.
7. I am indebted to Gene Hollon for this anecdote.
8. Chris Wilson, *The Myth of Santa Fe: Tourism, Ethnic Identity, and the Creation of a Modern Regional Tradition* (Albuquerque: University of New Mexico, 1997).
9. Elliott West, *The Way to the West: Essays on the Central Plains* (Albuquerque: University of New Mexico, 1995), 156, 146.
10. Maureen Harrington, "Love of Land Is Gospel in Abbey's Novel Dogma," *Denver Post,* April 3, 1988.

11. Jan Golab, "Blue Heaven: Former Los Angeles Police Moving to Idaho," *Los Angeles Magazine,* June 1995.

12. "A Long Way from the Rat Race," *U.S. News and World Report,* October 30, 1995, 86–87.

13. See Albert Tucker, "The 'B' Western and Personal Behavior," *The Permian Historical Annual* 28 (December 1988): 111–117.

14. "Kiddies in the Old Corral," *Time,* November 27, 1950, 30; and Jane and Michael Stern, *Way Out West* (New York: HarperCollins, 1993), 43.

15. Sterns, *Way Out West,* 43.

16. "Kiddies in the Old Corral," *Time,* 19–20.

17. Roy Rogers and Dale Evans, with Jane and Michael Stern, *Happy Trails: Our Life Story* (New York: Simon & Schuster, 1994), 140, 204; list from Robert W. Phillips, *Roy Rogers: A Biography, Radio History, Television Career Chronicle, Discography, Filmography, Comicography, Merchandising and Advertising History, Collectibles Description* (Jefferson, N.C.: McFarland, 1995).

18. Rogers, Evans, and Sterns, *Happy Trails,* 137–138; "Lone Ranger Actor Keeps Spirit Alive," *Denver Post,* November 11, 1996; Gene Autry, with Mickey Herskowitz, *Back in the Saddle Again* (Garden City, N.Y.: Doubleday, 1978), 184; and Rogers, Evans, and Sterns, *Happy Trails,* 201.

19. Autry, *Back in the Saddle,* 42; "Kiddies in the Old Corral," *Time,* 20; Rogers, Evans, and Sterns, *Happy Trails,* 198, 251; and George Morris and Mark Pollard, *Roy Rogers: King of the Cowboys* (San Francisco: HarperCollins, 1994), 6. For further indications of the tie between these men and the baby boomer generation, see Beth Harris, Associated Press, "First Singing Cowboy Dead at 91: Gene Autry, 1907–1998," *Boulder Daily Camera,* October 3, 1998; Richard Severo, "Roy Rogers, Singing Cowboy, Dies at 86," *New York Times,* July 7, 1998; and Cynthia L. Webb, Associated Press, "So Long, Cowboy: Hundreds of Fans Gather to Bid Farewell to 'King of Cowboys," *Denver Post,* July 12, 1998.

20. Edgar Marquess Branch et al., eds., *Mark Twain's Letters,* vol. 1, 1853–1866 (Berkeley: University of California Press, 1988), 133.

21. Richard F. Burton, *The City of the Saints and Across the Rocky Mountains to California,* ed. Fawn Brodie (New York: Knopf, 1963), 60–61.

22. Silver Wolf Walks Alone (Wendy Whiteman), *Sacred Sage: How It Heals* (Ashland, Va.: self-published, 1992), 18.

23. Ibid., 19, 1.

24. Ibid., 2–4.

25. Frederick Jackson Turner, *The Rise of the New West, 1819–1829* (New York: MacMillan, 1962).

26. Porter Bibb, *It Ain't As Easy As It Looks: Ted Turner's Amazing Story* (New York: Crown, 1993), 383, 385; and Geraldine Fabrikant, "Ted (Don't Fence Me In) Turner," *New York Times,* November 24, 1996.

27. Bibb, *It Ain't As Easy As It Looks,* 386.

28. Fabrikant, "Ted (Don't Fence Me In) Turner," *New York Times.*

29. Advertisements in *Sedona,* Summer 1996.

30. *Sedona: Journal of Emergence!,* July 1996, 1, 90.

31. Ibid., 60.

32. Ibid., 33, 2.

33. Norman Maclean, *A River Runs Through It* (Chicago: University of Chicago

Press, 1976), ix; and Ivan Doig, *This House of Sky: Landscapes of a Western Mind* (New York: Harcourt Brace Jovanovich, 1978).

34. "A Grudge Runs Through It," *Harper's,* February 1993, 35.
35. James Bryce, *The American Commonwealth,* ed. Louis Hacker (New York: Putnam's, 1959), vol. 2, 582–583.
36. John McCormick and Bill Turque, "American's Outback," *Newsweek,* October 9, 1989, 76–79.
37. Jordan Bonfante, "Boomtime in the Rockies: Sky's The Limit," *Time,* September 6, 1993, 20–26.
38. J. Francis Stafford, "The Heights of the Mountains Are His: The Development of God's Country," pastoral letter, November 24, 1994, 5–6.
39. Ray Ring, "The New West's Servant Economy," *High Country News,* April 17, 1995.
40. Lisa Jones, "The Region's New Pioneers Buoy the Economy and Live on the Edge," in "El Nuevo West," special issue, *High Country News,* December 23, 1996.
41. Stafford, "The Heights of the Mountains," 2–4.
42. Ibid., 6.

IV-D Believing in the American West

1. Michael Quinn, "Religion in the American West," in *Under an Open Sky: Rethinking America's Western Past,* William Cronon, George Miles, and Jay Gitlin, eds., (New York: Norton, 1992), 157–158.
2. Harold Driver, *Indians of North America,* 2d. ed. (Chicago: University of Chicago Press, 1969), 396.
3. Dean May, *Three Frontiers: Family, Land, and Society in the American West, 1850–1900* (New York: Cambridge University Press, 1994), 212, 215.
4. Eldon G. Ernst, "American Religious History from a Pacific Coast Perspective," in *Religion and Society in the American West,* ed. Carl Guarneri and David Alvarez (Lanham, Md.: University Press of America, 1987), 23.
5. Jim Bob Tinsley, *He was Singin' This Song* (Orlando: University Presses of Florida, 1981), 108.
6. Ferenc Morton Szasz, *The Protestant Clergy in the Great Plains and Mountain West, 1865–1915* (Albuquerque: University of New Mexico Press, 1988), 211. See also Sandra Sizer Frankiel, *California's Spiritual Frontiers: Religious Alternatives in Anglo-Protestantism, 1850–1910* (Berkeley: University of California Press, 1988), and Michael E. Engh, S.J., *Frontier Faiths: Church, Temple, and Synagogue in Los Angeles, 1846–1888* (Albuquerque: University of New Mexico Press, 1992).
7. Josiah Strong, *Our Country: Its Possible Future and Its Present Crisis* (1891; reprint, Cambridge: Harvard University Press, 1963), 192.
8. Ibid., 39.
9. Ibid., 212–214.
10. Ibid., 169–170.
11. Albert Weinberg, *Manifest Destiny: A Study of Nationalist Expansionism in American History* (1935; reprint, Gloucester, Mass: Peter Smith, 1958), 73, 128, 173, 283.

12. Michael F. Steltencamp, *Black Elk: Holy Man of the Oglala* (Norman: University of Oklahoma Press, 1993).

13. Daniel Sylvester Tuttle, *Missionary to the Mountain West: Reminiscences of Episcopal Bishop Daniel S. Tuttle* (1906; reprint, Salt Lake City: University of Utah Press, 1987), 91.

14. Ibid., 97.

15. Howard Thurman *Footsteps of a Dream: The Story of The Church for the Fellowship of All Peoples* (New York: Harper, 1959), 11, 31, 21, 40.

16. Ibid., 69–70, 21.

Index